PENGUIN CLASSICS

ALFRED THE GREAT

SIMON KEYNES, M.A., PH.D., LITT.D., was born in 1952 and educated at the Leys School and Trinity College, Cambridge. He was elected a Fellow of Trinity College in 1976, and was appointed Reader in Anglo-Saxon History, University of Cambridge, in 1992. He is the author of *The Diplomas of King Æthelred 'the Unready'* (1980), and of numerous articles on Anglo-Saxon history.

MICHAEL LAPIDGE, M.A., PH.D., LITT.D., was born in Canada in 1942, and has been living in Cambridge since 1969. He was appointed Elrington and Bosworth Professor of Anglo-Saxon, University of Cambridge, in 1991, and is a Fellow of Clare College. He has translated the Latin writings of Aldhelm, and is the author of numerous books and articles on Insular Latin literature.

ALFRED THE GREAT

Asser's *Life of King Alfred*
and other contemporary sources

TRANSLATED
WITH AN INTRODUCTION AND NOTES BY
Simon Keynes and Michael Lapidge

PENGUIN BOOKS

PENGUIN BOOKS

Published by the Penguin Group
Penguin Books Ltd, 27 Wrights Lane, London W8 5TZ, England
Penguin Books USA Inc., 375 Hudson Street, New York, New York 10014, USA
Penguin Books Australia Ltd, Ringwood, Victoria, Australia
Penguin Books Canada Ltd, 10 Alcorn Avenue, Toronto, Ontario, Canada M4V 3B2
Penguin Books (NZ) Ltd, 182–190 Wairau Road, Auckland 10, New Zealand

Penguin Books Ltd, Registered Offices: Harmondsworth, Middlesex, England

First published 1983
11 13 15 17 19 20 18 16 14 12

Set in Ehrhardt Monophoto
Printed in England by Clays Ltd, St Ives plc

Contents

Preface

The Penguin Classics series of translations is one of which King Alfred the Great would have heartily approved. Amid great difficulties, and among many other undertakings, he initiated a programme for the translation into English of 'certain books which are the most necessary for all men to know', and he made arrangements to ensure that they received wide circulation, all as part of his general plan for the revival of learning in England. It seems, therefore, especially appropriate that a volume which gathers together the principal written sources for the study of Alfred and his reign should find a place in the series, and we are grateful to the editor, Mrs Betty Radice, and to Donald McFarlan, of Penguin Books, for their encouragement and support.

King Alfred was also the first to acknowledge his indebtedness to others, and to appreciate the advantage of having 'a few learned men with you who would not disturb you in any way, but would assist you in your work'. We too should like to express our thanks to the many such men and women who have given freely and readily of their advice in connection with the preparation of this book: Peter Baker, Nicholas Brooks, Pierre Chaplais, Wendy Davies, David Dumville, Rosemary Graham, Kenneth Harrison, David Howlett, Alan Kennedy, Peter Kitson, Vivien Law, Stewart Lyon, Rosamond McKitterick, Janet Nelson, Oliver Padel, Raymond Page, Peter Sawyer, Dagmar Schneider, Richard Sharpe, Patrick Sims-Williams, Eric Stanley, Robin Waterfield and Patrick Wormald. But our greatest and most obvious debt is to the work of W. H. Stevenson, who laid the foundations for the modern study of Asser's *Life of King Alfred*, and Dorothy Whitelock, who did so much to advance knowledge and understanding of the Anglo-Saxons in general and of King Alfred in particular. Their track can still be seen, and we have followed.

April 1983

Simon Keynes
Michael Lapidge

Introduction

1. King Alfred the Great

The reign of King Alfred the Great (871–99) is among the most stirring periods of English history. It saw the kingdom of Wessex taken from the brink of Viking conquest to the threshold of an undertaking that led eventually to the political unification of England. It is a story of enduring personal interest, for Alfred himself emerges as a man who had to overcome considerable difficulties in effecting the survival of his kingdom, and whose practical intelligence and vision contributed both materially and spiritually to the future prosperity of his country.

The general pattern of events during the reign is clear. A Viking army, described by contemporaries as 'a great heathen army', invaded England in 865 and met little effective resistance as it passed through the ancient kingdoms of East Anglia, Northumbria and Mercia, forcing each in turn to sue for peace. It was only a matter of time before the Vikings turned their attention to Wessex, and indeed when Alfred became king of the West Saxons in 871 his kingdom was already in the throes of a desperate struggle against the invading army. Under Alfred's leadership the West Saxons fought and bargained for their survival, though their fate remained in the balance until Alfred's famous victory over the Vikings at Edington in 878. His success discouraged another Viking army, which had arrived in the Thames in the same year, from seeking its fortune in Wessex, and while that army directed its efforts to ravaging on the Continent, Alfred embarked on a comprehensive programme of reform. He devised a new system for the defence of his kingdom and overhauled procedures of royal government, but most remarkably he initiated a scheme for the encouragement of learning and involved himself personally in its implementation. When the Viking army returned to England in 892,

Alfred's defensive measures were put to the test, and soon proved their worth; the Vikings dispersed in 896, leaving Alfred free to concentrate in the remaining years of his life on furthering his programme of reform. It was then from the foundations laid by King Alfred that his successors in the tenth century were able to extend their authority over the areas that had previously succumbed to the Viking onslaught, and in the process to bring about the political unification of England. When judged in purely military and political terms, Alfred's achievement was impressive; when judged also in cultural terms, it was truly exceptional. It is no wonder that he has come to be known as King Alfred the Great.

The sources of our knowledge

The historian of Anglo-Saxon England is unusually fortunate in the extent and range of the primary source material available for the study of Alfred and his reign. First and foremost, there is the contemporary biography of the king written by Asser, a monk from (possibly bishop of) St David's in Wales who became his close associate and latterly bishop of Sherborne. This work affords the historian a vivid picture of Alfred in peace and war, and creates a striking impression of how the king ordered his own life; for no other pre-Conquest king does a comparable account of his rule survive.[1] Secondly, there is the *Anglo-Saxon Chronicle*, a series of annals compiled during Alfred's reign and continued thereafter, which provides for the late ninth century a detailed narrative of the king's military activities in the face of Viking invasion. Thirdly, there is a substantial collection of miscellaneous documentary material, including instruments of royal government (a law-code, a political treaty and several charters) and more personal records (letters to the king, and his own will). Finally, there are the literary works of King Alfred himself, comprising a small group of translations of books considered by him to be of particular importance. These are by no means slavish translations, of limited interest, for Alfred interspersed them all with reflections of his own on matters secular, religious and philosophic; they are accordingly of the greatest historical value, and provide a unique insight into the character and outlook of an early medieval king. To these written sources may be added the evidence of coins and archaeology, which make significant further contributions to our knowledge. The present book is intended to supply for the interested reader a collection of the written sources for the reign of King Alfred the Great, and should enable him to form his own judgement on the distinctive quality of King Alfred's rule.

The historical background

In order to place the reign of King Alfred in its historical context, it may be helpful to trace briefly three themes which together characterize the political history of Anglo-Saxon England in the first half of the ninth century. First, the change in the balance of power from a position that favoured Mercia to one that favoured Wessex; secondly, the alliance that developed between these two kingdoms; and thirdly, the course and impact of the Viking invasions.

The kingdom of Mercia had risen to the summit of its political fortunes during the reign of King Offa (757–96). The once independent rulers of the Hwicce (see Map 1, p. 59), of Sussex and of Kent gradually came under Offa's overlordship, and by the end of his reign he had assumed direct royal control over these kingdoms; it seems that he also managed to extend his sway over Lindsey, Surrey, Essex and East Anglia. It is unlikely, on the other hand, that he ever gained the submission of the kingdoms of Wessex and Northumbria, though towards the end of his reign one of his daughters married Beorhtric, king of Wessex (786–802), and another married Æthelred, king of Northumbria (774–8, 790–96); the point is of particular importance in the case of Wessex, for while Wessex was certainly overshadowed by Mercia throughout the eighth century, it appears that she was never overwhelmed, and this may have contributed in some way to her subsequent rise at Mercia's expense. The Mercian supremacy in the east and south-east was maintained after Offa's death for much of the first quarter of the ninth century, but the balance of power was then overturned in 825 at the battle of *Ellendun* (now Wroughton, in north-east Wiltshire): Egbert, king of Wessex (802–39), defeated Beornwulf, king of Mercia (823–5), and as a direct consequence the people of Kent, Surrey, Sussex, Essex and East Anglia submitted to King Egbert. Four years later, in 829, Egbert conquered the kingdom of Mercia and everything else south of the Humber, and in this connection the West Saxon chronicler exclaimed enthusiastically that 'he was the eighth king who was Bretwalda'.[2] In the same year Egbert led an army to Dore, in north Derbyshire, and secured the submission of the Northumbrians; in 830 he is said to have extended his authority over the Welsh.

Egbert's achievements in 825–30 established him momentarily in a position that no king before him had enjoyed, though he seems not to have tried or to have been able to consolidate whatever power he exercised in Mercia, East Anglia, Northumbria and Wales. Wiglaf, king of Mercia, recovered his kingdom in 830, but it is uncertain whether he did so by force or by Egbert's consent. There are various signs, however, that relations between Mercia and Wessex prospered during the following decades, and indeed that the two kingdoms reached some understanding to their mutual advantage which may fairly be termed an alliance. This understanding appears to be reflected in the coinage of Æthelwulf, king of Wessex (839–58), and of Berhtwulf, king of Mercia (840–52), for during the 840s the kings issued coins of similar type and even employed the same moneyers.[3] The existence of an alliance is further suggested by the chronicler's account of how Burgred, king of Mercia (852–74), sought and obtained Æthelwulf's assistance in subjecting the Welsh in 853, and by the fact that in the same year Æthelwulf gave Burgred his daughter in marriage. The alliance between Mercia and Wessex thus originated in the second quarter of the ninth century, and was fostered thereafter; in time it proved to be a critical factor in the struggle against the Vikings.

To judge from the *Anglo-Saxon Chronicle*, it was in the 830s that the Vikings really began to make their presence felt in southern England. They had first descended on the south coast towards the end of the eighth century, during the reign of Beorhtric of Wessex; on that occasion an unfortunate reeve from Dorchester went to meet the company of three ships of Northmen, thinking them to be traders, not raiders, and suffered violent death for his innocent mistake.[4] It is apparent from charter evidence that Viking raiders were active in Kent in the late eighth and early ninth centuries,[5] and they were certainly causing trouble across the Channel in Charlemagne's Francia at the same time. But the continuous record of their activities does not begin until 835, perhaps suggesting that it was only then and thereafter that Viking attacks were at the forefront of men's minds. Sheppey was ravaged in 835; in the following year the crews of thirty-five ships won a victory against King Egbert at Carhampton in

Somerset, but in 838 'a great naval force' which had joined up with Cornishmen was defeated by Egbert at Hingston Down; there were further raids between 840 and 845 (one involving the crews of thirty-three ships), with victories recorded on both sides. These early raids were probably conducted by bands which practised hit-and-run tactics, but in the 850s the nature of Viking activity seems to have taken on a new dimension, as the raiders began to stay in England over the winter. The chronicler records that Vikings stayed 'for the first time' on Thanet in the winter of 850–51, and 'for the first time' on Sheppey in the winter of 854–5, as if the fact of their stay on these occasions seemed in retrospect to have initiated a whole series of occasions on which they did the same, and which for their very recurrence were not in themselves worthy of note. Moreover, whereas the early raids were probably conducted by bands which ranged widely in size, from perhaps a hundred to as many as a thousand men, the more sustained invasions which began in the 850s probably involved armies of consistently greater size.[6] It is true that we cannot take literally the chronicler's statement that '350' ships stormed Canterbury and London in 851, but this figure does at least suggest that the ships were too numerous to count, and so that the fleet was unusually large; the Vikings in question put the Mercians to flight, but were then defeated at *Aclea* (in Surrey) by the West Saxons, who (in the words of the chronicler writing in Alfred's reign) 'inflicted the greatest slaughter on a heathen army that we ever heard of until this present day'. This may mean that the extent of the slaughter had never been surpassed, or that it was only surpassed in Alfred's reign; in either case it is apparent that it was considered to be a notable victory over what must have been a sizeable army.

The period of Alfred's youth

Alfred was born in 849 at Wantage in Berkshire. He was the youngest son of King Æthelwulf, by his first wife Osburh, and thus a grandson of King Egbert. He had four elder brothers, called Æthelstan, Æthelbald, Æthelberht and Æthelred, and one elder sister, Æthelswith. If we are to believe Asser, Alfred was a favourite child, and was brought up exclusively in the royal court under the care of his parents and tutors; since the court did not have a permanent base, we may imagine that Alfred spent the earliest years of his life in the company of his parents on their travels around the kingdom. He came to regret the fact that there were at the time no teachers available to instruct him in Latin learning and the 'liberal arts', and he is said to have remained 'ignorant of letters' during his youth; but he enjoyed listening to English poetry recited or read out to him by others, and had the ability to learn it easily by heart. In this connection, Asser tells the well-known story of how his mother promised to give a 'book of English poetry' to whichever of her sons could learn its contents first, whereupon Alfred took the book to his teacher, memorized the poems with his help, and then recited them to his mother (Asser, chapter 23). He also learnt the daily services, certain psalms and many prayers, and had his favourite passages copied out for him into a little book which he constantly kept by his side.

Alfred did not, however, spend all his childhood thirsting for knowledge in Wessex. In 853, when he was still only four years old, his father sent him to Rome, presumably in the expectation that he would derive some spiritual advantage from the experience; he was received there by Pope Leo IV, who accorded him great honour.[7] Two years later Alfred travelled to Rome for a second time, in company with his recently widowed father. They were entertained on the way by Charles the Bald, king of the Franks, and again on their return in 856, when Æthelwulf took Charles's daughter Judith as his second wife. We may suppose that these visits to Rome and to Carolingian France had some influence on Alfred's later life. His devotion to the papal see is shown by the several recorded occasions in the late 880s when he sent his alms and those of the West Saxons to Rome, and may also account in part for his choice of Pope Gregory's *Pastoral Care* as one of the books he translated. While staying at the Carolingian court Alfred must have wondered at the abundance and quality of the scholars in the Frankish kingdom, and perhaps he still remembered this thirty years later, when he resolved to revive learning in his own kingdom and turned to the archbishop of Rheims for help. Moreover, it is possible that his stay with Charles the Bald also awakened in him a general interest in Frankish affairs, and he may have made a special effort to ascertain in particular how the Carolingian kings had dealt with the Viking raiders, when confronted with the same problem himself.

In the years before Alfred's accession there were further developments in West Saxon history that were to affect the course of events during his reign. As a result of Egbert's victory at *Ellendun* in 825, the kingdom of Wessex had expanded eastwards to include Surrey, Sussex, Essex and Kent, and it was clearly felt for some time thereafter that the size of the enlarged kingdom was too great for one man to control; the question of the succession thus became a complex and sensitive issue, and played a central role in domestic politics in the later part of the ninth century. In his own lifetime Egbert had appointed his son Æthelwulf as king of Kent (presumably with responsibility for the other eastern provinces as well), and in the same way Æthelwulf had assigned all the eastern provinces to his eldest son Æthelstan when he succeeded to the West Saxon throne himself. Æthelstan died in the early 850s, leaving Æthelwulf in sole control, and shortly before his departure for Rome in 855 Æthelwulf divided the kingdom between his two eldest surviving sons, assigning Wessex to Æthelbald and the eastern provinces to Æthelberht. While Æthelwulf (and Alfred) were absent abroad, Æthelbald plotted to prevent his father's return, and although his schemes failed he did manage to retain the favoured western part of the kingdom, obliging his father to take over the eastern provinces from Æthelberht (Asser, chapter 12). But Æthelwulf evidently felt that he retained the right effectively to determine the succession to both parts of the kingdom, and sometime between 856 and 858 he had a document drawn up in which he made his wishes known. The document in question has not survived, but Asser's account of it (chapter 16) shows that Æthelwulf made provision for the division of the kingdom after his death between his sons Æthelbald and Æthelberht (as he had done previously in 855), thereby confirming the former in his possession of Wessex proper but restoring the latter to his control over the eastern provinces. Asser's account can be supplemented by remarks made by Alfred in his will, which, though they relate to the disposal of Æthelwulf's private property (not to the question of royal succession) seem nevertheless to reflect arrangements made for the succession itself. Æthelwulf apparently envisaged that the two parts of the enlarged kingdom would remain separate; that Æthelberht would establish a distinct branch of the royal family to hold the eastern kingdom; that Æthelbald, together with his younger brothers Æthelred and Alfred, would confine their interests to the western kingdom, and that these three brothers would succeed each other, leaving the survivor in sole control. Matters did not, however, turn out as intended. Æthelbald died in

860, and Æthelberht succeeded to the whole kingdom, probably because Æthelred (and Alfred) were themselves unable or unwilling at this stage to assume direct responsibility for Wessex; but as part of the modified arrangement, it was apparently understood that Æthelred and Alfred would eventually succeed (in turn) not only to the western but also to the eastern provinces. Æthelberht died in 865 and Æthelred succeeded to the whole kingdom. Alfred at once sought to safeguard his own interests by asking his brother for his share of their father's private property, though it is unlikely that he went so far as to propose a division of the kingdom itself. Æthelred refused the request, perhaps because he thought it desirable that as king he should retain all available property for his own use, but he did undertake to bequeath their father's private property to Alfred on his death; this undertaking was probably tantamount to the recognition of Alfred as heir-apparent, and indeed Asser makes it plain that he was regarded as such during Æthelred's reign. Further modifications to the arrangement were made soon afterwards to accommodate the interests of their respective children: the new terms ensured that the children of the brother who died first would receive generous provision from the surviving brother, but they left the way clear for the surviving brother to pass over his nephews in favour of his own children when deciding the succession to the kingdom. In the event, of course, Alfred survived (perhaps unexpectedly, since he was unhealthy), leaving the sons of Æthelred understandably disappointed, with little prospect of succeeding to the kingdom themselves; their claims were one of the first problems that Alfred had to face as king.

The arrangements surrounding the royal succession may have complicated matters in the years leading up to Alfred's accession, but they pale into insignificance beside the threat posed by the further activities of the Vikings. A 'great heathen army' arrived in England towards the end of 865, and took up winter quarters in East Anglia. The chronicler reports that the East Angles 'made peace' with them, which can probably be taken to imply that they paid tribute to the army in return for a promise to leave the kingdom. The Vikings at this stage were evidently content to oblige, for towards the end of 866 they moved northwards into Northumbria and established themselves at York. In 867 the Northumbrians 'made peace' with the Vikings and a puppet ruler was appointed, leaving the Vikings free to seek further fortune in Mercia; they took up winter quarters for 867–8 in

Nottingham. The reaction of Burgred, king of Mercia, is particularly interesting, for it represents another expression of the alliance between Mercia and Wessex that had developed during the previous decades. Burgred and his councillors asked Æthelred, king of Wessex, and his brother Alfred for help in fighting against the Vikings, but although a combined Mercian and West Saxon force then laid siege to the Vikings in Nottingham, no serious battle occurred, and the Mercians in turn 'made peace' with the enemy. The alliance was further strengthened at about the same time (in 868) by the marriage of Alfred himself to Ealhswith, whose father was a Mercian ealdorman and whose mother was a member of the Mercian royal family (Asser, chapter 29); and as before, the alliance was symbolized in the coinage, for in the later 860s kings Burgred and Æthelred issued coins almost identical in design and in some cases struck by the same moneyer.[8] The Vikings returned to York in the autumn of 868 and remained there for the greater part of 869; they then retraced their steps still further and took up winter quarters for 869–70 at Thetford, in the kingdom of East Anglia. This time, however, the East Angles were not prepared to countenance their presence or to make a second payment of tribute; the Vikings, for their part, may not anyway have been content to accept money and leave the kingdom in peace. So Edmund, king of East Anglia, fought against them, but he was captured and savagely killed; the Vikings were victorious, and 'conquered the land'. This conquest of East Anglia in 869–70 did not lead to the immediate settlement of the Vikings, and one imagines that at this stage they simply took control of the kingdom (perhaps installing another puppet ruler) and exploited it to their own advantage; for it seems that they were not yet ready to give up the prospect of making further gains elsewhere in England. Towards the end of 870 they moved westwards and established themselves at Reading, and from there struck deeper into the heartland of Wessex. During the opening weeks of 871 King Æthelred and his brother Alfred fought a series of battles against them, but despite an apparently notable victory at Ashdown they failed to achieve any decisive advantage. The situation was made still more desperate for the West Saxons by the arrival at Reading of a second Viking army, and by the death, after Easter, of Æthelred their king.

The reign of King Alfred

Alfred could hardly have come to the throne under more difficult circumstances. A Viking army was at large in the kingdom, and had just been reinforced by another; the fighting had already resulted in a heavy loss of men, the survivors were exhausted, and there was always the possibility that some would be tempted to throw in their lot with the invaders. Moreover, Alfred had his personal problems: a mysterious illness had afflicted him suddenly at his wedding in 868, and caused him continuous distress; he would have to deal with the claims of his two nephews for their share of the inheritance of King Æthelwulf; and a man of his known disposition can only have been unsettled by the poor quality of religious observance and by the sorry state of learning at the time of his accession. It comes as no surprise, therefore, when Asser tells us that Alfred initially had misgivings about his ability to cope, for it is plain from Alfred's own writings that he was not one to take his responsibilities lightly. He thought often and deeply about the burdens of royal government, and about the resources necessary for performing the task committed to him: he needed manpower, in the form of praying men and fighting men and working men, and he needed the means of their support, in the form of land, gifts, weapons, food, drink and clothing.[9] In 871 it must have seemed that the resources at his disposal were woefully inadequate.

The historian, with the advantage of hindsight, can distinguish three periods in Alfred's reign.

(i) The fight for survival (871–8)

A month after his accession, Alfred fought against the combined forces of the two Viking armies, at Wilton, and although he is said to have put the enemy to flight the battle ended with the Vikings having the upper hand. It seems then that Alfred realized there was no prospect of defeating the invaders decisively in the field, and that the only way out of the immediate danger was to come to terms with them: the chronicler reports that the West Saxons 'made peace' with the Vikings, which was probably his way of saying that they bought them off. The Vikings left Wessex and established their winter quarters for 871–2 at London, and again the Mercians 'made peace' with them; in this case it is known for certain that the making of peace involved the payment of money. In 872 the Vikings went to

Northumbria, apparently to restore their power there after a rebellion against Egbert, the puppet ruler whom they had installed in 867; but they established their winter quarters for 872–3 at Torksey in Lindsey, and yet again the Mercians 'made peace' with them. Towards the end of 873 they moved further into Mercia, taking up winter quarters at Repton in Derbyshire. Repton was evidently an important political and religious centre in the kingdom, since at least two Mercian kings – Æthelbald (716–57) and Wiglaf (827–40) – had been buried there; its significance was presumably well understood by the Vikings, and its choice as a base may thus reflect their determination on this occasion to take more than another payment of tribute. Recent excavations in the vicinity of the surviving Anglo-Saxon church at Repton have revealed traces of ramparts identified as part of the Viking camp, as well as multiple burials of warriors which show that the Viking occupation was attended by extensive bloodshed. According to the chronicler, the Vikings drove King Burgred from his kingdom and 'conquered all that land'; they installed a certain Ceolwulf as king in Burgred's place and made him undertake to hand over the kingdom whenever they should want it. By this stage the army that had arrived in 865 had been in the field and on the move for nine years, and it was perhaps essentially the survivors of this army who now decided that the time had come to settle down: so they returned to Northumbria and took up winter quarters for 874–5 somewhere on the river Tyne, and then 'conquered the land'; in 876 their leader Halfdan 'shared out the land of the Northumbrians, and they proceeded to plough and to support themselves', thereby bringing into existence the territory of the northern Danelaw, based on the Viking kingdom of York. The army that had arrived in 871 had itself been in the field for over three years, but it seems nevertheless that its leaders were still intent on bleeding the kingdom of Wessex. From Repton this army came back south and took up winter quarters for 874–5 at Cambridge, and remained there for a year, probably making whatever preparations were necessary.

The second invasion of Wessex began towards the end of 875. The Vikings established themselves at Wareham in 875–6, and Alfred soon came to terms: he is said to have 'made peace' with the enemy, and the Vikings for their part gave him hostages and swore oaths that they would leave his kingdom. However, the Vikings merely transferred their camp further westwards and took up winter quarters for

876–7 at Exeter; again Alfred came to terms, receiving more hostages and more sworn promises, and this time the Vikings honoured the agreement (at least temporarily), for in August 877 they crossed the border into Mercia and established camp at Gloucester. It is not clear how Alfred managed to survive the invasion of 875–7, nor why the Vikings were seemingly prepared to accept his terms; but it is possible that the Vikings agreed to a treaty in 876 merely to extricate themselves from Wareham, and then had to agree to another in 877 because their fleet had suffered heavily on the passage to Exeter and because Alfred had reacted swiftly in bringing his army there. It is also possible that the treaties in question were not quite as favourable to Alfred as the West Saxon chronicler, understandably loyal to his king, implies: he mentions Alfred receiving hostages and the Vikings swearing oaths, but he may well have been putting the best possible interpretation on events, and in the process he may have obscured some further desperate bargaining on the king's part. Alfred was probably keen to gain as much time as possible, for he must have hoped that the Vikings would eventually abandon their plans in Wessex and settle, like Halfdan's men, in the lands they had already conquered; and both sides may have been reluctant to risk a major battle, since much could be gained from negotiation and everything could be lost by defeat. It is likely, therefore, that the treaties of 876 and 877 entailed further payments of tribute by Alfred, and that the Vikings, as well as Alfred, received hostages. Once back in Mercia, the Vikings proceeded to share out some of the land, and to give some to Ceolwulf, so it seems that Alfred's hopes were fulfilled at least in part. The share of Mercia settled at this stage by the Vikings must have included the territory which came later to be known as that of the 'Five Boroughs' (Lincoln, Leicester, Nottingham, Stamford and Derby), as well as the land further south and south-east (around Northampton, Bedford and London). The share allotted to Ceolwulf corresponded to the more south-westerly part of the kingdom, and would have included the towns of Gloucester, Worcester and Warwick.

The settlement of part of Mercia in the autumn of 877 must have involved some dispersal of Viking manpower, but a sufficient number remained in arms to undertake a third invasion of Wessex in 878. In early January, according to the chronicler, the Vikings came stealthily to Chippenham 'and occupied and settled the land of the West Saxons, and drove a great part of the people across the sea, and they subdued and subjected to themselves most of the others, except King Alfred';[10] another group of Vikings invaded Devon at about the same time, but was apparently defeated by the local ealdorman. It is possible that the two Viking armies were operating in collusion with one another, and that their intention had been to capture King Alfred, who may himself have been celebrating Christmas at Chippenham (an important royal estate). Whatever the case, there can be no doubt that Alfred was caught completely unawares: the Vikings from Mercia had arrived under the cover of an apparently firm truce, at a time of year when an attack would have been least expected, and the element of surprise must have contributed in large measure to the extraordinary success that they evidently enjoyed. Alfred found himself in no position to offer any resistance, and was forced into hiding: according to the chronicler, he 'journeyed in difficulties with a small force through the woods and fen fastnesses', and Asser, locating these in Somerset, adds that the king 'had nothing to live on except what he could forage by frequent raids, either secretly or even openly, from the Vikings as well as from the Christians who had submitted to the Vikings' authority' (chapter 53). Knowing their king to be in such desperate straits (or perhaps not knowing him still to be alive), some of the West Saxons may have felt they had no option but to submit to the Vikings, while others may have chosen flight from Wessex as their preferred course of action; in that sense the Vikings effectively conquered the land, though it seems unlikely that they could have maintained much of a presence outside their base at Chippenham.

Alfred presently made a fortification at Athelney in the midst of the Somerset marshes, and from there he proceeded to fight against the enemy. The period spent by the king in his refuge became in course of time the most celebrated part of his reign, and gave rise to various popular stories which served to illustrate, variously, the depths to which he had sunk, the assistance he received from divine powers, and his resourcefulness in snatching victory from the jaws of defeat. The most famous, of course, is the story of how Alfred took temporary shelter in a swineherd's hut, neglected to turn some burning cakes, and was duly berated by the swineherd's wife; the story was an expression of the wretchedness of the king's predicament at this time, and it showed further how it was St Neot who rescued him from his troubles and brought him to victory (see Appendix I). According to another story, St Cuthbert of Lindisfarne came to Alfred disguised as a pilgrim, and asked for food; the king set aside half of all that he had, but when an attendant took him the food, the 'pilgrim' had mysteriously disappeared; moved by the king's generosity, Cuthbert then worked a miracle on the king's behalf and appeared to him in a vision offering advice on how to beat the Vikings and indeed promising him victory and future prosperity.[11] A third story relates how the king, accompanied by a single attendant, entered the Viking camp disguised as a minstrel, and surreptitiously gathered information about the enemy's plans; after several days he returned to Athelney, told his followers what he had learnt, and then led them to victory.[12]

The successful organization of West Saxon resistance to the Vikings is no less remarkable than the success of the Viking invasion in the first place. One can only suppose that it soon came to be known that King Alfred was still alive and kicking, and one has to imagine also that the Vikings were not thick enough on the ground to prevent the West Saxons from mustering their forces. In early May 878 Alfred left Athelney and rode to 'Egbert's Stone', east of Selwood, and was met there by the people of Somerset, Wiltshire and of part of Hampshire; the chronicler's remark, that these others 'rejoiced to see him', is both a suggestion of their former despair and a sign of their instinctive loyalty to the king. Two days later Alfred arrived with his army at Edington in Wiltshire, and there he fought against the Vikings and put them to flight. He pursued the enemy as far as its stronghold (at Chippenham) and camped in front of the gates. After a fortnight the Vikings capitulated. They gave hostages to Alfred, and on this occasion Alfred gave none to them; 'never before', comments Asser, 'had they made peace with anyone on such terms' (chapter 56). They also swore that they would leave Wessex immediately. The agreement was sealed symbolically three weeks later, when the Viking king Guthrum came with his leading men to Alfred at Aller, near Athelney; Alfred stood sponsor to Guthrum at his baptism, and a few days after that, when the ceremony was completed at Wedmore, Alfred honoured him and his companions with gifts. The turn of events which brought Alfred to this position of advantage is one of the more puzzling aspects of his reign. Alfred must have realized that the Viking invasion of 878 was aimed at nothing less than the conquest of his kingdom, so he can have had no choice but to fight; moreover, he may not in this instance have had access to the funds necessary for buying peace, as he had done on earlier occasions. The Vikings for their part cannot have been as numerous as they had been before, and may indeed have been outnumbered by the West Saxons. We remain ignorant, however, of the course of events at the battle of Edington itself, and it is accordingly uncertain whether we should attribute Alfred's victory to the quality of leadership displayed by either of the respective leaders, or more vaguely to the unforeseeable fortunes of war.

Towards the end of 878 the Viking army moved from Chippenham to Cirencester, and a year later it returned to East Anglia 'and settled there and shared out the land'. The settlement of East Anglia in 879–80 represents the third and final stage in the creation of what came to be known as the Danelaw, following the settlement of Northumbria in 876 and of the eastern parts of Mercia in 877. It emerges, therefore, that the creation of the Danelaw was not just a simple matter of conquest leading immediately to settlement: after an initial stage of exacting as much tribute as they could throughout England, the Vikings had turned to establishing direct political authority over the English kingdoms by military conquest, and their actual settlement was a development that occurred subsequently and over several years, as the Vikings tired of life in the field, and eventually as they despaired of achieving the ultimate goal of complete conquest. Nevertheless, in about fifteen years the Viking armies of 865 and 871 had transformed the map of Anglo-Saxon England, by overthrowing the ancient kingdoms of East Anglia, Northumbria and Mercia and by replacing them with new political structures of their own; their influence on the society of the areas where they settled was more subtle, but no less significant for that.[13]

(ii) The years of reconstruction and reform (878–92)

Besides forcing Guthrum's Vikings to abandon their plans in Wessex, Alfred's victory at Edington also discouraged a third Viking army that had arrived in the Thames estuary in 878 from making any attempt to invade Wessex on its own account; this army duly set sail for the Continent in the summer of 879, and occupied itself there for the next thirteen years.[14] After the traumatic events of the 870s,[15] Alfred enjoyed a period of relative freedom from external attack which lasted throughout the 880s and was only brought to an end when the Vikings returned from the Continent in 892. He took full advantage of the situation, for the period saw the inception of the programmes of military, cultural and civil reform which in combination express the distinctive character of his achievement.

The measures by which Alfred strengthened the kingdom's defences are nowhere described for their own sake, but it is clear none the less that he was responsible for the establishment of a number of burhs, or fortified sites, throughout England south of the Thames. Incidental remarks by Asser (chapter 91) reveal that the king was closely involved in all manner of building projects: he alludes to the building and rebuilding of royal halls, chambers and residences, but more significantly he also mentions the construction of cities, towns and fortifications; the reader is given to believe that the king had a hard time persuading his subjects to cooperate with him in the various projects, even though they were of vital importance. In chapter 92 Asser mentions a 'fortification' built at the king's command near Athelney, and the reference is demonstrably to one at Lyng in Somerset; elsewhere he mentions Wareham and Shaftesbury in terms which suggest that both places had been fortified by the time of writing (in 893). Moreover, the account of the campaign against the Viking army in the 890s, given in the *Anglo-Saxon Chronicle*, presupposes the existence by that time of several other burhs, though only Exeter and Chichester are named. In fact an entire network of burhs in southern England, including all those mentioned above, is described in the document known as the *Burghal Hidage*, and although this appears to date from the reign of Edward the Elder (899–924) there can be no doubt that the network was substantially the creation of King Alfred himself.[16] In recent years, great advances have been made in the identification on the ground of the burhs named in the *Burghal Hidage* (see Map 3, p. 61), and it is now possible to understand the intentions that lie behind the document. The sites were strategically selected, and between them guarded the main routes into and through the kingdom of Wessex; moreover, they were distributed in such a way that most people would have been living within twenty miles or so of one such defended place. Above all, however, it emerges that considerable ingenuity was displayed in deciding precisely what type of burh would be most appropriate at each place. In some cases use was made of existing forts, whether Iron Age or Roman in origin, and in other cases new forts were built apparently from scratch; but most remarkable are the sites that are best described as fortified towns, some of which were themselves of Roman origin, while others were effectively new foundations, on promontory sites with irregular defences or on open sites with rectangular defences. In many cases, it seems, these new towns were provided with an internal grid of streets, designed to ensure ease of movement within the burh for defensive purposes; but the street systems would also have served the domestic needs of the inhabitants, and there can be little doubt that these new towns were from the first intended as permanent urban developments in their own right.[17] At once we appreciate the significance of Asser's rhetorical question, 'and what of the cities and towns to be rebuilt and of others to be constructed where previously there were none?' (chapter 91). It remains uncertain what provided the model for Alfred's burghal system. There was a tradition of fortification for defensive purposes in Mercia and, to a lesser extent, in Wessex as well, so it is possible that Alfred's forts and fortified towns were an extension of insular practice. On the other hand, there are some striking parallels between the Alfredian system and the defensive measures undertaken by the Frankish king Charles the Bald in the 860s; and given all the opportunities for the transmission of ideas from the Continent to England, it is difficult to resist the conclusion that Alfred was to some extent influenced by Carolingian example in the planning of his scheme, if not necessarily in its execution.[18] It was presumably in connection with his development of the burghal system, in the 880s, that Alfred reorganized his army: according to the *Chronicle* for 893, 'the king had divided his army in two, so that always half its men were at home, half out on service, except for those men who were to garrison the burhs'. The different elements of Alfred's reformed military organization complemented each other, and the way in which they operated in combination is well illustrated by the account in the *Chronicle* of the campaign against the Viking army which returned to England in 892.

Alfred's practical measures for the defence of Wessex undertaken in the 880s would protect the kingdom from the threat of further Viking attack; but if his military reforms can be regarded as prevention, there is reason to regard his programme for the revival of religion and learning as the intended cure. In one of his own writings, Alfred looked back to the seventh century as a Golden Age when religion and learning flourished, and when kings 'not only maintained their peace, morality and authority at home but also extended their territory outside'.[19] It was clearly felt, however, that the Church had fallen into serious decay during the ninth century, and although some laid the blame on the Viking invasions, others attributed the decline to general failings on the part of the English themselves.[20] The quality of learning in England had also declined, to such an extent that there were not many men capable of understanding Latin north of the Humber, and very few south of the Humber; at the time of Alfred's accession there was not a single one south of the Thames (that is, in Wessex itself).[21] Alfred seems to have regarded the Viking invasions as a form of divine punishment for the decline, and his endeavours to revive religion and learning can thus be seen as an attempt on his part to strike at the heart of the problem and thereby to ensure peace and prosperity in the future.

Alfred's first concern was to recruit learned men to make up for the lack of scholars in Wessex. To judge from Asser's account of this activity (chapters 77–9), the king turned initially to the neighbouring kingdom of Mercia and from there secured the services of Werferth (bishop of Worcester), Plegmund (whom he appointed archbishop of Canterbury in 890), and Æthelstan and Werwulf (described as priests and chaplains); it is not known when these men joined the king, nor indeed whether they did so at one and the same time, but it seems most likely that they came in the early 880s.[22] Asser then states that since the king's desire for learning was still not satisfied, he 'sent messengers across the sea to Gaul to seek instructors' and as a result secured the services of Grimbald and John, both described as priests and monks. John can probably be identified as John the Old Saxon (whom Alfred appointed abbot of Athelney), so it may well be that he came from a monastery in the eastern Frankish kingdom (Germany); but otherwise nothing is known of the circumstances in which he joined Alfred in Wessex. We are relatively well informed, however, about Grimbald, thanks largely to a letter addressed by Fulco, archbishop of Rheims (883–900), to King Alfred. It would appear that Alfred had written to Fulco lamenting the sorry state of the ecclesiastical order in England and seeking the archbishop's help and advice in improving the situation; he had sent to Rheims a sizeable embassy to make his case, and accompanied his request with the gift of some fine hunting dogs. The choice of Alfred's envoys had fallen on a certain Grimbald, who was a monk at St Bertin's in Flanders; it is not clear how they had come to hear of him, but it may have been through Fulco himself, who had been abbot of St Bertin's from 878 to 883. Fulco was clearly reluctant to part with Grimbald, not least because he had intended to make him a bishop as soon as the opportunity arose; nevertheless, he put the service of the Church above his own personal feelings and decided to authorize Grimbald's departure, but only after the envoys had undertaken to ensure that Grimbald would be accorded due honour and that his teaching would be respected. It is apparent from the patronizing tone of his letter that Fulco considered himself to be doing Alfred a great favour, and that he was determined to make Alfred aware of it by emphasizing Grimbald's qualities and prospects, and by stipulating in no uncertain terms that the king should give him every support. Fulco's letter cannot be closely dated, but it seems likely that the negotiations began in about 885 and that Grimbald arrived in England in 886 or soon thereafter;[23] one imagines that John (the Old Saxon) came at about the same time. The only other scholar known to have been recruited by Alfred is Asser himself, and it emerges from Asser's own detailed account of the circumstances in which he joined the king that protracted and complicated negotiations were involved. His first visit to the king took place at Dean in Sussex and lasted just four days; Asser was at that time a monk at St David's in Wales (and he may indeed have been bishop of St David's: see below, p. 52), and on this occasion he insisted that he would have to take advice from members of his community, though he promised to return with an answer in six months' time. He then tells us that he spent just over a year lying ill at Caerwent, but apparently soon after the illness had abated he came to Alfred again, and began to read aloud to the king. The community at St David's evidently hoped to benefit from Asser's presence at the West Saxon court, for through his intercession with Alfred they might gain some relief from the attacks inflicted upon them by the king of Dyfed; so with their blessing Asser agreed to spend six months of every year with Alfred in Wessex, though on this particular occasion he remained for eight. (He may subsequently have altered this arrangement in order to spend more of his time in Wessex, especially after he became a bishop.) Again the chronology of these events is obscure, but there is some reason to believe that his first visit occurred in the opening months of 885, that the second visit lasted from May to December 886, and that the first of the regular visits thereafter began in the latter half of 887.[24]

It was with the help of these men that Alfred began to implement his plan for the revival of learning in England. Grimbald, John, Asser and the Mercians would have been educated in different intellectual traditions, and one imagines that they each had something individual to contribute to the discussions that must frequently have taken place at Alfred's court.[25] One suspects also that they brought with them manuscripts of works that had never been or were no longer available in England, and so set in motion the gradual re-stocking of English libraries after everything had been left 'ransacked and burned' by the Vikings.[26] Alfred's learned advisers busied themselves reading aloud to the king, doubtless explaining passages of particular interest or difficulty; his own understanding of Latin and of the written word would have improved steadily under their guidance. According to Asser, a significant development occurred in 887, when the king 'first began through divine inspiration to read and to translate at the same time, all on one and the same day' (chapter 87); this appears to refer to a miraculous occasion when the king suddenly learned how to read Latin and to translate it into English, but to judge from Asser's further elaboration of the point (chapters 88–9) the reference is rather to an occasion when he resolved to perfect these skills for himself as a means of instructing others. If so, it may have been at about this time that Alfred decided to involve himself personally in a general scheme to produce translations of selected Latin works, for the instruction of all.

Alfred describes the purpose and scope of this scheme in the preface to his translation of Gregory's *Pastoral Care*, which takes the form of a letter addressed by the king to each of the bishops to whom a copy of the work was to be sent. Alfred laments the decline of Latin learning, and proposes a deceptively simple solution: 'Therefore it seems better to me – if it seems so to you – that we too should turn into the language that we can all understand certain books which are the most necessary for all men to know, and accomplish this, as with God's help we may very easily do provided we have peace enough, so that all the free-born young men now in England who have the means to apply themselves to it, may be set to learning (as long as they are not useful for some other employment) until the time that they can read English writings properly. Thereafter one may instruct in Latin those whom one wishes to teach further and wishes to advance to holy orders.' Of the books which were translated in this general scheme as being 'most necessary for all men to know', Alfred himself is believed to have been primarily responsible for four: Gregory's *Pastoral Care*, Boethius's *Consolation of Philosophy*, St Augustine's *Soliloquies* and the first fifty psalms of the Psalter. In addition, several translations were prepared by other scholars at this time, apparently as part of Alfred's scheme: Gregory's *Dialogues*, Orosius's *Histories against the Pagans* and Bede's *Ecclesiastical History*. Some other Old English prose writings which survive from this period should possibly be considered in the context of Alfred's educational scheme as well. It may be helpful briefly to describe each of the works in question.[27]

Gregory the Great was elected pope on 3 September 590 and died on 12 March 604; a man with a genius for organization and administration, he effectively laid the foundations of medieval ecclesiastical government.[28] His *Liber Regulae Pastoralis* (or *Pastoral Care*, as it is usually called) was written soon after his accession to the papacy.[29] It consists of four books and is concerned with the qualities necessary in the man who would be a shepherd of souls: it examines the character, motives and virtues which such a man must have as well as the responsibilities he must undertake, and stresses the need for continual reflection and examination of conscience. The book was immensely popular throughout the Middle Ages,[30] providing in effect the spiritual guidance for secular clergy which the *Rule of St Benedict* provided for monks. It was translated into Greek by Anastasius II, patriarch of Antioch, in 602, and it is not surprising that Alfred should have wished to make it available in translation to his English clergy. But although the *Pastoral Care* is addressed to the clergy, much of its discussion has more general application, and we need not doubt that Alfred took many of its precepts personally to heart. For example, Gregory's insistence on learning as a qualification for those in positions of responsibility finds a direct echo in Alfred's insistence (as reported by Asser, chapter 106) that ealdormen and reeves should devote themselves wholeheartedly to the study of wisdom. Similarly, Gregory's remarks on the chastening effect of tribulations, or on the cares of those responsible for government, or on the need for constancy in the face of the worldly distractions which tempt the ruler – all these concerns will have seemed specifically relevant to Alfred himself. Perhaps as a result of the importance which Alfred attached to the *Pastoral Care*, it was the first work to be translated as part of his general scheme; for a similar reason, perhaps, the translation adheres faithfully to Gregory's text. Alfred made special provision to have the translation circulated to all his bishops, and the success of this provision is reflected in the number of copies preserved to the present day.

Boethius's *Consolation of Philosophy* (in Latin *De Consolatione Philosophiae*) was one of the most important and influential books of the Latin Middle Ages.[31] Boethius was a noble Roman who rose to one of the highest offices of Roman government, serving as 'master of the offices' (*magister officiorum*) under the barbarian king Theodoric (493–526). Boethius, however, was suspected by Theodoric of treasonable associations with the Greek government in Byzantium, and was consequently imprisoned and savagely executed in 525. While in prison awaiting execution he composed the *Consolation of Philosophy*. The work is conceived as a dialogue between Boethius and the Lady Philosophy (who appears to the prisoner in a vision); with Philosophy's guidance, Boethius is able to proceed from maudlin reflections on the injustice and unhappiness of his lot to a just and true appreciation of the role of fate and divine providence in the universe. The work is not overtly Christian (though Boethius himself was unquestionably Christian and occasionally quotes the Bible in the *Consolation* without indicating his source), but its view of providence is not incompatible with a Christian viewpoint. Even today the work could be read with profit by those afflicted by Fortune's adversity, and it is not surprising that it should have had a strong personal appeal to Alfred, harassed and afflicted as he was by Vikings and illness. The twelfth-century historian William of Malmesbury reports that Asser helped Alfred with the translation of Boethius by expounding the text to him in simple prose. With the guidance of Asser (and perhaps of others as well) Alfred produced a fairly free translation of Boethius's text, often drawing on ancillary sources to illuminate passages where Boethius's classical references would have been obscure to a medieval audience; he also attempted to make the work more overtly Christian in conception than the original had been, for example by recasting it in the form of a discussion between Wisdom and Mind and by adding at various points reflections (often of a very homely nature) on the order of the universe and man's capacity for understanding God. More so than in the case of the *Pastoral Care*, Alfred's translation of Boethius reveals the mind of a translator who has pondered deeply on the significance of his text and who has recast its sophisticated philosophical problems in terms at once familiar and immediately comprehensible. Although not always a faithfully accurate translation, it is a valuable index to the king's mental concerns.

The *Soliloquies* (Latin *Soliloquia*) of St Augustine (354–430) belong to a small group of Augustine's early works which are cast in the form of dialogues and which treat individual philosophical problems in considerable detail.[32] The *Soliloquies* are a dialogue between St Augustine's mind and reason (*ratio*) on the question of the soul's immortality. They would not today be considered among Augustine's most important works, nor even a work 'most necessary for all men to know'; nevertheless, the concerns of the *Soliloquies* form a splendid complement to those passages in Alfred's translation of Boethius where the king, departing markedly from the text before him, speculates at length on the soul's immortality and its means of knowing God. The translation of the *Soliloquies* serves Alfred as a pretext for recording his own reflections on the human soul; in other words, it is a translation only in a loose sense of the word. Alfred follows Book I of Augustine's work and the first part of Book II, but thereafter he departs from the text and draws material from a variety of sources. In the preface to his translation Alfred compares his undertaking to that of a builder making many trips to the forest to select timber for his building works; so too Alfred makes many trips to the Church Fathers – he specifically names Augustine, Gregory and Jerome – to select the materials for constructing an eternal home for the soul. These authors and others (notably Boethius) are used in Alfred's version of the *Soliloquies*; yet at points where no patristic source can be identified, it is possible that we have the personal reflections of Alfred himself on his soul's immortality.

Alfred was also responsible for a prose translation of the first fifty psalms of the Psalter. William of Malmesbury reports that Alfred was at work on a translation of the psalms at the time of his death; and one surviving prose version of the first fifty psalms shares so many stylistic features with the other translations by Alfred mentioned above that there can be no doubt that he was its author. There are good reasons why the king might have undertaken a translation of the Psalter. In the first place, during the early Middle Ages the Latin Psalter was the elementary text *par excellence* for instruction in Latin;[33] Alfred would thus have regarded an English translation of

the Psalter as indispensable to his programme for the revival of
religion and learning. More pertinent, perhaps, is the fact that the
psalms (particularly the first fifty) contain King David's lamentations
in the face of severe oppression by his (foreign) enemies and his
assertions of the need to embrace learning and place trust in God.
Alfred will have been intimately familiar with the Psalter, possibly
knowing it by heart, since as Asser tells us (chapters 24 and 76) he had
the invariable habit of listening to the daily office and of participating
in recitation of the psalms. He will obviously have been struck by the
similarities between King David's plight and his own sufferings at
the hands of the Vikings, and been especially receptive to the psalmist's admonitions to embrace learning. From this point of view, it is
possible to regard Alfred's translation of the Psalter as a personal
handbook of consolation and guidance in times of affliction.

   These four works were translated into English by Alfred himself;
but three further works were translated by others, seemingly as part
of the king's programme to make available the books most necessary
for all men to know. The first of these was certainly prepared in
collaboration with the king, namely the translation of Gregory's *Dialogues* (Latin *Dialogi*) by Bishop Werferth of Worcester; Asser tells
us (chapter 77) that Werferth undertook the translation 'at the king's
command'. Gregory's *Dialogues* (written in 593) consist of conversations between the pope and an old friend, Peter, a deacon.[34] The
point of departure for the conversations is that, whereas many holy
anchorites had achieved renown in the East through their miracles,
Italy could boast no such saints. Gregory accordingly sets out to
describe the lives and miracles of numerous Italian saints in order to
put the record straight. Many of the saints he describes are utterly
obscure, but Paulinus of Nola and St Benedict (the founder of Western monasticism, to whom the whole of Book II is devoted) were
widely venerated in Anglo-Saxon England as well as in the rest of
Europe. The final book of the *Dialogues* is concerned (among other
things) with the soul's immortality, a question which continually
exercised Alfred, as we have seen. Another work of late antiquity
widely read during the Middle Ages was Orosius's *Histories against
the Pagans* (Latin *Historiae adversus Paganos*).[35] Paulus Orosius was a
Spaniard by birth who moved to Africa in the early fifth century and
was there befriended by St Augustine. His work was written at
Augustine's suggestion in the aftermath of Alaric the Goth's sack of

Rome in 410, and was intended to refute the belief then prevalent among pagans that times were better in the past and that Rome's present troubles were due to her abandonment of the pagan gods; it is in effect a potted history of the world from the Creation to the year 417. The Old English translation was made during Alfred's reign by an anonymous West Saxon.[36] The translator was clearly not Alfred himself, but was evidently working in collaboration with the king, for at one point he includes a description of the White Sea that reportedly had been given by a sailor named Ohthere to King Alfred.[37] Like some of Alfred's own translations, the Old English Orosius is a rather free rendering, almost at times a paraphrase, of the Latin original: the translator deletes (and confuses) many details in the original, adds a good deal of explanatory matter and generally overhauls Orosius's polemic against the pagans so that the work reads more like a forth-right demonstration of God's guiding role in world history. In this way it could have been thought a useful companion-volume to Bede's *Ecclesiastical History* (Latin *Historia Ecclesiastica*), another work which was translated into English at approximately this time. Bede's *Ecclesiastical History* (finished in 731) is primarily concerned with the establishment of the Christian Church among the English from the arrival of St Augustine (of Canterbury) in 597 up to Bede's own day.[38] The work was widely read all over Europe, but may have had an especial appeal to King Alfred: it gave an account of the happy times in the later seventh century, which Alfred was so concerned to re-create; it provided the English as a whole with a sense of their common past, which would have been of some comfort in times of adversity; and one of its central ideas, that from support of the Church comes worldly prosperity, was as important to Alfred as it had been to Bede. The dialect of the Old English Bede is Anglian, which suggests that its author was a Mercian; and given both its late-ninth-century dating as well as the fact that it was apparently distributed to various scriptoria from a central source much in the manner of Alfred's *Pastoral Care*, it is not unreasonable to think of the Old English Bede as the product of one of Alfred's Mercian helpers, though absolute certainty in the matter is at present unattainable.[39]

Finally, two other Old English prose works should be mentioned in the context of Alfred's revival of learning. The first is the so-called *Leechbook* of Bald, an extensive compilation in two books of medical recipes from various sources.[40] The first book

gives eighty-eight simple cures for various ailments listed roughly
from head to foot; the second contains a similarly large number of
remedies (the exact number is uncertain because the unique manuscript is defective) of a somewhat more 'scientific' nature, including
much discussion of symptoms, causes and so on. The compiler of
the book is unknown; the 'Bald' to whose name it is attached was
apparently the owner (a practising physician or 'leech'?) for whom
it was copied. What is interesting is that one sequence of remedies
in Book II for internal disorders of various kinds is said to have
been sent by Elias, patriarch of Jerusalem, to King Alfred.[41] It is
not improbable, then, that the compilation of Bald's *Leechbook* took
place during Alfred's reign. The second work of interest in this
connection is the Old English *Martyrology*, another extensive prose
compilation which contains notices of some two hundred saints.
The compilation was an original undertaking of immense scope and
genuine scholarly application, for the anonymous compiler apparently assembled and collated an impressive variety of sources; he
drew, in effect, on a very substantial library. The date of the compiler's activity cannot be determined exactly: certainly later than
800 and certainly earlier than the late ninth century, the date of
the earliest surviving manuscript. The compiler could, therefore,
have been a contemporary of King Alfred, and the recent editor of
the work has drawn attention to its lexical and stylistic similarities with the Mercian translations of Alfred's reign (Werferth's
translation of Gregory's *Dialogues* and the Old English Bede).[42]
It remains to be seen whether any direct links between the Old
English *Martyrology* and Alfred's educational programme can be
discovered.

    This list of books will seem a curious, even idiosyncratic, choice to
have served as the basis for a programme of educational reform.[43] In
certain cases (notably Augustine's *Soliloquies*) it seems clear that the
choice was determined by the king's personal predilections rather
than by the book's status as a classic of Christian literature. But
although the choice of books may reflect personal taste to some
extent, it is also clear that the task of making the books available in
translation was very much a joint enterprise by Alfred and his collaborators. In one telling passage of the *Soliloquies* Alfred deliberately
altered a passage in which Augustine had stressed the need for privacy
and tranquillity when writing so as to describe 'a private place free

from all other distractions, and a few learned men with you who would not disturb you in any way, but would assist you in your work'.[44] The chronicler Æthelweard implies that the king's translations were given public readings, no doubt among the close circle of collaborators in the first instance. In the preface to his translation of the *Pastoral Care* Alfred acknowledges the assistance of no fewer than four helpers: Plegmund, Asser, Grimbald and John; presumably the other translations were completed with similar assistance.[45] The project was a large one, and it occupied a number of men for a number of years, a decade at least. The general scheme was apparently conceived in 887 (above, p. 28). The chronology of the various translations cannot be precisely determined, but the *Pastoral Care* was probably the first of Alfred's own translations to be completed, perhaps by as early as 890; the Boethius translation is later than the *Pastoral Care*, and the *Soliloquies* in turn are probably later than the Boethius, on which they appear to draw.[46] Given that the Psalter translation is incomplete, William of Malmesbury's report that Alfred was translating the Psalter at the time of his death (in 899) may well be correct. Werferth's translation of the *Dialogues* was complete at the latest by 893, the year in which Asser wrote his *Life* of the king. The Old English Orosius could well have been complete by as early as 890 or 891.[47] In any case, it is one of the most impressive achievements of Alfred's reign that so extensive a programme of translation could be designed and executed in the space of little more than a decade.

Another important aspect of King Alfred's programme for the revival of learning was his establishment of a school, apparently as an integral part of the royal household, for the education not only of his own children but also of the sons of his leading men and others of lesser birth. The emphasis was evidently on training in literacy, particularly the reading of works in English, and one imagines that the translations of the 'books which are the most necessary for all men to know' featured prominently in the curriculum. The object of the exercise was, in general, to ensure that those who would eventually occupy the offices of worldly power and religious authority in the kingdom would be properly qualified to discharge their responsibilities, for they would be able to pursue for themselves the study of divine wisdom (Asser, chapter 106); Alfred had considerable difficulties with his own generation of officials, who had not had the benefit of this kind of education, and he was determined that their successors should be better trained, in the interests of all.[48] At the same time, however, it seems likely that Alfred hoped to gain some advantage in more practical areas of government and administration. He was certainly a king who gave much attention to perfecting the government of his kingdom (to judge from Asser's account in chapters 99–102 of his arrangements for the division of his annual income and for the organization of the royal household), and he may well have been aware of the benefits to be derived from a new generation of literate royal officials: they would be able to read any written instructions that they might receive, and perhaps to write their own as well, while those who had judicial responsibilities would be able to refer for guidance on matters of principle and procedure to the written laws.[49] Anglo-Saxon royal government had always relied heavily on oral communication, and continued to do so until the end of the Anglo-Saxon period; but there is evidence that increasing use was made of written documents for administrative purposes during the tenth and eleventh centuries, and it is conceivable that Alfred's educational policy established the wider regard for literacy which made this possible.[50]

Alfred's concern to improve the quality of religious life in his kingdom is amply attested by his initiative in the provision of translations of important books, and by his desire that those intended for holy orders should be taught Latin; but he seems nevertheless to have stopped short of attempting a more general reform of the Church. His own foundation of two religious houses, at Athelney and Shaftesbury, suggests a desire on his part to set an example of personal piety, rather than an attempt to set in motion a new monastic movement: his house for monks at Athelney was presumably founded as a symbol of gratitude for deliverance in his most dangerous hour, and his house for nuns at Shaftesbury, which he entrusted to his own daughter Æthelgifu, was perhaps conceived as an expression of his family's faith. It is apparent that a fair number of religious houses had survived into the late ninth century, and the king gave financial support to many of them, perhaps even to all;[51] but despite Asser's admission that they 'do not maintain the rule of monastic life in any consistent way' (chapter 93), there is no evidence that Alfred himself was dissatisfied with the form of religious life practised in them, nor indeed that any attempt was made to impose regular observances upon them. It would, however, be unreasonable to judge Alfred's measures by the standards of the reform movement which prospered under royal patronage in the central decades of the tenth century: Alfred's priority was simply to revive the standards of religious life and learning, and he could hardly go much further than that; more- over, he did not have the material resources to spare for a more lavish display of munificence towards the Church. What he did manage to achieve under such difficult circumstances is remarkable enough: in the 890s he gave thanks for the 'learned bishops' who were by then 'nearly everywhere',[52] and the evidence for the rapid multiplication and dissemination of copies of the various works produced in his reign is another reflection of success. One should add that the stimulus given by King Alfred to the religious life created conditions in which the visual arts were able to flourish: the revival of learning provided new opportunities for the decorators of manuscripts, while the mate- rial support for the Church provided the same for sculptors and architects; metalworkers and exponents of other artistic skills would also have prospered under such circumstances, and all would have been influenced by the 'craftsmen from many races' (Asser, chapter 101) who were employed by the king. One suspects that the result, in context, was nothing less than a cultural renaissance.[53]

King Alfred's plans for the defence of Wessex and for the revival of religion and learning were initiated in the years following his victory at Edington in 878 and were still in the course of imple- mentation when the Viking army returned from the Continent in 892; yet as if these plans were not enough to occupy his attention, the king was simultaneously engaged in other activities of equal importance. In the early 880s Alfred managed to gain recognition as overlord of Mercia, though it is not clear how this was achieved. He had appar- ently maintained amicable relations with the rulers of Mercia in the 870s, for he continued the practice of his predecessors in issuing coinage shared first with King Burgred (his brother-in-law) and then with King Ceolwulf (the one to whom the Vikings had entrusted Mercia following Burgred's expulsion in 874).[54] Ceolwulf's reign ended in unknown circumstances in 879, but it seems that a certain Æthelred soon gained the position of ealdorman of western Mercia, and charter evidence reveals that he had acknowledged Alfred's over- lordship by 883. Alfred's next move was calculated to serve the inter- ests of both Wessex and Mercia, and it set the seal on their relations.

When the Vikings had settled in eastern Mercia in 877 they had very probably taken control of London, and for as long as the city remained in Viking hands neither the West Saxons nor the Mercians could feel secure. The danger would have been especially apparent in 885, when a Viking force had assembled at Benfleet, on the north bank of the Thames estuary, threatening a strike further upriver and thence inland. In fact this never materialized, but none the less Alfred was quick to react: in 886 he took the offensive against the Vikings of London, and managed to capture the city after a siege; he restored its defences, and made arrangements for the settlement there of a permanent garrison. Alfred then entrusted London to the control of Ealdorman Æthelred, thereby respecting its former status as a Mercian town; soon thereafter, it seems, Æthelred was married to Alfred's daughter Æthelflæd, further strengthening the alliance between Wessex and Mercia.[55]

The capture of London in 886 precipitated an event of the utmost significance in Alfred's reign: as the chronicler records, 'all the English people that were not under subjection to the Danes submitted to him', or as Asser puts it, 'all the Angles and Saxons ... turned willingly to King Alfred and submitted themselves to his lordship' (chapter 83). This submission appears to represent some kind of ceremonial commitment made by all Englishmen outside the Danelaw to recognize Alfred as their ruler and leader in the struggle against the Vikings, and to support him in all his endeavours; one imagines that it involved West Saxons, Mercians and others alike, and it is possible that they were required to take an oath of loyalty to the king.[56] The occasion may have been regarded (by some) as marking the emergence among the English of a sense of common identity, under a common leader, in a common cause, for there are signs that such an attitude, however grandiose and anachronistic it may seem, was indeed current in the aftermath of the general submission of 886. Sometime between 886 and 890 King Alfred concluded a treaty with Guthrum, king of the Vikings in East Anglia, and the prologue associates Alfred with 'the councillors of all the English race', as if he were regarded as the leader of more than the West Saxons alone. It is also significant that in certain charters of the late 880s and early 890s Alfred is styled 'king of the Angles and of the Saxons', or 'king of the Anglo-Saxons',[57] apparently reflecting his enhanced authority as king of both peoples, or perhaps simply representing a position which those in the king's circle were anxious to promote on his behalf.

The same spirit of unity under Alfred's leadership appears to pervade two major works which can probably be assigned to this period: Alfred's law-code and the *Anglo-Saxon Chronicle*. Alfred's law-code affords valuable evidence of those matters which the king considered to be of particular importance for ensuring social and political order: for example, he lays great stress on the keeping of oaths; he announces severe punishment for treachery to a lord, and especially for treachery to the king; and he specifies procedures for the settlement of feuds without undue bloodshed. But the law-code was evidently intended to be more than a collection of pronouncements on matters of current concern to the king. The act of law-making was a public display of a king's royal power, and provided an opportunity for him to express his political and ideological aspirations in legal form. The code begins with translated extracts from the Mosaic Law, and continues with an account of how this Law was subsequently modified for application to Christian nations and augmented by successive councils of the Church. In this way Alfred places his own activity as a law-giver in what he regards as its proper context, effectively implying that the legislation which follows stands in the same tradition and represents that of the new chosen people.[58] But who were the people in question? Alfred is styled 'king of the West Saxons', yet he seems to be conscious of a wider conception of his position. He acknowledges his debt to the earlier West Saxon, Mercian and Kentish laws of Kings Ine, Offa and Æthelberht, and thus it seems that he thought of himself as successor to all three traditions of royal legislation. Since Alfred's legislation was apparently the first attempt at a codification of law for the best part of a century, it would have represented a dramatic assertion of his role as the shepherd and guardian of an amalgamated English people.

The *Anglo-Saxon Chronicle* was not 'published' until after the return of the Viking army from the Continent in the autumn of 892,[59] but the main work of compilation must have started some time before, since the *Chronicle* was available to Asser writing in 893 and does not give the impression of having been produced in a hurry. The compilers present a view of history seen very much from a West Saxon perspective, but to no greater extent, perhaps, than would be expected given their natural sympathies as West Saxons themselves, the range of sources likely to have been at their disposal, and the

reality of West Saxon power at the time of compilation. It seems
more significant that they expended considerable effort in putting
together a synopsis of early Christian and Roman history to provide a
background for their main subject; that they borrowed material from
Bede's *Ecclesiastical History* to trace the advance of Christianity
among the various peoples of England in the seventh century; and
that they did what may be considered their best to incorporate historical traditions and to supply information on royal genealogy and
regnal succession not only for Wessex but for other kingdoms as well.
As the product of such extensive research, involving both translation
from Latin sources and the collection of diverse kinds of material,
the *Chronicle* represents a notable intellectual achievement in its own
right, and it is accordingly difficult to dissociate its production from
the circle of learned men around the king. It is obvious that the actual
work of compilation was done by Englishmen, but it is possible that
the idea of assembling all the material and producing a history on this
scale should be attributed at least in part to the influence of one of
Alfred's Frankish helpers: there was certainly a strong tradition among
the Franks of historical writing in the form of annals, and a man like
Grimbald of St Bertin's may well have urged the compilation of a
chronicle soon after his arrival in England, while Frankish influence
would also account for the extent and quality of the information on
continental affairs incorporated particularly in the annals for the
880s.[60] Moreover, the *Chronicle* fits naturally among the other historical works produced in Alfred's reign (and presumably under his
direction): it complements the translations of Orosius's *Histories
against the Pagans* and Bede's *Ecclesiastical History*, and indeed there
is some evidence that the man responsible for the Orosius was himself
acquainted with the *Chronicle*.[61] It should be emphasized, however,
that King Alfred need not have been involved personally in the work
of compilation, so we cannot assume that the *Chronicle* was in that
sense an 'official' production. We should also resist the temptation to
regard it as a form of West Saxon dynastic propaganda, written for
the consumption of the West Saxons in particular and intended to
arouse their support for King Alfred at a time when the very survival
of his dynasty was at stake.[62] It reads more like an attempt at a
history of the English people as a whole, showing how they shared a
common past stretching back to the beginning of the Christian era,
but demonstrating at the same time how the West Saxon kings had

assumed the lead. The *Chronicle* thus accords well with the wider
conception of Alfred's position known to have been current at precisely the time of its compilation: it projected an image of history of
which the king and his circle would have approved, for it gave expression in historiographical terms to the political aspirations which
cast Alfred as 'king of the Anglo-Saxons'.

(iii) A kingdom defended (892–9)

The Vikings who had been active on the Continent since 879 suffered
a serious defeat at the battle of the river Dyle in 891, and a famine in
the following year forced them to return to the coast of Flanders,
whence they presently embarked for England. The Vikings landed in
Kent, and were soon joined by another army, also with many years'
experience on the Continent. The two fleets were estimated to com-
prise 250 and 80 ships respectively, and even when due allowance
is made for exaggeration and for the presence in the ships of women,
horses and provisions, it is difficult to resist the conclusion that the
combined force numbered at least three or four thousand men.

The return of the Vikings to England appears to have occasioned
the 'publication', in late 892 or early 893, of the *Anglo-Saxon Chronicle*, presumably because its compilers felt that their view of the past
was particularly apposite at a moment of such grave national crisis,
when it would have been essential to strengthen in any way possible
the resolve of the English to unite under Alfred's leadership against
the common enemy. Moreover, it seems likely that it was precisely
the appearance of the *Chronicle* at this time that prompted Asser to
write his *Life of King Alfred*; the fact that he was able to gain access
to a copy almost as soon as it became available, and then use it as the
basis of a biography dedicated to the king, further encourages the
belief that the *Chronicle* was itself a product of the court circle. But
whereas the *Chronicle* was written for a readership composed of
Alfred's English subjects, Asser's *Life* was apparently intended to
serve a different, though complementary, purpose. By the time Asser
was writing in 893, all the rulers of the Welsh had submitted to King
Alfred, so the Welsh themselves had become a significant group
among the king's subjects; the *Life of King Alfred* was evidently
written with a Welsh readership in mind, and its purpose may have
been to convey to them some idea of the personal qualities and
military achievements of their English overlord. It is interesting that

Asser styles Alfred 'king of the Anglo-Saxons' throughout, indicating his own awareness of the significance of recent political developments and suggesting his concern to point out to the Welsh that Alfred stood for a new sense of unity among the English. It is also important to notice that he casts the Vikings as 'pagans' and the English as 'Christians',[63] thereby presenting the struggle between them as a holy war and enabling the Welsh to identify themselves more readily with Alfred's cause. Of course there is no evidence that the *Anglo-Saxon Chronicle* and Asser's *Life of King Alfred* were ever brought into service for the purposes outlined above; the *Chronicle* does appear to have been copied quite frequently at an early stage, implying that it achieved a degree of circulation, but Asser's *Life* may not even have been finished. So far as their 'purpose' is concerned, both may be little more than exercises in wishful thinking, not truly representative of the realities of the situation but at least affording some idea of the thoughts of learned men in the court circle as they responded to the new crisis.

Our knowledge of the warfare in the 890s is derived from the first continuation of the *Anglo-Saxon Chronicle*, covering the years from 893 to 896; the details are best followed in the chronicler's own words, for he manages to convey a particularly vivid impression of Viking action and English reaction during the course of the campaign. It may be helpful, however, to draw attention to certain points of interest which arise from the chronicler's account. In the first place, the Vikings who arrived in 892 received much support from those who had previously settled in Northumbria and East Anglia, and when they were not actually operating together as a single army, the different Viking forces struck simultaneously in different parts of the country and thus stretched the English defences to the limit. Secondly, when the account of Viking activity in the 890s is compared with the account of their activity in the 870s, it is immediately apparent that the character of the conflict between Vikings and English has changed, and that the change was brought about directly by the defensive measures undertaken by King Alfred in the 880s. The Vikings no longer have complete freedom of movement through the country: wherever they go, they find themselves confronted by the local garrisons based on the burhs, and at the same time they are often pursued or besieged by mobile sections of the English army kept on service in the field. The Vikings were very effective as raiders, but they were less well suited to a war of attrition against a firmly entrenched and highly organized opposition: the English could draw on the resources of the countryside for sustenance and reinforcements, and were able therefore to maintain constant and relentless pressure on the enemy. Thirdly, the description of the events at Buttington in 893 shows that the West Saxons, Mercians and Welsh did collaborate with one another against the Vikings, while the description of the naval engagement in 896 reveals the presence of Frisians among the English forces: it is significant that on both occasions the chronicler refers to the 'Christians' collectively, suggesting that their common religious identity was seen as the basis of such combined operations. Fourthly, the chronicler's account of the campaign shows Alfred personally at the height of his powers as a military leader, affording three famous examples of his practical resourcefulness: Alfred's division of the army (annal 893), his investigation of the Viking position near Hertford in order to establish how best to prevent their escape (annal 895), and his order for the construction of long-ships according to his own design (annal 896). Finally, it should be emphasized that the Vikings were never decisively defeated, and eventually gave up in despair: they must have realized that for all their efforts they had made little impression on the English, and in the summer of 896 those who had sufficient resources to start a new life opted to settle in the Danelaw, while those who had nothing returned to the Continent in further search of fortune.

Little is known of events in the last three years of Alfred's reign (897–9), for apart from a couple of obits the annals in the *Anglo-Saxon Chronicle* are completely blank; one of the most dramatic periods of English history simply peters out in apparent anticlimax. But if the dispersal of the Vikings in 896 left all quiet on the West Saxon front, it would be mistaken to infer that Alfred spent his last years in peaceful inactivity. He cannot have known that there would be no further invasions from across the sea for many years, and he would certainly not have imagined that the Vikings settled in the Danelaw would remain docile in the foreseeable future. It is likely, therefore, that more work was done to improve the burghal defences of England, and that Alfred impressed on his son Edward, his daughter Æthelflæd and his son-in-law Æthelred the necessity of continuing the process of the reconquest of the Danelaw, which he had started by taking control of London in 886; in fact one document reveals that arrangements for the fortification of Worcester were still under consideration in the 890s,[64] and another shows that the king held a meeting in 898 or 899 to discuss the 'restoration' of the city of London.[65] Meanwhile, Alfred must also have been engaged in further work of translation: his translation of Gregory's *Pastoral Care* was probably circulated in the early 890s, but his translations of Boethius's *Consolation of Philosophy*, of St Augustine's *Soliloquies*, and of part of the Psalter, were made during the closing years of his reign. These translations thus reflect the intellectual preoccupations of the king as he neared the end of his life, and as he continued his quest for knowledge of divine wisdom, both for his own sake and for the benefit of others.

When Alfred died, aged about fifty, on 26 October 899, his achievements were far from secure; it remained for those who came after him to ensure that the promise of his reign was properly fulfilled. The Anglo-Saxon kingdom eventually taken over by William the Conqueror was forged in the tenth century by men like Æthelstan and Edgar; but if the furnace they used was originally constructed by Egbert of Wessex, it was Alfred who had kept the embers glowing during the worst of the storms and who had then raised the fire.

The cult of King Alfred

King Alfred belongs to a very select group of medieval rulers who are known popularly as 'the Great', though in at least one important respect he stands apart from the others. Charles, king and subsequently emperor of the Franks (768–814), was called 'the Great' already in the first half of the ninth century, though it was not for another two hundred years or so that 'Carolus Magnus' appeared in the more familiar form 'Charlemagne' in the French *chansons de geste*; Otto, king and emperor of the Germans (936–73), was similarly called 'the Great' within fifty years of his death. Alfred, by contrast, was something of a late developer. The earliest occurrences of his epithet 'the Great' are in references to the king made by historians writing in the sixteenth century, and the style was not popularized until the Latin version of Sir John Spelman's *Life of Alfred the Great* was published in 1678, followed by the original English version in 1709.[66]

It is important to ask, therefore, whether Alfred's greatness was perceived by his contemporaries and immediate successors, or whether it was only apparent to those who had the advantage of hindsight. Asser himself was certainly fulsome in his praise of the king, and as would be expected of a close associate he focused his attention on Alfred's personal qualities, dwelling on the king's piety, generosity, courage, perseverance, justice and wisdom; but as befits a contemporary observer, he need not have been immediately concerned to reflect in objective terms on the significance of anything that the king had achieved. Asser's views were undoubtedly shared by other contemporaries: Wulfsige, bishop of Sherborne, expressed his admiration for the king in Old English verse (below, p. 187), and a foreigner, who may have been John the Old Saxon, did the same in two Latin acrostics (below, p. 192). The notice of Alfred's death in the *Anglo-Saxon Chronicle* describes him as 'king over the whole English race, except for that part which was under Danish rule', while the chronicler Æthelweard, writing towards the end of the tenth century, refers to 'the magnanimous Alfred . . . king of the Saxons, unshakeable pillar of the western people, a man replete with justice, vigorous in warfare, learned in speech, above all instructed in divine learning':[67] again the emphasis is on Alfred's personal distinction, as if this more than anything else set him apart from other kings. Æthelweard goes on to mention Alfred's translation of 'unknown numbers of books', and the homilist Ælfric, at about the same time, similarly refers to 'the books which King Alfred wisely translated from Latin into English, which are obtainable';[68] so the fruits of Alfred's labours were much appreciated, and indeed it is clear that the translations were studied throughout the tenth and eleventh centuries.[69]

There is, on the other hand, no evidence from the Anglo-Saxon period that Alfred was raised above his fellow kings in the estimation of his countrymen. Although Asser's *Life of King Alfred* was known in the later Anglo-Saxon period, it did not become as popular as one might otherwise expect; perhaps this should be understood as a reflection on the work itself, and not on the subject, but it is instructive to compare the apparently limited circulation of Asser's *Life* with the wide dissemination enjoyed on the Continent by Einhard's *Life of Charlemagne*, known from several manuscripts written in the ninth and tenth centuries (and from many later medieval ones). It is also interesting to observe that when King Æthelred the Unready (978–1016) was choosing names for his sons (having decided, evidently, to restrict himself to the names of his predecessors on the throne), he started with 'Æthelstan', then went back to 'Egbert', and then followed King Æthelstan's successors with 'Edmund', 'Eadred',

'Eadwig', 'Edgar' and 'Edward'; only then, having used the name of his own immediate predecessor, did he revert to 'Alfred' as the name for his eighth and youngest son. If only on this evidence (and admittedly it is not much), it may be that the real heroes in the late tenth century were Æthelstan (who destroyed the formidable Norse–Celtic alliance at the battle of *Brunanburh* in 937) and Egbert (who broke the long-lasting Mercian supremacy at the battle of *Ellendun* in 825). Æthelred might not have considered it appropriate to give his own father Edgar more prominence, but others were less inhibited. In the early eleventh century, the homilist Ælfric singled out three kings in England who were 'often victorious through God': the first (chronologically) was Alfred, 'who often fought against the Danes, until he won the victory and protected his people'; the second was Æthelstan, 'who fought against Olaf and slew his army and put him himself to flight, and afterwards lived in peace with his people'; but the third was Edgar, 'the noble and resolute king, [who] exalted the praise of God everywhere among his people, the strongest of all kings over the English nation'.[70] Alfred may, therefore, have been regarded as just one of a series of extremely capable kings in the ninth and tenth centuries, who between them turned the kingdom of Wessex into the unified kingdom of England; and since his part in this collective achievement was basically survival, his contribution may have been eclipsed to a great extent by the more tangible and spectacular contributions of his successors. Memories of Æthelstan and Edgar would have to fade before Alfred could come into his own.

The further development of King Alfred's reputation is a subject worthy of study in its own right. It is likely that tales of Alfred's wars and wisdom circulated orally before the Conquest, and were handed down in popular tradition to later generations, but it is difficult now to distinguish any remnant of such tales from the purely fictional and imaginary elements in the literary accounts of Alfred which survive. The Anglo-Norman historians, in the first half of the twelfth century, were primarily responsible for determining later medieval knowledge of Anglo-Saxon history, and they served King Alfred well: Orderic Vitalis regarded Alfred as 'the first king to hold sway over the whole of England' and considered that 'in goodness, nobility, and states-manship he stood head and shoulders above all the kings of England who came before and after him';[71] 'Florence' of Worcester was among those who incorporated material derived from Asser's *Life of King*

Alfred in their accounts of the king, otherwise based on the *Anglo-Saxon Chronicle*, and in this way the details of Alfred's personal qualities entered the mainstream of written historical tradition; William of Malmesbury claimed that local inhabitants still pointed out the places associated with King Alfred, and provided some important information on the king's literary activities; while Henry of Huntingdon was moved to celebrate Alfred's achievements in verse.[72] The stories told about the king multiply thereafter in bewildering confusion, crediting him with all manner of accomplishments and steadily improving with each retelling. Most were probably fabricated from the best of motives, and exemplify or elaborate some undoubtedly authentic aspect of the king's character; but a few, like Alfred's supposed role in the foundation of Oxford University,[73] were invented for less laudable purposes. One of the most persistent themes was Alfred's wisdom. His reputation in this respect may have originated in Asser's *Life*, where he is called *veredicus*, 'truthful' (chapter 13), and where references to his love of wisdom abound; but he is called 'the wise King Alfred' in an alleged writ of Æthelred the Unready,[74] which may testify to the existence of an independent and popular tradition. The early Middle English poem *The Proverbs of Alfred* is a collection of precepts for good conduct uttered by the king (called 'England's darling') in an assembly at Seaford in Sussex, and other supposedly Alfredian words of wisdom occur in the poem *The Owl and the Nightingale*; both poems illustrate the tendency in the twelfth and thirteenth centuries to attribute wise sayings to the king, but alas there is no reason to believe that any of the sayings derive from Alfred himself.[75]

As the stories multiplied and improved, Alfred's fame came easily to surpass that of all other Anglo-Saxon kings: perhaps a king whose personal qualities had made such a strong impression on his contemporaries would be expected to rise in popular estimation above kings known only from the bare record of their achievements, once those achievements had themselves been overtaken by subsequent events; perhaps as later generations began to indulge in historical reflection the singular importance of Alfred's contribution to English history came into sharper focus, once it was seen how his heroic stand against the Viking invaders had made all else possible; or perhaps it was simply the concentration of so many virtues in the person of Alfred that gave him his special appeal. Alfred came to be known as 'the

Great' during the sixteenth century; his reputation prospered mightily thereafter, though he was admired by different people for different reasons. In the seventeenth century he was held up as a mirror of princely behaviour: Sir John Spelman's *Life* was apparently written for the edification of Charles I in 1642–3, and when published in 1678 was dedicated to Charles II. In the eighteenth century he was credited by radical thinkers with the foundation of the democratic and popular forms of government held to have been characteristic of the Anglo-Saxon past and to have been destroyed by the tyranny of the Normans.[76] He was celebrated widely in novels, poems and plays (in fact it was in *Alfred: a Masque*, produced in 1740, that the song 'Rule Britannia' made its first appearance), and artists too found inspiration in the stirring events of his reign.[77] During the reign of Queen Victoria the love of all things Germanic gave the cult of Alfred a further boost, and he was venerated not only as the founder of the British navy but also as the founder of the British Empire. The millenary of his birth was enthusiastically commemorated in 1849, and a statue of the king was subsequently unveiled at Wantage;[78] what was regarded by some as the millenary of his death, in 1901,[79] was marked by more celebrations which culminated with the unveiling of another statue, at Winchester.[80] The legendary king who emerged into the twentieth century is far removed from the historical king of the late ninth century, and it was the legendary king who was acclaimed as Alfred the Great; but while historical tradition has a way of distorting the truth, in this case there can be no doubt that justice was done.

2. *Asser and his* Life of King Alfred

Asser's *Life of King Alfred* is the earliest known biography of an Anglo-Saxon king, and as such is an invaluable source for the study of early England. But whereas Asser's biography throws precious light on his subject's life, the life of the royal biographer is unfortunately obscure.

Asser was a Welshman, from St David's in the kingdom of Dyfed. His name, curiously enough, is not Welsh but Hebrew, and was evidently adopted from the Old Testament figure Aser (Asher), the eighth son of Jacob (see Genesis xxx, 13, etc.). The custom of adopting Old Testament names was fairly common in medieval Wales (numerous Welshmen named Abraham, Daniel, Iago/Jacob, Isaac, Samson, etc., are encountered in Welsh records), and in fact the name Asser is by no means a rarity.[81] Nevertheless, it is perhaps worth asking why the name Asser should have been chosen among so many others. In his treatise on the meaning of Hebrew names, St Jerome explains that the name Asser means 'blessed' or 'blessedness'.[82] There is evidence that Jerome's treatise was studied with care in ninth-century Wales,[83] and it is therefore perhaps significant that the meaning of the Hebrew name Asser corresponds exactly to that of the Welsh name Gwyn (Old Welsh Guinn). A learned Welshman named Gwyn who had some familiarity with Jerome's treatise might well have adopted the name Asser in religion, at the time he was tonsured. However, although the name Gwyn is very common nowadays, it is not as widely attested in early Welsh sources, so the question of Asser's Welsh name (if indeed he had one) must be left open.

   Contemporary sources other than the *Life of King Alfred* supply a very few fleeting references to Asser's activities in Wessex. King Alfred himself explicitly acknowledges the help of 'Asser my bishop' in translating Gregory's *Pastoral Care* (below, p. 126), and the scholarly assistance given by Asser to the king is confirmed by the twelfth-century historian William of Malmesbury, who notes that Asser helped Alfred to translate Boethius's *Consolation of Philosophy*.[84] Episcopal lists show that Asser was bishop of Sherborne.[85] Wulfsige, his predecessor in the lists, attests a charter dated 892 (below, p. 181), but there is no evidence for the position thereafter until Asser makes his first appearance as a witness in a charter dated 900; he otherwise occurs among the witnesses to several charters issued in the early years of the tenth century.[86] Asser's succession to the see of Sherborne can thus be dated no more closely than between 892 and 900, but it is apparent that he was already a bishop before he succeeded Wulfsige, since Wulfsige is known to have received a copy of the *Pastoral Care* (in which Asser is described as a 'bishop').[87] It is possible that he had been made a suffragan bishop within the diocese of Sherborne before he was elevated to the bishopric itself,[88] but it can also be argued that he had been ordained as bishop of St David's before he first came to Wessex (see below). A set of Welsh annals kept at St David's records the death of Asser under the year 908,[89] and the *Anglo-Saxon Chronicle* states simply that 'Asser, who was bishop of Sherborne' died in 909.[90]

It is possible to flesh out this skeleton of bare facts with the autobiographical details supplied by Asser himself in his *Life of King Alfred*, but before doing so it is necessary to apply one more stripe to a horse not yet but nearly dead, namely, the hypothesis that the *Life* is not the authentic work of a late-ninth-century Welshman named Asser, but rather the work of a later forger. This hypothesis has been propounded in various forms during the past 150 years,[91] most recently in 1964 by V. H. Galbraith.[92] His case was promptly and comprehensively demolished by Dorothy Whitelock,[93] but Galbraith's richly deserved prestige as a medieval historian has ensured that suspicion still lingers in some quarters, and hence it is necessary briefly to review the main points at issue. Galbraith argued that the text contains serious anachronisms, and he fastened on two in particular: that Asser repeatedly describes Alfred as *rex Angul-Saxonum* (a title which, in his opinion, only became current in the late tenth century), and that Asser refers specifically in chapter 81 to the 'diocese' (translating *parochia*), and hence by implication to the 'bishopric', of Exeter (a see which was not created until much later, in 1050). Galbraith went on to suggest that the forger was none other than the Leofric who became bishop of Devon and Cornwall in 1046, who was instrumental in transferring his episcopal seat from Crediton to Exeter in 1050, and who died in 1072.[94] Leofric's motive in allegedly forging the work was to promote or to justify the re-establishment of his see at Exeter, by showing that such an arrangement had a distinguished precedent. He was, moreover, a Welshman, and the *Life of King Alfred* is certainly by a Welshman; and he had a library available to him at Exeter which included many of the works cited in the *Life*.

Galbraith's arguments make compelling reading, but they collapse on further investigation. He seems not to have realized that the regnal style *rex Angul-Saxonum* ('king of the Anglo-Saxons') was indeed current in royal charters issued in the late 880s and early 890s (above, p. 38), and hence the usage is unquestionably Alfredian and entirely appropriate. He seems also to have overlooked the fact that *parochia* was a term frequently employed by Celtic-Latin authors to designate the *jurisdiction* of a church or monastery and has nothing to do with a bishop or his bishopric (below, p. 262 note 181, and p. 264 note 193); hence there is no necessary reference here to the diocese, or bishopric, of Exeter. Both Galbraith's alleged anachronisms are therefore illusory. The case against Leofric is equally insecure. It is far from certain that Leofric was a native speaker of Welsh,[95] as the author of the *Life of King Alfred* certainly was; and even if he were, it is doubtful that he could have known that Asser was a Welshman or would have considered him a suitable person on whom to foist the forgery, since little information about Asser would have been available to him. And while it is true that there are certain books in common between those cited in the *Life of King Alfred* and those present in Leofric's library, it cannot be said that the overlap is significant: books like Sedulius's *Carmen Paschale* and Gregory's *Regula Pastoralis* were so widely studied in Anglo-Saxon England that they could have been found in any monastic library.[96] Leofric had no specialized collection, and one might as well argue that the other books cited in the *Life of King Alfred* (including works by Aldhelm, Virgil, Augustine and Einhard: see below) do not appear to have been owned by Leofric.[97] One should add that there is powerful evidence that the now lost Cotton manuscript of the *Life* was written in about 1000 (below, pp. 223–5), and that the work was already known and being used in the first half of the eleventh century (below, p. 57); so it is difficult to believe that the work was not written until the middle of the eleventh century. Moreover, if the text is studied closely, it will be seen that in countless respects information conveyed by Asser can be corroborated by a variety of independent and contemporary sources, and it is simply inconceivable that a later forger could have produced a work which accords so well with the other evidence available; in the notes accompanying our translation of Asser we have wherever possible drawn attention to evidence of this nature. In short, the case against the authenticity of Asser's *Life of King Alfred* does not stand up to scrutiny, and any lingering doubts should be laid peacefully to rest.

We may now return to the subject of Asser himself. We learn from the *Life of King Alfred* that Asser was a native Welshman who had been brought up, trained, tonsured and eventually ordained at St David's (chapter 79). On the face of it, these remarks would appear to imply simply that Asser was a monk and a priest. However, near the end of the same chapter he couples his own name with that of a kinsman of his, one 'Archbishop' Nobis (a bishop of St David's who died in 873 or 874: see below, p. 262 note 182), in the context of discussing bishops who had been expelled from the see of St David's by King Hyfaidd of Dyfed. Taken together the two observations have suggested to some commentators that the ordination in question was episcopal, not merely sacerdotal, in character, and that Asser had in fact been ordained as bishop of St David's by the time he met King Alfred.[98] It is worth noting that Gerald of Wales (or Giraldus Cambrensis, as he is often called) lists Asser among the bishops of St David's in his *Itinerarium Cambriae*, written in 1191.[99] If Gerald's evidence is trustworthy, then Asser may indeed have been bishop of St David's when he first met King Alfred – which would explain why Asser was evidently reluctant to be away from St David's for more than six months in any year and how Alfred could refer to him as 'my bishop' in the preface to the *Pastoral Care*, written before Asser succeeded Wulfsige at Sherborne. It has to be admitted, however, that the argument is tenuous, and Asser's exact status when he came to Alfred's kingdom must remain uncertain.

Asser was summoned by King Alfred from the 'remote, western-most parts of Wales' (chapter 79), and he met the king for the first time on the royal estate at Dean (in Sussex), probably in 885 (above, p. 27). We have no means of knowing how Asser's name or reputation came to Alfred's attention. The kings of several southern Welsh kingdoms, including Hywel ap Rhys of Glywysing and Hyfaidd of Dyfed, had some time previously submitted themselves to King Alfred's over-lordship, and it is possible that Asser, who describes the submissions of these kings in some detail (chapter 80), had taken part in the negotiations which must have been involved. In this connection it is interesting to note that a charter of King Hywel ap Rhys, which has been dated *c.* 885, is witnessed by several *clerici*, including a bishop and a certain Asser, and if this Asser is identical with the author of the *Life of King Alfred* then we have evidence (albeit slight) of a link between the biographer and one of the kings who submitted himself to Alfred's overlordship.[100] Asser's first extended stay with Alfred lasted eight months and probably ended in late December 886; during this period Asser read aloud to the king 'whatever books he wished and which we had at hand', and when Asser was about to leave, the king gave him charge of two monasteries, at Congresbury and Banwell in Somerset (chapter 81). Thereafter Asser seems to have divided his

time between Alfred's kingdom and St David's. He was with the king
on an auspicious occasion in November 887 when Alfred supposedly
learnt how to read Latin (see above, p. 28), and at some stage he was
given charge of the monastery of Exeter with all its jurisdiction in
Wessex and Cornwall (chapter 81); he evidently travelled quite widely
in southern England, both on his own and in company with the king,
and he participated fully in the social and intellectual life that went
on in the royal court;[101] nothing, however, is known of his activities
during his presumed periodic returns to Wales. As we have already
seen, he became bishop of Sherborne some time between 892 and
900, and he died in 908 or 909.

The *Life of King Alfred* was written by Asser in 893 (see chapter
91). It is crucial evidence of Welsh learning in the second half of the
ninth century, for, apart from Asser's *Life*, we have no more than a
handful of manuscripts of uncertain origin on which to base any
assessment.[102] One should bear in mind, however, that the state of
the author's learning as revealed by the *Life* is likely to be the product
not only of his initial training in Wales but also of his later association
with continental scholars at Alfred's court, making it difficult to
decide under which circumstances he acquired knowledge of the
various works that he certainly used. The version of the Bible cited
by Asser was, on at least two occasions, the 'Old Latin' (*Vetus Latina*)
translation, as opposed to Jerome's 'Vulgate' translation.[103] The 'Old
Latin' Bible enjoyed some currency in late antiquity (it is cited by St
Patrick and Gildas, both of whom were educated in Roman Britain),
but during the early Middle Ages it was gradually replaced by the
Vulgate. The process of replacement, in England and on the Continent, was complete by the eighth century. Asser's knowledge of the
'Old Latin' Bible is most likely to derive from his early training at St
David's, and that he should still be quoting from it towards the end
of the ninth century suggests that St David's was, in this respect at
least, a cultural backwater. The texts studied by Asser are otherwise
conventional enough. He is able to quote from various patristic
sources (Gregory, chapter 102, and Augustine, chapter 103). Of Latin
poetry he was evidently familiar with Virgil,[104] and he certainly knew
the *Carmen Paschale* of Caelius Sedulius (chapter 1), one of the staple
texts of the medieval curriculum. Asser had also read Aldhelm's massive prose *De Virginitate*, a work which became established in the
continental school curriculum as a result of the efforts of Anglo-

Saxon missionaries abroad;[105] it is interesting to note that it was apparently known at St David's as well. In addition to these school texts, Asser seems to have become acquainted with various historical texts. He probably knew the *Historia Brittonum*,[106] a work composed in Wales in the early ninth century, and perhaps Bede's *Historia Ecclesiastica* as well.[107] He also knew Einhard's *Vita Caroli* (*Life of Charlemagne*),[108] and he appears to have known the anonymous *Vita Alcuini*.[109]

The list of works known or cited by Asser is not suggestive of exceptional learning by any means. The quality of his Latin prose supports a similar conclusion: it shows Asser as a man with considerable stylistic pretensions but without any mastery of prose style. His sentences are frequently long and sprawling (in this respect Asser had studied Aldhelm too closely), his syntax unclear and his exposition garbled.[110] And as is often the case with authors whose overall command of Latin is insecure, Asser took care to embellish his prose with learned-looking words of various sorts: thus grecisms (for example, *graphium*, chapter 11), archaisms (for example, *oppido*, chapter 8, or *suapte*, chapter 80) and various other rare words (such as the noun *subsequutrix*, chapter 13, or the verb *conscindo*, chapter 85) adorn his writing. Above all Asser seems to have been obsessed with a love of polysyllabic adverbs, to the point that scarcely a sentence lacks one: we find adverbs terminating in -*iter*, such as *annualiter* (chapter 100), *incommutabiliter* (chapter 103), *ordinabiliter* (chapter 16), *tenuiter* (chapter 104) and *vituperabiliter* (chapter 15); or adverbs in -*im*, such as *densatim* (chapter 88), *elucubratim* (chapter 77), *suatim* (chapter 56) and *succinctim* (chapter 73); or simply terminating in -*e*, such as *indebite* (chapter 16) and *opprobriose* (chapter 72). The list of such adverbs could be extended almost indefinitely. Such vocabulary gives Asser's prose the baroque flavour which is quite common in Insular Latin authors of the early Middle Ages.[111]

Among the unusual words used by Asser are several which seem peculiar to Frankish Latin sources: for example, *cambra* in lieu of the usual *camera* (chapters 88 and 91; cf. modern French *chambre*), *capellanus* (chapters 77 and 104; cf. modern French *chapelain*) and *senior* in the sense of 'lord' (chapters 13 and 97; cf. modern French *seigneur*). Words such as these led Stevenson to suggest that Asser had received some part of his education on the Continent in Francia.[112] The suggestion is a possible, but by no means the only, explanation. We know that the scholars assembled at Alfred's court were of very diverse linguistic backgrounds, and it is reasonable to assume that Latin was the common speech among them, at least in the early stages before they learnt English.[113] The Latin spoken at court by a Frank such as Grimbald must necessarily have included everyday words like *cambra*, *capellanus* or *senior*, and there is no reason why Asser (or any of the other scholars at court) should not have adopted such words into his personal vocabulary. And if it is permissible to assume a close relationship between Grimbald and Asser at Alfred's court, then Grimbald may equally well have been Asser's source for the special knowledge he displays of recent Frankish history and for some detailed information concerning Frankish sites.[114] So too Asser may have been indebted to Grimbald for his knowledge of the Frankish Latin texts which are cited in the *Life of King Alfred*, such as Einhard's *Life of Charlemagne* and the anonymous *Vita Alcuini*. In short, close intellectual contact with Grimbald is sufficient to explain the Frankish features of Asser's text, and there is no need to postulate for him a period of study in Francia.

However Asser acquired his knowledge of Einhard's *Life of Charlemagne*, it is likely that his reading of it suggested to him the possibility of writing a biography of King Alfred. Asser quotes from the *Life of Charlemagne* at various points in his narrative (chapters 16, 73 and 81), but he does not imitate it slavishly.[115] His *Life of King Alfred* is a highly idiosyncratic biography which falls, roughly speaking, into two unequal parts: the first covers the period of Alfred's life up to 887 (chapters 1–86), the second consists of a general appreciation of the quality of his rule (chapters 90–106), and the two parts are separated by a brief but crucial passage in which Asser describes his own contribution to Alfred's activities (chapters 87–9). For the period up to 887 Asser based his work principally on a version of the *Anglo-Saxon Chronicle*, translating the annals into Latin and supplementing the chronological framework with whatever information he could glean either from Alfred himself or from members of his court and family, such as the details of Alfred's childhood (chapters 22–5) and the account of the wicked queen Eadburh (chapters 14–15). This part of the work also covers Alfred's illnesses (chapter 74), his children (chapter 75) and his recruitment of learned helpers, including Asser himself (chapters 76–81); it ends with a translation of the *Chronicle*'s annals for 886 and 887 (chapters 82–6). For the period after 887

Asser abandons the *Chronicle* altogether: it was in 887 that Alfred
learnt how to read Latin under his tutelage (chapters 87–9), and
henceforth Asser was able to draw on his direct experience of the
king; this was evidently preferable to the mundane and difficult
business of sustaining the chronological narrative any further.[116]
The second part of the work (chapters 90–106) is thus concerned
essentially with the distinctive character of King Alfred's rule, notably
his encouragement of religion, his careful organization of his own
affairs, and his deep interest in justice and the pursuit of wisdom.
The work terminates abruptly in chapter 106 without any concluding
remarks or epilogue of any sort; and although Asser outlived his
subject by a decade or so, he never returned to record Alfred's significant achievements against the Vikings in the 890s or his death in
899. We cannot tell why this was so;[117] but it should always be borne
in mind that what has been transmitted to us is apparently an incomplete draft rather than a polished work in its finished state.[118]

To some extent it is permissible to see Asser's *Life of King Alfred*
simply as an expression of the biographer's personal respect for his
subject: the constant harping on Alfred's exceptional qualities and the
emphasis given to the difficulties which he had to overcome may
threaten at times to defeat the patience of the modern reader, but
there can be no doubt that all the praise and admiration was deeply
felt. However, it is evident that the *Life of King Alfred* was written
principally for the benefit of readers (and listeners) in Wales. That
Asser had a Welsh audience uppermost in his mind is clear not only
from his concern to explain the local geography of the places that he
mentions (see, for example, chapters 3–5), but especially from the
various occasions on which he provides an explanation in Welsh of an
English place-name: Nottingham, for example, 'is called *Tig Guocobauc* in Welsh or *Speluncarum Domus* ['house of caves'] in Latin'
(chapter 30), and Exeter is '*Cairuuisc* in Welsh, or *civitas Exae* ['city
of the Exe'] in Latin' (chapter 49).[119] Such information would have
been inscrutable and unnecessary to an Anglo-Saxon audience, and
while it would not have been of much help even to the Welsh, at least
it might have made them feel more at home. Indeed, it was argued
above (pp. 41–2) that Asser intended his *Life of King Alfred* to reassure
the Welsh that they had submitted themselves to a wise, just, effective
and Christian king.

Although the work was written for a Welsh audience, there is no evidence that it ever circulated in Wales. What limited circulation the work did enjoy was entirely in England; but even in England it does not seem to have been known to more than a handful of medieval authors. This may be because Asser apparently never completed the work and hence made no arrangements to have it copied and distributed; for it might well be argued that the manuscript transmission derives entirely from Asser's incomplete draft. Only one medieval manuscript of the work is known to have survived into modern times, written at an unidentified place about the year 1000; the manuscript is known as Cotton Otho A.xii, but unfortunately it was destroyed by fire in 1731 (see below, pp. 223–5). In the late tenth or early eleventh century, Byrhtferth of Ramsey had access to a copy of the work and incorporated large sections of it into his historical miscellany; there is some possibility that it was the Cotton manuscript which Byrhtferth used.[120] The anonymous author of the *Encomium Emmae*, a biography of Queen Emma (wife first of King Æthelred the Unready and then of Cnut) written in the early 1040s, was apparently acquainted with the *Life of King Alfred*; unfortunately one cannot tell how he came to know the work, or in what form he knew it, but the fact that he was a monk of St Bertin's in Flanders does not exclude the possibility that he had been introduced to it in England.[121] In the early twelfth century Asser's *Life* was used by a chronicler known as Florence (or perhaps more correctly, John) of Worcester, who incorporated long extracts from it into his chronicle; again, it is possible that 'Florence' was using the Cotton manuscript itself.[122] In the second quarter of the twelfth century, an anonymous chronicler at Bury St Edmunds produced the compilation now known (misleadingly) as the *Annals of St Neots*.[123] The text of Asser cited in this work seems in some places to be more accurate than that of the Cotton manuscript, and it is possible therefore that the Bury chronicler had access to a different copy.[124] Finally, mention must be made of a curious statement by Gerald of Wales in his *Life of St Æthelberht*, written probably at Hereford during the 1190s: 'And Asser, the historian and reliable narrator of the deeds of King Alfred, says that as the miracles and signs increased at the tomb of the martyr [St Æthelberht], King Offa sent two bishops in whom he had the greatest confidence to Hereford, in order to investigate the truth of the reports.'[125] No such incident is found in Asser's *Life of King Alfred* as we have it. Are we to assume that Gerald had access to a version of the work quite unlike that which has been preserved? Or that he knew another historical work by Asser, now lost? Or has Gerald simply fabricated the incident and invoked the name of Asser in order to give it some verisimilitude? In the present state of our knowledge it is impossible to answer any of these questions with confidence, though awareness of Gerald's working habits might perhaps incline us to answer the last one in the affirmative.

Further research on the medieval historians who made use of Asser's *Life of King Alfred* will doubtless throw valuable light on the history of Asser's text, but such research is unlikely dramatically to change the picture sketched briefly above. Asser's *Life of King Alfred* never reached its intended audience in Wales, perhaps because Asser abandoned the work incomplete, and it never circulated in England in more than one or possibly two manuscript copies. The *Life* may not have been well known in its own right, but the eleventh- and twelfth-century historians who used it ensured that Asser's efforts had not been in vain.

Map 1. The Vikings in England, 865–78

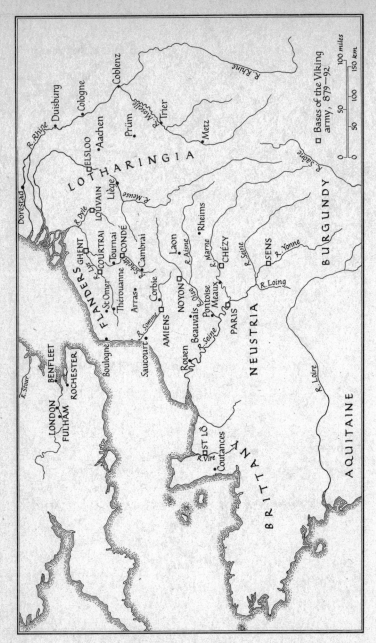

Map 2. *The Vikings on the Continent, 879–92*

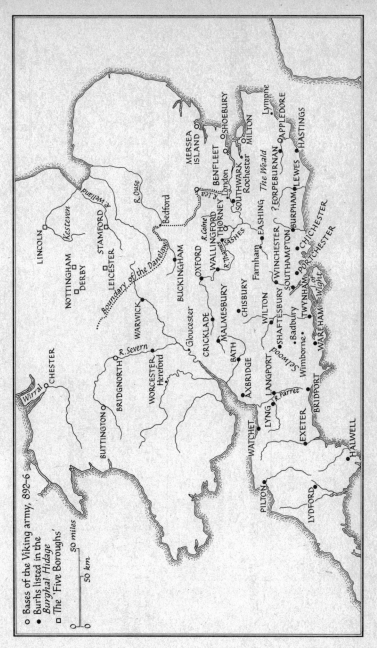

Map 3. The Vikings in England, 892–6

Bases of the Viking army, 892–6
Burhs listed in the
Burghal Hidage
The 'Five Boroughs'

50 miles

50 km

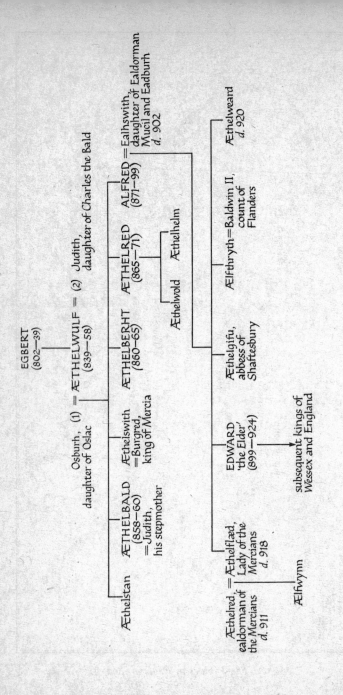

Genealogy of the Kings of Wessex

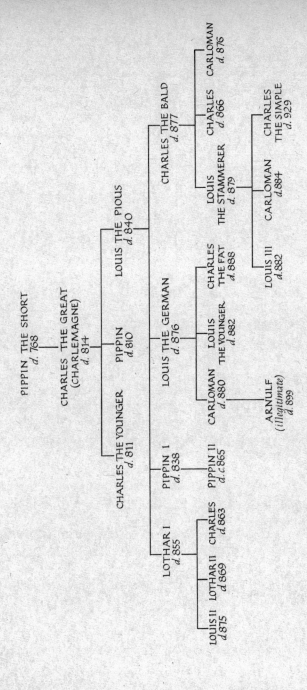

Genealogy of the Carolingian Kings

I

ASSER'S
LIFE OF KING ALFRED

DOMINO MEO VENERABILI PIISSIMOQUE·
OMNIVM BRITTANNIE INSVLAE xpiano
RVM· RECTORI· ælFRED· ANGLORVM SAXO
NVM· REGI· ASSER· OMNIVM· SERVO
RVM DEI VLTIMVS· MILLE MODAM
ADVOTA DESIDERIORVM· VTRIVSQVE
VITAE· PROSPERITATEM·

ANNO DOMINICAE
INCARNATIONIS. DCCC.XLIX. natuſ
eſt ælfreð anguſ ſaxonum rex in uilla
regia que dicitur inuanating uuill a paga
que nominatur berrocſcire que paga taliter
uocatur aberrocſilua ubi buxuſ habundan
tiſſime naſcitur cuiuſ geneſlogia taliſ taliſerie

*Facsimile of the beginning of Asser's Life of King Alfred in Cotton
Otho A.xii, written c. 1000. (The facsimile was published in 1722, a few
years before the manuscript itself was destroyed by fire: see pp. 223–5.)*

1. In the year of the Lord's Incarnation 849 Alfred, king of the
Anglo-Saxons,[1] was born at the royal estate called Wantage,[2] in the
district known as Berkshire (which is so called from Berroc Wood,
where the box-tree grows very abundantly).[3] His genealogy is woven
in this way:[4] King Alfred was the son of King Æthelwulf, the son of
Egbert, the son of Ealhmund, the son of Eafa, the son of Eoppa, the
son of Ingild. Ingild and Ine, the famous king of the West Saxons,
were two brothers; Ine journeyed to Rome, and honourably ending
this present life there he entered the heavenly land to reign with
Christ. They were the sons of Cenred, the son of Ceolwold, the son
of Cutha, the son of Cuthwine, the son of Ceawlin, the son of
Cynric, the son of Creoda, the son of Cerdic, the son of Elesa, the
son of Gewis (after whom the Welsh call that whole race the Gewisse),[5] the son of Brand, the son of Bældæg, the son of Woden, the
son of Frithuwald, the son of Frealaf, the son of Frithuwulf, the son
of Finn, [the son of] Godwulf, the son of Geat (whom the pagans
worshipped for a long time as a god). The poet Sedulius mentions
Geat in his poem *Carmen Paschale*, as follows:[6]

Since the pagan poets sought in their fictions to swagger either in high-
flowing measure, or in the wailing of tragedy's speech, or with comedy's
absurd Geta, or by means of any sort of verse whatever to relate the violent
crimes of evil deeds and sing of monumental wickedness, and with scholarly
application commit these many lies to paper: why should I – a poet accustomed
to chanting the measures of the harp in the manner of David, and of taking
my place in the holy chorus and hymning heavenly melodies in pleasing
diction – be silent concerning the renowned miracles of Christ who brought
us salvation?

Geat was the son of Tætwa, the son of Beaw, the son of Sceldwa, the
son of Heremod, the son of Itermon, the son of Hathra, the son of
Hwala, the son of Bedwig, the son of Seth, the son of Noah, the son
of Lamech, the son of Methuselah, the son of Enoch, [the son of
Jared], the son of Mahalaleel, the son of Cainan, the son of Enos, the
son of Seth, the son of Adam.

2. Concerning his mother's family. Alfred's mother was called Osburh, a most religious woman, noble in character and noble by birth. She was the daughter of Oslac, King Æthelwulf's famous butler.[7] Oslac was a Goth by race,[8] for he was descended from the Goths and Jutes, and in particular, from the line of Stuf and Wihtgar, two brothers – indeed, chieftains – who, having received authority over the Isle of Wight from their uncle King Cerdic and from Cynric his son (their cousin), killed the few British inhabitants of the island whom they could find on it, at the place called *Wihtgarabyrig*;[9] for the other inhabitants of the island had either been killed before or had fled as exiles.[10]

3. In the year of the Lord's Incarnation 851 (the third of King Alfred's life),[11] Ceorl, ealdorman of Devon, fought with the men of Devon against the Vikings[12] at the place called *Wicganbeorg*,[13] and the Christians had the victory. And in the very same year, for the first time, the Vikings spent the winter on the Isle of Sheppey (which means 'island of sheep'),[14] situated in the river Thames between Essex and Kent, but nearer to Kent than to Essex; an excellent monastery is established on the island.[15]

4. In the same year a great Viking army, with 350 ships, came into the mouth of the river Thames, and ravaged Canterbury (the city of the men of Kent) [and London][16] (situated on the northern bank of the river Thames, on the boundary of Essex and Middlesex, though the city properly belongs to Essex); they put to flight Berhtwulf, king of the Mercians, who with all his army had come to do battle against them.

5. After these things had happened there, the Viking army moved on to Surrey (a district situated on the southern bank of the river Thames, to the west of Kent). Æthelwulf, king of the Saxons, and his son Æthelbald, with the whole army, fought for a very long time at the place called *Aclea* (that is, 'oak field');[17] and there, when battle had been waged fiercely and vigorously on both sides for a long time, a great part of the Viking horde was utterly destroyed and killed, so much so that we have never heard of a greater slaughter of them, in any region, on any one day, before or since; the Christians honourably gained the victory and were masters of the battlefield.

6. In the same year Æthelstan [18] and Ealdorman Ealhhere slaughtered a great Viking army at Sandwich in Kent, and captured nine ships from their fleet; the others escaped by flight.

7. In the year of the Lord's Incarnation 853 (the fifth of King Alfred's life), Burgred, king of the Mercians, sent messengers to Æthelwulf, king of the West Saxons, asking him for help, so that he could subject to his authority the inland Welsh, who live between Mercia and the western sea and who were struggling against him with unusual effort. As soon as King Æthelwulf had received his embassy, he assembled an army and went with King Burgred to Wales, where immediately on entry he devastated that race and reduced it to Burgred's authority. When he had done this, he returned home.

8. In the same year King Æthelwulf sent his son Alfred to Rome in state, accompanied by a great number of both nobles and commoners. At this time the lord Pope Leo was ruling the apostolic see; he anointed the child Alfred as king, ordaining him properly, received him as an adoptive son and confirmed him. [19]

9. Also in the same year Ealdorman Ealhhere, with the men of Kent, and Huda, with the men of Surrey, fought vigorously and fiercely against the Viking army on the island called Thanet in English and *Ruim* in Welsh; [20] the Christians initially had the upper hand, but the battle there lasted for a long time and many men on both sides fell or were drowned in the water. Both those ealdormen died there. After Easter in this year, Æthelwulf, king of the West Saxons, gave his daughter to Burgred, king of the Mercians, as queen, at the royal estate called Chippenham, [21] and the marriage was conducted in royal style.

10. In the year of the Lord's Incarnation 855 (the seventh of the king's life), a great Viking army stayed for the entire winter on the Isle of Sheppey. [22]

11. In the same year Æthelwulf, the esteemed king, freed the tenth part of his whole kingdom from every royal service and tribute, and as an everlasting inheritance he made it over on the cross of Christ to the Triune God, for the redemption of his soul and those of

his predecessors.[23] He also travelled to Rome that year in great state, taking his son Alfred with him, for a second time on the same journey, because he loved him more than his other sons;[24] there he remained for a whole year. After this, he returned to his homeland, bringing with him Judith, daughter of Charles [the Bald], king of the Franks.[25]

12. However, while King Æthelwulf was lingering overseas, even for so short a time, a disgraceful episode – contrary to the practice of all Christian men – occurred in the western part of Selwood.[26] For King Æthelbald[27] and Ealhstan, bishop of Sherborne, along with Eanwulf, ealdorman of Somerset, are reported to have plotted that King Æthelwulf should never again be received in the kingdom on his return from Rome. A great many people ascribe this wretched incident, unheard of in all previous ages, to the bishop and the ealdorman alone, at whose instigation it is said to have taken place. There are also many who attribute it solely to arrogance on the part of King Æthelbald, because he was grasping in this affair and in many other wrongdoings, as I have heard from the report of certain men, and as was demonstrated by the outcome of the following event. When King Æthelwulf was returning from Rome, his son Æthelbald, with all his councillors – or rather co-conspirators – attempted to perpetrate a terrible crime: expelling the king from his own kingdom; but God did not allow it to happen, nor would the nobles of the whole of the Saxon land have any part in it. For, in order that the irremediable danger to the Saxon land – civil strife, as it were, with father and son at war, or indeed with the whole people rebelling against both of them – might not become more horrible and cruel as each day passed, the previously united kingdom was divided between father and son through the indescribable forbearance of the father and with the agreement of all the nobles. The eastern districts were assigned to the father, but the western districts were assigned to the son. So that iniquitous and grasping son ruled where by rightful judgement the father should have done; for the western part of the Saxon land has always been more important than the eastern.

13. When, therefore, King Æthelwulf returned from Rome, the entire nation was so delighted (as was fitting) at the arrival of their

lord that, had he allowed it, they would have been willing to eject his
grasping son Æthelbald from his share of the whole kingdom, along
with all his councillors. But displaying great forbearance and wise
counsel (as I have said), so that no danger should befall the kingdom,
Æthelwulf did not wish this to be done; and without any disagreement
or dissatisfaction on the part of his nobles, he ordered that Judith,
the daughter of King Charles [the Bald] whom he had received from
her father, should sit beside him on the royal throne until the end of
his life, though this was contrary to the (wrongful) custom of that
people. For the West Saxons did not allow the queen to sit beside the
king, nor indeed did they allow her to be called 'queen', but rather
'king's wife'.[28] The elders of the land maintain that this disputed and
indeed infamous custom originated on account of a certain grasping
and wicked queen of the same people, who did everything she could
against her lord and the whole people, so that not only did she earn
hatred for herself, leading to her expulsion from the queen's throne,
but she also brought the same foul stigma on all the queens who came
after her. For as a result of her very great wickedness, all the inhabitants of the land swore that they would never permit any king to reign
over them who during his lifetime invited the queen to sit beside him
on the royal throne. And because many do not know (I suspect) how
this perverse and detestable custom, contrary to the practice of all
Germanic peoples, originally arose in the Saxon land, I think I should
explain it a little more fully. I have heard the explanation from my
lord the truthful Alfred, king of the Anglo-Saxons, who still often
tells me about it; and he likewise had heard it from many reliable
sources, indeed to a large extent from men who remembered the
event in all its particulars.

14. There was in Mercia in fairly recent times a certain vigorous
king called Offa, who terrified all the neighbouring kings and provinces around him, and who had a great dyke built between Wales
and Mercia from sea to sea.[29] Beorhtric, king of the West Saxons,
received in marriage his daughter, called Eadburh.[30] As soon as she
had won the king's friendship, and power throughout almost the
entire kingdom, she began to behave like a tyrant after the manner of
her father – to loathe every man whom Beorhtric liked, to do all
things hateful to God and men, to denounce all those whom she
could before the king, and thus by trickery to deprive them of either

life or power; and if she could not achieve that end with the king's compliance, she killed them with poison. This is known to have happened with a certain young man very dear to the king, whom she poisoned when she could not denounce him before the king. King Beorhtric himself is said to have taken some of that poison unawares: she had intended to give it not to him, but to the young man; but the king took it first, and both of them died as a result.

15. Accordingly, when King Beorhtric was dead, since Eadburh was unable to stay any longer among the Saxons, she sailed overseas with countless treasures and went to Charlemagne, the very famous king of the Franks.[31] As she stood before the throne, bearing many gifts for the king, Charlemagne said to her: 'Choose, Eadburh, whom you wish between me and my son, who is standing with me on this throne.' She, foolishly replying without thinking, said: 'If the choice is left to me, I choose your son, as he is younger than you.' Charlemagne smiled and replied to her: 'Had you chosen me, you would have had my son; but because you have chosen my son, you will have neither him nor me.' He did however give her a large convent of nuns in which, having put aside the clothing of the secular world and taken up that of nuns, she discharged the office of abbess – but only for a few years. For just as she is said to have lived recklessly in her own country, so was she seen to live still more recklessly among a foreign people. When at long last she was publicly caught in debauchery with a man of her own race, she was ejected from the nunnery on Charlemagne's orders and shamefully spent her life in poverty and misery until her death; so much so that in the end, accompanied by a single slave boy (as I have heard from many who saw her) and begging every day, she died a miserable death in Pavia.[32]

16. King Æthelwulf lived two years after he returned from Rome; during which time, among many other good undertakings in this present life, as he reflected on his going the way of all flesh, he had a testamentary – or rather advisory – document drawn up, so that his sons should not quarrel unnecessarily among themselves after the death of their father.[33] In this document he took care to have properly committed to writing a division of the kingdom between his sons (namely the two eldest), of his own inheritance between his sons, daughter and kinsmen, and of such money as should remain after his

death between his soul,[34] sons and his nobles. I have decided to record, for posterity to imitate, a few of the many aspects of this wise policy, in particular those which are understood to pertain principally to the needs of the soul. It is not necessary to mention the other details of his disposition to men in this short work, for fear its readers or those wishing to listen to it should find its verbosity distasteful.[35] And so, for the benefit of his soul (which from the first flower of his youth he was keen to care for in all respects), he enjoined on his successors after him, right up to the final Day of Judgement, that for every ten hides[36] throughout all his hereditary land one poor man (whether native or foreigner) should be sustained with food, drink and clothing; on this condition, however, that the land should be occupied by men and livestock, and not be waste. He also ordered that every year a great sum of money, namely three hundred mancuses,[37] should be taken to Rome, and be divided up there in this way: one hundred mancuses in honour of St Peter, especially for the purchase of oil with which all the lamps in that apostolic church were to be filled on Easter eve, and likewise at cockcrow; one hundred mancuses in honour of St Paul, on the same terms, for the purchase of oil for filling the lamps in the church of St Paul the Apostle on Easter eve and at cockcrow; and one hundred mancuses for the universal apostolic pope.

17. Once King Æthelwulf was dead,[38] Æthelbald, his son, against God's prohibition and Christian dignity, and also contrary to the practice of all pagans, took over his father's marriage-bed and married Judith, daughter of Charles [the Bald], king of the Franks, incurring great disgrace from all who heard of it;[39] and he controlled the government of the kingdom of the West Saxons for two and a half lawless years after his father.[40]

18. In the year of the Lord's Incarnation 860 (the twelfth of King Alfred's life), Æthelbald [died] and was buried at Sherborne, and Æthelberht, his brother, annexed to his control Kent, Surrey and also Sussex, as was right.[41] In his days a great Viking army, arriving from the sea, aggressively attacked and laid waste the city of Winchester. When they were returning to the ships with immense booty, Osric, ealdorman of Hampshire, with his men, and Ealdorman Æthelwulf, with the men of Berkshire, opposed them strenuously. Battle was

joined in earnest; the Vikings were cut down everywhere and, when they could resist no longer, they took to flight like women, and the Christians were masters of the battlefield.[42]

19. So after governing in peace, love and honour for five years, Æthelberht went the way of all flesh, to the great sorrow of his people; and he lies buried honourably beside his brother, at Sherborne.

20. In the year of the Lord's Incarnation 864,[43] the Vikings spent the winter on the Isle of Thanet, and concluded a firm treaty with the men of Kent. The men of Kent undertook to give them money to ensure that the treaty was kept. Meanwhile, however, the Vikings, like crafty foxes, secretly burst out of their camp by night, broke the treaty and, spurning the promise of money (for they knew they could get more money from stolen booty than from peace), laid waste the entire eastern district of Kent.

21. In the year of the Lord's Incarnation 866 (the eighteenth of King Alfred's life), Æthelred, brother of King Æthelberht, took over the government of the kingdom of the West Saxons. In the same year, a great Viking fleet arrived in Britain from the Danube, and spent the winter in the kingdom of the East Saxons (which in English is called East Anglia),[44] where almost the whole army was supplied with horses. But (to speak in nautical terms)[45] so that I should no longer veer off course – having entrusted the ship to waves and sails, and having sailed quite far away from the land – among such terrible wars and in year-by-year reckoning, I think I should return to that which particularly inspired me to this work: in other words, I consider that some small account (as much as has come to my knowledge) of the infancy and boyhood of my esteemed lord Alfred, king of the Anglo-Saxons, should briefly be inserted at this point.

22. Now, he was greatly loved, more than all his brothers, by his father and mother – indeed, by everybody – with a universal and profound love, and he was always brought up in the royal court and nowhere else. As he passed through infancy and boyhood he was seen to be more comely in appearance than his other brothers, and more pleasing in manner, speech and behaviour. From the cradle onwards,

was gifted from
the beginning

in spite of all the demands of the present life, it has been the desire for wisdom, more than anything else, together with the nobility of his birth, which have characterized the nature of his noble mind; but alas, by the shameful negligence of his parents and tutors he remained ignorant of letters until his twelfth year, or even longer.[46] However, he was a careful listener, by day and night, to English poems, most frequently hearing them recited by others, and he readily retained them in his memory. An enthusiastic huntsman, he strives continually in every branch of hunting, and not in vain; for no one else could approach him in skill and success in that activity, just as in all other gifts of God, as I have so often seen for myself.[47]

23. One day, therefore, when his mother was showing him and his brothers a book of English poetry which she held in her hand, she said: 'I shall give this book to whichever one of you can learn it the fastest.' Spurred on by these words, or rather by divine inspiration, and attracted by the beauty of the initial letter in the book, Alfred spoke as follows in reply to his mother, forestalling his brothers (ahead in years, though not in ability): 'Will you really give this book to the one of us who can understand it the soonest and recite it to you?' Whereupon, smiling with pleasure she reassured him, saying: 'Yes, I will.' He immediately took the book from her hand, went to his teacher and learnt it.[48] When it was learnt, he took it back to his mother and recited it.

24. After this he learnt the 'daily round', that is, the services of the hours, and then certain psalms and many prayers; these he collected in a single book, which he kept by him day and night, as I have seen for myself; amid all the affairs of the present life he took it around with him everywhere for the sake of prayer, and was inseparable from it.[49] But alas, he could not satisfy his craving for what he desired the most, namely the liberal arts; for, as he used to say, there were no good scholars in the entire kingdom of the West Saxons at that time.[50]

25. He used to affirm, with repeated complaints and sighing from the depths of his heart, that among all the difficulties and burdens of his present life this had become the greatest: namely, that at the time when he was of the right age and had the leisure and the capacity for

learning, he did not have the teachers. For when he was older, and more incessantly preoccupied by day and night with – or rather harassed by – all kinds of illnesses unknown to the physicians of this island,[51] as well as by the cares (both domestic and foreign) of the royal office, and also by the incursions of the Vikings by land and sea, he had the teachers and scribes to some small extent, but he was unable to study. Nevertheless, just as he did not previously desist from the same insatiable desire, among the difficulties of the present life, from infancy right up to the present day (and will not, I dare say, to the end of his life),[52] so too he does not yet cease to yearn for it.

26. In the year of the Lord's Incarnation 867 (the nineteenth of King Alfred's[53] life), the Viking army went from East Anglia to the city of York (which is situated on the northern bank of the river Humber).

27. At that time a great dispute, fomented by the devil, had arisen among the Northumbrians, as always happens to a people which has incurred the wrath of God. The Northumbrians at that time (as I have said) had expelled from the kingdom their rightful king, called Osberht, and had established at the kingdom's summit a certain tyrant called Ælle, who did not belong to the royal line. But, when the Vikings arrived, by divine providence and with the support of the best men, for the good of all, the dispute had calmed down slightly; Osberht and Ælle combined forces and assembled an army, and went to the city of York. On their arrival, the Vikings immediately took to flight, and endeavoured to defend themselves within the fortifications of the city. When the Christians noticed their flight and panic, they too determined to pursue them within the fortifications of the city and to breach the wall; and this they did. For in those days the city did not yet have firm and secure walls. After the Christians had breached the wall as they had intended, and the majority of them had got into the city along with the Vikings, the Vikings, driven on by grief and necessity, attacked them fiercely, cut them to pieces, put them to flight, and overthrew them inside and outside. Virtually the entire force of Northumbrians was annihilated there, and the two kings were killed; but the remainder, who escaped, made peace with the Vikings.[54]

28. In the same year Ealhstan, bishop of the church of Sherborne, after he had ruled the bishopric honourably for fifty years,[55] went the way of all flesh; he was buried in peace at Sherborne.

29. In the year of the Lord's Incarnation 868 (the twentieth of King Alfred's life), the same much-esteemed King Alfred, at that time accorded the status of 'heir apparent',[56] was betrothed to and married a wife from Mercia, of noble family, namely the daughter of Æthelred (who was known as Mucil), ealdorman of the *Gaini*.[57] The woman's mother was called Eadburh, from the royal stock of the king of the Mercians. I often saw her myself with my very own eyes for several years before her death. She was a notable woman, who remained for many years after the death of her husband a chaste widow, until her death.[58] *character opposite that of her mother*

30. In the same year the Viking army left Northumbria, came to Mercia and reached Nottingham (which is called *Tig Guocobauc* in Welsh, or *Speluncarum Domus* ['house of caves'] in Latin);[59] and they spent the winter that year in the same place. Immediately upon their arrival there, Burgred, king of the Mercians, and all the leading men of that people sent messengers to Æthelred, king of the West Saxons, and to his brother Alfred, humbly requesting that they help them, so that they would be able to fight against the Viking army; they obtained this easily. For the brothers, promptly fulfilling their promise,[60] gathered an immense army from every part of their kingdom, went to Mercia and arrived at Nottingham, single-mindedly seeking battle. But since the Vikings, protected by the defences of the stronghold, refused to give battle, and since the Christians were unable to breach the wall, peace was established between the Mercians and the Vikings, and the two brothers, Æthelred and Alfred, returned home with their forces.

31. In the year of the Lord's Incarnation 869 (the twenty-first of King Alfred's life), the Viking army rode back to Northumbria and went to the city of York, and remained there for a whole year.

32. In the year of the Lord's Incarnation 870 (the twenty-second of King Alfred's life), the Viking army mentioned above passed through Mercia to East Anglia, and spent the winter there at a place called Thetford.

33. In the same year, Edmund, king of the East Angles, fought fiercely against that army. But alas, he was killed there with a large number of his men,[61] and the Vikings rejoiced triumphantly; the enemy were masters of the battlefield, and they subjected that entire province to their authority.

34. In the same year Ceolnoth, archbishop of Canterbury, went the way of all flesh; he was buried in peace in the same city.[62]

35. In the year of the Lord's Incarnation 871 (the twenty-third of King Alfred's life), the Viking army of hateful memory left East Anglia, went to the kingdom of the West Saxons, and came to the royal estate called Reading (situated on the southern bank of the river Thames, in the district called Berkshire).[63] On the third day after their arrival there, two of their earls, with a great part of the force, rode out for plunder, while the others constructed a rampart between the two rivers Thames and Kennet, on the right-hand [southern] side[64] of the same royal estate. Æthelwulf, ealdorman of Berkshire, confronted them with his followers at a place called Englefield, and battle was joined there resolutely on both sides. When both sides had held out there for a long time, and when one of the Viking earls had been killed[65] and a great part of the army overthrown, the others took to flight and the Christians won the victory and were masters of the battlefield.

36. Four days after these things had happened there, King Æthelred and his brother Alfred combined forces, assembled an army, and went to Reading. When they had reached the gate of the stronghold by hacking and cutting down all the Vikings whom they had found outside, the Vikings fought no less keenly; like wolves they burst out of all the gates and joined battle with all their might. Both sides fought there for a long time, and fought fiercely, but alas, the Christians eventually turned their backs, and the Vikings won the victory and were masters of the battlefield; and the Ealdorman Æthelwulf mentioned above fell there,[66] among others.

37. The Christians were aroused by the grief and shame of this, and four days later, with all their might and in a determined frame of mind, they advanced against the Viking army at a place called Ash-

down (which means *mons fraxini* ['hill of the ash'] in Latin).[67] But the Vikings, splitting up into two divisions, organized shield-walls of equal size (for they then had two kings and a large number of earls), assigning the core of the army to the two kings and the rest to all the earls.[68] When the Christians saw this, they too split up the army into two divisions in exactly the same way, and established shield-walls no less keenly. But as I have heard from truthful authorities who saw it, Alfred and his men reached the battlefield sooner and in better order: for his brother, King Æthelred, was still in his tent at prayer, hearing Mass and declaring firmly that he would not leave that place alive before the priest had finished Mass, and that he would not forsake divine service for that of men; and he did what he said. The faith of the Christian king counted for much with the Lord, as shall be shown more clearly in what follows.

38. Now the Christians had decided that King Æthelred and his forces should engage the two Viking kings in battle, while his brother Alfred and his troops should submit to the fortunes of war[69] against all the Viking earls. Matters were thus firmly arranged on both sides; but since the king was lingering still longer in prayer, and the Vikings were ready and had reached the battlefield more quickly, Alfred (then 'heir apparent') could not oppose the enemy battle-lines any longer without either retreating from the battlefield or attacking the enemy forces before his brother's arrival on the scene. He finally deployed the Christian forces against the hostile armies, as he had previously intended (even though the king had not yet come), and acting courageously, like a wild boar,[70] supported by divine counsel and strengthened by divine help, when he had closed up the shield-wall in proper order, he moved his army without delay against the enemy.[71]

39. But it should be made clear at this point to those unaware of the fact, that the battlefield was not equally advantageous to both contending parties. The Vikings had taken the higher position first, and the Christians were deploying their battle-line from a lower position. A rather small and solitary thorn-tree (which I have seen for myself with my own eyes) grew there, around which the opposing armies clashed violently, with loud shouting from all, one side acting

wrongfully and the other side set to fight for life, loved ones and country. When both sides had been fighting to and fro, resolutely and exceedingly ferociously, for quite a long time, the Vikings (by divine judgement) were unable to withstand the Christians' onslaught any longer; and when a great part of their forces had fallen, they took to ignominious flight. One of the two Viking kings and five earls were cut down in that place, and many thousands on the Viking side were slain there too – or rather, over the whole broad expanse of Ashdown, scattered everywhere, far and wide: so King Bagsecg was killed, and Earl Sidroc the Old, Earl Sidroc the Younger, Earl Osbern, Earl Fræna, and Earl Harold; and the entire Viking army was put to flight, right on till nightfall and into the following day, until such time as they reached the stronghold from which they had come. The Christians followed them till nightfall, cutting them down on all sides.

40. A[72] further fourteen days after these things had happened there, King Æthelred, together with his brother Alfred, combined their forces for a battle against the Vikings, and went to Basing. They clashed violently on all fronts, but after a long struggle the Vikings gained the victory and were masters of the battlefield. When the battle was over, another Viking army came from overseas and attached itself to the band.[73]

41. After Easter [15 April] in the same year, King Æthelred went the way of all flesh, having vigorously and honourably ruled the kingdom in good repute, amid many difficulties, for five years; he was buried at Wimborne Minster and awaits the coming of the Lord, and the first resurrection with the just [cf. Revelation xx, 6, and Luke xiv, 14].

42. In the same year Alfred, who until that time (while his brothers were alive) had been 'heir apparent',[74] took over the government of the whole kingdom as soon as his brother had died, with the approval of divine will and according to the unanimous wish of all the inhabitants of the kingdom. Indeed, he could easily have taken it over with the consent of all while his brother Æthelred was alive, had he considered himself worthy to do so, for he surpassed all his brothers both in wisdom and in all good habits; and in particular because he was a

great warrior and victorious in virtually all battles. When a month had
passed after he had begun to reign, almost unwillingly[75] (for indeed
he did not think that he alone could ever withstand such great ferocity
of the Vikings, unless strengthened by divine help, since he had
already sustained great losses of many men while his brothers were
alive), he fought most vigorously, with a few men who were easily
outnumbered, against the entire Viking army at a hill called Wilton
(which is situated on the southern bank of the river *Guilou* [Wylye],[76]
from which that whole district takes its name). When both sides had
been fighting violently and resolutely on all fronts for much of the
day, the Vikings realized of their own accord the complete danger
they were in, and, unable to bear the onslaught of their enemies any
longer, they turned tail and fled. But alas, scorning the small number
of pursuers,[77] they advanced again into battle, and seizing victory
they were masters of the battlefield. Nor should it seem extraordinary
to anyone that the Christians had a small number of men in the
battle: for the Saxons were virtually annihilated to a man in this
single year in eight[78] battles against the Vikings (in which eight
battles one Viking king and nine earls, with countless men, were
killed), leaving aside the innumerable skirmishes by day and night
which Alfred, and the individual ealdormen of that race, with their
men, and also very many king's thegns, had fought ceaselessly and
intently against the Vikings. How many thousands of the Viking
army were killed in these frequent skirmishes (quite apart from those
who were slaughtered in the eight battles mentioned above) is not
known, except to God alone.

43. Also in the same year, the Saxons made peace with the Vikings,
on condition that they would leave them;[79] and this the Vikings did.

44. In the year of the Lord's Incarnation 872 (the twenty-fourth
of King Alfred's life), the Viking army went to London and spent the
winter there; and the Mercians made peace with them.[80]

45. In the year of the Lord's Incarnation 873 (the twenty-fifth of
King Alfred's life), the Viking army left London and moved on to
the province of the Northumbrians, and they spent the winter there
in the district known as Lindsey;[81] and the Mercians again made
peace with them.

46. In the year of the Lord's Incarnation 874 (the twenty-sixth of King Alfred's life), the Viking army left Lindsey, went to Mercia, and spent the winter at a place called Repton. They forced Burgred, king of the Mercians, to abandon his kingdom against his wish, to go abroad and to set out for Rome, in the twenty-second year of his reign. He did not live long after he had arrived at Rome: he died there and was honourably buried in the church of St Mary, in the Saxon quarter,[82] where he awaits the coming of the Lord, and the first resurrection with the just [cf. Revelation xx, 6, and Luke xiv, 14]. After his expulsion the Vikings reduced the whole kingdom of the Mercians to their authority; however, by a wretched arrangement they entrusted it to a certain foolish king's thegn, who was called Ceolwulf, on these terms of custody, that whenever they should wish to have it again, he should hand it over peacefully to them. He gave hostages to them under the terms of this arrangement, and he swore that in no way would he wish to countermand their intentions, but would be obedient in all respects.[83]

47. In the year of the Lord's Incarnation 875 (the twenty-seventh of King Alfred's life), the Viking army left Repton and split up into two bands. One band, under Halfdan, set out for the province of the Northumbrians, and spent the winter there beside the river Tyne; it subdued the entire province of the Northumbrians, and also ravaged the Picts and the men of Strathclyde. The other band, under three Viking kings (Guthrum, Oscetel and Anwend), went to a place called Cambridge, and spent the winter there.[84]

48. In the same year King Alfred fought a naval battle at sea against six[85] Viking ships; he captured one of them, and the others escaped by flight.

49. In the year of the Lord's Incarnation 876 (the twenty-eighth of King Alfred's life), the Viking army left Cambridge by night;[86] they went to a fortified site called Wareham (a convent of nuns situated in the district called *Durngueir* in Welsh and Dorset in English, between the two rivers *Frauu* [Frome] and Tarrant, in a very secure position except on the west, where it is joined to the mainland).[87] King Alfred firmly made a treaty with the army, the condition being that they should leave him;[88] the army, without any dispute,

gave him as many picked hostages as he alone chose,[89] and they also took an oath, on all the relics in which the king placed the greatest trust after God Himself (and on which they had never before been willing to take an oath to any race),[90] that they would immediately leave his kingdom. But one night, practising their usual treachery, after their own manner, and paying no heed to the hostages, the oath and the promise of faith, they broke the treaty, killed all the [hostages][91] they had, and turning away they went unexpectedly to another place, called Exeter in English (*Cairuuisc* in Welsh, or *civitas Exae* ['city of the Exe'] in Latin), situated on the eastern bank of the river *Uuisc* [Exe],[92] near the southern sea which runs between Gaul and Britain. There they spent the winter.

50. In the same year Halfdan, king of one part of the Northumbrians, shared out the whole province between himself and his men, and together with his army cultivated the land.[93]

51. *For this chapter, and the events of 877, see Notes.*[94]

52. In the year of the Lord's Incarnation 878 (the thirtieth of King Alfred's life), the Viking army left Exeter and went to Chippenham, a royal estate[95] situated in the left-hand [northern] part[96] of Wiltshire, on the eastern bank of the river called *Abon* [Avon] in Welsh;[97] and they spent the winter there. By strength of arms they forced many men of that race to sail overseas, through both poverty and fear, and very nearly all the inhabitants of that region submitted to their authority.

53. At the same time King Alfred, with his small band of nobles and also with certain soldiers and thegns, was leading a restless life in great distress amid the woody and marshy places of Somerset. He had nothing to live on except what he could forage by frequent raids, either secretly or even openly, from the Vikings as well as from the Christians who had submitted to the Vikings' authority.[98]

54. In the same year the brother[99] of Ivar and Halfdan sailed with twenty-three ships from Dyfed (where he had spent the winter), after slaughtering many of the Christians there, and came to Devon;

there, acting on an erroneous assumption, he met an unhappy death with 1,200 men, at the hands of the king's thegns and in front of the stronghold at *Cynuit* [Countisbury].[100] For many of the king's thegns, with their followers, had shut themselves up for safety inside this stronghold; and when the Vikings saw that the stronghold was unprepared and altogether unfortified (except for ramparts thrown up in our fashion),[101] they made no attempt to storm it, since by the lie of the land that place is very secure from every direction except the east, as I myself have seen. Instead they began to besiege it, thinking that those men would soon give way, forced by hunger, thirst and the siege, since there is no water near the stronghold. But it did not turn out as they thought. For the Christians, long before they were liable to suffer want in any way, were divinely inspired and, judging it much better to gain either death or victory, burst out unexpectedly at dawn against the Vikings and, by virtue of their aggressiveness, from the very outset they overwhelmed the enemy in large part, together with their king, a few escaping by flight to the ships.

55. In the same year, after Easter [23 March], King Alfred, with a few men, made a fortress at a place called Athelney,[102] and from it with the thegns of Somerset he struck out relentlessly and tirelessly against the Vikings. Presently, in the seventh week after Easter [4–10 May], he rode to Egbert's Stone, which is in the eastern part of Selwood Forest (*sylva magna* ['great wood'] in Latin, and *Coit Maur* in Welsh);[103] and there all the inhabitants of Somerset and Wiltshire and all the inhabitants of Hampshire – those who had not sailed overseas for fear of the Vikings[104] – joined up with him. When they saw the king, receiving him (not surprisingly) as if one restored to life after suffering such great tribulations, they were filled with immense joy. They made camp there for one night. At the break of the following dawn the king struck camp and came to a place called Iley,[105] and made camp there for one night.

56. When the next morning dawned he moved his forces and came to a place called Edington,[106] and fighting fiercely with a compact shield-wall against the entire Viking army, he persevered resolutely for a long time; at length he gained the victory through God's will. He destroyed the Vikings with great slaughter, and pursued those who fled as far as the stronghold, hacking them down; he seized

everything which he found outside the stronghold – men (whom he killed immediately), horses and cattle – and boldly made camp in front of the gates of the Viking stronghold with all his army.[107] When he had been there for fourteen days the Vikings, thoroughly terrified by hunger, cold and fear, and in the end by despair, sought peace on this condition: the king should take as many chosen hostages as he wanted from them and give none to them; never before, indeed, had they made peace with anyone on such terms.[108] When he had heard their embassy, the king (as is his wont)[109] was moved to compassion and took as many chosen hostages from them as he wanted. When they had been handed over, the Vikings swore in addition that they would leave his kingdom immediately, and Guthrum, their king, promised to accept Christianity and to receive baptism at King Alfred's hand;[110] all of which he and his men fulfilled as they had promised. For three weeks later Guthrum, the king of the Vikings, with thirty[111] of the best men from his army, came to King Alfred at a place called Aller, near Athelney. King Alfred raised him from the holy font of baptism, receiving him as his adoptive son; the unbinding of the chrisom on the eighth day[112] took place at a royal estate called Wedmore.[113] Guthrum remained with the king for twelve nights after he had been baptized, and the king freely bestowed many excellent treasures[114] on him and all his men.

57. In the year of the Lord's Incarnation 879 (the thirty-first of King Alfred's life), the Viking army left Chippenham, as promised, and went to Cirencester (called *Cairceri* in Welsh),[115] which is in the southern part of the land of the Hwicce,[116] and remained there for one year.

58. In the same year a great Viking army, sailing from foreign parts, came to the river Thames and made contact with the army further upstream,[117] but nevertheless they spent the winter at a place called Fulham, near the river Thames.

59. In the same year there was an eclipse of the sun between nones and vespers, but nearer to nones.[118]

60. In the year of the Lord's Incarnation 880 (the thirty-second of King Alfred's life), the Viking army left Cirencester and went

to East Anglia; they divided up the province and began to settle there.

61. In the same year the Viking army which had spent the winter at Fulham left the island of Britain, setting out again across the sea, and went to eastern Francia; and they stayed for one year at a place called Ghent.[119]

62. In the year of the Lord's Incarnation 881 (the thirty-third of King Alfred's life), the Viking army went further still into Francia. The Franks fought against them and, once the battle was over, the Vikings procured horses and became a mounted force.[120]

63. In the year of the Lord's Incarnation 882 (the thirty-fourth of King Alfred's life), the Viking army drew its ships much further upstream into Francia, along the river Meuse, and stayed there one year.[121]

64. In the same year Alfred, king of the Anglo-Saxons, launched a naval attack on the high seas against the Viking ships; he captured two of the ships, having killed everyone on board. The two commanders of the other two ships who, with all their crews, were very much exhausted by the fight and by their wounds, laid down their arms and on bended knee with submissive pleas gave themselves up to the king.

65. In the year of the Lord's Incarnation 883 (the thirty-fifth of King Alfred's life), the Vikings drew their ships along the river Scheldt, and sailed upstream to a convent of nuns called Condé; they remained there one year.[122]

66. In the year of the Lord's Incarnation [885][123] (the thirty-seventh of King Alfred's life), the Viking army split up into two bands: one band set out for eastern Francia, and the other, coming to Britain, entered Kent and besieged the city which in English is called Rochester, situated on the eastern bank of the river Medway.[124] The Vikings immediately constructed a strong fortification for themselves in front of its entrance, but they were unable to capture the city because the citizens defended themselves courageously until King

Alfred arrived, bringing them relief with a large army. Thereupon the Vikings, abandoning their fortress and leaving behind in it all the horses they had brought with them from Francia – not to mention the greater part of their prisoners – fled quickly to their ships at the king's sudden arrival. The English immediately seized the prisoners and horses left behind by the Vikings. For their part the Vikings were forced by this unavoidable turn of events to return that same summer once again to Francia.[125]

67. In the same year Alfred, king of the Anglo-Saxons, transferred his fleet and its complement of fighting men from Kent to East Anglia,[126] in order to plunder that area. When they arrived at the mouth of the river Stour, thirteen[127] Viking ships rigged for battle immediately advanced to meet them. A sea-battle was joined: there was savage fighting everywhere. All the Vikings were killed and all their ships (together with all their booty) were captured. As the victorious royal fleet was about to go home,[128] the Vikings who lived in East Anglia assembled ships from everywhere and met it in the mouth of the same river; there was a naval encounter and the Vikings had the victory.

68. In the same year a boar[129] brought Carloman, king of the western Franks, to a gruesome end, goring him savagely with its tusks while he was engaged in a boar-hunt. His brother Louis [III] had died the previous year. He too was king of the Franks: for both the brothers were sons of Louis [the Stammerer], king of the Franks. This Louis had died in the year of the solar eclipse, which was mentioned above; moreover, he was the son of Charles [the Bald], king of the Franks, whose daughter Judith was given as queen – by paternal consent – to Æthelwulf, king of the West Saxons.[130]

69. In the same year a great Viking army arrived from Germany in the territory of the Old Saxons (as they are called in English).[131] These Old Saxons joined forces with the Frisians and valiantly fought the Vikings twice in the same year. In these two battles the Christians, through the bounty of heavenly mercy, had the victory.[132]

70. Also in this same year Charles [the Fat],[133] king of the Alemanni, acceded by universal acclamation to the kingdom of the west-

ern Franks and to all those kingdoms – excepting only the kingdom of
Brittany – which are between the Mediterranean and that marine gulf
which lies between the Old Saxons and the Gauls.[134] This Charles
was the son of King Louis [the German], who in turn was the brother
of Charles [the Bald], king of the Franks, father of the Queen Judith
mentioned above. The two brothers were the sons of Louis [the
Pious], who in turn was the son of the old and wise Charlemagne,
who was himself the son of Pippin.[135]

71. In the same year Pope Marinus of blessed memory went the
way of all flesh. He had generously released the Saxon quarter[136] in
Rome from all tribute and tax, as a result of the friendship and
entreaties of Alfred, king of the Anglo-Saxons. On that occasion the
pope also sent many gifts to King Alfred, among which he gave not a
small piece of that most holy and venerable Cross, on which our Lord
Jesus Christ hung for the salvation of all mankind.[137]

72. In that same year the Viking army, which had settled in East
Anglia, broke in a most insolent manner the peace which they had
established with King Alfred.

73. Accordingly, in order that I may return to that point from
which I digressed – and so that I shall not be compelled to sail past
the haven of my desired rest as a result of my protracted voyage[138] –
I shall, as I promised, undertake, with God's guidance, to say
something (albeit succinctly and briefly, as far as my knowledge
permits) the life, behaviour, equitable character and, without
exaggeration, the accomplishments of my lord Alfred, king of the
Anglo-Saxons, after the time when he married his excellent wife
from the stock of noble Mercians – briefly, I say, so that I do not
offend with my protracted narrative the minds of those who are
scornful of information of any sort.[139]

74. When, therefore, he had duly celebrated the wedding which
took place ceremonially in Mercia in the presence of countless persons
of both sexes, and after the feasting which lasted day and night, he
was struck without warning in the presence of the entire gathering by
a sudden severe pain that was quite unknown to all physicians. Certainly it was not known to any of those who were present on that

occasion, nor to those up to the present day who have inquired how such an illness could arise and – worst of all, alas! – could continue so many years without remission, from his twentieth year up to his fortieth and beyond. Many, to be sure, alleged that it had happened through the spells[140] and witchcraft of the people around him; others, through the ill-will of the devil, who is always envious of good men; others, that it was the result of some unfamiliar kind of fever; still others thought that it was due to the piles, because he had suffered this particular kind of agonizing irritation even from his youth.

Now on a previous occasion when, by divine will, he had gone to Cornwall to do some hunting and, in order to pray, had made a detour (as is his wont) to a particular church in which St *Gueriir*[141] lies in peace (and now St Neot lies there as well)[142] – for even from his childhood he was an enthusiastic visitor of holy shrines, to pray and give alms – he lay prostrate in silent prayer a long while in order to beseech the Lord's mercy, so that Almighty God in his bountiful kindness might substitute for the pangs of the present and agonizing infirmity some less severe illness, on the understanding that the new illness would not be outwardly visible on his body, whereby he would be rendered useless and contemptible. For he feared leprosy or blindness, or some other such disease, which so quickly render men useless and contemptible by their onslaught. When he had finished praying, he set out the way he had started, and shortly thereafter – just as he had asked in his prayers – he felt himself divinely cured from that malady, in such a way that it was going to be completely eliminated, even though the holy suppliant, devout in prayer and continual supplication of God, had contracted the malady in the first flowering of his youth.

For (if I may speak briefly and cursorily – although I go back to the beginning – of the kindly disposition of his mind towards God) when in the first flowering of his youth before he had married his wife, he wished to confirm his own mind in God's commandments, and when he realized that he was unable to abstain from carnal desire, fearing that he would incur God's disfavour if he did anything contrary to His will, he very often got up secretly in the early morning at cockcrow and visited churches and relics of the saints in order to pray; he lay there prostrate a long while, turning himself totally to God, praying that Almighty God through His mercy would more staunchly strengthen his resolve in the love of His service by means of some illness which he would be able to tolerate – not, however, that God would make him unworthy and useless in worldly affairs. When he had done this frequently with great mental devotion, after some time he contracted the disease of piles through God's gift; struggling with this long and bitterly through many years, he would despair even of life, until that time when, having finished his prayers, God removed it from him completely.

But, alas, when it had been removed, another more severe illness seized him at his wedding feast (as I have said), which plagued him remorselessly by day and night from his twentieth year until his forty-fifth; and if at any time through God's mercy that illness abated for the space of a day or a night or even of an hour, his fear and horror of that accursed pain would never desert him, but rendered him virtually useless – as it seemed to him – for heavenly and worldly affairs.[143]

75. As I was saying, sons and daughters were born to him by his wife: namely Æthelflæd the first-born, and after her Edward, then Æthelgifu followed by Ælfthryth, and finally Æthelweard (leaving aside those who were carried off in infancy by an untimely death and who numbered . . .[144]). Æthelflæd, when the time came for her to marry, was joined in marriage to Æthelred, ealdorman of the Mercians;[145] Æthelgifu, devoted to God through her holy virginity, subject and consecrated to the rules of monastic life, entered the service of God;[146] Æthelweard,[147] the youngest of all, as a result of divine wisdom and the remarkable foresight of the king, was given over to training in reading and writing under the attentive care of teachers, in company with all the nobly born children of virtually the entire area, and a good many of lesser birth as well. In this school books in both languages – that is to say, in Latin and English – were carefully read; they also devoted themselves to writing, to such an extent that, even before they had the requisite strength for manly skills (hunting, that is, and other skills appropriate to noblemen), they were seen to be devoted and intelligent students of the liberal arts.[148] Edward[149] and Ælfthryth[150] were at all times fostered at the royal court under the solicitous care of tutors and nurses, and indeed with the great love of all; and to the present day they continue to behave with humility, friendliness and gentleness to all compatriots and foreigners, and with great obedience to their father. Nor, amid the

other pursuits of this present life which are appropriate to the nobility, are these two allowed to live idly and indifferently, with no liberal education, for they have attentively learned the Psalms, and books in English, and especially English poems, and they very frequently make use of books.

76. Meanwhile the king, amidst the wars and the numerous interruptions of this present life – not to mention the Viking attacks and his continual bodily infirmities – did not refrain from directing the government of the kingdom;[151] pursuing all manner of hunting; giving instruction to all his goldsmiths and craftsmen as well as to his falconers, hawk-trainers and dog-keepers; making to his own design[152] wonderful and precious new treasures[153] which far surpassed any tradition of his predecessors; reading aloud from books in English and above all learning English poems by heart; issuing orders to his followers: all these things he did himself with great application to the best of his abilities. He was also in the invariable habit of listening daily to divine services and Mass, and of participating in certain psalms and prayers and in the day-time and night-time offices, and, at night-time, as I have said, of going (without his household knowing) to various churches in order to pray.[154] He similarly applied himself attentively to charity and distribution of alms to the native population and to foreign visitors of all races, showing immense and incomparable kindness and generosity to all men, as well as to the investigation of things unknown.[155] Wherefore many Franks, Frisians, Gauls,[156] Vikings, Welshmen, Irishmen and Bretons subjected themselves willingly to his lordship, nobles and commoners alike;[157] and, as befitted his royal status, he ruled, loved, honoured and enriched them all with wealth and authority, just as he did his own people. He was also in the habit of listening eagerly and attentively to Holy Scripture being read out by his own countrymen, or even, if the situation should somehow arise, of listening to these lessons in the company of foreigners. With wonderful affection he cherished his bishops and the entire clergy, his ealdormen and nobles, his officials[158] as well as all his associates. Nor, in the midst of other affairs, did he cease from personally giving, by day and night, instruction in all virtuous behaviour and tutelage in literacy to their sons, who were being brought up in the royal household and whom he loved no less than his own children.

But as if he derived no consolation from all these things, and suffered no greater distress of any kind inwardly and outwardly (and he did, to the extent that he would cry out in anguish by day and night to the Lord and to all those who were known to him on terms of intimacy), he used to moan and sigh continually because Almighty God had created him lacking in divine learning and knowledge of the liberal arts. In this respect he resembled the holy, highly esteemed and exceedingly wealthy Solomon, king of the Hebrews, who, once upon a time, having come to despise all renown and wealth of this world, sought wisdom from God, and thereby achieved both (namely, wisdom and renown in this world), as it is written, 'Seek ye therefore first the kingdom of God, and his justice, and all these things shall be given to you' [Matthew vi, 33].[159] But God, who is ever the observer of our internal desires and the instigator of all our thoughts and good intentions, and also – so that these good intentions may be fulfilled – a most generous overseer (for He never initiates any good intention, nor does He bountifully bring it to fulfilment, unless the person appropriately and rightly desires it to be so), stimulated King Alfred's intelligence from within, not from without, as it is written, 'I will hear what the Lord God speaks in me' [Psalm lxxxiv, 9], so[160] that he could acquire helpers in this good intention of his, who would be able to help him attain to the desired wisdom and enable him to fulfil his wishes whenever possible. Accordingly, just like the clever bee[161] which at first light in summertime departs from its beloved honeycomb, finds its way with swift flight on its unpredictable journey through the air, lights upon the many and various flowers of grasses, plants and shrubs, discovers what pleases it most and then carries it back home, King Alfred directed the eyes of his mind far afield and sought without what he did not possess within,[162] that is to say, within his own kingdom.

77. At that point God (being unable to tolerate so well-intentioned and justifiable a complaint any longer) sent some comforts for this royal intention – certain luminaries, as it were: Werferth,[163] the bishop of Worcester, a man thoroughly learned in holy writings who at the king's command translated for the first time the *Dialogues* between Pope Gregory and his disciple Peter from Latin into the English language, sometimes rendering sense for sense, translating intelligently and in a very polished style;[164] then Plegmund,[165] arch-

bishop of Canterbury, a Mercian by birth and an estimable man richly endowed with learning; and also Æthelstan and Werwulf, both priests and chaplains, Mercians by birth and learned men.[166] King Alfred summoned these four men to him from Mercia,[167] and showered them with many honours and entitlements in the kingdom of the West Saxons (not counting those which Archbishop Plegmund and Bishop Werferth already possessed in Mercia). The king's desire for knowledge increased steadily and was satisfied by the learning and wisdom of all four men. By day or night, whenever he had any opportunity, he used to tell them to read aloud from books in his presence – indeed he could never tolerate being without one or other of them – and accordingly, he acquired some acquaintance with almost all books, even though he could not at this point understand anything in the books by himself. For he had not yet begun to read anything.

78. However, since the royal 'greed' (which was entirely praise-worthy!) in this respect was not yet satisfied, he sent messengers across the sea to Gaul to seek instructors. From there, he summoned Grimbald,[168] a priest and monk and a very venerable man, an excellent chanter, extremely learned in every kind of ecclesiastical doctrine and in the Holy Scriptures, as well as being distinguished by his virtuous behaviour. Similarly, he summoned John,[169] also a priest and monk, a man of most acute intelligence, immensely learned in all fields of literary endeavour, and extremely ingenious in many other skills. Through their teaching the king's outlook was very considerably broadened, and he enriched and honoured them with great authority.

79. At about this time I too was summoned by the king from the remote, westernmost parts of Wales, and I came to the Saxon land. When I had taken the decision to travel across great expanses of land to meet him, I arrived in the territory of the right-hand [southern][170] Saxons, which in English is called Sussex, accompanied by some English guides. There I saw him for the first time[171] at the royal estate which is called Dean.[172] When I had been warmly welcomed by him, and we were engaged in discussion, he asked me earnestly to commit myself to his service and to become a member of his household,[173] and to relinquish for his sake all that I had on the left-hand [northern] and western side of the Severn. He promised to pay me greater compensation for it (which indeed he was to do). I replied

that I could not enter such an agreement incautiously and without due consideration. For it struck me as unfair to abandon those very holy places in which I had been brought up, trained, tonsured and eventually ordained, in favour of some other worldly honour and position, unless I were under constraint and compulsion. He replied to my remark: 'If it is not agreeable to you to come on these terms, at least grant me one half of your services, whereby you would be with me for six months each year and the same length of time in Wales.' To which I replied in the following terms: that even this I could not promise casually and rashly without being able to take the advice of my people.[174] But when I perceived that he greatly desired to have my services (for whatever reason I knew not!), I promised that I would come back to him in six months' time, health permitting, with an answer which would be acceptable to me and my people, and agreeable to him. Since this reply seemed acceptable to him, I gave him my undertaking to return at the agreed time; and on the fourth day I left him and rode off home.

However, a short while after I had left him, I was seized by a violent fever in the monastery of Caerwent;[175] in which I suffered for twelve months and a week, by day and night without any remission or hope of recovery. So when I had not returned to him at the agreed time (as I had promised), he sent letters to me asking the cause of my delay and urging me to ride quickly to him. But since I was unable to ride to him, I sent a letter back to explain the cause of my delay and to reaffirm my intention of keeping my promise, if only I could recover from the illness. Accordingly, when the illness finally abated, I pledged myself to the king's service as I had promised, with the understanding and consent of all our people, for the benefit of that holy place and everyone living there,[176] on the condition that for six months of every year I would remain with him – either, if I could, I would spend six months at a stretch, or else would take it in turns, spending three months in Wales and three months in the Saxon land; thus the latter would derive benefit in every respect from the learning[177] of St David,[178] to the best of my abilities at least. For our people were hoping that, if I should come to Alfred's notice and obtain his friendship through some such arrangement, they might suffer less damaging afflictions and injuries[179] at the hands of King Hyfaidd[180] (who often assaulted that monastery and the jurisdiction[181] of St David, sometimes by expelling those bishops

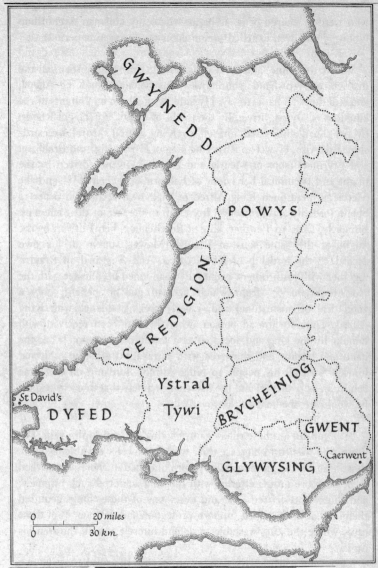

GWYNEDD

POWYS

CEREDIGION

Ystrad
Tywi

St David's

DYFED

BRYCHEINIOG

GWENT

Caerwent

GLYWYSING

0   20 miles
0   30 km

Map 4. Wales in the late ninth century

The political affiliation of Ystrad Tywi is uncertain, for it was connected at different times with either Dyfed or Ceredigion; in the late ninth century it probably formed part of Dyfed.

who were in charge of it, as happened to my kinsman Archbishop Nobis;[182] he even expelled me on occasion during this period).

80. At that time, and for a considerable time before then, all the districts of right-hand [southern] Wales belonged to King Alfred, and still do.[183] That is to say, Hyfaidd, with all the inhabitants of the kingdom of Dyfed, driven by the might of the six[184] sons of Rhodri [Mawr], had submitted himself to King Alfred's royal overlordship. Likewise, Hywel ap Rhys (the king of Glywysing) and Brochfael and Ffyrnfael (sons of Meurig and kings of Gwent), driven by the might and tyrannical behaviour of Ealdorman Æthelred[185] and the Mercians, petitioned King Alfred of their own accord, in order to obtain lordship and protection from him in the face of their enemies. Similarly, Elise ap Tewdwr, king of Brycheiniog, being driven by the might of the same sons of Rhodri [Mawr], sought of his own accord[186] the lordship of King Alfred. And Anarawd ap Rhodri, together with his brothers, eventually abandoned his alliance with the Northumbrians[187] (from which he had got no benefit, only a good deal of misfortune) and, eagerly seeking alliance with King Alfred, came to him in person; when he had been received with honour by the king and accepted as a son in confirmation[188] at the hand of a bishop, and showered with extravagant gifts, he subjected himself with all his people to King Alfred's lordship on the same condition as Æthelred and the Mercians, namely that in every respect he would be obedient to the royal will.

81. Nor did all these rulers gain the king's friendship in vain. For those who wished to increase their worldly power were able to do so; those who wished an increase of wealth obtained it; those who wished to be on more intimate terms with the king achieved such intimacy; and those who desired each and every one of these things acquired them. All of them gained support, protection and defence[189] in those cases where the king was able to defend himself and all those in his care.

Therefore, when I arrived in his presence at the royal estate known as *Leonaford*,[190] I was honourably received by him, and on that occasion I remained with him at court for eight months, during which time I read aloud to him whatever books he wished and which we had to hand. For it is his peculiar and most characteristic habit either to read books aloud himself or to listen to others doing so – by day and night, amid all other mental preoccupations and physical ailments. When I repeatedly sought permission from him to return and was unable to obtain it by any means, and had finally decided to demand this permission no matter what, I was summoned to him at daybreak on Christmas Eve, and he presented me with two documents in which there was a lengthy list of everything which was in the two monasteries [191] named Congresbury and Banwell in English. [192] On that same day he granted those two monasteries to me, with all the things which were in them, as well as an extremely valuable silk cloak and a quantity of incense weighing as much as a stout man. He added that the giving of these trifles would not prevent him from giving me greater gifts at a future time. Indeed with the passage of time he unexpectedly granted me Exeter with all the jurisdiction pertaining to it in Saxon territory and in Cornwall, [193] not to mention the countless daily gifts of worldly riches of every sort which it would be tedious to recount at this point for fear of boring my readers. [194] But let no one think that I have mentioned these gifts here out of some form of pride or self-esteem or for the sake of acquiring greater prestige: I testify in God's presence that I have *not* done so for this reason, but rather to reveal to those who do not know the king how lavish in his generosity he is. He then immediately gave me permission to ride out to those two monasteries so well provided with goods of all sorts, and from there to return home. [195]

82. In the year of the Lord's Incarnation 886 (the thirty-eighth of King Alfred's life), the Viking army fled from the territory [of the eastern Franks] [196] once again and came to the territory of the western Franks; taking their ships along the river Seine and going a long way up-river, they reached the city of Paris. They spent the winter there, and established their camp on both sides of the river near the bridge, so that they could prevent the citizens from crossing the bridge (for Paris is situated on a small island in the middle of the river), and laid siege to the city for that entire year. But, because God mercifully protected the citizens and they defended themselves courageously, the Vikings could not breach the fortifications. [197]

83. In this same year Alfred, king of the Anglo-Saxons, restored the city of London splendidly – after so many towns had been burned

and so many people slaughtered[198] – and made it habitable again; he
entrusted it to the care of Æthelred, ealdorman of the Mercians. All
the Angles and Saxons – those who had formerly been scattered
everywhere and were not in captivity with the Vikings[199] – turned
willingly to King Alfred and submitted themselves to his lordship.[200]

84. In the year of the Lord's Incarnation 887 (the thirty-ninth of
King Alfred's life), the Viking army left the city of Paris without
damaging it, simply because they had been unable to accomplish their
ends any other way; rowing under the bridge, they steered their fleet
upstream against the Seine a long way until at length they arrived at
the mouth of the river Marne. Then, leaving the Seine, they altered
their course at the mouth of the Marne and sailed up it a long time
and a long way until they finally arrived – not without difficulty – at
a place called Chézy, which is a royal estate.[201] They stayed at Chézy
for a whole year. The following year they entered the mouth of the
river Yonne and remained there a further year – not without extensive
damage to that region.[202]

85. In that same year Charles [the Fat], king of the Franks, went
the way of all flesh; but Arnulf, his brother's son, had expelled him
from the kingdom six weeks before his death. As soon as he was dead,
five kings were consecrated and the empire was torn up into five
parts.[203] Nevertheless, the principal seat of the realm fell to Arnulf
– rightly and deservedly (but for the fact that he had sinned shamefully in expelling his uncle). The other four kings also promised
fealty and obedience to Arnulf, as was only fitting: for none of those
four kings had any hereditary right to the kingdom on his father's
side, only Arnulf. In short, five kings were consecrated immediately
upon the death of Charles [the Fat], but the overall authority remained
in the hands of Arnulf.[204] The division of the empire, then, was as
follows: Arnulf took the lands east of the Rhine; Rudolf took the
inland part of the kingdom; Odo took the western kingdom; and
Berengar and Guy between them took Lombardy as well as the other
territories on that side of the mountains. They did not, however,
preserve those extensive kingdoms thus defined peacefully among
themselves: on two occasions they waged all-out war against each
other, and very frequently took turns at laying waste the other kingdoms, and each of them drove the other from his realm.[205]

86. In the very same year in which the Viking army left Paris and went to Chézy, Æthelhelm, ealdorman of Wiltshire, took to Rome the alms of King Alfred and the [West] Saxons.[206]

87. It was also in this year that Alfred, king of the Anglo-Saxons, first began through divine inspiration to read [Latin] and to translate at the same time, all on one and the same day.[207] But in order that this process may be understood more clearly by those who are uninformed, I shall take pains to explain the reasons for this late start.

88. One day when we were sitting together in the royal chamber discussing all sorts of topics (as we normally did), it happened that I was reading aloud some passage to him from a certain book. As he was listening intently to this with both ears and was carefully mulling it over in the depths of his mind, he suddenly showed me a little book[208] which he constantly carried on his person, and in which were written the day-time offices and some psalms and certain prayers which he had learned in his youth. He told me to copy the passage in question into the little book. When I heard this and[209] realized his natural good-will on the one hand as well as his devout enthusiasm for the pursuit of divine wisdom, I stretched out my palms to the heavens and gave mighty (albeit silent) thanks to Almighty God,[210] who had sown such great enthusiasm for the pursuit of learning in the king's heart. But, when I could find no empty space in the little book in which I might copy the passage – for it was completely filled with all manner of things – I hesitated slightly, mainly because I was eager to draw the king's excellent intelligence to a fuller understanding of passages of Holy Scripture. When he urged me to copy the passage as quickly as possible, I said to him: 'Would it meet with your approval if I were to copy out the passage separately on another sheet of parchment? For we don't know whether we might at some point find one or more similar passages which you would like; and if this were to happen unexpectedly, we'd be glad to have kept it separate.' He listened to this and said that he agreed with my advice. When I heard his reply I was delighted, and quickly prepared a quire[211] for the purpose, and copied the passage near the quire's beginning – not without some prompting from him! And that very same day I copied into the same quire at his request no fewer than three other passages

pleasing to him, just as I had foreseen. Thereafter during our daily discussions, while searching to this end, as we found other equally pleasing passages the quire grew full, and rightly so, just as it is written, 'The just man builds on a modest foundation and gradually proceeds to greater things',[212] or like the busy bee, wandering far and wide over the marshes in his quest, eagerly and relentlessly assembles many various flowers of Holy Scripture, with which he crams full the cells of his heart.[213]

89. Now as soon as that first passage had been copied, he was eager to read it at once and to translate it into English, and thereupon to instruct many others, just as we are admonished by the example of that fortunate thief who recognized the Lord Jesus Christ – his Lord and indeed Lord of all things – hanging next to him on the venerable gallows of the Holy Cross, and petitioned Him with earnest prayers.[214] Turning his fleshly eyes only (he could not do anything else, since he was completely pinned down with nails), he called out in a reverential voice: 'Christ, remember me when thou shalt come into thy kingdom' [Luke xxiii, 42]. This thief first began to learn the rudiments of Christian faith on the gallows; the king likewise[215] (even though in a different way, given his royal station), prompted from heaven, took it upon himself to begin on the rudiments of Holy Scripture on St Martin's Day [11 November] and to study these flowers[216] collected here and there from various masters and to assemble them within the body of one little book (even though they were all mixed up) as the occasion demanded. He expanded it so much that it nearly approached the size of a psalter. He wished it to be called his *enchiridion* (that is to say, 'hand-book'), because he conscientiously kept it to hand by day and night. As he then used to say, he derived no small comfort from it.

90. But, just as it was written by a certain wise man a long time ago, 'The minds of those in whom there is conscious concern for ruling are ever alert',[217] I think I should be particularly alert, since I have just suggested a comparison (albeit of different degree) between the fortunate thief and the king: for the gallows are hateful to anyone who finds himself in trouble. But what can he do, if he cannot extricate himself from it, or even run away, or by some manner of means improve his lot by remaining there? He ought

therefore to endure – willy-nilly – in pain and sorrow what he is suffering.

91. King Alfred has been transfixed by the nails of many tribulations, even though he is invested with royal authority: from his twentieth year until his forty-fifth (which is now in course)[218] he has been plagued continually with the savage attacks of some unknown disease, such that he does not have even a single hour of peace in which he does not either suffer from the disease itself or else, gloomily dreading it, is not driven almost to despair. Moreover, he was perturbed – not without good reason – by the relentless attacks of foreign peoples, which he continually sustained from land and sea without any interval of peace. What shall I say of his frequent expeditions and battles against the Vikings and of the unceasing responsibilities of government? What of his daily involvement[219] with the nations which lie from the Mediterranean to the farthest limit of Ireland? – for I have even seen and read letters sent to him with gifts from Jerusalem by the patriarch Elias.[220] And what of the cities and towns to be rebuilt and of others to be constructed where previously there were none? And what of the treasures[221] incomparably fashioned in gold and silver at his instigation? And what of the royal halls and chambers marvellously constructed of stone and wood at his command? And what of the royal residences of masonry, moved from their old position and splendidly reconstructed at more appropriate places by his royal command?[222] And what[223] of the mighty disorder and confusion of his own people – to say nothing of his own malady – who would undertake of their own accord little or no work for the common needs of the kingdom?

Yet once he had taken over the helm of his kingdom, he alone, sustained by divine assistance, struggled like an excellent pilot to guide his ship laden with much wealth to the desired and safe haven of his homeland, even though all his sailors were virtually exhausted; similarly, he did not allow it to waver or wander from course, even though the course lay through the many seething whirlpools of the present life. For by gently instructing, cajoling, urging, commanding, and (in the end, when his patience was exhausted) by sharply chastising those who were disobedient and by despising popular stupidity and stubbornness in every way, he carefully and cleverly exploited and converted his bishops and ealdormen and nobles, and his thegns most dear to him, and reeves as well (in all of whom, after the Lord and the king, the authority of the entire kingdom is seen to be invested, as is appropriate), to his own will and to the general advantage of the whole realm.[224] But if, during the course of these royal admonitions, the commands were not fulfilled because of the people's laziness, or else (having been begun too late in a time of necessity) were not finished in time to be of use to those working on them (I am speaking here of fortifications commanded by the king which have not yet been begun, or else, having been begun late in the day, have not been brought to completion[225]) and enemy forces burst in by land and sea (or, as frequently happens, by both!), then those who had opposed the royal commands were humiliated in meaningless repentance by being reduced to virtual extinction. I say 'meaningless repentance' on the authority of Scripture, where numberless persons who had performed foul deeds were frequently struck down by a severe calamity and thus had cause for sorrow. But even though (to follow up the example[226] of the excellent authority) they are, alas, pitifully driven to despair and, having lost their fathers, spouses, children, servants, slaves, handmaidens, the fruits of their labours and all their possessions, are reduced to tears, what use is their accursed repentance, when it cannot help their slaughtered kinsfolk, nor redeem those captured from a hateful captivity, nor even occasionally be of use to themselves who have escaped, since they no longer have anything by which to sustain their own life? Those who were severely afflicted, therefore, are contrite in untimely repentance, and are sorry that they had negligently scorned the royal commands; now they loudly applaud the king's foresight and promise to make every effort to do what they had previously refused – that is, with respect to constructing fortresses and to the other things of general advantage to the whole kingdom.[227]

92. At this point I do not think that I can profitably bypass the intention and resolve of his most excellent enterprise, which he never allowed himself to overlook no matter whether things were going well or badly. For when in his usual manner he had taken stock of what was most essential for his soul, amid his other good deeds performed by day and night (on which he concentrated attentively and fully), he ordered two monasteries to be constructed.

One of these was for monks and was located at a place called

Athelney,[228] which is surrounded by swampy, impassable and extensive marshland and groundwater on every side. It cannot be reached in any way except by punts or by a causeway which has been built by protracted labour between two fortresses. (A formidable fortress of elegant workmanship was set up by the command of the king at the western end of the causeway.)[229] In this monastery he gathered monks of various nationalities from every quarter, and assembled them there.

93. The reason is that, at first, he had no noble or free-born man of his own race who would of his own accord undertake the monastic life, except for children, who could not as yet choose good or reject evil because of the tenderness of their infant years – not surprisingly, since for many years past the desire for the monastic life had been totally lacking in that entire race (and in a good many other peoples as well!), even though quite a number of monasteries which had been built in that area still remain but do not maintain the rule of monastic life in any consistent way. I am not sure why: either it is because of the depredations of foreign enemies whose attacks by land and sea are very frequent and savage, or else because of the people's enormous abundance of riches of every kind, as a result of which (I suspect) this kind of monastic life came all the more into disrespect.[230] In any case Alfred took pains to assemble monks of various nationalities in that monastery.

94. In the first place, he appointed John,[231] a priest and monk of Old Saxon origin, as abbot; and thereafter certain priests and deacons from across the sea. Among these (since he had not yet achieved the number he desired), he acquired a number of people of Gallic origin;[232] he ordered that certain of their children be educated in the monastery and at a later time be raised to the monastic order. In that monastery too I saw someone of Viking parentage who had been brought up there, and who, as quite a young man, was living there in the monastic habit – and he was assuredly not the last of them to do so.[233]

95. On one occasion a crime was perpetrated in that monastery which I would not commit to the oblivion of silence, mute in its taciturnity (even though the crime itself is unworthy to be recorded),

since throughout scripture the foul deeds of the unrighteous are sown among the holy deeds of the righteous, like cockle and tares in the crop of wheat:[234] the good deeds, that is, so they may be praised, followed, emulated, and their imitators may be esteemed worthy of every holy honour; the evil deeds, on the other hand, that they may be disparaged, cursed and entirely shunned, and their imitators reproached with all hatred, contempt and punishment.

96. On a particular occasion, then, a priest and a deacon of Gallic origin from among those monks mentioned above were aroused by envy at the devil's prompting against their abbot, the said John; they were secretly embittered to such a degree that, in the manner of the Jews, they ambushed and betrayed their lord by treachery. In their treachery, they instructed two slaves of the same Gallic race (who became involved for a bribe) to the effect that, during the night when everyone was sleeping soundly in blissful bodily peace, they would enter the unlocked church armed, and would close it again after them in the normal way and, hidden in the church, would await the approach of the abbot; and when the abbot would quietly enter the church alone in order to pray, as he usually did, and would lie down on the ground in front of the holy altar on bended knees, they would attack him savagely and kill him on the spot; then they would drag his lifeless body away and dump it at the door of a certain whore, to make it seem as if he had been killed in the course of whoring. They devised this plan, adding crime to crime, as it is said: 'The last error shall be worse than the first' [Matthew xxvii, 64]. But divine mercy, which is always ready to help the innocent, frustrated to a large degree this evil plan of evil men, so that everything did not turn out as they had planned.

97. When all the evil plan had been clearly expounded and outlined by the evil conspirators to their evil accomplices,[235] when the night had arrived and was thought propitious, and a promise of impunity had been given, the two armed villains shut themselves in the church to await the abbot's arrival. At midnight John entered the church secretly as usual (so that no one would know) in order to pray, and bowed down on bended knees before the altar; then the two villains attacked him suddenly with drawn[236] swords and wounded him severely. But he, being a man of customary sharp intelligence and (as I have heard

about him from several sources) a man with some experience in the
martial arts – had he not set his mind on a higher course – rose briskly
to meet them as soon as he heard their commotion and before he saw
them or was wounded by them. He called out and resisted them as
best he could, shouting that they were devils and not men: he could
not think otherwise, since he did not believe that men would attempt
such a thing. However, he was wounded before his own men arrived:
they had been awakened by the uproar but, having heard the word
'devils', were frightened and did not know what to do either. They
and the two betrayers of their lord (in the manner of the Jews) all ran
helter-skelter to the doors of the church; but before John's men got
there, the villains had fled as quickly as possible to the depths of the
nearby marsh, leaving the abbot half-dead. The monks picked up
their half-dead master and carried him home with lamentation and
sadness. Nor did the deceitful conspirators shed fewer tears than the
innocent. For God's mercy was unwilling for such a crime to go
unpunished: the villains who had committed this deed, as well as all
those who had instigated so great a crime, were captured and bound
and underwent a terrible death through various tortures.

Now that I have reported these events, allow me to return to my
proper subject.

98. King Alfred ordered the other monastery to be built near the
east gate of Shaftesbury[237] as a residence suitable for nuns. He
appointed as its abbess his own daughter Æthelgifu, a virgin consecrated to God; and many other noble nuns live with her in the same
monastery, serving God in the monastic life.

Alfred abundantly endowed these two monasteries with estates of
land and every kind of wealth.

99. When these affairs had been settled, he thought to himself in
his usual manner about what more he might add that would be more
in keeping with his holy resolve: and this resolve,[238] initiated not
without profit and profitably conceived, was quite profitably sustained. For he had once heard a passage in scripture to the effect that
the Lord had promised to repay His tithe many times over, and had
faithfully kept this promise.[239] Encouraged by this example and
desiring to excel the practice of his predecessors, this man of holy
resolve promised devoutly and faithfully with all his heart to give to

God one half of his service, both by day and by night, and one half of all the riches which, acquired by right, steadily accrued to him during the year.[240] And in so far as human intelligence is able to discriminate and remain alert, he thoughtfully and intelligently sought to fulfil this vow. But in order that, in his usual way, he might be able to avoid what we are cautioned against in another passage of Holy Scripture – 'If thou offer aright, but dost not divide aright, thou sinnest' [Genesis iv, 7][241] – he considered how he might justly divide what he had generously promised to God. As Solomon says: 'The heart of the king' (that is, his wisdom) 'is in the hand of the Lord' [Proverbs xxi, 1]. Having received this wisdom from on high, Alfred commanded his thegns to divide the revenue from all taxation in any one year into two equal parts in the first instance.

100. When the revenues had been divided in this way, he decreed that the first part should be reserved for secular affairs. He ordered this in turn to be divided into three portions. He paid out the first portion every year to his fighting men and likewise to his noble thegns who lived at the royal court in turns, serving him in various capacities.[242] Now the royal household was systematically managed at all times by means of three shifts: for the king's followers were sensibly divided into three groups, so that the first group lived at the royal court for one month, performing its duties by day and night; when the month was up and the next group had arrived, the first returned home and spent two months there, each man seeing to his own private affairs. The second group, when a month had passed and the third group had arrived, likewise went home in order to spend two months there. And this third group, once its month's service was over and the first group had returned, went home to spend two months there. By this arrangement the administration in the royal court is taken in turns at all times.[243]

101. To such men the king granted the first of these three portions, but to each according to his own rank and even to his own office.[244] The second portion he gave to his craftsmen, who were skilled in every earthly craft[245] and whom he had assembled and commissioned in almost countless quantity from many races. With admirable generosity, in a praiseworthy manner and – as it is written, 'God loveth a cheerful giver' [II Corinthians ix, 7] – with a cheerful disposition, he

paid out the third portion to foreigners of all races who came to him from places near and far and asked money from him (or even if they did not ask), to each one according to his particular station.

102. The second part of all his riches, however, which accrued to him annually from every form of taxation and were assigned to the treasury,[246] he marked out for God in full devotion (as I explained a short while ago). He instructed his thegns to divide it carefully into four equal portions, on the understanding that the first portion of the subdivision would be judiciously expended on the poor of every race who came to him. In this connection he recalled that, in so far as human judgement could make provision, the opinion of the holy Pope Gregory ought to be followed, where he makes the following shrewd observation concerning the distribution of alms: 'Do not give little to whom you should give much, nor much to whom little is due, nor nothing to whom you should give something, nor something to whom nothing is due.'[247] The second portion he bestowed on the two monasteries which he himself had instituted, and to those serving God within them (I spoke more fully about these a short while ago). The third portion was to be given to the school, which he had assiduously assembled from many nobles of his own race and also from boys not of noble birth.[248] He gave the fourth portion to neighbouring monasteries throughout the Saxon land and Mercia; and in certain years, by turns, depending on his resources, he either made a grant at once or agreed to make such a grant on a subsequent occasion (given life and favourable circumstances) to churches and the servants of God dwelling within them in Wales and Cornwall, Gaul, Brittany, Northumbria, and sometimes even in Ireland.

103. When the king had systematically arranged these matters in this way, being mindful of that saying of Holy Scripture that 'he who wishes to give alms ought to begin from himself',[249] he reflected thoughtfully on what he might offer to God in the way of service of his own body and mind, for he had decided to make an offering to God in this respect no less than in that of external riches.[250] That is to say, he had promised to render to God, of his own accord and with all his strength, in so far as his health and resources and abilities would allow, one half of his mental and bodily effort both by day and

night. But because he could not in any way accurately estimate the duration of the night hours because of darkness, nor of the day-time hours because of the frequent density of rain and cloud, he began to reflect on how he might be able (sustained by God's mercy) to preserve the substance of his vow unfailingly until he died, by means of some enduring principle, without any kind of uncertainty.

104. When he had thought about these things for some time, he at last hit upon a useful and intelligent solution. He instructed his chaplains[251] to produce an ample quantity of wax, and, when they had brought it, he told them to weigh it against the weight of pennies on a two-pound balance. When a sufficient amount of wax, equivalent in weight to seventy-two pennies, had been measured out, he told the chaplains to make six candles out of it, each of equal size, so that each candle would be twelve inches long and would have the inches marked on it. Accordingly, once this plan had been devised, the six candles were lit so as to burn without interruption through the twenty-four hours of each day and night in the presence of the holy relics of a number of God's chosen saints which the king always had with him everywhere. But because of the extreme violence of the wind, which sometimes blew day and night without stopping through the doors of the churches or through the numerous cracks in the windows, walls, wall-panels and partitions, and likewise through the thin material of the tents, the candles on occasion could not continue burning through an entire day and night up to the same hour that they had been lighted the evening before; when this happened it caused the candles to burn up more quickly than they should, so that they had finished their course before their appointed hour. Alfred considered how he might be able to exclude such draughts of wind; and when he had ingeniously and cleverly devised a plan, he ordered a lantern to be constructed attractively out of wood and ox-horn – for white ox-horn, when shaved down finely with a blade, becomes as translucent as a glass vessel. Once this lantern had been marvellously constructed from wood and horn in the manner I have described, and a candle had been placed inside it at night so that it shone as brightly without as within, it could not be disturbed by any gust of wind, since he had asked for the door of the lantern to be made of horn as well. When the apparatus had been constructed in this way, the six candles could burn one after the other without interruption through the course of

the twenty-four hours – neither more quickly nor more slowly. And once these candles were consumed, more were lighted.[252]

105. When these arrangements had been properly carried out in every respect, he was eager to observe the half of his service, just as he had promised to God, and even to increase it, in so far as his means and abilities – and of course his health – would allow. He was a painstaking judge in establishing the truth in judicial hearings,[253] and this most of all in cases concerning the care of the poor, on whose behalf he was wonderfully solicitous day and night, amid all the other obligations of this present life. Throughout the entire kingdom the poor had either very few supporters or else none at all, except for the king himself: not surprisingly, since nearly all the magnates and nobles of that land had devoted their attention more to worldly than to divine affairs; indeed, everyone was more concerned with his own particular well-being in worldly matters than with the common good.[254]

106. King Alfred used also to sit[255] at judicial hearings for the benefit both of his nobles and of the common people, since they frequently disagreed violently among themselves at assemblies of ealdormen or reeves, to the point where virtually none of them could agree that any judgement reached by the ealdormen or reeves in question was just.[256] Under pressure of this intransigent and obdurate disagreement, the separate parties could undertake to submit to the king's judgement, a procedure which both parties quickly hastened to implement. However, if anyone considered that some injustice (as he saw it) might arise in the case, he would not willingly submit to the decision of such a judge, although by force and stipulation of the law[257] he would be constrained to be present, even against his will. For he knew that none of his malice could remain there unexposed for long – not surprisingly, since the king was an extremely astute investigator in judicial matters as in everything else. He would carefully look into nearly all the judgements which were passed in his absence anywhere in his realm, to see whether they were just or unjust; and if he could identify any corruption in those judgements, he would ask the judges concerned politely, as is his wont, either in person or through one of his other trusted men, why they had passed so unfair a sentence – whether through ignorance or because of some

other malpractice (that is to say, either for love or fear of the one party or for hatred of the other, or even for the sake of a bribe).[258] Accordingly, if the judges in question were to confess after all that they had indeed passed judgement in such a way because they had not known better in the circumstances, then the king, admonishing their inexperience and foolishness with discretion and restraint, would reply as follows: 'I am astonished at this arrogance of yours, since through God's authority and my own you have enjoyed the office and status of wise men, yet you have neglected the study and application of wisdom. For that reason, I command you either to relinquish immediately the offices of worldly power that you possess, or else to apply yourselves much more attentively to the pursuit of wisdom.' Having heard these words, the ealdormen and reeves were terrified and chastened as if by the greatest of punishments, and they strove with every effort to apply themselves to learning what is just. As a result nearly all the ealdormen and reeves and thegns (who were illiterate from childhood) applied themselves in an amazing way to learning how to read, preferring rather to learn this unfamiliar discipline (no matter how laboriously) than to relinquish their offices of power.[259] But if one of them – either because of his age or because of the unresponsive nature of his unpractised intelligence – was unable to make progress in learning to read, the king commanded the man's son (if he had one) or some relative of his, or even (if he had no one else) a man of his own – whether freeman or slave – whom he had caused to be taught to read long before, to read out books in English to him by day and night, or whenever he had the opportunity. Sighing greatly from the bottom of their hearts, these men regretted that they had not applied themselves to such pursuits in their youth, and considered the youth of the present day to be fortunate, who had the luck to be instructed in the liberal arts, but counted themselves unfortunate because they had not learned such things in their youth nor even in their old age, even though they ardently wished that they had been able to do so. But I have explained this concern for learning how to read among the young and old in order to give some idea of the character of King Alfred.[260]

II

THE *ANGLO-SAXON CHRONICLE,*
888–900

The contemporary annals in the Anglo-Saxon Chronicle *form the basis for the narrative history of Alfred's reign. Asser, writing his* Life of King Alfred *in 893, incorporates a full translation of the annals from 851 to 887, thus covering the years of Alfred's childhood and a part of his reign. In the following pages a translation is provided of the remaining 'Alfredian' annals, from 888 to 900. These have been divided up into three sections, for reasons explained on pp. 277–81 below. The passages translated are among the earliest surviving examples of connected English prose; it is not surprising, therefore, that the style might in certain respects seem primitive to the modern reader.*

Annals 888–92

888 In this year Ealdorman Beocca [1] took the alms of the West Saxons and of King Alfred to Rome. [2] And Queen Æthelswith, [3] who was King Alfred's sister, died, and her body lies in Pavia. And in the same year Archbishop Æthelred [4] and Ealdorman Æthelwold [5] died, in the same month.

889 In this year there was no expedition to Rome, except that King Alfred sent two couriers with letters.

890 In this year Abbot Beornhelm [6] took the alms of the West Saxons and of King Alfred to Rome. And Guthrum, the northern king, died. His baptismal name was Æthelstan; he was King Alfred's godson, and he lived in East Anglia, and was the first to settle that land. [7]

And in the same year the Viking army went from the Seine to Saint-Lô, which lies between the Bretons and the Franks; and the Bretons fought against them and had the victory, and drove them into a river and drowned many of them. [8]

891 In this year the Viking army went eastwards, and King Arnulf with the East Franks and the Saxons and Bavarians fought against the mounted force before the ships arrived, and put it to flight. [9]

And three Irishmen [10] came to King Alfred in a boat without any oars from Ireland, whence they had stolen away because they wished to go on pilgrimage for love of God, they cared not where.[11] The boat in which they travelled was made from two and a half hides;[12] and they took with them only enough food for seven days. And after seven days they came to land in Cornwall, and then went immediately to King Alfred. Their names were Dubslaine, Macbethath and Maelin-muin.[13] And Suibne, the greatest teacher among the Irish, died.[14]

And the same year, after Easter [4 April], around the Rogation Days[15] or before, appeared the star which is called in Latin *cometa*.[16] Some men say that it is in English a 'long-haired' star, because a long stream of light trails from it, sometimes on one side, sometimes on every side.[17]

892 In this year the great Viking army, about which we spoke earlier,[18] went back from the eastern kingdom westward to Bou-logne, and there they were provided with ships, so that they trans-ported themselves across, horses and all, in one journey,[19] and then came up into the estuary of the Limen[20] with 250[21] ships. This estuary is in eastern Kent, at the east end of the great wood which we call *Andred* [the Weald]. The wood from east to west is 120 miles long, or longer, and thirty miles wide. The river about which we spoke before flows out of that forest. They rowed their ships up the river as far as the forest, four miles from the outer part of the estuary, and there they attacked a fortification located in the marsh-land.[22] A few commoners[23] were present inside, and it was only half-made.[24] Then shortly afterwards Hastein came up the Thames estuary with eighty ships and made a fortification for himself at Milton,[25] and the other Viking army made one at Appledore.[26]

Annals 893–6

893 In this year, which is to say about twelve months after the Vikings had made the fortification in the eastern kingdom,[1] and the Northumbrians and East Angles had given oaths to King Alfred, and the East Angles had given six hostages,[2] nevertheless, contrary to those pledges, whenever the other Viking armies [those at Appledore and Milton] set out in full force, then they went as well, either with them or on their own. And then King Alfred assembled his army and

advanced so that he encamped between the two Viking armies at a
point where he had the best access both to the forest stronghold [at
Appledore] and to the river stronghold [at Milton], so that he could
reach either one if they chose to make for any open country. Then
the Vikings set out afterwards through the forest in small bands and
riding companies, along whatever side was then undefended by the
English army; and they were also pursued by other troops almost
every day, either by day or by night, both from the English army and
also from the burhs.[3] The king had divided his army in two, so that
always half its men were at home, half out on service, except for
those men who were to garrison the burhs.[4] The Viking army did not
set out all together from those encampments more often than twice:
the one time when they first landed, before the English army had
been assembled; the other time when they wished to move from those
encampments. Then they seized a large amount of booty and wished
to carry it north across the Thames into Essex to meet the ships.[5]
Then the English army intercepted them from in front and fought
against them at Farnham and put the Viking army to flight and
recovered the booty;[6] and they fled across the Thames, without using
any ford, and then up the Colne to an islet.[7] The English army then
surrounded them there for as long as they had provisions. But they
had by then completed their period of service and used up their
provisions, and the king was then on the way there with the division
which was in service with him.[8] While he was on his way there, and
the other English army was going home (and the Danes were staying
there because their king had been wounded in the battle so that they
could not move him), then those who live in Northumbria and East
Anglia assembled some hundred ships, and went south around the
coast; and some forty ships went north around the coast and besieged
a fortification on the north coast of Devon; and those who went
south around the coast besieged Exeter.[9]

When the king heard this, he turned west towards Exeter with all
the English army, except for a very small number of people who
continued eastwards. These people went on until they came to London
and then, with the townsmen[10] and the reinforcements which came
to them from the west, they went east to Benfleet.[11] Hastein had
already arrived with his army (the one which had previously been at
Milton), and the great army which had previously been at Appledore
on the Limen estuary had by then arrived as well. Hastein had

previously made the fortification at Benfleet; he was then away on a plundering raid, and the great army was at home [in the fortification]. Then the English arrived and put the Viking army to flight and stormed the fortification and seized everything that was inside it, in the way of goods, women, and children as well, and they brought everything to London; and they either broke up or burned all the ships, or brought them to London or Rochester. And Hastein's wife and his two sons were brought to the king; and he gave them back again, because one of them was his godson and the other the godson of Ealdorman Æthelred.[12] They had stood sponsor to them before Hastein came to Benfleet, and Hastein had given Alfred hostages and oaths; and likewise the king had given him a good deal of money, and did so again when he returned the boy and the woman. But as soon as the [Milton] Vikings arrived at Benfleet and the fortification was made, Hastein went plundering in Alfred's kingdom – that very part for which Æthelred, his son's godfather, was responsible; and afterwards, he was out plundering in that same kingdom a second time when his fortification was stormed.

The king turned west with the English army towards Exeter, as I said before: the Viking army had laid siege to the burh, and on his arrival they returned to their ships. While he was occupied against that army there in the west, and the Viking armies [Hastein's Milton/ Benfleet army, and the Appledore/Benfleet army] had both gathered at Shoebury in Essex and had made a fortification there, they both went together up the Thames and a great reinforcement came to them, both from the East Angles and from the Northumbrians. They then went up the Thames until they arrived at the Severn, then up along the Severn. Then Ealdorman Æthelred and Ealdorman Æthelhelm and Ealdorman Æthelnoth,[13] and the king's thegns who were then at home at the fortifications, assembled from every burh east of the Parret, and both west and east of Selwood, and also north of the Thames and west of the Severn,[14] and also some part of the Welsh people.[15] When they had all assembled, they overtook the Viking army from the rear at Buttington on the bank of the Severn,[16] and surrounded them on all sides there in a stronghold. Then, while they remained for many weeks on both sides of the river (and the king was in the west in Devon, occupied against the naval force), the Vikings were sorely pressed by famine and had devoured most of their horses (the rest had died of hunger); they then came out against the men who were encamped on the eastern side of the river and fought against them, and the Christians had the victory. And the king's thegn Ordheah[17] was killed there, as well as many other king's thegns; and there was a mighty slaughter of the Danes there,[18] and the part that got away were saved by taking flight.

When they came to their fortification and to their ships in Essex, the survivors again assembled a great army from the East Angles and Northumbrians at the beginning of the winter, and they made safe their women and their ships and their property in East Anglia; and they went continuously by day and night until they arrived at a deserted city in Wirral, which is called Chester.[19] Then the English army could not overtake them from the rear before they were inside the fortification; but they surrounded the fortification for two days or so, and seized all the cattle that were left outside, and killed the men whom they had been able to cut off outside the fortification, and burned all the corn in the whole neighbourhood or else used it up for their horses. And that was about twelve months after they had come here from across the sea.

894 And then immediately after that, in this year, the Viking army went from Wirral into Wales, because they could not remain there: that was because they had been deprived of both the cattle and the corn which they had plundered. When they turned back from Wales with the booty they had seized there, they crossed Northumbria and East Anglia (so that the English army could not reach them) until they came to the eastern part of Essex, to an island out in the sea called Mersea.

And when the Viking army which had besieged Exeter turned back for home, they ravaged up in Sussex near Chichester, and the townsmen[20] put them to flight and killed many hundreds of them and captured some of their ships.

Then that same year, at the beginning of winter, the Danes who were established on Mersea rowed their ships up the Thames and then up the Lea. That was about two years after they came here from across the sea.

895 In the same year the Viking army made a fortification on the Lea, twenty miles above London.[21] Then afterwards in the summer a large number of the townsmen[22] and also of other people set out until they arrived at the Danes' fortification; and there they were put to flight and some four of the king's thegns were killed. Then afterwards at harvest time the king encamped in the vicinity of the burh [London] while they reaped their corn, so that the Danes could not deny them the harvest. Then one day the king rode up along the river, and looked to see where the river could be obstructed so that the Danes would not be able to bring the ships out. And the English did as follows: they made two fortifications, on the two sides of the river.[23] When they had just started this work, and had encamped alongside, the Viking army realized that they would not be able to bring the ships out. Then they abandoned the ships and went overland until they reached Bridgnorth on the Severn, and there they made a fortification. The English army then rode west after the Viking army; and the men from London fetched the ships, and they broke up all they could not take away, and they brought to London those which were serviceable. And the Danes had made their women safe in East Anglia before they set out from the fortification. They remained at Bridgnorth that winter. That was about three years after they came here from across the sea into the estuary of the Limen.

896 Then afterwards, in the summer of this year, the Viking army dispersed, some into East Anglia, some into Northumbria; and those who were without property[24] got themselves ships and went south across the sea to the Seine.[25]

The Viking army had not – by God's grace! – afflicted the English people to a very great extent; but they were much more severely afflicted during those three years by the mortality of cattle and men,[26] and most of all by the fact that many of the best king's thegns who were in the land died during those three years: among them Swithwulf, bishop of Rochester;[27] and Ceolmund, ealdorman of Kent;[28] and Beorhtwulf, ealdorman of Essex;[29] and Wulfred, ealdorman of Hampshire;[30] and Ealhheard, bishop at Dorchester;[31] and Eadwulf, a king's thegn in Sussex;[32] and Beornwulf, the town-reeve of Winchester;[33] and Ecgwulf, the king's horse-thegn;[34] and many more besides them, though I have named the most distinguished.

That same year the Viking armies from East Anglia and Northumbria greatly harassed Wessex along the south coast with marauding bands, most of all with the warships which they had built many years before. Then King Alfred ordered 'long-ships' to be built with which to oppose the Viking warships. They were almost twice as long as the others. Some had sixty oars, some more. They were both swifter and more stable, and also higher, than the others. They were built neither on the Frisian nor on the Danish pattern, but as it seemed to Alfred himself that they would be most useful.[35]

Then on a certain occasion in the same year six Viking ships came to the Isle of Wight and did considerable damage there, both in Devon and all along the sea-coast. Then the king ordered his men to set out with nine of the new ships, and they blocked them off in the estuary from the seaward end.[36] Then the Vikings went out with three ships against them; and three were beached further up the estuary on dry land: the men had gone off inland. Then the English captured two of the three ships at the mouth of the estuary and killed the men. The other one escaped: the men on that one were also killed, except five; these got away because the English ships ran aground. Moreover, they had run aground very awkwardly: three ran aground on that side of the channel where the Danish ships were beached, and all the others on the other side, so that none of them could get to the others. But when the water had ebbed many furlongs from the ships, the Danes from the three beached ships then went to the other three English ships which were stranded on their side, and there they then fought. The following were killed there: Lucuman, the king's reeve;[37] and Wulfheard the Frisian and Æbbe the Frisian and Æthelhere the Frisian;[38] and Æthelferth, the king's *geneat*;[39] and of all the Frisians and English, sixty-two [were killed], and of the Danes, 120.[40] Then, however, the flood-tide came first to the Danish ships before the Christians could push theirs off, and so they rowed out and away.[41] They were wounded by then to such an extent that they were unable to row past Sussex, but there the sea cast two of the ships on to the land, and the men were taken to Winchester to the king, and he ordered them to be hanged there. And the men who were in the one remaining ship made it back to East Anglia, severely wounded.

That same summer no fewer than twenty ships, with men and all, perished along the south coast. That same year Wulfric, the king's horse-thegn, died; he was also the Welsh-reeve.[42]

Annals 897–900

897 In this year Æthelhelm, ealdorman of Wiltshire, died nine days before midsummer;[1] and in this year Heahstan, who was bishop of London, died.[2]

900 In this year Alfred son of Æthelwulf died six days before All Saints' Day.[3] He was king over the whole English people, except for that part which was under Danish rule; and he held that kingdom for twenty-eight and a half years.[4] And then his son Edward succeeded to the kingdom.[5]

Then Æthelwold, his father's brother's son,[6] seized the residences at Wimborne[7] and Twynham[8] without the permission of the king and his councillors.[9] Then the king rode with the army until he encamped at Badbury[10] near Wimborne, and Æthelwold stayed inside the residence with the men who had submitted to him; and he had barricaded all the gates against him, and said that he would either live there or die there. Then meanwhile he stole himself away during the night, and came to the Viking army in Northumbria, and the king ordered them to ride after him, and then he could not be overtaken.[11] Then the woman was captured whom he had previously taken without the king's permission and contrary to the orders of the bishops, for she had previously been consecrated as a nun.[12]

And in this same year Æthelred, who was ealdorman of Devon, died, four weeks before King Alfred.[13]

III

EXTRACTS FROM THE WRITINGS OF KING ALFRED

The preface to Werferth's translation
of Gregory's Dialogues

Asser, writing in 893, tells us that Werferth, bishop of Worcester and 'a man thoroughly learned in holy writings', translated the Dialogues of Pope Gregory into English 'at the king's command' (chapter 77). Although the surviving Old English translation of the Dialogues does not bear Werferth's name, it must surely be his, since it is accompanied by the prose preface (translated below) in King Alfred's name stating the reasons for the king's command to have the work translated. Furthermore, Asser mentions that Werferth was a Mercian, and the language of the translation has certain Anglian dialectal features that show its author to have been a Mercian. The Dialogues, therefore, will have been one of the earliest works translated at Alfred's instigation. Like Alfred's own translation of the Pastoral Care, Werferth's work was apparently distributed to various ecclesiastical centres in the kingdom: in one manuscript a verse preface by Bishop Wulfsige of Sherborne (translated below, p. 187) replaces Alfred's present prose preface, giving a clear indication that Alfred had sent a copy of Werferth's work to Wulfsige.

I, Alfred, honoured with the dignity of kingship through Christ's gift, have clearly perceived and frequently heard from statements in holy books that for us, to whom God has granted such a lofty station of worldly office, there is the most urgent necessity occasionally to calm our minds amidst these earthly anxieties and direct them to divine and spiritual law. And therefore I sought and petitioned my true friends[1] that they should write down for me from God's books the following teaching concerning the virtues and miracles of holy men, so that, strengthened through the exhortations and love they contain, I might occasionally reflect in my mind on heavenly things amidst these earthly tribulations.[2]

From the translation of Gregory's Pastoral Care

Alfred's translation of Gregory's Regula Pastoralis *was probably the earliest of the translations undertaken by the king himself; it may date from as early as* c. *890 (see above, p. 35). The work is concerned with the spiritual and intellectual qualities necessary in any man who is responsible for the government of others. Gregory's text was principally directed to the holders of ecclesiastical office, but his words are frequently couched in terms that would be equally applicable to the holders of secular office, and one may see at once why the work had such an appeal for King Alfred and why he undertook to make its lessons available to the bishops of his realm. In the prose preface to the work, Alfred explains why he has undertaken to translate this and other works, and the procedures by which he intends to have it circulated. This preface is consequently a cardinal document in our understanding of King Alfred and of the literary culture of late Anglo-Saxon England in general. We have translated the prose preface and the brief verse preface which follows it in the manuscripts; in addition, we have included modern English versions of two chapters of Alfred's translation of the* Regula Pastoralis *(chapters III and IV) in order to convey some impression of the work itself.*

Prose Preface

King Alfred sends words of greeting lovingly and amicably to [. . .].[1]

And I would have it known that very often it has come to my mind what men of learning there were formerly throughout England, both in religious and secular orders; and how there were happy times then throughout England;[2] and how the kings, who had authority over this people, obeyed God and his messengers; and how they not only maintained their peace, morality and authority at home but also extended their territory outside; and how they succeeded both in warfare and in wisdom; and also how eager were the religious orders both in teaching and in learning as well as in all the holy services

which it was their duty to perform for God; and how people from
abroad sought wisdom and instruction in this country; and how nowadays, if we wished to acquire these things, we would have to seek
them outside.[3] Learning had declined so thoroughly in England that
there were very few men on this side of the Humber who could
understand their divine services in English, or even translate a single
letter from Latin into English: and I suppose that there were not
many beyond the Humber either. There were so few of them that I
cannot recollect even a single one south of the Thames when I succeeded to the kingdom.[4] Thanks be to God Almighty that we now
have any supply of teachers at all![5] Therefore I beseech you to do as
I believe you *are* willing to do: as often as you can, free yourself from
worldly affairs so that you may apply that wisdom which God gave
you wherever you can. Remember what punishments befell us in this
world when we ourselves did not cherish learning nor transmit it to
other men.[6] We were Christians in name alone, and very few of us
possessed Christian virtues.[7]

When I reflected on all this, I recollected how – before everything
was ransacked and burned – the churches throughout England stood
filled with treasures and books. Similarly, there was a great multitude
of those serving God.[8] And they derived very little benefit from
those books, because they could understand nothing of them, since
they were not written in their own language. It is as if they had said:
'Our ancestors, who formerly maintained these places, loved wisdom,
and through it they obtained wealth and passed it on to us. Here one
can still see their track, but we cannot follow it.'[9] Therefore we have
now lost the wealth as well as the wisdom, because we did not wish to
set our minds to the track.[10]

When I reflected on all this, I wondered exceedingly why the good,
wise men who were formerly found throughout England and had
thoroughly studied all those books, did not wish to translate any part
of them into their own language.[11] But I immediately answered
myself, and said: 'They did not think that men would ever become so
careless and that learning would decay like this; they refrained
from doing it through this resolve, namely they wished that the more
languages we knew, the greater would be the wisdom in this land.'
Then I recalled how the Law was first composed in the Hebrew
language, and thereafter, when the Greeks learned it, they translated
it all into their own language, and all other books as well. And so too

the Romans, after they had mastered them, translated them all
through learned interpreters into their own language. Similarly all the
other Christian peoples turned some part of them into their own
language.[12] Therefore it seems better to me – if it seems so to you –
that we too should turn into the language that we can all understand
certain books which are the most necessary for all men to know,[13]
and accomplish this, as with God's help we may very easily do
provided we have peace enough, so that all the free-born young men
now in England who have the means to apply themselves to it, may be
set to learning (as long as they are not useful for some other employment)[14] until the time that they can read English writings properly.
Thereafter one may instruct in Latin those whom one wishes to teach
further and wishes to advance to holy orders.

When I recalled how knowledge of Latin had previously decayed
throughout England, and yet many could still read things written in
English, I then began, amidst the various and multifarious afflictions
of this kingdom, to translate into English the book which in Latin is
called *Pastoralis*, in English 'Shepherd-book', sometimes word for
word, sometimes sense for sense,[15] as I learnt it from Plegmund my
archbishop, and from Asser my bishop, and from Grimbald my
mass-priest and from John my mass-priest.[16] After I had mastered
it, I translated it into English as best I understood it and as I could
most meaningfully render it; I intend to send a copy to each bishopric
in my kingdom; and in each copy there will be an *æstel*[17] worth fifty
mancuses. And in God's name I command that no one shall take that
æstel from the book, nor the book from the church. It is not known
how long there shall be such learned bishops as, thanks be to God,
there are now nearly everywhere. Therefore I would wish that they
[the book and the *æstel*] always remain in place, unless the bishop
wishes to have the book with him, or it is on loan somewhere, or
someone is copying it.

Verse Preface[18]

Augustine brought this work from the south over the salt sea to the
island-dwellers, exactly as the Lord's champion, the pope of Rome,
had previously set it out. The wise Gregory was well versed in many
doctrines through his mind's intelligence, his hoard of ingenuity.
Accordingly, he won over most of mankind to the guardian of the

heavens, this greatest of Romans, most gifted of men, most celebrated for his glorious deeds.

King Alfred subsequently translated every word of me [19] into English and sent me south and north to his scribes; he commanded them to produce more such copies from the exemplar, so that he could send them to his bishops, because some of them who least knew Latin had need thereof.

Chapter III
Concerning the burden of government, and how the ruler must despise all hardships and must recoil from any sense of security

We have said these things [20] in few words because we wished to indicate how great is the burden of teaching, so that someone who is unworthy of it will not dare to undertake it, lest through desire for renown in this world he take on the leadership of the damned. St James the Apostle reproved this when he said, very appropriately, 'Brothers, let there not be too many masters among you' [James iii, 1]. For this very reason the mediator Himself of God and men, that is Christ, avoided undertaking earthly rule – He Himself who surpasses all wisdom of the higher spirits and ruled in Heaven before the world was created! It is written in the gospel that the Jews came and wished to make Him king by force. When the Saviour realized that, He avoided them and hid Himself. Who could more easily rule men *religious* without fault than He who created them? He did not avoid authority *allusion* because anyone else was more worthy, but rather He wished to set us an example, so that we are not too greedy for it; and also, He wished to suffer for us. He did not wish to be king, and He came of His own will to the Cross. He shunned the glory of royal authority and chose the punishment of that most abominable death, so that we who are His limbs would learn from Him to shun the allurements of this earth, and also would not fear its horrors and its dangers, and for the sake of truth would love work and fear prosperity and avoid it. For in prosperity a man is often puffed up with pride, whereas tribulations

chasten and humble him through suffering and sorrow. In the midst
of prosperity the mind is elated, and in prosperity a man forgets
himself; in hardship he is forced to reflect on himself, even though he
be unwilling. In prosperity a man often destroys the good he has done;
amidst difficulties he often repairs what he long since did in the way
of wickedness. Very often a man is responsive to the lessons of adversity, even though he previously refused to respond to his instructor's
morals and precepts. But even though afflictions teach and instruct
him, if he acquire the kingdom, he immediately becomes perverted
with pride at the people's reverence for him, and becomes accustomed
to flattering praise. Thus King Saul:[21] at first he declined the throne,
and reckoned himself to be wholly unworthy of it. But as soon as he
assumed the power of the kingdom, he swelled up with pride and
became enraged at that same Samuel who formerly had brought him
to the throne and consecrated him; accordingly Samuel announced
Saul's sins before the people, since thanks to them he had been
unable to control him; and when Samuel wished to leave, Saul seized
him and tore his clothing and dishonoured him. So too David, who
was pleasing to God in nearly every respect:[22] as soon as he no longer
had the burden of so many afflictions, he suffered the wound of
pride, and exhibited this very savagely in the murder of Uriah, a
member of his own household, because of his disgusting desire for
Uriah's wife. The very man who previously had pardoned so many
crimes against his person thus became uncontrollably eager for that
good man's death, without there having been any crime or hostility
against him. This same David refrained from injuring Saul who
reduced him to such great misery and drove him from his land:[23]
when David had him completely in his power in the cave, he cut a piece
from his cloak as a sign that he had power over him, and nevertheless let
him go because of his former loyalty. This same David exposed his own
army to great danger and sent many a man to his death, when he plotted
to kill his own faithful and guiltless follower. The crime would have
kept him far from the company of all other holy men, if once again his
toil and tribulations had not helped him.

Chapter IV
How the administration of authority and government often distracts the mind of the ruler

Very often the manifold cares of assumed leadership trouble the heart, and when the mind is divided between many things at once, it is less firmly fixed in each case, and also less effective. Concerning this the wise Solomon said: 'My son, do not dissipate your mind on too many things, and the same is true of your labours' [cf. Ecclesiasticus xi, 10]. For it often happens that when a man loses the awe and constancy which he ought to have within him, his mind tempts him to a great many useless activities. He is anxious about them, preoccupied with them, and forgets himself when he sets his mind on these useless activities far more than he ought. He is like the man on a journey who is occupied with other affairs to the point where he no longer knows where he wanted to go and is unable to realize what he is losing in delay all the time that he is hesitating, and how much he errs in so doing. Hezekiah, king of the Israelites, did not suppose that he sinned when he led the foreign ambassadors into his treasury and showed them his hoard of gold.[24] But nevertheless he experienced God's anger in the misery which came to his son, Manasses, after his own days on earth. And yet he thought it no sin! Often, when someone happens to do something great and glorious and those who are subject to him consequently magnify and praise him, then he becomes puffed up in pride and thoroughly calls down his Judge's anger upon himself, even though he does not show it in evil deeds. Nevertheless the Judge is forced to anger by his vanity: the Judge who knows all our innermost thoughts also judges them. We can conceal our thoughts and desires from men, but not from God. Consider the Babylonian king, Nebuchadnezzar, who was greatly puffed up in spirit because of his authority and circumstances when he rejoiced at the mighty size and splendour of the city he had built, and exalted himself in his pride above all other men and spoke silently in his mind:[25] 'Is this not the great Babylon which I myself built for my throne and my majesty, for my own adornment and glory, with my own might and strength?' [Daniel iv, 27]. The invisible Judge very quickly heard his silent voice and answered him very plainly with the punishments with which He very quickly afflicted him. God reproved and reproached his arrogance when He deprived him of his worldly authority and returned him to the irrational animals and so, perverting his mind, He associated him with the beasts of the field: thus, through this severe decree, Nebuchadnezzar relinquished his humanity. To the very same man who thought that he was above all other men it happened that he himself did not know that he *was* a man! Nevertheless, although I recount this example, I do not blame great works nor legitimate power: I blame the fact that, because of them, a man will become arrogant in spirit. Rather, I would fortify the weakness of their hearts and control the will of those incompetent, so that none of them would dare rashly to seize power or leadership, and so that those who cannot stand firmly on level ground do not attempt so dangerous an ascent.

wants to make sure leaders will do so — he must think himself very competent to lead

From the translation of Boethius's
Consolation of Philosophy

Boethius's Consolation of Philosophy *was one of the most widely studied books of the early Middle Ages, and it is not surprising that it should have found a sympathetic translator in King Alfred. Cast in the form of a dialogue between Boethius and the Lady Philosophy, its discussion proceeds in alternating prose and verse from Boethius's self-pitying comments on the injustice of Fortune to Philosophy's exposition of the divine order of the universe. Although Boethius's conception of divine order is not at odds with a Christian viewpoint, his work is not explicitly Christian. In translating the work, Alfred was concerned to elicit an overtly Christian message from it. Accordingly, unlike his translation of the* Pastoral Care *(which for the most part is closely literal), Alfred's translation of Boethius displays considerable freedom of handling. At many points, for example, Alfred replaces autobiographical passages in Boethius with lengthy reflections on man's means of comprehending God and His divine order; he recasts the work as a dialogue between the inquirer's mind and the personification Wisdom. All the passages which have been translated below represent additions made by Alfred to the translation, and as such are an invaluable guide to the king's mental preoccupations.*

Prose Preface

King Alfred was the translator of this book: he turned it from Latin into English, as it now stands before you. Sometimes he translated word for word, sometimes sense for sense,[1] so as to render it as clearly and intelligibly as he could, given the various and multifarious worldly distractions which frequently occupied him either in mind or in body. These occupations, which beset him during his days on the throne that he had accepted, are virtually countless; nevertheless, when he had mastered[2] this book [the *De Consolatione Philosophiae*] and turned it from Latin into English prose, he subsequently rendered it into verse, as has now been done.[3] And now he beseeches and in

God's name implores each of those whom it pleases to read this book, to pray for him and not to blame him if they can interpret it more accurately than he was able: for every man must say what he says and do what he does according to the capacity of his intellect and the amount of time available to him.

VII.5 [Wisdom speaking]:[4] 'How, then, will you reply to worldly blessings if they say to you: "What, Mind, do you blame us for? Why are you angry with us? In what way have we offended you? Look, you started desiring us, not us you; you set us on the throne of your Creator when you sought from us the good which you should have sought from Him. You say that we have deceived you, but we could well say that you have deceived us, given that, as a result of your desire and your greed, the Creator of all things is to reject us. So you are more guilty than we are, both because of your own wrongful desires and also because through your fault we cannot obey our Creator's will; for He granted us to you in order that you might enjoy us in accord with His commandments, not in order to fulfil your own desire for greediness." Answer me now, said Wisdom, as you will: I await your answer.'

XVII. When Wisdom had sung this song,[5] he fell silent; and then Mind answered, and said as follows: 'Look, Wisdom, you know that desire for and possession of earthly power never pleased me overmuch, and that I did not unduly desire this earthly rule, but that nevertheless I wished for tools and resources for the task that I was commanded to accomplish, which was that I should virtuously and worthily guide and direct the authority which was entrusted to me. You know of course that no one can make known any skill, nor direct and guide any authority, without tools and resources; a man cannot work on any enterprise without resources. In the case of the king, the resources and tools with which to rule are that he have his land fully manned: he must have praying men, fighting men and working men.[6] You know also that without these tools no king may make his ability known. Another aspect of his resources is that he must have the means of support for his tools, the three classes of men. These, then, are their means of support: land to live on, gifts, weapons, food, ale, clothing, and whatever else is necessary for each of the three classes of men. Without these things he cannot maintain the tools, nor without the tools can he accomplish any of the things he was commanded to do. Accordingly, I sought the resources with which to exercise the authority, in order that my skills and power would not be forgotten and concealed: because every skill and every authority is soon obsolete and passed over, if it is without wisdom; because no man may bring to bear any skill without wisdom. For whatever is done unthinkingly, cannot be reckoned a skill. To speak briefly: I desired to live worthily as long as I lived, and to leave after my life, to the men who should come after me, the memory of me in good works.'[7]

XXIV.3 [Wisdom speaking]: 'Then I say that true friends are the most precious of all this world's blessings: they are not even to be reckoned as worldly goods but as divine, since worthless fate does not bring them forth, but rather God, who created them naturally as kinsmen. For in this world a man desires everything else because he may thereby acquire either power or worldly pleasure, except a faithful friend. One loves a friend sometimes out of affection, sometimes out of trust, even though no other return is expected from him. Nature joins and cements friends together with an inseparable love. But in this world's fortunes and its present wealth one makes enemies more often than friends.'

XXV [Wisdom speaking]: 'There is no created thing that does not wish that it could arrive once more at its source, namely at peaceful rest and security. This rest is with God: indeed it *is* God. But every creature turns about itself like a wheel; and it turns precisely so that it returns to where it previously was, and becomes what it formerly was . . .'

XXVII.2 [Wisdom speaking]: 'Wisdom is the highest virtue, and it has within it four other virtues: one is caution, the second moderation, the third courage and the fourth justice. Wisdom renders those who love it wise and honourable and temperate and patient and just, and it fills him who loves it with every good quality. Those who have authority in this world cannot do likewise; they cannot from all their wealth grant virtue to those who love it,[8] if they have it not by nature.'

XXVII.3 [Wisdom speaking]: 'The empty hopes and fancies of foolish men suppose that power and prosperity are the highest good;

but it is quite otherwise. When rich men are either in a foreign land or in the company of wise men in their native land, both the wise men and the foreigners count their riches for naught, since they realize that they owe their position not to any ability but to the praise of foolish people. But if they derived any trace of particular or natural good from their power, they would retain this even if they forfeited the power: they would not forfeit this natural good, but it would always adhere to them and they would always behave honourably, no matter what land they found themselves in.'

XXXIV.5 [Wisdom speaking]: 'There is only one God, who is the base and foundation of all kinds of good:[9] from Him they all come and they return again to Him, and He rules them all. Although He is the origin and foundation of all good men and all good things, yet the kinds of good which come from Him are manifold: just as all the stars are illuminated and brightened by the sun, some none the less are more, some less bright. So too the moon, which shines only as brightly as the sun illuminates it: when the sun shines directly on the moon, then it becomes fully bright.'

XXXIV.11 [Wisdom speaking]: 'You can ascertain from many things that Nature is very great. It is the very greatness of Nature that all our bodily strength comes from the food which we consume, and nevertheless the food passes through the body and out. But its flavour and its strength pass into every sinew, just as flour is sifted: the flour creeps through each opening and the siftings are separated.'

XXXV.3 Then Wisdom said: 'Through goodness God created all things, because He Himself rules everything which we said was good; and He alone is the steady ruler and steersman and rudder and helm, because He guides and governs all creation just as a good steersman guides a ship.' Then I said: 'I now confess to you that I have found a door where previously I saw a little chink, whereby I was able to see with difficulty a tiny ray of light in this darkness. And yet you previously showed me the door; but I couldn't find the way any better, except that once I saw the ray of light glimmer I groped about for it. I said earlier in this book that I didn't know what the origin of all creation was: you explained to me that it was God. Then I said I knew nothing about its end, but you told me once again that it was

God. Then I said that I knew not how He governed all creation. But you have now explained it to me very clearly, as if you had pulled open the door which I had been looking for.'

XLI.5 [Wisdom speaking]: 'Man perceives things one way through his eyes, another way through his ears, differently again through his imagination, and differently yet again through his intelligence, through sure reason. There are many motionless living creatures, such as shell-fish, which nevertheless have some measure of reason, because they could not live at all if they had no particle of reason. Some can see, some hear, some feel, some smell. But mobile animals are more similar to men, because they have everything which the immobile creatures have, and more besides: that is, they approximate to men. They love what men love and hate what they hate, and flee from what they hate and seek what they love. Men, then, have every attribute which we mentioned above, and also in addition the great gift of intelligence. Angels, however, have pure reason. Therefore creatures are created so that the immobile do not exalt themselves above the mobile, nor contend with them; nor may mobile creatures rise above men, nor men above angels; nor may angels contend with God. But it is a pity that the great part of mankind does not seek after what is granted to them, namely intelligence, nor after what is above them, the possession of angels and wise men, namely pure reason. Rather, most men imitate animals in that they desire worldly pleasure as animals do. And if we had any particle of indubitable reason as angels have, then we might realize that this reason is far better than our intelligence. Even though we may reflect a good deal, we have little perfect understanding free from doubt; but for the angels there is no doubt concerning any of the things which they perceive. Their perception, therefore, is much better than our intelligence is, as our intelligence is better than the animals', or than any part of the understanding which is granted to them, whether mobile or immobile. But let us have our mind set as high as we can on loftier things, set towards the crowning apex of the highest understanding, so that you may most swiftly and easily return to your native land, whence you formerly came. There your mind and intelligence may see clearly what now is in doubt, either with respect to divine providence (which we have often discussed above), or to our own free will, or to all other things.'

XLII [Wisdom speaking]: 'Therefore we must investigate God with all our might, so that we may know what He is. Although it is not within our capacity to know what He is like, we ought nevertheless to inquire with the intellectual capacity which He gives us, just as we previously stated that one should understand everything according to one's intellectual capacity, given that we cannot understand everything as it really is. Every creature, both rational and irrational, reveals that God is eternal, because so many creatures so great and fair would never subject themselves to a lesser creature or to lesser authority than themselves, nor even to one equally great.' Then I said: 'What is eternity?' Wisdom said: 'You ask me something vast and difficult to understand; if you wish to know, you should first have your mind's eye pure and clear. But I cannot conceal anything which I know. Do you know that there are three things on this earth? One is transitory, having both beginning and end; and I know nothing of that which is transitory, nor of its beginning nor its end. Another thing is eternal, having a beginning but no end; and I know when such things begin and that they never end: that is to say, angels and men's souls. The third is eternal, without end and without beginning: that is God. Between these three there is a great difference; but if we are to investigate it all, then we will arrive late at the end of this book, or never at all. But one thing you should of necessity know on this point, namely, why God is called the "highest eternity".' Then I said: 'Why?' Then he said: 'Because we know very little concerning what was before our time, except through memory and inquiry, and even less concerning what comes after us. Only one thing is certainly present to us, namely that which now exists. But to God all is present: what was before, what is now, and what shall be after us. All is present to Him. His prosperity does not wax, nor does it ever wane. He does not ever recollect anything, because He never forgets. He does not seek anything, nor reflect on anything, because He knows everything. He seeks nothing, because He has lost nothing. He pursues nothing, because nothing can escape Him. He fears nothing, because there is nothing greater nor even equal to Him. He is always giving, yet He never diminishes in any respect. He is always Almighty, because He always wills good and never evil. He needs nothing. He is always vigilant, nor does He ever sleep. Similarly, He is always gentle. He is always eternal, because there never has been a time in which He did not exist, nor will there ever be one. He is always free, nor is He ever compelled to any work. Because of His divine power He is present everywhere. No man can measure His magnitude: it is not in any case to be conceived corporeally but spiritually, as is wisdom and righteousness, because He is that Himself. What, then, are you men proud of, or why do you vaunt yourselves against so mighty a power? For you can accomplish nothing against Him, because the Eternal and Almighty One sits always on the throne of His authority, from where He can see everything; and He rewards every man with due justice according to his works. Therefore it is not in vain that we trust in God, because He is not changeable as we are. Rather, pray to Him meekly, because He is very generous and very merciful. Lift up your hearts to Him with your hands, and pray for what is just and what is necessary, because He will not reject you. Scorn evil and flee from it as quickly as you can; love the virtues and follow them. You have a very great need to act well, because what you do you do always in the presence of Eternal and Almighty God: He sees it all and He requites it all.'

Concluding prayer

Lord God Almighty, maker and ruler of all creatures, I beseech You on behalf of Your mighty mercy, and through the sign of the Holy Cross, and through St Mary's maidenhood, and through St Michael's obedience, and through the love and merits of all Your saints, that You guide me better than I have done towards You; and direct me according to Your will and my soul's need better than I myself am able; and strengthen my mind to Your will and to my soul's need, and confirm me against the devil's temptations; and keep far from me foul lust and all iniquity; and protect me from my enemies visible and invisible; and teach me to perform Your will, that I may inwardly love You before all things with pure thought and clean body, for You are my Creator and my Redeemer, my sustenance, my consolation, my trust and my hope. Praise and Glory be to You now and forever, world without end. Amen.

From the translation of Augustine's Soliloquies

More so even than in the case of his Boethius translation, Alfred's version of the Soliloquies *is a very free rendering of the original; in effect, Augustine's work serves as a point of departure for Alfred's reflections on the human soul, its immortality and its knowledge of God after death. Alfred's Book I and the first part of Book II follow Augustine's text fairly closely (though with certain additions), but discussion in the remainder of Book II and all of Book III ranges widely and is drawn from various authorities, including works by Augustine, Jerome, Gregory and Boethius. Accordingly, the following translation includes the Alfredian additions to Books I and II together with Book III in its entirety.*

Preface

[...]¹ I then gathered for myself staves and props and tie-shafts, and handles for each of the tools that I knew how to work with,² and cross-bars and beams, and, for each of the structures which I knew how to build, the finest timbers I could carry. I never came away with a single load without wishing to bring home the whole of the forest, if I could have carried it all – in every tree I saw something for which I had a need at home. Accordingly, I would advise everyone who is strong and has many wagons to direct his steps to that same forest where I cut these props, and to fetch more for himself and to load his wagons with well-cut staves, so that he may weave many elegant walls and put up many splendid houses and so build a fine homestead, and there may live pleasantly and in tranquillity both in winter and summer – as I have not yet done!³ But He who instructed me, to whom the forest was pleasing, may bring it about that I may abide more comfortably both in this temporary dwelling by this road as long as I am in this life, and also in the eternal home that He has promised us through the writings of St Augustine and St Gregory and St Jerome, and through many other holy fathers:⁴ as I believe He

will, through the merits of all these saints, both make this present
road easier than it was before, and in particular will illuminate the
eyes of my mind so that I can discover the most direct way to the
eternal home and to eternal glory and to the eternal rest which is
promised to us through those holy fathers. So may it be!

Nor is it any wonder that a man should work with such materials,
both in transporting them and in building with them; but every man,
when he has built a hamlet on land leased to him by his lord and with
his lord's help, likes to stay there some time, and go hunting, fowling
and fishing; and to employ himself in every way on that leased land,
both on sea and land, until the time when he shall deserve bookland [5]
and a perpetual inheritance through his lord's kindness. May the
bounteous benefactor, who rules both these temporary habitations as
well as those eternal abodes, so grant! May He who created both and
rules over both grant that I be fit for both: both to be useful here and
likewise to arrive there.

St Augustine, bishop of Carthage [*recte* Hippo], produced two
books through his own meditations; these books are called *Soliloquia*,
that is, they concern the reflections and doubts of his mind, how his
reason answered his mind when his mind was in doubt about
something or wished to know something which previously it had been
unable to comprehend clearly.

from *Book I*

ST AUGUSTINE: To what shall I entrust whatever I acquire, if not
to my memory?

REASON: Is your memory so powerful that it can contain everything
that you reflect on and that you command it to retain?

ST AUGUSTINE: No, not at all; neither my nor any man's memory is
powerful enough to retain everything entrusted to it.

REASON: Then commit it to letters and write it down. But it seems
to me, nevertheless, that you are not well enough to write it all
down; and even if you *were* well enough, you would need to have a
private place free from all other distractions, and a few learned
men with you who would not disturb you in any way, but would
assist you in your work. [6]

*

[St Augustine's Prayer to God]: [7] All the creatures which You created serve You. Every good soul is subject to You. According to Your command the heavens revolve and all the stars hold their course; according to Your command the sun brings forth the bright day, and the moon brings light at night. By analogy You govern and control all this world so that all creatures change like day and night. You rule the year and arrange it through the alternation of the four seasons, that is, spring, summer, autumn and winter. Each of these alternates with the other and revolves, so that each of them is once again what it previously was and where it previously was. And thus do all stars change and revolve in the same way, and so too the sea and its waters. In the same way all creatures change. Some, however, change in another way, so that the same ones do not return again to where they were, nor indeed become what they were. But others come in place of them, as leaves on trees; and apples and grass and plants and trees grow old and wither, and others come and wax green and grow and ripen, whereupon they begin again to wither. And likewise all beasts and birds, all of which are too lengthy to enumerate here. So too men's bodies grow old and age, just as other creatures do. And just as they live more worthily than trees or other animals, so too they will arise more worthily on the Day of Judgement, so that never thereafter shall their bodies die nor grow old. And even though the body had decayed before that time, yet the soul was always alive since the time it was first created.

*

REASON: [8] For these reasons it is essential that you look directly with your mind's eyes at God, just as directly as the ship's anchor-cable is stretched in a straight line from the ship to the anchor; and fix your mind's eyes on God as the anchor is fixed in the ground. Even though the ship is on the waves out at sea, it is safe and sound if the cable holds, because one of its ends is fixed in the ground and the other is fixed to the ship. [9]

ST AUGUSTINE: What is it that you refer to as the 'mind's eyes'?

REASON: Reason, in addition to the other virtues.

ST AUGUSTINE: What are these other virtues?

REASON: Wisdom, humility, caution, moderation, justice, mercy, discretion, constancy, benevolence, chastity and temperance. With these anchors you should fix in God the cable so that it will hold the ship of your mind.

ST AUGUSTINE: May the Lord God make me act in accordance with your teaching! If only I could! But I cannot understand how I am to acquire these anchors, or how I am to fix them, unless you instruct me more clearly.

REASON: I could well teach you; but first I should ask how many of this world's desires you have relinquished for God. After you have told me that, then I will be able to say to you without any doubt that you have acquired as many of these anchors as you have relinquished those worldly desires.

ST AUGUSTINE: How can I relinquish that which I know and am familiar with and have been accustomed to since childhood, and love that which is unfamiliar to me except by hearsay? I think, however – if what you have told me about were as familiar to me as what I see – that I would love the one and renounce the other.

REASON: I am astonished that you speak in this way. Consider now, if your lord's letter and his seal came to you,[10] whether you could say that you could not recognize him by this means, and could not thereby know his intention. If, then, you say that you *can* recognize his intention thereby, say next which seems more proper to you: that you follow his intention, or that you follow the wealth which he previously gave you in addition to his friendship.

ST AUGUSTINE: Whether I will or not, I must speak the truth, unless I wish to lie. If I lie, then God knows it. Therefore I dare speak nothing but the truth, in so far as I am able to know it. It seems to me better to renounce the gift and follow the giver, who acts for me as the guardian both of the wealth and of his friendship – unless I can have both. I should like, however, to have both if I could – to have the wealth and also to follow his intention.

REASON: You have answered me correctly. But I should like to ask you whether you think that you can have all that you now possess without also having your lord's friendship.

ST AUGUSTINE: I do not suppose that there is anyone so foolish as to think that.

REASON: You understand it correctly. But I would like to know whether you think that what you have is temporal or eternal.

ST AUGUSTINE: I never thought that it was eternal.

REASON: What then do you think about God and about the anchors we were discussing: are they like the temporal things, or are they eternal?

ST AUGUSTINE: Who would be so insane as to dare to say that God is not eternal?

REASON: If, then, He is eternal, why do you not love the eternal Lord more than the temporal? Look, you know that the eternal Lord does not abandon you, unless you depart from Him; but you must necessarily depart from the other one whether you will or not: either you must leave him or he you. I hear, however, that you love him exceedingly, and likewise fear him and behave properly: you do so quite rightly and quite appropriately. But I wonder why you do not love the other much more – Him who grants you both the friendship of the worldly lord and of Himself, and eternal life after this world. The Lord is the ruler of both, of yourself and of the lord whom you love so immeasurably.

ST AUGUSTINE: I confess to you that I would love Him above all other things, if only I could understand and know Him as well as I wished. But I can only comprehend Him a very little or not at all, and yet, when I reflect on Him and when any inspiration about the eternal life comes to me, then I do not love any jot of this present life in preference to that other, nor even love it to the same degree.

*

REASON: Faith, Hope and Charity – these are the three anchors which hold fast the ship of the mind amidst the dangers of the waves. The mind, however, has great consolation from that in which it trusts, and knows well that the mishaps and misfortunes of this world are not eternal. So the ship's pilot, when the ship rides most unsteadily at anchor and the sea is at its stormiest, knows with certainty that calm weather is to follow. Three things are necessary for the eyes of every soul: the first is that they be healthy; the second, that they observe what they wish to see; the third, that they are able to see that which they observe. For all three God's assistance is essential, for a man can neither do good nor anything else without His assistance. Therefore God is continually to be entreated that He may continually offer assistance; therefore too it is His undertaking to inspire us and moreover to persuade us that first of all we should wish to do well, and thereafter to work using us to do what He will, until such time as we accomplish it with His help. And indeed

He works with us as with certain insignificant tools, just as it is written that God is a co-worker with everyone who strives after good [cf. I Corinthians iii, 9]. We know that no one can accomplish anything good unless God work with him; and yet no one should remain so idle as not to undertake something with the abilities that God gives him.

*

REASON: Consider now that with the eyes of your body you are able to see three things pertaining to the sun: one is that it exists, the second that it shines, and the third, that it illuminates many things with its light. All the things that are bright reflect that light when the sun shines on them, each in its own way; but those things which are dull do not reflect their light back to the sun even though it shines on them. But nevertheless the sun *does* shine on them; and even though someone may look directly at it, he cannot see it exactly as it is. You can consider all this with respect to God, and more besides: He is the high sun; with His own light He is continually illuminating not only the sun which we see with our bodily eyes but also all creatures, both spiritual and terrestrial. Therefore it seems to me that he is foolish indeed who expects to be able to perceive God exactly as He is, during the time he is in this world. Truly, I think that no one is so foolish as to become sad because he cannot see and comprehend this sun – which we view with corporeal vision – exactly as it is. But everyone rejoices at least in what he can comprehend according to the capacity of his understanding.[11] He acts wisely who desires to comprehend the Eternal and Almighty Sun; but he behaves foolishly if he expects to comprehend it utterly while he is in this world.

*

REASON: Consider now, in the case of men who come to the king's estate where he is then in his residence, or to his assembly, or to his army, whether it seems to you that they all come there by the same route. I think, rather, that they arrive by very many routes: some come from very far away, and have a lengthy journey on a very bad and difficult road; some have a very long journey but a very direct and very good road. Some have a very short journey which is neverthe-less rough, difficult and filthy; some have a short, smooth and direct journey. And yet they are all coming to the one lord, some with ease, some with difficulty. They neither come there with a similar ease, nor are they similarly at ease when they get there. Some are received with greater reverence and greater familiarity than others, some with less; some with virtually none, except for the one fact, that he loves them all.[12] So it is with respect to wisdom: everyone who desires it and is eager for it may come to it and dwell in its household and live in its company; nevertheless, some are close to it, some farther away. It is likewise with the estates of every king: some men are in the chamber, some in the hall, some on the threshing-floor, some in prison, and yet all of them live through the one lord's favour, just as all men live under the one sun and by its light see everything that they see: some see very sharply and very clearly; some see anything only with difficulty, some are stareblind, and yet enjoy the sun. But just as this visible sun illuminates the eyes of our body, so does wisdom illuminate the eyes of our mind, that is, our understanding; and just as the eyes of the body are healthier when they take in more of the sun's light, so it is with the mind's eyes, that is, the understanding.

*

REASON: But that which you call truth is God. He always was, and ever shall be, immortal and eternal. God has in Himself all virtues, wholly and perfectly. He has fashioned two eternal creatures, namely angels and the souls of men;[13] to these He has granted a certain portion of eternal gifts, such as wisdom and righteousness, and other things that are too many for me to enumerate. To the angels He grants in accordance with their nature; to the souls of men He gives similar gifts, to each in accordance with its nature. They need never relinquish gifts such as these, for they are eternal. He likewise grants to men many and variously fine gifts in this world, even though they are not eternal; they are nevertheless serviceable for as long as we are in this world. Do you now perceive that souls are immortal?

from *Book II*

REASON: Now you know that you exist, and also that you are alive, and you know that you know something, even though you are far

more ignorant than you might wish; and you wish also to know a
fourth thing, whether all these three things are eternal or not, or
whether any one of them is eternal; or, if they all are eternal,
whether any of them after this life would do one of two things,
increase or decrease in eternity.

ST AUGUSTINE: You have quite rightly anticipated all my curiosity.

REASON:[14] What, then, are you still doubtful about? Did you not
previously agree that God was eternal and almighty, and had created
two rational and eternal creatures, as we said before, namely angels
and the souls of men, to which He has granted eternal gifts? They
need never relinquish these gifts. If, then, you remember this and
believe it, then you know without doubt that you exist and that you
will always exist, and always will have some knowledge, even though
you may be ignorant of some of the things you wish to know. So
you now know about the three things that you inquired about,
firstly, whether you would always exist; secondly, whether you would
always live;[15] and thirdly, whether you would always know
something, whether after the separation of the body and the soul
you would know more than you now know, or less. Now that you
know these three, we shall pursue inquiry about the fourth, until
you know about it as well.

ST AUGUSTINE: You explain everything in a very orderly manner,
but I still wish to tell you what I certainly believe and what I still
have some doubt about. Now I have no doubt whatever about
God's eternity and His omnipotence, for it cannot be otherwise
with respect to the Trinity and Unity, which is without beginning
and end. Indeed I cannot believe otherwise, because He has
fashioned creatures so great and manifold and wondrous to behold,
and He governs them all and controls them all; and at the one time
He adorns them with exquisitely delightful appearances, at another
He strips and disfigures them again. He rules the kings who have
the greatest dominion on this earth, who are born and die like other
men. He permits them to rule as long as He wills it. For these and
many similar reasons, I do not know how I could doubt His eternity.
Nor do I have any doubt whatever about our souls' vitality. But I
still have some doubts about their eternity, about whether they live
forever.

*

REASON: I wonder why you desire so eagerly to know with such certainty what no man in the prison of this present life can ever know as certainly as you wish; though many have worked in this present life to understand it more clearly than others, many have only believed it on the word of these and other truthful men. No man can ever understand all that he might wish to know before the soul is separated from the body – nor indeed before the Day of Judgement – as clearly as he desires. And yet the holy fathers who lived before us knew a good deal about the things you were asking about, namely, about the immortality of men's souls. It was so abundantly clear to them that they had no doubt whatever when they renounced this present life so that they could rejoice in the future life when the body and soul have been separated; [16] and indeed [17] they suffered the greatest of torments in this world so that they would have a greater reward in the eternal life. Through the sayings of such men they should believe who cannot understand it as clearly as they could.

*

REASON: Now I know that at this very time you have a lord whom you trust in all things better than yourself; so too does many a slave who has a less powerful lord than you have. And I know that you also have many friends whom you trust well enough, even though you do not trust them as well as you trust your lord. How does it strike you if this lord of yours tells you some news which you have never heard before, or says that he saw something which you have never seen? Do you think that you would doubt his statement in any way, simply because you never saw it for yourself?

ST AUGUSTINE: No, of course not; there is no story so incredible that, if he told it to me, I would not believe him. In fact I have many companions whom I would believe if they told me something they had themselves seen or heard, just as if I had seen or heard it myself.

*

REASON: I now perceive that you trust the higher lord better. But I would like to know whether you think that your worldly lords had wiser and more truthful thegns than the higher lords. Do you trust yourself and your companions better than the apostles, who were Christ's own thegns? Or the patriarchs? Or the prophets, through whom God Himself said what He wished to His people?

ST AUGUSTINE: No, no: I don't trust ourselves anywhere near as well as I trust them.

REASON: What, then, did God speak of more often, or what did He declare more truly through His prophets to His people, than the soul's immortality? Or what were the apostles and all the holy fathers speaking of, if not the eternity of souls and their immortality?

*

REASON: I wonder why you could ever suppose that men's souls are not eternal, because you realize clearly enough that they are the highest and most blessed of all God's creation; and likewise you know well enough that He does not allow any of His creatures to pass entirely away so that it becomes nothing, not even the most worthless of all. Rather, He beautifies and adorns all creatures, and then again deprives them of beauty and adornment, and then again renews them. Furthermore, all things change in such a way that they pass away and then immediately come again and return once more to that same beauty and loveliness in the sight of men that they possessed before Adam sinned. Now you may perceive that no creature passes so utterly away that it does not come again, nor is destroyed so utterly that it becomes nothing. Why then do you suppose – given that the most insignificant creatures do not utterly pass away – that the most blessed creature, the soul, should pass away entirely?

ST AUGUSTINE: Alas, I am so overcome with miserable forgetfulness that I cannot remember what previously I knew well. I seem to recall that you had explained it clearly enough through this one example, even if you had said no more.

REASON: Look inside yourself for the examples and the indications, and then you may know properly what you wished to know and what I explained to you through external examples. Ask your own mind why it is so willing and eager to know what formerly existed, before you were born or indeed before your grandfather was born; and likewise ask it why it knows that which is now present to it and which it sees and hears every day; or why it wishes to know what will happen after us. Then I suspect that it will answer you, if it is rational, and will reply that it wishes to know what was before us because it has always existed since the time that God created the first man; and that it therefore strives after what it formerly was, and strives to know what it formerly knew, even though it is now so weighed down with the burden of this body that it cannot know all it formerly knew. And I suspect that it will say to you that it knows what it sees and hears in this place, because it is here in this world; and I also suspect that it will say that it wishes to know what will happen after our days because it knows that it shall exist forever.

ST AUGUSTINE: I think that you have now stated clearly enough that every man's soul exists now and shall always exist, and has always existed since the time that God first created the first man.

REASON: There is no doubt that souls are immortal. Believe your own reason, and believe Christ the Son of God, and believe all His saints, because they were very reliable witnesses, and believe your own soul, which through its own reason tells you continually that it is within you. It likewise tells you that it is eternal, because it strives after eternal things. It is not so foolish a creature as to seek what it cannot find, nor to strive after what it cannot possess or what does not belong to it. Abandon now your unjustifiable doubt: it is sufficiently clear that you are eternal and shall exist forever.

Book III

ST AUGUSTINE: Now you have completed the discourses which you selected from the two previous books, but you have not yet given me an answer to what I last asked you about, namely, my intellect.[18] I asked you whether, after the separation of the body and the soul, it would increase or decrease, or would do both, as it did previously.

REASON: Did I not say that you should look for it in the book we were discussing [Augustine's *De Videndo Deo*]?[19] Learn that book; you will then find it there.

ST AUGUSTINE: I am not at leisure now to examine all that book. But I wanted you to tell me [. . .][20]

[REASON: . . .] But the mind is weighed down and occupied with the body, so that we are unable with the mind's eye to see anything exactly as it is, in the same way that you can only see the sun's brilliance at times when the clouds are darting between it and you, even though it is shining very brightly where it is. And even if there were no cloud between it and you, you could not see it with full clarity exactly as it is, because you are not where it is. Your body cannot be there; your bodily eyes cannot come anywhere near, nor even look directly at it. In fact we cannot even see the moon – which is nearer to us – exactly as it is. We know that it is larger than the earth, and yet it sometimes seems no larger than a shield because of its distance.

Now you have learned that we cannot see anything in this world exactly as it is with our bodily eyes or with the eyes of the mind. However, from the part of it which we can see we ought to believe in the part which we cannot see. For without any doubt it is promised to us that, as soon as we depart from this world and the soul escapes from the prison of the body and is delivered,[21] we shall know every single thing which we now wish to know, and much more than the ancients, the wisest of all men in this world, could know. And after the Day of Judgement it is promised to us that we may be able to see God clearly, to see Him exactly as He is, and henceforth to know Him forever as perfectly as He now knows us. Thereafter there shall never be any deficiency of wisdom in us. He who permits us to know Him will not conceal anything from us. Rather, we shall then know all that we now wish to know, and also all that we do not now wish to know. We shall all see God, both those who here are worst and those who here are best. All the good shall see Him, to their comfort and joy and honour and peace and glory; and the evil shall see Him no less than the good, though to their great misery, because they shall see the glory of the good, so that their own misery will seem the greater to them, because they did not wish by following their Father's teaching to merit the same glory during the time they were in this world. And the good shall similarly see their torments, so that their own glory will seem the greater to them. The evil shall see God in the same way as the guilty man who is condemned by some king: when he sees the king and his favourites, then his punishment seems the greater to him. So too the king's dear ones see his torment in such a way that their own favour seems ever the greater to them. However, no one ought to suppose that all those who are in hell have similar torments, nor that all those who are in heaven have similar glory. Rather, everyone has either torment or glory (depending on where he is) according to his merits. The like have their like. Likewise, it is not to be supposed that all men have similar wisdom in heaven. Rather, everyone has it according as he has earned it here: as he works harder here and more eagerly strives after wisdom and righteousness, so he has more of it there, and so too greater favour and greater glory. Has it now been clearly enough explained concerning wisdom and the vision of God?

ST AUGUSTINE: Yes. I do well believe that we need not relinquish any of the wisdom which we now possess, even though the soul and the body separate. But I believe that our intellect will thereby be much increased, even though we cannot before the Day of Judgement know all that we would wish to know. Rather, I believe that after the Day of Judgement nothing shall be hidden from us, neither of what takes place in our lifetime, nor of what was before us, nor of what shall be after us. You have now given me many precepts, and I have myself seen written in holy books far more than I can relate, or indeed even remember. You also showed me such honest witnesses that I can do nothing else but believe them; for, if I do not believe *weaker* testimony,[22] then I know very little or nothing at all. What *do* I know, except that I wish we understood about God as clearly as we wished? [. . .][23]

[. . .] might or could in this world, or whether they had any remembrance of the friends whom they left behind them in the world. Then Reason responded to its own reflections and said: Why do you suppose that the departed good, who have complete freedom and know everything that they wish to know either in this present life or in the future – why do you suppose that they have no recollection of their friends in this world, when the evil Dives feared on his friends' behalf the very same punishments in hell's torments which he himself had merited?[24] He it was of whom Christ said in His gospel [Luke xvi, 19–31] that he requested Abraham to send Lazarus the beggar to drip water with his little finger on to his tongue and thereby to quench his thirst. Then Abraham said: 'No, my child, no! Remember instead that you deprived him of all benefits while both of you were in the body, and you had every bounty and he had every misfortune. He cannot now do more to comfort you than you did then for him.' Then Dives said: 'Abraham, if that cannot be, send Lazarus to my five brothers who are still on earth where I was, so that he may tell them what torments I am suffering and may teach them to beware that they do not come here.' Then Abraham said: 'No, no. They have books of the holy fathers always with them on earth: let them study them and believe them. If they do not believe them, then they would not believe Lazarus either, even if he were to come to them.'

We are now able to perceive that both the good men and the evil who have departed know all that happens in this world and all that will come to pass, and also everything in the world in which they are. They know the most part, even though they do not know everything before the Day of Judgement, and they have a very good recollection of their kinsmen and friends in this world. And the good help the good, each the other, in so far as they can. But the good will not show mercy to their evil friends, because the evil do not wish to abandon their wickedness, any more than Abraham wished to have mercy on Dives, though he was of his own kin, because he realized that he was not as obedient to God as he ought properly to have been. The evil, then, can do neither their friends nor themselves any good, because formerly, when they were in this world, they helped neither themselves nor their friends who had passed away before them. Rather, the situation is the same for them as it is for the men who in this life are brought to a king's prison and who every day may see their friends and ask of them what they wish, and the friends can none the less be of no use to them: they either do not wish to help them, or cannot. Accordingly, the evil will have the greater torment in the world to come the more they realize the prosperity and glory of the good, and also the more that they remember all the honours which they enjoyed in this world, and likewise recognize the honours which those who live after them in this world will have.

The good, then, who have complete freedom, see both their friends and their enemies, just as in this world powerful men often see both their friends and enemies together. They see and perceive them in the same way even though they do not love them. And again, the righteous, when they are out of this world, frequently remember both the good and the evil which they experienced in this world, and rejoice exceedingly that they did not forsake their Lord's will, either in easy or in difficult matters, during the time they were in this world. Likewise, a powerful man in this world may have expelled one of his favourites from him, or against both their wishes the man may have been banished, and the man might then experience many torments and many misfortunes on his journey of exile, and return nevertheless to the same lord with whom he previously had been, and be received there with greater honour than he had formerly been. At that point he will recall the misfortunes which he experienced on his journey of exile, and yet will not be any the more unhappy for that.

But I myself have seen or heard[25] things reported by men far less reliable than were those holy fathers who said the things we are discussing. Am I not bound in such cases to do one of two things: either to trust some men, or trust none? I suppose that I know who built Rome, and also many other things which took place before our days, so many that I cannot enumerate them all. Yet I do not *know* who built Rome because I saw it myself, nor indeed do I know of what kin I am, nor who was my father or my mother, except by hearsay. I know that my father begot me and that my mother bore me: but I do not know it because I saw it for myself, but because it was reported to me. Nevertheless the men who told me were not such reliable men as were those holy fathers who related the things which we were investigating for so long: and yet I believe it.

Therefore a man strikes me as very foolish and very ill-advised who does not seek to increase his understanding while he is in this world, and at the same time does not wish and desire that he may come to that eternal life where nothing shall be concealed from us.

Here end the sayings which King Alfred selected from the book which in Latin is called *De Videndo Deo* and in English, *On Seeing God*.

From the prose translation of the Psalter

King Alfred was a layman of exceptional religious devotion: as Asser tells us (chapter 76), he was 'in the invariable habit of listening daily to divine services and Mass, and of participating in certain psalms and prayers and in the day-time and night-time offices' (above, p. 91). Given that the offices consist largely of psalmody, Alfred cannot but have been thoroughly familiar with the Psalter. Many psalms represent King David's anguished outpourings to God for help against his foreign enemies and for sustenance in his pursuit of divine knowledge. Alfred will have been struck by similarities between King David's situation and his own, and it is not misleading to regard Alfred's translation of the Psalter as an act of personal devotion. Alfred translated only the first fifty psalms, and was possibly prevented by death from completing the task. His translations are closely literal. We include a selection of psalms (II, III, IX, XIII and XLV) in order to illustrate the qualities to which Alfred may have responded personally. The Introductions to each psalm were compiled by Alfred from various sources and help to give a personal immediacy to their recitation.

Psalm II

The text of the following psalm is called *psalmus Dauid*, that is, 'David's Psalm' in English. It is so called because David in this psalm lamented and complained to the Lord about his enemies, both native and foreign, and about all his troubles. And everyone who sings this psalm does likewise with respect to his own enemies. So too did Christ with respect to the Jews.[1]

1. Why do all nations rage, and why do they contemplate useless undertakings?
2. And why do the kings of the earth rise up, and noblemen[2] come

together against God, and against him whom He chose as lord and anointed? They say,

3. 'Let us break their bonds, and cast away their yoke from us.'

4. 'What avails their talk,' said the prophet, 'though they speak in this manner?[3] For God who is in heaven derides them, and the Lord confounds them.

5. And He calls out to them in His anger, and confuses their scheme.'

6. And I nevertheless am placed by God as king over His holy Mount Sion, for the purpose of teaching His will and His law.

7. For the Lord said to me: 'You are my son – I begot you this very day.

8. Ask me, and I shall deliver the enemy peoples for your inheritance, and I shall extend your authority over their boundaries.

9. And I shall bring it about that you rule them with an iron rod; and I can destroy them as easily as the potter can a pot.'

10. Hear now, you kings, and learn, you judges who judge over the earth:

11. Serve the Lord and fear Him; rejoice in God, yet with awe.

12. Embrace learning, lest you incur God's anger and lest you stray from the right path.

13. For when His anger is kindled, then blessed are those who now trust in Him.

Psalm III

David sang this third psalm when he was lamenting Absalom his son, and he bewailed his misery to the Lord. Everyone who sings this psalm does likewise: he laments his tribulations, of either mind or body, to the Lord. Christ did likewise when He sang this psalm: He sang it of the Jews, and He lamented to the Lord about Judas Iscariot who betrayed Him.[4]

1. O Lord, why are there so many of my enemies who afflict me? Why do so many rise up against me? Many say to my spirit that it has no protection from its God.

2. But it is not as they say:[5] rather You without any doubt are my protection and my glory, and You lift up my head.

3. I called out to the Lord with my voice, and He heard me from His holy mountain.

4. Then I fell asleep and slept, and I got up again because the Lord awakened me and lifted me up.

5. Therefore I do not now fear the thousands of the enemy peoples, even though they surround me from without; but You, O Lord, arise, and make me safe, for You are my God.[6]

6. For You have slain all those who were wrongly against me, and have crushed the power of the wicked.

7. For all our salvation and all our hope is in You; and may Your blessing be over Your people!

Psalm IX

In the ninth psalm David prayed to the Lord and thanked Him that his son and other enemies as well had been unable to do him all the evil that they had intended against him. And by the same account every just man sings it with respect to his own enemies. Similarly, Christ sang it when the Jews wished to do Him more harm than they were able; so too did Hezekiah when his enemies could not dispose of him as they wished.[7]

1. I shall praise the Lord with all my heart: and I shall announce all Your wonders.

2. And I shall rejoice and exult, and extol Your name, Almighty God!

3. For You threw back my enemies; and they were weakened, and perished before Your face.

4. For you promulgate my judgement and my decree; and You did everything for me that I should have done. You sit on the high throne, You who always judge justly.

5. You chastise and terrify the enemy peoples who are oppressing us, and these unholy ones perish;[8] and You obliterate their name for ever and ever.

6. The plan and the scheme of our enemies has failed, when they ought to have brought it to completion;[9] and You have destroyed all their cities.[10]

7. And all memory of them passes away with the report; and the Lord abides forever in eternity.

8. And He prepares His seat of judgement; and He shall judge all the earth equally.

9. He shall judge all peoples with justice; He has become a sanctuary for those most in need.

10. And You are our helper, O Lord, in every need; for that reason all those who know Your name place their hope in You.

11. For You do not forsake any of those who seek You: therefore praise the Lord who dwells on Sion!

12. And announce His wonders among all peoples, because He is not forgetful of the prayers of the needy, but He is very mindful of the need to avenge their blood.

13. Have mercy on me, O Lord, and look on my weakness, on how miserable my enemies have made me; for You are the same God that raised me up from the gates of death, so that I proclaimed all Your glory at the gates of the city[11] of Jerusalem.

14. I will rejoice in Your protection, which You grant to me; and the enemy peoples persecuting me are trapped in the same difficulties which they had intended for me, and their feet are caught in the same snare which they had concealed and set for me.

15. For the Lord is revealed in just judgements; and the sinner is caught up in his own handiwork.

16. And the wicked shall be cast into hell, and all the nations who forget God.

17. For God does not forget those who need Him even to the end; nor does their patience give in until the end.

18. Arise, O Lord, so that the wicked man cannot achieve his ends, and see to it that judgement is passed on all peoples in Your presence.

19. O Lord, set some authority over them, so that they may learn to know that they are men.

20. O Lord, why did You go so far away from us, and why did You not wish to come to us at a time which was most pressing for us?

21. When the wicked man exults, then the poor man is consumed with want and afflicted and saddened as well; but the wicked shall be caught in the schemes they have devised.

22. For the sinner is praised wherever he works his evil will; and the evil bless him because of his evil deeds.

23. The sinner mocks the Lord, and because of the quantity of his wickedness he does not think that God can punish it.

24. For he does not place God before the sight of his mind; therefore all his ways and his work are wellnigh impure.

25. For he has no thought of God's judgement in his mind, so that he is able to govern and control all his enemies, and do to them what evil he will.

26. And he thinks to himself: 'There will never be any change in this situation, without great peril to my enemies.'

27. His mouth is always full of cursing and bitter words and deceit and treachery.

28. And beneath his tongue always lies the suffering and hardship of others; he always sits secretly in counsel with the rich so that he can destroy the innocent.

29. And he threatens the poor man with his eyes, and lies in wait secretly for him, as does a lion in his den.

30. He lies in wait in order to rob the poor, and longs to do so; and when he has caught the poor man with his snare, he afflicts him; and when he has subdued him, the poor man either begins to sink down of his own accord, or else He fells him.

31. He said to himself beforehand: 'God does not think on such things, but averts His eyes so that He never sees them.'

32. Arise, O Lord my God, and lift up Your hand against the wicked, and do not forget the needy in the end.

33. For the wicked man mocks the Lord, because he says to himself: 'God will not care, even though I behave in this way.'

34. 'Do you see now', said the prophet to the Lord, 'what misery and suffering we undergo and endure? Now it would be proper for You to punish them for it with Your own hands. I am a poor man, abandoned now to You: You are the supporter of those who have neither father nor mother.

35. You crush the arm and the might of the wicked; because, although someone might ask why the wicked man behaved thus, he could not explain it, nor would he wish to admit that he behaved wrongly.'

36. The Lord shall rule forever both in this world and in the world to come: therefore the wicked shall be destroyed in each of His kingdoms.

37. The Lord hears the wishes of those needing Him: and Your ear hears the desire of their hearts.

38. Now, O Lord, consider the needs of the poor and the humble, so that the wicked man no longer presumes to exalt himself on earth.

Psalm XIII

When David sang this thirteenth psalm, he lamented to the Lord in the psalm that in his time there should be so little faith, and so little wisdom should be found in the world. And so does every just man who sings it now: he laments the same thing in his own time. And so did Christ with respect to the Jews, and Hezekiah with respect to Rabsaces, king of the Assyrians.[12]

1. The wicked man says in his heart, 'There is no God who shall observe or punish this'; for saying that, people are defiled and corrupted in their evil desires.

2. There is no man who is altogether good, not a single one.

3. The Lord gazes down from heaven on the sons of men, and looks to see anyone who seeks Him or understands Him.

4. But they all flee from Him at once, and seek and affect to be idle and useless: accordingly, there is not one of them who is altogether good.

5. They are like tombs: pleasant on the outside and foul within. Their tongues produce great deceit; although they speak pleasantly, their thought and their will and their works are like the venom of the most poisonous kind of adder, the asp.

6. Their mouth is always full of curses and bitter words; their feet are very quick to shed blood needlessly out of evil intentions.

7. And their ways are always troubled; they desire with all their might the unhappiness of other men, and the very same thing happens to them. They seek no peace.

8. The fear of God is not present before their mind's eye. Why do they not realize, all those who work iniquity,

9. Those who wish to devour my people like a loaf, who do not beseech God with good works, why do they not realize that terror and misfortune shall come upon them when they least expect it?

10. Why do they not realize that God is with the righteous people? Why do you confound the thoughts of my poor self? – for God is my thought.

11. Who shall arise elsewhere from Sion in order to grant salvation to the Israelites but You, O Lord, who did away with the captivity of Your people?

12. Rejoice now, you people of Jacob, and be joyful, Israel!

Psalm XLV

David sang this forty-fifth psalm, thanking God that He had released him from his many afflictions. And he also prophesied that the men who are the two tribes, namely Judah and Benjamin, should do likewise, that they should thank God that He protected them from the siege and from the invasion of the two kings, Phacee son of Romelia and Rasin, king of Syria: it was not done through the merits of King Achaz, but through God's mercy and the merits of the elders it happened that the two kings were driven out by the King of the Assyrians. And he prophesied the same with respect to all righteous men who are first oppressed and then spared. And he prophesied the same with respect to Christ and the Jews.[13]

1. The Lord is our protection and our strength and our support in our tribulations, which have befallen us exceedingly.

2. Therefore we shall not fear, even though all the earth is oppressed and the mountains are cast into the middle of the sea.

3. Our enemies fell upon us so terribly that it seemed to us that all the earth shook with the tumult; and nevertheless they were frightened by God more severely than we; and their kings, lifted up like the mountains, were oppressed by God's might.[14]

4. Then God's fortress in Jerusalem rejoiced with the arrival of the shower which cleansed it. The Almighty consecrated His temple within the city: therefore the city shall never be altered as long as God remains unalterably in its midst.

5. God helped it very early in the morning; and the foreign peoples were afflicted, and their might was vanquished: the Almighty sent His word, and our land and our people were changed for the better, and they and their land for the worse.

6. The Lord, the God of armies, is with us, and our defender is Jacob's God.

7. Come and see God's work, and the wonders which He works here on earth.

8. He drives back from us every attack, far away beyond our borders; and He shatters our enemies' bows and crushes their weapons and burns their shields. Then God responded to the prophet's spirit, and said again through the prophet,

9. 'Relax now, and see that I alone am God, and raise me up above the foreign peoples: and even among these peoples am I exalted.'

10. The Lord, God of armies, is with us, and our defender is Jacob's God.

IV

MISCELLANEOUS SOURCES FOR THE REIGN OF KING ALFRED

Extracts from the laws of King Alfred

*Alfred's law-code was probably drawn up in the late 880s or early 890s.
It shows how the king sought to maintain social order, and at the same
time it expresses his wider political and ideological aspirations: see above,
p. 39.*

*The code begins with a list of chapter-headings numbered 1–120; of
these, 1–43 refer to Alfred's laws, and 44–120 refer to the appended laws
of Ine, king of the West Saxons (688–726).[1] There follows a series of
quotations translated from the book of Exodus, representing the Law
which Moses received from God on Mount Sinai, that is the Ten Commandments and the statutes which augmented them (Introduction,
Prologue–Int. 48, in the modern numeration); the quotations are from
Exodus xx, 1–3, 7–17, 23; xxi, 1–36; xxii, 1–11, 16–29, 31; and xxiii,
1–2, 4, 6–9, 13.[2] Alfred then considers how the Old Testament legislation
for the Jews was modified for application to Christian nations, citing the
letter sent by the Apostles to the Gentiles of Antioch, Syria and Cilicia,
given in Acts xv, 23–9 (Int. 49–Int. 49.5). The first numbered 'chapter'
of Alfred's code occurs at this point (Int. 49.6), and is a general affirmation
of the 'Golden Rule' (Matthew vii, 12) mentioned in Int. 49.5 (where it is
derived from Acts xv, 29 in the 'Western' text of the New Testament).
The extracts from the Bible now cease, and Alfred turns to review the
subsequent history of law-giving, before coming to the main part of his
own legislation.*

[Int. 49.7] Afterwards, when it came about that many peoples had
received the faith of Christ, many synods of holy bishops and also of
other distinguished councillors were assembled throughout all the
earth, and also throughout all the English people (after they had
received the faith of Christ).[3] They then established, through that
mercy which Christ taught, that for almost every misdeed at the first
offence secular lords might with their permission receive without sin
the monetary compensation, which they then fixed; only for treachery

to a lord did they dare not declare any mercy, since Almighty God
adjudged none for those who despised Him, nor did Christ, the Son
of God, adjudge any for the one who betrayed Him to death; and He
commanded everyone to love his lord as Himself.

[Int. 49.8] Then in many synods they fixed the compensations for
many human misdeeds, and they wrote them in many synod-books,
here one law, there another.

[Int. 49.9] Then I, King Alfred, gathered them together and ordered
to be written many of the ones that our forefathers observed – those
that pleased me; and many of the ones that did not please me I
rejected with the advice of my councillors, and commanded them to
be observed in a different way.[4] For I dared not presume to set down
in writing at all many of my own, since it was unknown to me what
would please those who should come after us. But those which I
found either in the days of Ine, my kinsman, or of Offa, king of the
Mercians, or of Æthelberht (who first among the English people
received baptism), and which seemed to me most just, I collected
herein, and omitted the others.[5]

[Int. 49.10] Then I, Alfred, king of the West Saxons, showed these
to all my councillors, and they then said that it pleased them all to
observe them.

[§ 1] 2. First we enjoin, what is most necessary, that each man keep
carefully his oath and his pledge.[6]

[§ 1.1] If anyone is compelled wrongfully to either of these, either to
treachery to a lord or to any unlawful aid, then it is better to leave it
unfulfilled than to carry it out.[7]

[§ 1.2] If, however, he pledges what it is right for him to carry out,[8]
and leaves it unfulfilled, he is with humility to hand over his weapons
and his possessions to his friends for keeping, and be forty days in
prison at a king's estate;[9] he is to do penance there as the bishop
prescribes for him, and his kinsmen are to feed him if he has no food
himself.

[§ 1.3] If he has no kinsmen and has not the food, the king's reeve is to feed him.

[§ 1.4] If he has to be forced thither and he refuses to go otherwise, when he is bound, he is to forfeit his weapons and his property.

[§ 1.5] If he is killed, he is to lie unpaid for.

[§ 1.6] If he escapes before the time, and he is captured, he is to be forty days in prison as he should have been before.

[§ 1.7] If he gets away, he is to be outlawed and to be excommunicated from all the churches of Christ.

[§ 1.8] If, however, there is any secular surety, he is to pay compensation for the breach of surety as the law directs him, and for the breach of pledge as his confessor prescribes for him.

[§ 2] *On taking sanctuary in* any one of the monastic houses to which the king's food-rent belongs,[10] *or in some other privileged community*; [§ 3] *On penalties for violating the surety or protection extended by king, archbishop, bishop or ealdorman.*

[§ 4] 5. If anyone plots against the king's life, by himself or by means of the harbouring of fugitives or his men,[11] he is to be liable for his life and all that he possesses.[12]

[§ 4.1] If he wishes to clear himself, he is to do it by [an oath equivalent to] the king's wergild.[13] *punishment*

[§ 4.2] Thus also we establish for all ranks, both *ceorl* and noble:[14] he who plots against his lord's life is in return to be liable for his life and all that he possesses, or is to clear himself by [an oath equivalent to] his lord's wergild.

[§ 5] *On taking sanctuary in a church consecrated by a bishop, and on penalties for thefts committed on certain holy days*; [§ 6] *On punishment for theft from a church.*

[§ 7] 8. If anyone fights or draws his weapon in the king's hall, and he is captured, it is to be at the king's judgement – either death or life, as he wishes to grant him.

[§ 7.1] If he gets away, and is afterwards captured, he is always to pay for himself according to his wergild, and he is to pay compensation, either wergild or fine, for the crime in accordance with what he deserves.

[§ 8] *On the penalty for bringing a nun out of a nunnery without permission,*[15] *and related matters*; [§ 9] *On the compensation due when a pregnant woman is killed, and on scales of fines in general.*

[§ 10] 11. If anyone lies with the wife of a twelve-hundred man, he is to pay 120 shillings compensation to the husband; to a six-hundred man, he is to pay 100 shillings compensation; to a *ceorl*, he is to pay forty shillings compensation.[16]

man of high standing

held land

[§ 11] *On penalties for assaulting women*; [§ 12] *On penalties for burning and felling wood belonging to another man*; [§ 13] *On accidental death caused by a falling tree*; [§ 14] *On the father's liability for the misdeeds of the deaf and dumb*; [§ 15] *On penalties for fighting, etc., in the presence of archbishop, bishop or ealdorman*; [§ 16] *On penalties for theft of cows or mares and for driving off their young*; [§ 17] *On the death of someone's dependant while being fostered by someone else*; [§ 18] *On penalties for assaulting nuns, and on penalties incurred by betrothed women of varying social status who commit fornication*; [§ 19] *On a man's liability in cases of crime committed with weapons lent by him to someone else, and on the obligations of those who repair weapons or tools belonging to others*; [§ 20] *On the loss of property lent to another man's monk, without the permission of the monk's lord*; [§ 21] *On the treatment of a priest who kills someone.*

[§ 22] 20. If anyone brings a charge in a public meeting of a king's reeve,[17] and afterwards wishes to withdraw it, he is to bring it against a more likely person, if he can; if he cannot, he is to forfeit his compensation.[18]

[§ 23] *On the owner's liability for offences committed by his dog*; [§ 24] *On the owner's liability for injury committed by his cattle*; [§ 25] *On punishments for raping slave-women*; [§§ 26–8] *On penalties for the murder of men of varying social status, committed by a member of a band, and on the liability of the other members of the band*; [§ 29] *On the penalty for raping a girl not of age*; [§ 30] *On the liability of the maternal kinsmen and associates of a man without paternal kinsmen who kills another man*; [§ 31] *On the distribution of the penalty due for killing a man without kinsmen*; [§ 32] *On the punishment for public slander*; [§ 33] *On procedure when a man accuses another man of failing to carry out a promise made in God's name.*

[§ 34] 31. Moreover, it is prescribed for traders: they are to bring before the king's reeve, at a public meeting, those men whom they are taking with them into the country, and it is to be established how many of them there are; and they are to take with them such men as they are able thereafter to bring to justice at a public meeting; and whenever it is necessary for them to have more men out with them on their journey, it is always to be made known, as often as may be necessary for them, to the king's reeve in the witness of the meeting.[19]

made to regulate those who came into country

[§ 35] *On the penalties for maltreating an innocent ceorl*; [§ 36] *On procedure when someone is wounded by a spear carried over a man's shoulder.*

[§ 37] 34. If anyone from one district wishes to seek a lord in another district,[20] he is to do so with the witness of the ealdorman in whose shire he previously served.

[§ 37.1] If he does so without his witness, he who receives him as his man is to pay 120 shillings as a fine; he is, however, to divide it, half to the king in the shire in which he previously served, and half in that to which he has come.[21]

[§ 37.2] If he has committed any crime where he was before, he who now accepts him as his man is to pay compensation for it, and 120 shillings to the king as a fine.

[§ 38] 35. If anyone fights at a meeting in the presence of the king's ealdorman, he is to pay wergild and fine in accordance with the law, and before that 120 shillings to the ealdorman as a fine.

[§ 38.1] If he disturbs a public meeting by drawing a weapon, he is to pay 120 shillings to the ealdorman as a fine.

[§ 38.2] If anything of this kind takes place in the presence of the deputy of the king's ealdorman, or in the presence of a king's priest, he is to pay thirty shillings as a fine.

[§ 39] 36. If anyone fights in the house of a *ceorl*, he is to pay six shillings compensation to the *ceorl*.

[§ 39.1] If he draws a weapon and does not fight, it is to be half as much.

[§ 39.2] If either of these things happens to a six-hundred man, the compensation is to amount to three times the compensation due to a *ceorl*; if to a twelve-hundred man, to double the compensation due to a six-hundred man.

[§ 40] The fine for forcible entry into the king's residence is 120 shillings; the archbishop's, ninety shillings; another bishop's or an ealdorman's, sixty shillings; a twelve-hundred man's, thirty shillings; a six-hundred man's, fifteen shillings; for forcible entry into a *ceorl*'s enclosure, five shillings.[22]

[§ 40.1] If anything of this kind takes place while the army is out, or during the Lenten fast, the compensation is to be doubled.

[§ 40.2] If anyone openly disregards the ecclesiastical laws during Lent without permission, he is to pay 120 shillings compensation.

[§ 41] In the case of a man who has bookland[23] *land given in charter* which his kinsmen left to him, we establish that he may not dispose of it outside his kindred, if there is a document or witness to show that it was the injunction of those men who acquired it in the first place and of those who gave it to him, that he could not do so;[24] and that is then to be declared in the witness of the king and of the bishop, in the presence of his kinsmen.[25]

[§ 42] 38. Moreover we command: the man who knows his enemy[26] to be dwelling at home is not to fight before he asks justice for himself.

[§ 42.1] If he has enough power to surround his enemy and besiege him at home, he is to keep him therein for seven days and is not to fight against him if the enemy is content to remain inside; and then after seven days, if the enemy is willing to surrender and give up his weapons, he is to keep him unharmed for thirty days and send notice about him to his kinsmen and to his friends.

[§ 42.2] If, however, the enemy reaches a church, it is then to be dealt with according to the privilege of the church, as we have declared above.[27]

[§ 42.3] If, however, he does not have enough power to besiege him at home, he is to ride to the ealdorman and ask him for support; if he is not willing to give him support, he is to ride to the king, before having recourse to fighting.

[§ 42.4] Also, if anyone encounters his enemy, and he did not previously know him to be at home: if he is willing to give up his weapons, he is to be kept for thirty days and his friends informed about him; if he is not willing to give up his weapons, then he may fight against him. If he is willing to surrender and to give up his weapons, and after that anyone fights against him, he [who does so] is to pay wergild or wound[28] in accordance with what he has done, and a fine, and is to have forfeited [his right to avenge] his kinsman.[29]

[§ 42.5] Moreover we declare that a man may fight on behalf of his lord, if anyone is fighting against the lord, without incurring a feud; similarly, the lord may fight on behalf of his man.

[§ 42.6] In the same way, a man may fight on behalf of his born kinsman, if anyone attacks him wrongfully, unless it is against his lord: that we do not allow.[30]

[§ 42.7] And a man may fight without incurring a feud if he finds another man with his lawful wife, behind closed doors or under the same blanket; or if he finds another man with his legitimate daughter or with his legitimate sister, or with his mother who was given as lawful wife to his father.

[§ 43] 39. These days are to be given to all free men, but not to slaves and unfree labourers:[31] twelve days at Christmas; and the day on which Christ overcame the devil [15 February]; and the anniversary of St Gregory [12 March]; and the seven days before Easter and the seven after; and one day at the feast of St Peter and St Paul [29 June]; and in harvest-time the whole week before the feast of St Mary [15 August]; and one day at the feast of All Saints [1 November]. And the four Wednesdays in the four Ember weeks[32] are to be given to all slaves, to sell to whomsoever they please anything of what anyone has given them in God's name, or of what they can earn in any of their spare time.

[§§ 44–77] *On the compensations due for injuries to the various parts of the body;*[33] *this section of the code is arranged as chapters 40–43, and the laws of King Ine, arranged as chapters 44–120, follow.*[34]

laws against noblemen
and religious men (clergy)

The treaty between Alfred and Guthrum

This document illustrates one aspect of King Alfred's political activity in the interval between his victory over Guthrum in 878 and the Viking invasion of 892: see above, pp. 37–9. It was drawn up in or soon after 886 (when Alfred seized London), since London is left under Alfred's control, and certainly before 890 (when Guthrum, king of the Vikings of East Anglia, died). It defines the boundary between 'English' England and the southern Danelaw, and regulates relations between the native population and the Danish settlers.

Prologue. This is the peace which King Alfred and King Guthrum and the councillors of all the English race and all the people who are in East Anglia have all agreed on and confirmed with oaths, for themselves and for their subjects, both for the living and for the unborn, who care to have God's favour or ours.

§ 1. First concerning our boundaries: up the Thames, and then up the Lea, and along the Lea to its source, then in a straight line to Bedford, then up the Ouse to Watling Street.[1]

§ 2. Next, if a man is slain, all of us estimate Englishman and Dane at the same amount, at eight half-marks of pure gold;[2] except the *ceorl* who occupies rented land and their freedmen – these also are estimated at the same amount, both at 200 shillings.[3]

§ 3. And if anyone accuses a king's thegn of manslaughter, if he dares to clear himself he is to do it with twelve king's thegns.[4] If anyone accuses a man who is of lesser degree than a king's thegn, he is to clear himself with eleven of his equals and with one king's thegn. And so in every suit which involves more than four mancuses; and if he dare not clear himself, he is to pay for it with threefold compensation, according to its valuation.[5]

§ 4. And that each man is to know his warrantor for men and for horses and for oxen.[6]

§ 5. And we all agreed on the day when the oaths were sworn that no slaves or freemen might go over to the army without permission, any more than any of theirs to us.[7] If, however, it happens that from necessity any one of them wishes to have traffic with us – or we with them – for cattle and for goods, it is to be permitted on this condition, that hostages shall be given as a pledge of peace and as evidence whereby it is known that no fraud is intended.[8]

The will of King Alfred

The will of King Alfred is the earlier of the two surviving wills of Anglo-Saxon kings; the other is that of King Eadred (946–55). The main concern of the will is the disposal of the king's private property, as distinct from the land which would not have been alienable in the same way (including, for example, any estates earmarked for the support of the king which would have passed automatically to the next holder of the office). The document begins with an account (in the first three paragraphs) of the arrangements made by King Æthelwulf in 856–8 for the disposal of his private property (cf. Asser, chapter 16) and of the various modifications to these arrangements effected by his sons between 860 and 871; see above, pp. 15–16. This introductory section serves to justify Alfred's title to the property, and he then indicates his wishes for its disposal after his death. The map of the estates mentioned in the will (Map 5, p. 176) reveals a clear strategy behind Alfred's own arrangements: his elder son Edward receives a series of important estates extending throughout Alfred's kingdom from Cornwall in the west to Kent in the east; his younger son Æthelweard also receives a widely distributed group of estates, though concentrated further south and behind the line of Edward's; his wife and daughters receive estates in the central part of the kingdom; but his nephews Æthelhelm and Æthelwold, and his kinsman Osferth, receive estates in its 'less important', eastern, part (cf. Asser, chapter 12). If only to judge from the relatively small number of estates he received, Æthelwold in particular would have had cause to feel aggrieved by this allocation of property, and his resentment is shown by his rebellion against Edward soon after Alfred's death (Anglo-Saxon Chronicle 900; above, p. 120). The will was apparently drawn up sometime between 872 and 888, and there are signs that it belongs to the 880s rather than the 870s (below, p. 313); it emerges from the text, however, that Alfred had made at least one earlier will, and it is possible that the first part of the present document (the first three paragraphs), which must be dated before 888, was retained from an earlier will in a revised version which included (as

*paragraph four to the end) an updated statement of the king's wishes for
the disposal of his property made nearer the time of his death on 26
October 899.*

I, King Alfred, by the grace of God[1] and on consultation with
Archbishop Æthelred[2] and with the witness of all the councillors of
the West Saxons, have been inquiring about the needs of my soul and
about my inheritance which God and my elders gave to me, and
about the inheritance which my father King Æthelwulf bequeathed
to us three brothers, Æthelbald, Æthelred and myself, stipulating
that whichever of us should live longest was to succeed to everything.[3]
But it happened that Æthelbald died; and Æthelred and I, with the
witness of all the councillors of the West Saxons, entrusted our share
to our kinsman King Æthelberht, on condition that he would restore
it to us as much under our control as it was when we entrusted it to
him; and then he did so, both that inheritance and what he had
obtained from the use of our joint property, as well as that which he
had himself acquired.[4]

Then it so happened that Æthelred succeeded to the kingdom,[5]
and I asked him in the presence of all our councillors that we might
divide the inheritance and he should give me my share. He then told
me that he could not divide it at all easily, for he had attempted to do
so many times before; and he said that after his lifetime he would
give to no person sooner than to me whatever he held as our joint
property and whatever he acquired.[6] And I was then readily a supporter of that.[7] But it came about that we were all oppressed by the
heathen army.[8] Then we spoke about our children, that they would
need some property, happen what might to the two of us in those
troubles. Then, when we were at an assembly at *Swinbeorg*,[9] we
agreed in the witness of the councillors of the West Saxons that
whichever of us should live longer should give to the other's children
the lands which we ourselves had obtained, and the lands which King
Æthelwulf gave to us during Æthelbald's lifetime, except those which
he bequeathed to us three brothers. And each of us gave to the other
his pledge, that whichever of us lived longer should succeed both to
the lands and to the treasures and to all the other's possessions except
that part which each of us had bequeathed to his children.[10]

But it came about that King Æthelred died.[11] Then no one made
known to me any will or testimony showing that the position was

other than as we had previously agreed before witnesses. When we now heard many disputes about the inheritance,[12] I brought King Æthelwulf's will to our assembly at *Langandene*,[13] and it was read before all the councillors of the West Saxons. When it had been read, I urged them all for love of me – and gave them my pledge that I would never bear a grudge against any one of them because they declared what was right – that none of them would hesitate, either for love or fear of me, to expound the common law, lest any man should say that I treated my young kinsmen wrongfully, the older or the younger.[14] And then they all pronounced what was right, and said that they could not conceive any juster title, nor could they find[15] one in the will. 'Now everything therein has come into your possession, so you may bequeath it and give it into the hand of kinsman or stranger, whichever you prefer.' And they all gave me their pledge and their sign manual[16] that no man, for as long as they lived, would ever change it in any way other than as I declare it myself at my last day.

I, Alfred, king of the West Saxons, by the grace of God and with this witness, declare what I desire concerning my inheritance after my lifetime. First, I grant to Edward my elder son[17] the land at Stratton in Triggshire,[18] and Hartland,[19] and all the booklands which Leofheah holds,[20] and the land at Carhampton,[21] at Kilton,[22] at Burnham,[23] at Wedmore[24] – and I entreat the community at Cheddar to choose him on the terms which we have previously agreed[25] – with the land at Chewton and what belongs to it;[26] and I grant him the land at Cannington,[27] at Bedwyn,[28] at Pewsey,[29] at Hurstbourne,[30] at Sutton,[31] at Leatherhead,[32] at Alton,[33] and all the booklands which I have in Kent.[34]

And the lands at the lower Hurstbourne[35] and at Chisledon[36] are to be given to Winchester on the terms previously settled by my father,[37] and my private property[38] which I entrusted to Ecgwulf at the lower Hurstbourne.

And to my younger son[39] the land at Arreton,[40] at Dean,[41] at Meon,[42] at Amesbury,[43] at Dean,[44] at Sturminster,[45] at Yeovil,[46] at Crewkerne,[47] at Whitchurch,[48] at Axmouth,[49] at Branscombe,[50] at Cullompton,[51] at Tiverton,[52] at *Mylenburnan*,[53] at Exminster,[54] at *Suðeswyrðe*,[55] and at Lifton and the lands which belong to it, namely all that I have in Cornwall except in Triggshire.[56]

And to my eldest daughter[57] the estate at Wellow;[58] to the middle

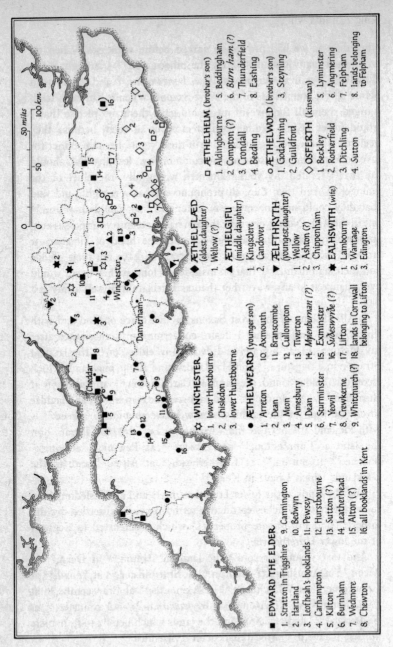

Map 5. *The estates mentioned in the will of King Alfred*

one [59] that at Kingsclere [60] and at Candover; [61] and to the youngest [62] the estate at Wellow, [63] at Ashton, [64] and at Chippenham. [65]

And to my brother's son Æthelhelm [66] the estate at Aldingbourne, [67] at Compton, [68] at Crondall, [69] at Beeding, [70] at Beddingham, [71] at *Burn ham*, [72] at Thunderfield, [73] and at Eashing. [74]

And to my brother's son Æthelwold [75] the estate at Godalming, [76] at Guildford, [77] and at Steyning. [78]

And to my kinsman Osferth [79] the estate at Beckley, [80] at Rotherfield, [81] at Ditchling, [82] at Sutton, [83] at Lyminster, [84] at Angmering, [85] and at Felpham [86] and the lands which belong to it.

And to Ealhswith [87] the estate at Lambourn, [88] at Wantage, [89] and at Edington. [90]

And to my two sons 1,000 pounds, 500 pounds each; to my eldest daughter, to the middle one, to the youngest and to Ealhswith, 400 pounds to the four of them, 100 pounds each. And to each of my ealdormen 100 mancuses, and to Æthelhelm, Æthelwold and Osferth likewise. And to Ealdorman Æthelred [91] a sword worth 100 mancuses. And to the men who serve me, to whom I have just now given money at Eastertide, 200 pounds are to be given and divided between them, to each as much as will belong to him according to the manner in which I have just now made distribution to them. [92] And to the archbishop 100 mancuses, and to Bishop Esne [93] and to Bishop Werferth [94] and to the bishop of Sherborne. [95] Likewise, 200 pounds is to be distributed for my sake, for my father and the friends for whom he used to intercede and I intercede, fifty to the mass-priests throughout all my kingdom, fifty to the poor servants of God, fifty to the poor and destitute, fifty to the church in which I shall rest. [96] I do not know for certain whether there is so much money, nor do I know whether there is more, though I suspect so. [97] If there is more, it is to be shared among all those to whom I have bequeathed money; and I desire that my ealdormen and my officials shall all be involved and shall distribute it thus.

Now I had previously written differently concerning my inheritance, when I had more property and more kinsmen, [98] and I had entrusted the documents to many men, and they were written with the same witness. Accordingly, I have now burnt all the old ones I could discover. Should any one of them be found, it stands for nothing, for I desire that it shall be as stated now, with God's help.

And I desire that the persons who have those lands should observe the directions which stand in my father's will to the best of their ability.[99] And I desire that if I have any money unpaid to any men, my kinsmen should certainly repay it. And I desire that the persons to whom I have bequeathed my bookland should not dispose of it outside my kindred after their lifetime, but I desire that after their lifetime it should pass to my nearest of kin, unless any of them have children; then I prefer that it should pass to the child in the male line as long as any is worthy of it.[100] My grandfather had bequeathed his land on the spear side and not on the spindle side.[101] If, then, I have given to any one on the female side what he acquired, my kinsmen are to pay for it, if they wish to have it during the lifetime [of the holders];[102] otherwise, it should go after their lifetime as we have previously stated. For this reason I say that they are to pay for it, because they are receiving my property, which I may give on the female side as well as on the male side, whichever I please.[103]

And I pray in the name of God and of his saints that none of my kinsmen or heirs oppress any of the dependants among those whom I have supported;[104] and the councillors of the West Saxons pronounced it right for me that I could leave them free or servile, whichever I should choose. But I desire for the love of God and for the needs of my soul that they be entitled to their freedom and their free choice. And in the name of the living God I command that no man should oppress them either with claims for money or with anything, in such a way that they cannot choose whatever lord they desire. And it is my will that the community at Damerham[105] be given their landbooks and their freedom to choose such lord as is dearest to them, for my sake and for Ælfflæd[106] and for the friends for whom she used to intercede and I intercede. Moreover, a payment in livestock is to be made for the needs of my soul, such as can be and as is also appropriate and as you wish to give on my behalf.[107]

King Alfred's charter for Ealdorman Æthelhelm

An Anglo-Saxon charter is typically a document by which a king granted land on privileged terms to a specified individual or religious house. About 1,000 charters survive from the Anglo-Saxon period as a whole, but of these no more than one third date from before the tenth century. About one tenth of the total number still exist in their original form, written on a separate sheet of parchment in handwriting contemporary with the date of the document. The remainder are preserved only as copies of originals now lost, normally made by monastic scribes in the later medieval period; it is naturally difficult to be certain of the authenticity of charters preserved in this way, since monks were not averse to 'improving' their title to an estate by altering the original text, or indeed by forging a document outright.

Unfortunately, not one charter of King Alfred has survived in its original form; but of the thirteen preserved in later copies, ten have some claim to authenticity in whole or in part. The example translated below is accepted as genuine. By this document Alfred granted an estate at North Newnton in Wiltshire to Æthelhelm, ealdorman of Wiltshire, in 892. The charter includes a section describing the boundaries of the estate in question, and these are seen from Map 6 to correspond to those of the modern parish. The list of witnesses is particularly interesting: it includes two of the priests recruited by King Alfred in the 880s (see Asser, chapters 77–8), and it accords special titles to three other witnesses, illustrating Asser's remarks (chapters 100–101) on the different royal officials who belonged to the king's household.

[*Rubric*] This is the charter of the ten hides at North Newnton which Alfred booked [1] to Æthelhelm his thegn [2] in perpetual inheritance.

In the name of the Lord. I, Alfred, by the bountiful clemency of the high-throned creator and governor of all things, king of the Anglo-Saxons, [3] concede and grant to Æthelhelm [4] my faithful ealdorman a small piece of land in eternal inheritance, [5] that is ten hides in the place called North Newnton. [6] And the aforesaid piece of land

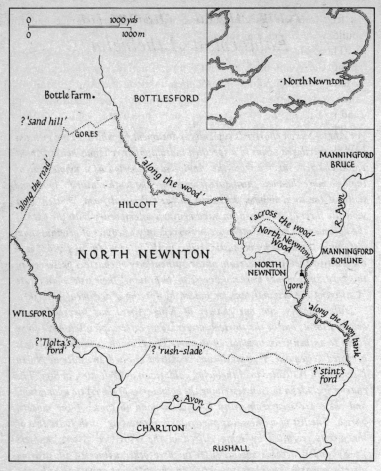

Map 6. Ealdorman Æthelhelm's estate at North Newnton, Wiltshire. The dotted line traces the modern parish boundary (see below, p. 328 note 8)

is free from all worldly burdens, except military service and the building of bridge and fortress.[7]

These are the boundaries of the estate mentioned above. First, along the Avon bank to stint's ford; then to rush-slade; then to Tiolta's ford; then to Wilsford; then so along the road to sand hill; then to Bottle; then along the wood; then across the wood to the gore; and so back to the Avon.[8]

The writing of this charter was done in the year of the Lord's Incarnation 892, the tenth indiction,[9] with the consent of these witnesses whose names are recorded below.

> Alfred, king of the Saxons
> Wulfsige,[10] bishop
> Wulfred,[11] ealdorman
> Æthelred,[12] ealdorman
> Edward,[13] king's son
> John, priest
> Werwulf, priest [14]
> Deormod, *cellerarius*
> Ælfric, *thesaurarius*
> Sigewulf, *pincerna* [15]
> Byrnstan, thegn
> Berhtmund, thegn
> Wulfsige, thegn
> Æthelm, thegn
> Æthelhelm, thegn
> Oswald, thegn
> Uhtferth, thegn
> Ocea, thegn
> Byrhthelm, thegn [16]

For those who maintain and consent to this our grant, may peace remain perpetual; but to those who challenge or try to break it, woe! and a portion with the traitor Scariot.[17]

The letter of Fulco, archbishop of Rheims, to King Alfred

This letter shows how King Alfred secured the services of one of the several scholars who participated in his scheme for the revival of learning in England; for the historical background, see above, pp. 25–8. The letter was probably written in about 886, in response to a request from King Alfred for help; Archbishop Fulco informs the king that Grimbald, a monk from St Bertin's (in Saint-Omer, Flanders), is about to be sent to England, and expresses his high opinion of Grimbald's qualities and his hope that he will be well treated. It should be compared with Asser's Life of King Alfred, *chapter 78.*

To Alfred, the most glorious and most Christian king of the English, Fulco,[1] by the grace of God archbishop of Rheims and servant of the servants of God, wishes both the ever-victorious sceptres of temporal rule and the eternal joys of the celestial kingdom.

First of all, of course, I give thanks to the Lord God our 'father of light' and author of all good, 'from whom the best and perfect gift' [James i, 17] is granted to everyone, who through the grace of the Holy Spirit has willed not only that the light of knowledge of Him should shine in your heart, but has also deigned to kindle the fire of love for Him. Enlightened and kindled by this, you attend to the good of the kingdom divinely entrusted to you, seeking or safeguarding its peace with warlike weapons and divine support, and also, with your mind continually on religious matters, you take care to increase the dignity of the ecclesiastical order with spiritual weapons. Accordingly, I beseech heavenly mercy with ceaseless prayers in order that He who anticipates and kindles your heart to this end may make you get your wish, fulfilling your intention in good measure [cf. Psalm cii, 5] whereby in your time peace may be increased for your kingdom and people, and likewise in order that the ecclesiastical order (which in many respects, as you say, has fallen into ruin, whether by the frequent invasion and onslaught of Vikings, or through decrepitude, or through the carelessness of its bishops or the ignorance of those subject to them)[2] may through your diligence and industry be reformed, improved and extended as quickly as possible.

And since you particularly wish that this may come about through my help, and since you seek advice and support over here from my see, over which St Remigius – truly the apostle of the Franks – presides, I believe this to have transpired not without divine guidance: for, just as the Frankish peoples were once freed from manifold error by St Remigius and were found worthy to acknowledge the worship of the one true God, so too the English people seek to acquire a similar man from his see and of his teaching, through whom they may learn to beware superstitions, trim away excesses and eradicate the evils springing up everywhere from inborn habits and barbaric custom, and thus, walking through the Lord's field, learn to pluck the flowers and beware the serpent.

For St Augustine, the first bishop of your people, sent to you by St Gregory your apostle, was unable to demonstrate in a short space of time all the decrees of the apostolic ordinances, nor did he wish suddenly to burden an uncultivated and barbarous people with new and unfamiliar laws: he knew how to look to their weakness and with the apostle to say as it were to children in Christ, 'I have given you milk to drink, not food' [I Corinthians iii, 2]. And so too Peter and James, 'who seemed to be pillars' [Galatians ii, 9], in the company of Barnabas and Paul and other elders, did not wish to burden the primitive Church flowing to the faith of Christ from many peoples, with a heavier yoke, except to urge them 'to abstain from things sacrificed, from fornication, from things strangled and from blood' [Acts xv, 29]: and I know it was done this way with you in the first instance.[3]

Indeed, the educating of barbaric savagery in order for it to be nourished on divine knowledge had need of this alone; and faithful and wise servants, set over the Lord's family, knew well how to pay out the measure of wheat to their fellow servants in due season [cf. Luke xii, 42], that is, in order to captivate their listeners. But with the passage of time and with Christianity growing, the holy Church neither wished to be content with these measures, nor ought to have been: rather, it derived its model from the apostles, its teachers and founders, who, after the evangelical teaching was spread out and extended from the heavenly teacher Himself, did not consider it

superfluous and useless but rather beneficial and helpful to instruct
the faithful more perfectly with the frequent exhortations of their
letters and to confirm them more securely in the true belief, and to
hand over to them more bountifully a way of living and a pattern of
religion.

Nevertheless the Church itself, whether disturbed by adversities or
sustained by good fortune, never ceased to seek the benefit of the
sons whom it begets daily for Christ, and to further their progress,
whether in private or in public, through the flaming fire of the Holy
Spirit. Hence councils were frequently summoned not only from
neighbouring cities and provinces but also from lands across the sea;
hence synodal decrees were frequently issued; hence holy canons
were established and consecrated by the Holy Spirit.[4] Through all
these the catholic faith is mightily strengthened and the inviolate
unity of ecclesiastical peace is preserved and its order rightfully
established: for it is unlawful for any Christian to trespass against
them; so too is it especially and particularly unspeakable for clerics
and priests to ignore them. Since, for reasons mentioned above, the
beneficial and religious observation and ever-cherished transmission
of them was either not fully observed among your peoples, or else has
largely fallen into disuse, it seemed pleasing to your best (and, I
think, divinely inspired) judgement and authority and royal wisdom
to consult with my insignificant self on these matters and to seek the
see of St Remigius, through whose merits and teaching the see, like
the true Church over all the churches of Gaul, has from his time
onward always flourished and excelled with religion and learning.

And since you were about to seek and request these things from us
and did not wish to appear as if sponging and empty-handed, your
royal authority has deigned to honour me with a magnificent gift, one
always useful and particularly apposite to the business in hand: concerning which I praise heavenly providence in great amazement and
give no small thanks to your generosity.

For you have sent to me some dogs which – though well-bred
and excellent, yet corporeal and mortal – are intended for
driving away the fury of visible wolves with which, among other
scourges sent to us through God's just judgement, our country greatly
abounds. You seek from me not corporeal but spiritual dogs – not
those which the prophet reproaches, saying, 'Dumb dogs, unable to
bark' [Isaiah lvi, 10], but those of which the psalmist says, 'The

tongue of your dogs may be red with the blood of your enemies' [Psalm lxvii, 24] – dogs which undoubtedly would know how and be suitable to bark out mighty growls on their master's behalf, and continually guard his flock with extremely vigilant and attentive watches, and keep far hence the savage wolves of the impure spirits who threaten and devour our souls. From the number of such watch-dogs you seek from us one in particular by the name of Grimbald, a priest and monk, to be appointed to this office and to superintend the administration of pastoral care.[5] The universal Church assuredly bears witness on his behalf: it nourished him from his earliest years in true faith and holy religion, and promoted him by ecclesiastical custom through the various grades to the honour of priesthood,[6] proclaiming him to be most worthy of a bishopric, and suitable too, in that he could instruct others. But since I had rather hoped that he would achieve that distinction in our kingdom, and since I had previously decided to arrange this at some opportune moment with Christ's consent – particularly so that the man whom I had had as a faithful son I could continue to have as a companion in my administration and as a most reliable assistant in every ecclesiastical concern[7] – I do not allow him to be torn from me without immense grief (if I may say so) and to be separated from my sight across such great distances of land and sea.

But, on the other hand, because love knows no cost, nor faith any detriment, and no distances on earth separate those whom the bond of true love binds, I have most willingly agreed to the request made by you, to whom I can deny nothing; nor do I begrudge him to you in whose advancement I rejoice as in my own and whose bounties I regard as my own. For I know that one God is being served in all places, and that there is one catholic and apostolic Church, whether it is at Rome or across the sea. Therefore it is my duty to yield him to you in accordance with ecclesiastical law, and yours to receive him honourably. On conditions and terms favourable as much to the glory of your kingdom as to the honour of my church and episcopacy he is to be sent to you, together with those who have chosen him[8] and with certain other noblemen and magnates of your realm, both bishops and priests and deacons as well as religious laymen. They are to profess and promise aloud to me in the presence of all my church that they will accept him with appropriate honour all the days of his life, and that they have the intention of maintaining unalterably all their days the canonical decrees and ecclesiastical injunctions handed down by the apostles and other apostolic men of the church, which they can now hear and observe from me, and afterwards can learn from their pastor and teacher [Grimbald] in the form handed on by us.[9] When they have done this with the divine blessing and the authority of St Remigius through my ministry and the laying on of hands, receiving him properly ordained according to ecclesiastical custom and fully instructed in all learning, they shall joyfully take him with the honour due to him to their own home,[10] delighted that they are to enjoy his patronage all their days and to be instructed always by his learning and example.

Because 'the members are mutually careful one for another, and if one member rejoices, all rejoice, or if one suffers, all members suffer' [I Corinthians xii, 25–6], I straightway commend him considerately and specifically to your royal highness and most provident grace, so that whatsoever he can discover that is appropriate to the credit of the Church and the instruction of your people, he will be able always to teach – with free authority and without constraint – and fulfil in deed, lest someone (which God forbid!), guided by some devilish impulse with jealousy of malice and ill-will, should occasion a quarrel or incite dissension. It will be your responsibility to oversee this in general and utterly to repress such men (if perchance they should appear) with royal censure, and to restrain their barbaric savagery with the bridle of your authority. It will be his responsibility always to think with pastoral concern of the welfare of those entrusted to him, and to lead them along after him with love rather than to compel them with fear.

May your distinguished authority, holy compassion and unconquerable strength always rejoice and flourish in Christ, the King of Kings and Lord of Lords.

Bishop Wulfsige's preface to the translation of Gregory's Dialogues

This Old English poem was evidently composed as a preface to accompany a manuscript copy of Werferth's Old English translation of the Dialogues of Gregory the Great (see above, p. 32). Gregory's Dialogues were one of the most popular works of the Latin Middle Ages, principally for the account they contain of the life and miracles of St Benedict (who is one of the saints whose help is implored in the poem). As we learn from the poem, its author was Wulfsige, a friend of King Alfred and Asser's predecessor as bishop of Sherborne (the exact dates of his episcopacy are unknown, the outer limits being 879 and 900); we also learn that Alfred had sent to Wulfsige an exemplar of the Werferth translation to be copied, and that the occasion for Wulfsige's poem was the copying of this exemplar. In the poem Wulfsige begs the reader's prayers both for himself and for Alfred, his 'ring-giver'.

He who sets out to read me [1] through will close [2] me with appropriate recompense. If he wishes many good examples of the spiritual life, he may find them in me in order that he may very easily ascend to the heavenly home where there is ever joy and rapture – bliss in those dwellings for those who may see the Son of God Himself with their own eyes. That may the man perceive whose mind is sound and then through his understanding trusts in the help of these saints and carries out their example – as this book explains.

Bishop Wulfsige commanded me to be written, the poor servant of Him who created all majesty and is also the Ruler of each of His creatures – one eternal God of all creation. The bishop who had this copy made [3] (which you are now holding in your hands and looking at) begs that you beseech help for him from those saints whose memories are here recorded, and that God Almighty, who wields power over every kingdom, forgive him the sins which he formerly committed, and also that he may come to rest with

Him and likewise with his ring-giver who gave him the[4] exemplar:
Alfred of the English, the greatest treasure-giver of all the kings
he has ever heard tell of, in recent times or long ago, or of any
earthly king he had previously learned of.

Æthelweard's account of the closing
years of Alfred's reign

*Æthelweard was ealdorman of the western shires in the last quarter of the
tenth century. His* Chronicle *is a translation into Latin of a manuscript
of the* Anglo-Saxon Chronicle *which has not survived, doubtless with
some additions provided by Æthelweard himself. His account of the years
from 893 to 899 is apparently independent of the corresponding annals in
the manuscripts which have survived (translated above, pp. 114–20), and
is therefore an important source for the period. Æthelweard's Latin text
has been poorly transmitted and is frequently corrupt; moreover, his
intended meaning is often obscured by his stylistic pretensions. In the
following translation, no attempt has been made to disguise textual difficulties; those passages rendered hopelessly corrupt through transmission
have been left untranslated.*

[893] And that then made up the number of years from the
Saviour's glorious birth to 900, excepting only seven. And after
Easter [1] [8 April] of that year the army which had arrived from [2]
Gaulish parts breaks camp, and by following the hiding-places of a
certain vast forest which is commonly called *Andredesuuda* [the
Weald], they get as far as the western English, and step by step they
devastate the provinces thereabouts, that is, Hampshire and Berkshire.
These matters are then made known to Prince Edward,[3] the son of
King Alfred. He had just been conducting a campaign [4] throughout
the southern parts of England; but afterwards the western English [5]
are also equipped.[6] The engagement takes place [7] at Farnham, with
the dense throngs (?) shrieking with threats.[8] Without delay, the
youth jump to it (?);[9] attacked [10] with weapons, they [. . .];[11] they
are duly liberated by the prince's arrival, just as, after the usual
onslaught of predators,[12] animals are taken back to [13] the pastures
with the shepherd's help. There the tyrant [the Viking leader] is
wounded; they drive the filthy crowds of his supporters across [14] the
river Thames to northern parts. Meanwhile, the Danes are held under

siege in Thorney, 'island of the stake'.[15] Having set out from the city of London, King Æthelred[16] supplied the prince with reinforcements. The Vikings now request the establishment of peace and a treaty. Hostages are given. They duly agree to leave the kingdom of the aforesaid king.[17] The deed and the word are fulfilled at the same time. At length they set out for the eastern parts of England, under the control of the army dwelling there, namely in the realm of the former king, St Edmund; and their ships sail round to them, from the Limen estuary to Mersea, a place in Kent,[18] with favourable winds.[19]

In the course[20] of the same year the treaty[21] is broken; the savage Hastein with a large force ravages all the lands of the Mercians from Benfleet, until they came to the borders of the Welsh.[22] The army then residing in the eastern area gives them assistance, and the Northumbrian army similarly. The distinguished Ealdorman Æthelhelm then[23] attacks them openly with a cavalry force,[24] together with Ealdorman Æthelnoth and the western army of the English. Afterwards King Æthelred of the Mercians joins them, assisting with a mighty army. They wage war by turns[25] through the effort of both peoples; then the youth of the English afterwards obtain the field of victory. These things done at Buttington are still proclaimed by old men. Moreover, further effort[26] is seen as foolish[27] by the Danes: they confirm the peace a second time; they do not refuse [to give] hostages; they promise to withdraw from that region.

In the same year the Danish[28] rampart at Benfleet collapses, without the intention[29] of the inhabitants; they divide their year's[30] booty among themselves. When these things had happened, Sigeferth, a pirate from the Northumbrians,[31] set out with a great fleet; he twice ravages along the coast on the one outing, and afterwards sets his sails for his own home.[32]

[894]   And when two years were ended since the time when the mighty fleet had come from the fortress at Boulogne,[33] and had been brought into Lympne, an English town, Ealdorman Æthelnoth then set out from the western part of England.[34] At the city of York he comes upon the enemy who are plundering[35] no small territories in the kingdom of the Mercians to the west of Stamford; that is, between the waters of the river *Weolod* [Welland] and the thickets of the wood which is commonly called Kesteven.[36]

[895]   And with the span of one year passing, Guthfrith, king of
the Northumbrians [the Vikings of Northumbria], died on the feast
of St Bartholomew, the apostle of Christ [24 August]. His body
is entombed in the city of York in the cathedral.[37]

[899]   Meanwhile, four years after the time when the aforemen-
tioned king had died, a great and mighty dissension arose among the
English who[38] then remained among the foul[39] throngs of the Northumbrians [the Vikings of Northumbria].[40]

Finally, in the same year, the magnanimous Alfred passed from
the world, king of the Saxons, unshakeable pillar of the western
people, a man replete with justice, vigorous in warfare, learned in
speech, above all instructed in divine learning. For he had translated
unknown numbers of books from rhetorical Latin speech into his
own language – so variously and so richly, that [his] book of Boethius
would arouse tearful[41] emotions not only in those familiar with it but
even in those hearing it [for the first time]. For the king died on the
seventh day before the feast of All Saints;[42] his body lies at peace in
Winchester. Now, reader, say 'O Christ our Redeemer, save his soul'.

Two acrostic poems on King Alfred

The two poems translated here are preserved in a manuscript contemporary with Alfred's lifetime. They are written in the form of double acrostics (that is, the first and last letters of each line spell out a word or words, often the name of the dedicatee of the poem). The first poem is addressed to Christ, but bears the name AELFRED as its left-hand legend; the second is addressed to the king himself and bears the name ELFRED as its left-hand legend. In both poems the king's name was to have formed the right-hand legend as well, but the complexities of the form defeated the poet and the effect was not fully achieved. The poems were apparently composed by a foreigner in Alfred's entourage, possibly by John the Old Saxon (see above, p. 26), whom we know to have written one other similar acrostic poem.

[To Christ:]

It is my intention to run through some amazing events. You reside in the starry citadel: but You will return swiftly thence as Judge – even as the Law taught figurally, You are foretold awesomely – and the mass of the universe shall burn at once in searing flame. O King, You made it so. But, Great One, You seize the wise man from these flames – just as,[1] triumphing, You Yourself destroyed chaos [death] – in order that he may enjoy the Divine Visage beyond the stars forever.

[To Alfred:]

Behold, may all the Graces descend from heaven upon you! You shall always be joyous, Alfred, through the happy walks of life. May you bend[2] your mind to heavenly affairs; be disgusted with trappings. Rightly do you teach, hastening from the deceptive charm of worldly things. See, you apply yourself ever to gain the shining talents:[3] run confidently through the fields of foreign learning![4]

The Burghal Hidage

The network of burhs, or fortified sites, described in the Burghal Hidage
*was essentially the product of King Alfred's programme for the defence of
Wessex, undertaken in the 880s: see above, pp. 24–5. The document
begins by listing all the burhs which formed part of the network, indicating
how many hides (of land) 'belonged', or were assigned, to each. The basis
of the assessment is explained in the second paragraph: the number of
hides assigned to a burh was determined by the length of its defensive wall,
on the principle that each pole (5½ yards) of wall was to be manned by
four men and that one man would be supplied from one hide. Thus, for
example, the statement '500 hides belong to Portchester' means that the
defences of Portchester were of such a length that 500 men were required
for the garrison, and these men were to be provided from land assessed at
500 hides in the vicinity of the burh.*

324 hides belong to *Eorpeburnan*;[1] to Hastings belong 500 hides; to
Lewes belong 1,300[2] hides; to Burpham belong 720 hides;[3] to Chichester belong 1,500 hides. Then 500 hides belong to Portchester; 150
hides belong to Southampton; to Winchester belong 2,400 hides; to
Wilton belong 1,400 hides; to Chisbury[4] belong 700[5] hides, and to
Shaftesbury likewise;[6] to Twynham[7] belong 500 hides less 30 hides;
to Wareham belong 1,600 hides; to Bridport[8] belong 800 hides less
40 hides; to Exeter belong 734 hides; to Halwell belong 300 hides; to
Lydford belong 150 hides less 10 hides; to Pilton[9] belong 400 hides
less 40 hides; to Watchet belong 513 hides; to Axbridge belong 400
hides; to Lyng belong 100 hides; to Langport belong 600 hides; to
Bath belong 1,000 hides; 1,200[10] hides belong to Malmesbury; to
Cricklade belong 1,400[11] hides; 1,500[12] hides to Oxford; to Wallingford belong 2,400 hides; 1,600 hides belong to Buckingham; to
Sashes[13] belong 1,000 hides; 600[14] hides belong to Eashing; to
Southwark belong 1,800 hides.[15]

For the maintenance and defence of an acre's breadth of wall, sixteen hides are required: if every hide is represented by one man, then every pole can be manned by four men.[16] And so for the maintenance of twenty poles of wall, eighty hides are required; and for a furlong, 160 hides are required, according to the same reckoning as I set out above. For two furlongs, 320 hides are required; for three furlongs, 480 hides. Then for four furlongs, 640 hides are required; for the maintenance of a circuit of five furlongs of wall, 800 hides are required; for six furlongs, 960 hides are required; for seven furlongs, 1,120 hides; for the maintenance of a circuit of eight furlongs of wall, 1,280 hides; for nine furlongs, 1,440 hides; for ten furlongs, 1,600 hides are required; for eleven furlongs, 1,760 hides are required; for the maintenance of a circuit of twelve furlongs of wall, 1,920 hides are required. If the circuit is greater, the additional amount can easily be established from this account, for 160 men are always required for one furlong so that every pole is manned by four men.

APPENDICES

Appendix I
Alfred and the Cakes

Without any doubt the best-known story concerning King Alfred is the account of how the king, while snatching a few days' anonymous refuge at the house of a herdsman during the period of his greatest misfortunes, was so preoccupied with his troubles that he failed to notice some loaves of bread burning in the oven: for this he was duly berated by the herdsman's wife. The story does not, however, originate in Asser's *Life of King Alfred*, and its authenticity cannot, therefore, be guaranteed; indeed, the story is probably best considered as one of the many legends which Alfred's fame attracted at a later time.

The earliest surviving version of the story is contained in an anonymous *Vita S. Neoti*, a work apparently composed not long after the transfer, probably in the late tenth century, of the relics of St Neot from their original location in Cornwall to a priory at Eynesbury (soon renamed St Neots) in Huntingdonshire; see further below, p. 254 note 142. Because the Latin text of the *Vita S. Neoti* has not been printed since 1809 (and then in a very unreliable edition: Whitaker, *The Life of Saint Neot*, pp. 339–65), and has never been translated, we have thought it best to provide a translation based on a fresh collation of the manuscript sources; a new edition of the text, by M. Lapidge, is forthcoming. In the five surviving manuscripts of the *Vita S. Neoti* the story of Alfred and the Cakes is as follows:

There is a place in the remote parts of English Britain far to the west, which in English is called Athelney and which we refer to as 'Athelings' Isle'; it is surrounded on all sides by vast salt marshes and sustained by some level ground in the middle. King Alfred happened unexpectedly to come there as a lone traveller. Noticing the cottage of a certain unknown swineherd (as he later learned), he directed his path towards it and sought there a peaceful retreat; he was given refuge, and he stayed there for a number of days, impoverished, subdued and content with the bare necessities. Reflecting patiently that these things had befallen him through God's just judgement, he remained there awaiting God's mercy through the intercession of His servant Neot; for he had conceived from Neot the hope that he nourished in his heart. 'Whom the Lord loves', says the apostle, 'He chastises; He scourges every son whom He adopts' [Hebrews xii, 6]. In addition to this, Alfred patiently kept the picture of Job's astonishing constancy before his eyes every day. Now it happened by chance one day, when the swineherd was leading his flock to their usual pastures, that the king remained alone at home with the swineherd's wife. The wife, concerned for her husband's return, had entrusted some kneaded flour to the husband of sea-borne Venus [Vulcan, the fire god, that is, the oven]. As is the custom among countrywomen, she was intent on other domestic occupations, until, when she sought the bread from Vulcan, she saw it burning from the other side of the room. She immediately grew angry and said to the king (unknown to her as such): 'Look here, man,

You hesitate to turn the loaves which you see to be burning,
Yet you're quite happy to eat them when they come warm from the oven!'

But the king, reproached by these disparaging insults, ascribed them to his divine lot; somewhat shaken, and submitting to the woman's scolding, he not only turned the bread but even attended to it as she brought out the loaves when they were ready.

The outline of the story is clearly visible here, even though it has been embellished considerably by pretentious literary artifice (such as the two hexameter lines – a favourite device of this author – and the reference to 'the husband of sea-borne Venus'). Since throughout the *Vita S. Neoti* the anonymous author was at pains to establish the historicity of St Neot by reference to historical figures such as King Alfred, the invention of the story of Alfred and the Cakes should probably be laid at his door.

At some point in the late eleventh or early twelfth century, the *Vita S. Neoti* served as the basis for a vernacular homily on St Neot, which is preserved among a collection of homilies in the mid-twelfth-century manuscript B.L. Cotton Vespasian D.xiv; the whole collection is printed by Warner, *Early English Homilies*, and the homily on St Neot is found on pp. 129–34. The author departed from his source in many respects, and it is interesting to see how he has recast the story of Alfred and the Cakes:

When King Alfred . . . learned that the Viking army was so strong and so close to England, he immediately took to flight in terror and abandoned all his soldiers and his chieftains, and all his people, his treasures and treasure-chests, and looked to his own safety. He went in stealth along hedges and lanes, through woods and open fields, until through God's guidance he arrived safe and sound at Athelney, and sought refuge in a swineherd's house, and was willingly obedient both to him and to his evil wife. Now it happened one day that the swineherd's wife heated her oven, and the king sat beside it, warming himself by the fire, the household being unaware that he was the king. Then the evil wife suddenly became angry, and in a filthy temper said to the king: 'Turn the loaves over so that they don't burn, because I see every day that you have a huge appetite.' He immediately obeyed the evil wife, because perforce he had to. Then the good king called out to his Lord with great sorrow and lamentation, begging His mercy.

It is interesting to note here how King Alfred has assumed the character of a deserter, and the swineherd's wife – who is scarcely characterized at all in the *Vita S. Neoti* – has become an 'evil wife'. It is the mark of a good anecdote both that it bears re-telling and that it can be flexibly adapted to the intentions of various story-tellers.

Another adaptation of the account in the *Vita S. Neoti* was incorporated into the so-called *Annals of St Neots*. The title of this compilation is misleading: in fact the annals in their present form appear to have been compiled at Bury St Edmunds during the second quarter of the twelfth century (the sole surviving manuscript of these annals, now Cambridge, Trinity College MS R.7.28, was written there at that time). The *Annals of St Neots* are principally concerned with East Anglian history (see Hart, 'The East Anglian Chronicle'), but in his account of the events of 878, covering the movements of the Viking army and Alfred's retreat to Somerset, the annalist saw fit to interpolate the story of Alfred and the Cakes as he found it in the *Vita S. Neoti*. This time the story is greatly abbreviated and its emphasis focused on Alfred (for the text, see Stevenson, *Asser*, p. 136):

And, as may be read in the *Vita S. Neoti*, he remained for some time at the house of one of his herdsmen. Now it happened one day that a countrywoman (the wife, that is, of his herdsman) was getting ready to bake bread, and the king, sitting by the fire, was busy preparing a bow and arrows and other instruments of war. And when that unhappy woman spied the loaves of bread burning in the fire, she ran over quickly and removed them, rebuking the unconquerable king and saying, 'Look here, man,

You hesitate to turn the loaves which you see to be burning,
Yet you're quite happy to eat them when they come warm from the oven![5]

That unhappy woman did not in any way realize that he was King Alfred who fought so many battles against the Vikings and gained so many victories from them.

The annalist has emphasized Alfred's warlike character at the expense of his reflective character: whereas the hagiographer's Alfred sat meditating on Holy Scripture and on the example of Job, the annalist's Alfred busies himself preparing weapons. The annalist has preserved nothing of the hagiographer's story except the general outline and the two hexameter lines expressing the woman's expostulation.

But the story as found in the *Vita S. Neoti* would also admit of considerable expansion. For the sake of comparison it is worth while to consider a somewhat later version found in the *Chronicle* attributed to John of Wallingford, which was composed at St Albans near the middle of the thirteenth century (see Vaughan, *The Chronicle Attributed to John of Wallingford*, p. 33). Here every suggestion present in the *Vita S. Neoti* has been teased out at length:

But King Alfred chose to yield to the spirit of the prophecy rather than oppose the raging enemy and risk certain slaughter of his own men; reflecting that the situation had arisen because of his own sins and those of his people, he sought humbly (as he was obliged to do) to bear the yoke of the Lord's injunction which St Neot had imposed through his prophecy. Therefore he retreated, prudently afraid and wisely fugitive, and came to Athelney, which place is in the remote parts of England to the far west, and is called 'the land of nobles' by the Britons. It is in the midst of salt marshes, having in its interior some welcome level ground. Accordingly, he arrived there, and, amid the surging storms of misfortune, embracing that patience which rejoices in adversity, he stood up strong at least in that one place: he stuck out his tongue to the mockeries of the ill-luck he could not avoid [cf. Juvenal, *Satire* 10.52-3] and fixed firmly in his mind the saying which he had heard repeated by the saint [St Neot], namely, that 'the mighty shall be mightily tormented' [Wisdom vi, 7], and the words of the apostle, that God 'scourges every son whom He adopts' [Hebrews xii, 6]. He placed before his eyes the just compensations of the holy Job and Tobias, who amid so many adversities had praised the Lord's justice. He hid out in the cottage of a swineherd, and in this remote station he patiently awaited the day of consolation predicted by St Neot and pending in God's will. Meanwhile it happened that he remained at the house and

the little old wife of the swineherd, thinking about the return of her husband (who was in the pastures with his herd), had placed some bread in
the warm ash to be baked there, and then turned to other necessary chores
while the bread was in the ashes. She forgot about the bread until she was
reminded of it by the burning smell. The old woman dropped what she
was doing in the meantime and ran over, and said impatiently to the man
whom she saw sitting there: 'What sort of careless man are you, who neg-
lects to attend to burning bread? Never have I seen so negligent a man –
one who doesn't even know how to turn ash-baked bread – and yet when
it's put in front of you you'll no doubt rush to consume it! Why were you
so slow to attend to it when it was burning?' The king, patiently taking in
the words of reproach, replied: 'It is as you say, good hostess, for I would
be exceedingly slow even if I knew how to deal with ash-baked bread.'
And thereupon he involved himself in the baking operation and stretched
out his extremely unskilled hand, and kept watch until the bread was sufficiently baked. Here I shall leave it to one's imagination to reflect how
awesome was the majesty of him who undid the belts of other kings and
caused their loins to be bound with ropes, and how agreeably desirable is
that humble poverty, content always with its own resources, to whose
refuge the king had turned.

The chronicler was so concerned with elaborating the story in all
ways possible that he got somewhat muddled in choosing between a
portrait of the majestic king with the patience of Job and a fumbling
baker's apprentice.

Whatever the individual merits of the various versions quoted
above, it was that in the *Annals of St Neots* which was known to
Matthew Parker, who was the first to print Asser's *Life of King
Alfred*, in 1574 (see below, p. 226). Parker noticed the similarities
between the *Annals* and Asser's *Life*, and deduced that the *Annals*
were themselves written by Asser (when in fact it was the later
compiler of the *Annals* who had made use of the *Life*); moreover, he
had a far less scrupulous attitude towards the integrity of a text than
a modern editor should have, and accordingly interpolated the story
of Alfred and the Cakes exactly as he found it in the *Annals* at the
appropriate point in his text of Asser's *Life*. Parker was followed in
this respect by Camden (1602) and Wise (1722), and although the
latter drew attention to the non-occurrence of the story in the manuscript of the *Life*, he explained that it was the manuscript that was
defective. Petrie (1848) enclosed the story within square brackets, and
was thus the first editor to mark it as an interpolation; Stevenson

(1904) marked it as such more clearly, by printing it in small italics. But the 'damage' had been done: already popular before the sixteenth century, and then for long accepted on the highest authority as having been told by Asser himself, the story of Alfred and the Cakes gained wide circulation and attained the fame which it enjoys to the present day.

Appendix II
The Alfred Jewel

The Alfred Jewel was found in 1693 at North Petherton in Somerset; it was given to the University of Oxford in 1718, and is now kept in the Ashmolean Museum. For a full account, see Hinton, *Ornamental Metalwork*, pp. 29–48.

The jewel (reproduced on the cover of this book) comprises a pear-shaped gold frame enclosing a transparent piece of rock crystal super-imposed on a figurative design in cloisonné enamel; a plate of gold is fixed at the back, with a plant- or tree-like design and basket-work hatching incised upon it; a gold extension in the form of an animal head is attached to the narrower end of the frame, and a short hollow tube or socket protrudes from the animal's mouth; a gold rivet passes through the socket. There is an inscription in openwork lettering around the edge of the frame, which reads: + AELFRED MEC HEHT GEWYRCAN ('Alfred ordered me to be made'). The enamel design represents, against a blue background, a half-length or seated male figure wearing a green sleeveless tunic and holding, one in each hand, the stems of objects that terminate with what appear to be flowers. The jewel is just under $2\frac{1}{2}$ inches (6.4 cm) in length, and about $1\frac{1}{2}$ inches (3.2 cm) at its greatest width; its main body is about $\frac{1}{2}$ inch (1.3 cm) thick; the socket protruding from the animal head is about $\frac{3}{8}$ inch (1 cm) deep and about $\frac{3}{16}$ inch (0.5 cm) in internal diameter.

While there can be no certainty in the matter, it is difficult to resist the traditional identification of the Alfred named in the inscription as King Alfred the Great. The available dating criteria (art-historical and linguistic) are compatible with the assumption that the jewel was made in the second half of the ninth century. It was found in an area strongly associated with King Alfred, only four miles from Athelney where he took refuge in 878, where he built a fortress and where he founded a monastery (Asser, chapters 55 and 92). The quality of its workmanship is appropriate to an object commissioned by a king, and

King Alfred himself is known to have had goldsmiths in his service
to whom he gave instruction (Asser, chapter 76). The fact that
Alfred is not styled 'king' in no way weakens the identification, for
the title may have been omitted merely for lack of space, and parallels exist for inscriptions naming known individuals without specifying their rank. The Mercian forms (*mec* and *heht*) in the inscription
are easily explained in an Alfredian context by the king's well-attested
use of Mercian helpers (Asser, chapter 77), while the Carolingian
technique of enamelling can be understood in terms of the king's
employment of craftsmen 'from many races' (Asser, chapter 101).
There are no obvious alternative candidates for the identification, and
certainly none that provides a better historical context for the interpretation of the iconography of the jewel and the assessment of its
function.

The figure depicted in cloisonné enamel on the front of the jewel
has been interpreted variously as a portrayal of Christ, one of His
saints (particularly St Cuthbert or St Neot), the Pope, Alexander the
Great, or simply Alfred himself; the interpretations of the objects
held by the figure vary accordingly, from flowers to sceptres (or, in
the case of Alexander the Great, poles with joints of meat impaled
upon them). The closest art-historical parallels that are likely to be
relevant may be said to favour two possible interpretations (which
need not be mutually exclusive). First, the figure is a portrayal of
Christ, holding two floral-headed sceptres; no significance need be
attached to the absence of a nimbus, since depictions of Christ without
a nimbus, though unusual, are not unknown. Secondly, the figure
is a personification of Sight; this interpretation is suggested by
comparison with the central figure on the Fuller Brooch in the
British Museum, which certainly represents Sight (see Wilson,
Ornamental Metalwork, pp. 91–8 and 211–14; the figure holds two
cornucopias, horns of plenty, overflowing with flowers and representing the fruits of the earth). The first interpretation is perhaps to
be preferred, if only because it springs more easily to mind; it has
been argued further (by Howlett, 'The Iconography of the Alfred
Jewel') that the figure signifies Christ as the incarnate form of the
Wisdom of God (cf. I Corinthians i, 24), and that the design on the
back of the jewel represents Wisdom as the Tree of Life (cf. Proverbs
iii, 13, 18).

The function of the jewel is something of a mystery. The rivet which passes through the socket protruding from the animal's mouth suggests that the jewel was originally fixed on the end of a thin rod which either became detached in antiquity or was made of some perishable material like wood or ivory; this rod may itself have been attached to something more substantial. A socket with rivet hole is similarly incorporated in the Minster Lovell Jewel (also in the Ashmolean Museum); this jewel, though smaller than the Alfred Jewel and without any apparently significant decoration or Alfredian association, may therefore have been intended to serve the same purpose. Various suggestions for the function of the Alfred Jewel have been put forward, ranging from the head of a dress-pin to the central jewel in a crown. The most popular theory depends on a passage in King Alfred's preface to his translation of Pope Gregory's *Pastoral Care* (above, p. 126): 'I intend to send a copy [of the book] to each bishopric in my kingdom; and in each copy there will be an *æstel* worth fifty mancuses. And in God's name I command that no one shall take that *æstel* from the book, nor the book from the church.' The exact meaning of the word *æstel* is uncertain, but both context and etymology suggest 'book-marker': it was obviously something closely associated with a book, and it probably derives from Latin (*h*)*astula*, 'small spear' or 'splinter' (cf. Old Irish *astul*, glossed 'a book's sliver or spear'); in the early eleventh century *æstel* was used as a gloss for *indicatorium*, 'pointer', and in the thirteenth century it was itself glossed *festuca*, 'stalk' or 'stick'. (For further discussion of the word, see Howlett, 'Alfred's *Æstel*', and Harbert, 'King Alfred's *Æstel*'.) An *æstel* would thus seem to have been a rod-like pointer, perhaps used for following the line while reading (cf. Dodwell, *Anglo-Saxon Art*, p. 32), or for inserting in a book at a desired place; but since each *æstel* sent out by Alfred is said to have been worth fifty mancuses, one has to suppose that each was expensive to make and so was presumably associated physically with a valuable jewel or piece of gold ornament. The Alfred Jewel at once presents itself as possibly the more valuable end of such an object, while both interpretations of its iconography (Sight, or the Wisdom of God) would seem equally and entirely appropriate.

The *æstel* theory is undeniably attractive, but it is not so irresistible that we should close our minds to further lines of speculation. There remains the possibility, for example, that the whole assembly (jewel plus rod) was a symbol of office. It would assuredly be vain to imagine that we could be so fortunate as to have here a fitting from

King Alfred's royal rod or sceptre, but we can hardly exclude the
possibility that other office-holders would have had their own symbols
of office, which they received from the king as a mark of their
authority. Of course there is no means of telling what office (if any)
might have been represented by the Alfred Jewel. One should bear in
mind, however, that its presumed Christian symbolism is compatible
with both secular and ecclesiastical office; several undoubtedly 'secular' objects from the Anglo-Saxon period (for example, certain rings
and seal-matrices) are decorated with overtly Christian designs. If the
jewel does depict Christ as the incarnate form of the Wisdom of
God, it would certainly express the very essence of the Alfredian
conception of worldly authority. Alfred knew from Pope Gregory's
Pastoral Care that for those in positions of responsibility learning was
an essential qualification and instruction was a primary duty. In one
of his own works he wrote: 'Therefore a man never attains virtue and
excellence through his power; rather he attains power and authority
through his virtue and excellence . . . Study wisdom, therefore, and
when you have learned it, do not neglect it, for I say to you without
hesitation that you can attain authority through wisdom' (translated
from Sedgefield, *King Alfred's Old English Version of Boethius*, p. 35).
Alfred strove to apply these principles in his own case, by devoting
himself wholeheartedly to the study of wisdom and by seeking to
improve the standard of learning among his people. Moreover he is
known to have reproached his ealdormen and reeves for neglecting
the study and application of wisdom, and to have commanded them
'either to relinquish immediately the offices of worldly power that
you possess, or else to apply yourselves much more attentively to the
pursuit of wisdom' (Asser, chapter 106). A king who conceived of
worldly power in this way might well have regarded the Alfred Jewel
as a fitting symbol of worldly office. But if the interpretation of the
jewel as a reading-aid still seems preferable, one should remember
that the bishops who received copies of the *Pastoral Care* would not
be alone in requiring help: the king's secular officials, who were
forced to learn how to read, would need all the help they could get.

NOTES
TO INTRODUCTION
AND TEXT

In the notes which follow, books and articles are cited by abbreviated titles; for full bibliographical details, see the list of references on pp. 345–59. In references to certain primary sources, the following abbreviations are used:

ASC = *Anglo-Saxon Chronicle*, cited by annal number according to the corrected chronology adopted in Whitelock et al., *Anglo-Saxon Chronicle*. When it is necessary to specify a particular manuscript, we follow the conventional system of letters (see below, pp. 276–7); thus '*ASC* MS 'A' s.a. 900' is a reference to the 'A' manuscript of the *Chronicle*, for the year (*sub anno*) 900.

CÆ = Campbell, *Chronicle of Æthelweard*. This is a Latin translation of a version of the *Anglo-Saxon Chronicle*, made towards the end of the tenth century; see further below, pp. 334–5.

DB = *Domesday Book*, vol. I, cited according to the foliation in the standard edition published in 1783 (which follows that of the manuscript itself). Texts and translations of the surveys of individual counties are available in the series *Domesday Book*, ed. John Morris (Chichester, 1975–).

EHD = Whitelock, *English Historical Documents* c. *500–1042*, with number of text or document.

HE = Bede's *Historia Ecclesiastica Gentis Anglorum*, available in a translation by Sherley-Price, *Bede: A History of the English Church and People*.

PL = Migne, *Patrologiae Cursus Completus. Series (Latina) Prima*.

S = Sawyer, *Anglo-Saxon Charters*, with number of document; each entry in this catalogue supplies full details of printed texts and (where available) of translations.

SEHD = Harmer, *Select English Historical Documents*, with number of document.

In references to manuscripts, B.L. = London, British Library.
All biblical quotations are taken from the Douai-Rheims version (1582–

1609), an English translation based on the Latin 'Vulgate' text of Jerome (rather than on the original Hebrew and Greek text, as in the case of the Authorized Version), for it was the Vulgate text that was current during the early Middle Ages.

INTRODUCTION (*pp. 9–58*)

1. The only other contemporary biography of an Anglo-Saxon king is the one of Edward the Confessor (1042–66), edited and translated by Barlow, *Life of King Edward*. Though a fascinating work in its own way, it does not convey such a clear impression of the king's personal involvement in royal government. Asser's *Life of King Alfred* should be compared with the ninth-century biographies of Frankish kings: see, for example, Thorpe, *Two Lives of Charlemagne*.

2. In expressing his enthusiasm for Egbert as a king of exceptional power, the chronicler simply added Egbert's name to a list of seven important kings devised in the first instance by Bede (*HE* ii, 5); but it is unlikely that Bede and the chronicler were recording succession to a recognized political office. Bede's choice of kings seems to be personal, and does not do justice to the power exercised by the Mercian kings Penda and Wulfhere in the seventh century. Moreover, he leaves the nature of their position rather vague, crediting them with *imperium* ('sovereignty') or *ducatus* ('leadership'). The chronicler similarly makes no attempt to recognize the power exercised by the Mercian kings Æthelbald and Offa in the eighth century, and thus distorts political reality even further. By calling Egbert 'Bretwalda' ('ruler of Britain') he also creates the (misleading) impression that a specific office, with its own title, was involved; but while this is the form of the word in *ASC* MS 'A', the variant forms in the other manuscripts raise the possibility that the chronicler originally wrote something like *brytenwealda*, which means 'wide ruler'.

3. See North, *English Hammered Coinage*, pp. 70–71 and 89–90, and Lyon, 'Some Problems in Interpreting Anglo-Saxon Coinage', pp. 180–81.

4. *CÆ*, pp. 26–7; Vikings attacked the monastery of Lindisfarne in Northumbria at about the same time. Charlemagne was not so easily fooled: see Thorpe, *Two Lives of Charlemagne*, p. 158. King Alfred learnt the lesson: he treated traders in general, and Viking traders in particular, with due circumspection (see his law-code, § 34, and the Treaty between Alfred and Guthrum, § 5). The Vikings themselves may not have appreciated the distinction between trading and raiding: there were professional traders among them, and professional raiders, but there were also men who made a living from a combination of both activities.

5. See Brooks, 'Development of Military Obligations', pp. 79–80.

6. The size of the Viking armies active in England in the second half of the

ninth century is the subject of keen debate among historians. Much depends on the interpretation of the statements in the *Chronicle* about the numbers of ships in the Viking fleets, and then on the presumed capacity of the ships. The chronicler (or chroniclers) evidently recognized a distinction between relatively small and relatively large fleets, and while he could provide apparently exact numbers for the former, he gave only rough estimates for the latter, or simply described them as 'great'. His 'accurate' figures for small fleets range up to thirty-five, and refer invariably to raiding parties or to detachments of the main force. The Viking armies described as 'great' (including those which arrived in 865, 871 and 892) would thus seem to have been considerably larger: no figures are given for the armies of 865 and 871 (though '120' ships were lost at Swanage in 877), but the army of 892 came in '250' ships (soon joined by 'eighty' more). There is reason to believe that the ships used in these expeditions often carried between thirty and fifty men (more, perhaps, when being used as troop-carriers): references to casualties from known numbers of ships point to crews of this order (*ASC* s.a. 878 and 896); the ships built by Alfred in 896 were 'twice' as long as the Viking ships and had sixty oars or more; the Gokstad ship itself, which dates from this period, has thirty-two oars. Thirty-five ships with crews of thirty men apiece would amount to a force of about 1,000 men; making all due allowance for the presence of some smaller ships in the fleets, for supplies and non-combatants, and for exaggeration, it follows that the larger fleets may have carried two or three thousand men (though perhaps not many more). For further discussion of these and the other related issues, see Sawyer, *Age of the Vikings*, pp. 123–31; Brooks, 'England in the Ninth Century'; and Sawyer, *Kings and Vikings*, pp. 93–4.

7. See Asser, chapter 8, and below, p. 232 note 19. Alfred may have been sent to Rome as part of a deputation charged with establishing good relations between King Æthelwulf and the Pope; it is also possible that as the king's youngest son, with little prospect of becoming king himself, Alfred was being prepared for eventual admission into the Church (though it would be unusual at this date for a king's son, as opposed to a king's daughter, to enter the religious life).

8. See North, *English Hammered Coinage*, pp. 72 and 91–2, and Lyon, 'Some Problems in Interpreting Anglo-Saxon Coinage', pp. 180–81.

9. See Alfred's remarks in his translation of Boethius's *Consolation of Philosophy*, above, pp. 132–3.

10. *ASC* MS 'B' s.a. 878. For different interpretations of this passage, see Davis, 'Alfred the Great: Propaganda and Truth', pp. 170–72, and Whitelock, 'Battle of Edington', pp. 9–10.

11. The story is first attested as a mid-eleventh-century, or later, interpolation in the anonymous *Historia de Sancto Cuthberto*, an account of St

Cuthbert and of the fortunes of his community originally compiled in about the middle of the tenth century: see Arnold, *Symeonis Monachi Opera Omnia* I, pp. 204–6, and Craster, 'The Patrimony of St Cuthbert', pp. 177–8. William of Malmesbury (see next note) has the same story in a slightly different form.

12. The story first occurs in William of Malmesbury's *Gesta Regum*, a general history of the English written in the early 1120s: see Stubbs, *Willelmi Malmesbiriensis Monachi De Gestis Regum Anglorum* I, p. 126. It is probably apocryphal, not least because William tells a similar story of a Viking leader before the battle of *Brunanburh* in 937 (ibid., p. 143; translated in *EHD* no. 8).

13. For general studies of the Danish settlements, see Sawyer, *Age of the Vikings*, pp. 148–76, and Loyn, *Vikings in Britain*, pp. 113–37. Note that the different parts of the Danelaw came into being in significantly different circumstances (at least if we take the *Chronicle* at face value): East Anglia was 'conquered' by the 865 army in 869–70, but 'settled' by what remained of the 871 army in 880; Mercia was 'conquered' by the combined 865 and 871 armies in 874–5, but 'settled' by part of the 871 army in 877; Northumbria was 'conquered' by the 865 army in 875 and 'settled' by the same in 876; the settlers in East Anglia and Northumbria were joined in 896 by parts of the 892 army. Of course, the composition of the armies in question may not have been quite as stable as this view implies; the point is that in general terms the circumstances of settlement varied from one main area of the Danelaw to another, so that its nature and effect may have varied accordingly.

14. For the movements of this army on the Continent, see below, pp. 250–67, notes 119–24, 197 and 202, and pp. 282–4, notes 8–9 and 19. The Vikings may have hoped initially to take advantage of the confused political situation in the Carolingian empire, following the death of Louis the Stammerer on 10 April 879: for details, see Halphen, *Charlemagne and the Carolingian Empire*, pp. 314–17.

15. An unusually large number of coin-hoards were deposited (and not recovered by their owners) during the later 860s and the 870s, particularly in the eastern and northern parts of England; the greater incidence of hoarding during these years, compared with earlier and later periods, must reflect in some way the traumas associated with the Viking invasions. For a list of the hoards in question, see Dolley, *Hiberno-Norse Coins*, pp. 21–3 and 48–9; see also Hill, *Atlas of Anglo-Saxon England*, p. 43.

16. Alfred may have embarked on the construction of his burghal system as early as 880 (see below, p. 340 note 6), but the work probably took place over many years: one fortification was 'half-made' when stormed in 892 (*ASC*, above, p. 114), and Asser writes of the project (in 893)

as if it were still a matter of current concern; see also above, pp. 43–4.

17. For further information, see Biddle, 'Towns', pp. 124–34; Hinton, *Alfred's Kingdom*, pp. 30–41; Radford, 'Pre-Conquest Boroughs'; Hill, *Atlas of Anglo-Saxon England*, pp. 85–6; and Campbell et al., *The Anglo-Saxons*, pp. 152–3.

18. Charles the Bald's plans for defence were announced in his capitularies issued at Pîtres in 862 and 864; the *Annals of St Bertin*, especially for 868 and 869, show how some of the measures were implemented. For further information, see Vercauteren, 'Comment s'est-on défendu, au ixᵉ siècle dans l'Empire franc contre les invasions normandes?'; Brooks, 'Development of Military Obligations', p. 81; Wallace-Hadrill, 'The Vikings in Francia'; Hodges, 'Trade and Market Origins', pp. 223–6; and Sawyer, *Kings and Vikings*, pp. 88–90.

19. From Alfred's preface to his translation of Gregory's *Pastoral Care*, above, p. 124.

20. See Asser, chapter 93, and Fulco's letter to Alfred (above, pp. 182–3).

21. See Alfred's preface to his translation of Gregory's *Pastoral Care*, above, p. 125, and Asser, chapters 24–5. Of course there is a possibility that Alfred was exaggerating the extent of decline in order to emphasize the need for reform; see Campbell et al., *The Anglo-Saxons*, pp. 142–4 and 147–8.

22. It is apparent from Asser's remarks that the Mercians came sometime before the recruitment of Grimbald, John and Asser in 885–6 (see following notes).

23. Grimbald was still at St Bertin's in September 885, but he was in England by 888 (see below, p. 332 notes 6 and 10); Asser himself implies that he was 'summoned' at about the same time as Grimbald, which would give further reason for placing Grimbald's arrival in about 886 (see next note).

24. The only fixed point in the chronology of Asser's relations with Alfred is the (alleged) fact that it was in Asser's presence on 11 November 887 that Alfred began to read Latin (chapters 87–9). It would appear that this event occurred after the first and second visits described in chapters 79 and 81. If we then assume that it occurred during the first return after the second visit, it would follow that the second visit (which lasted for eight months and ended soon after Christmas: chapter 81) lasted from May to December 886; that Asser's illness at Caerwent lasted from sometime during the opening months of 885 until a date just over a year later; and so that the first visit took place in early 885. If Alfred began to read on a subsequent return, the chronology would have to be pushed further back; if, on the other hand, he began to read during Asser's second visit (as suggested by Grierson, 'Grimbald of St Bertin's', pp. 546–7), then the first visit would have to be moved forward to early 886.

Whatever the case, it does seem to be significant that Asser places his account of Alfred's recruitment of learned helpers between his annals for 885 and 886.

25. Given the diverse linguistic backgrounds of the scholars assembled around Alfred (Frankish, Old Saxon, English and Welsh), it is difficult to imagine how the discussions were conducted in the early stages: presumably in Latin, since it would have been a while before the various foreigners were able to converse in English.

26. See Alfred's preface to his translation of Gregory's *Pastoral Care*, above, p. 125. A glance at Gneuss, 'A Preliminary List', shows that about fifty manuscripts survive which are thought to have been written on the Continent in the ninth century and to have found their way to England before 1100. These manuscripts deserve detailed examination in the context of Alfred's revival of learning, since some of them may well have been brought to England by his continental helpers. They include a manuscript of Prudentius (Cambridge, Corpus Christi College M S 223), which was apparently at St Bertin's in the second half of the ninth century and which may, therefore, have been brought to England by Grimbald himself (see Grierson, 'Grimbald of St Bertin's', p. 553; but cf. Ker, *Catalogue*, p. 92). It is difficult not to think of Grimbald again in connection with several other manuscripts written at (or in the vicinity of) Rheims and apparently imported into Anglo-Saxon England: Cambridge, Corpus Christi College M S 272 (Psalter, Litany and prayers); Cambridge, Pembroke College M S 308 (Hrabanus Maurus, *In Epistolas Pauli*); Hereford, Cathedral Library, O. iii. 2 (works by Jerome, Gennadius, Isidore, Augustine and Cassiodorus); B.L. Royal 15. A. xxxiii (Remigius, *In Martianum Capellam*); B.L. Royal 15. B. xix (Bede, *De Temporum Ratione*); and Utrecht, Universiteitsbibliotheek M S 32 (Psalter). Another manuscript, now Oxford, Bodleian Library, Rawlinson C. 697 (works by Aldhelm and Prudentius), was written in north-eastern Francia in the late ninth century, and contains the unique copy of an acrostic poem arguably by John the Old Saxon (below, p. 260 note 169). A ninth-century pocket gospel-book (Bern, Burgerbibliothek M S 671), written somewhere in the Celtic parts of Britain, was in England by the early tenth century and contains two acrostic poems on Alfred (below, p. 338).

27. For further discussion of these works, see Plummer, *Life and Times of Alfred*, pp. 139–96; Whitelock, 'Prose of Alfred's Reign', and idem, 'William of Malmesbury on the Works of King Alfred'; Wallace-Hadrill, *Early Germanic Kingship*, pp. 141–8; and Bately, *Literary Prose of King Alfred's Reign*.

28. For a general study, see Richards, *Consul of God*. Bede gives an account of Gregory's life in *HE* ii, 1 (including the famous story of his meeting with the English slave-boys in the market place at Rome).

29. The Latin text is printed in *PL* 77, cols. 13–128; it is translated by H. Davis, *St Gregory the Great: Pastoral Care*. For Alfred's translation, see below, p. 293.

30. For example, Bede urged Archbishop Egbert of York to read the *Pastoral Care* (*EHD* no. 170), and Alcuin, in a letter written in 796 to Archbishop Eanbald of York, referred to it as 'a mirror of a bishop's life and a cure for the wounds inflicted by the devil's wiles' (Allott, *Alcuin*, p. 11). Pope Honorius urged King Edwin of Northumbria to employ himself 'in frequent readings from the works of Gregory' (*HE* ii, 17).

31. The Latin text is edited by Bieler, *Boethii Philosophiae Consolatio*; it is translated by Watts, *Boethius: The Consolation of Philosophy*. For Alfred's translation, see below, p. 296. There are two recent studies of Boethius and his works: Chadwick, *Boethius*, and Gibson, *Boethius*.

32. These works are discussed by Brown, *Augustine of Hippo*, especially pp. 115–27. The Latin text of the *Soliloquia* is printed in *PL* 32, cols. 869–904; it is translated by Burleigh, *Augustine: Earlier Writings*, pp. 23–63. For Alfred's translation, see below, p. 299.

33. See Riché, 'Le Psautier'. For Alfred's translation, see below, p. 301.

34. The Latin text is edited by Moricca, *Gregorii Magni Dialogi Libri IV*; it is translated by Zimmerman, *Saint Gregory the Great: Dialogues*. Details of the Old English translation are given below, pp. 292–3.

35. The Latin text is edited by Zangemeister, *Pauli Orosii Historiarum adversum Paganos Libri VII*; it is translated by Deferrari, *Paulus Orosius: The Seven Books of History Against the Pagans*.

36. It is edited by Bately, *Old English Orosius*; this edition includes a full discussion of the translator's treatment of Orosius's text (pp. xciii–c), and an account of the other sources to which he appears to have had access (pp. lx–lxxii). The Old English text is translated into modern English, by Benjamin Thorpe, in Pauli, *Life of Alfred the Great*, pp. 238–528.

37. Bately, *Old English Orosius*, pp. 13–16; translated by Swanton, *Anglo-Saxon Prose*, pp. 33–5.

38. The Latin text is edited (with translation) by Colgrave and Mynors, *Bede's Ecclesiastical History*; there is a translation by Sherley-Price, *Bede: A History of the English Church and People*.

39. The Old English Bede is edited (with a translation into modern English) by Miller, *The Old English Version of Bede's Ecclesiastical History*. Its authorship is discussed by Whitelock, 'The Old English Bede'; the manner of its distribution is one of the questions raised by Whitelock, 'Chapter-Headings in the Old English Bede', especially pp. 277–8.

40. The *Leechbook* is preserved in a manuscript of mid-tenth-century date, now B.L. Royal 12. D. xvii, edited in facsimile by Wright, *Bald's*

Leechbook. The text is printed (with a translation) by Cockayne, *Leech-doms* II, pp. 2–299; some of the recipes are translated by Swanton, *Anglo-Saxon Prose*, pp. 180–85. The manuscript contains medical remedies arranged in three books; however, since the colophon assigning the work to Bald occurs at the end of Book II, and since the form of the remedies in Book III is entirely different from that of the remedies in Books I–II, it is apparent that Bald's *Leechbook* itself consists only of Books I and II.

41. See further below, p. 270 note 220.

42. See Kotzor, *Das altenglische Martyrologium*, pp. 363–7, 400–405, 421–5, and especially pp. 243 and 453–4. The sources used by the compiler have been the subject of a series of studies by Cross: see particularly, 'Apostles in the *Old English Martyrology*' and 'The Influence of Irish Texts and Traditions on the *Old English Martyrology*'.

43. On the choice of books translated, see Wallace-Hadrill, *Early Germanic Kingship*, p. 142, and Davis, 'Alfred the Great: Propaganda and Truth', p. 180; of course, one cannot exclude the possibility that other books were translated, of which no copies survive. A fragment of a 'ninth-century' Anglo-Saxon manuscript, described in an early twentieth-century sale catalogue, is said to have contained 'a portion of a constitutional treatise, apparently on the kingdom of the Franks', but the accuracy of the description cannot be guaranteed and the identity of the work cannot be established, since the fragment is now lost; see Collins, *Anglo-Saxon Vernacular Manuscripts in America*, pp. 66–7.

44. Above, p. 139.

45. Asser is said to have helped Alfred with the translation of Boethius: see below, p. 297. Werferth may similarly have had some assistance in translating Gregory's *Dialogues*: see below, p. 293 note 1.

46. On the relative chronology of the translations, see Whitelock, 'Prose of Alfred's Reign', especially pp. 73–7. In his preface to the *Pastoral Care*, Alfred clearly envisages that 'books' would be translated as part of the scheme, so the choice may have been made at the outset and work may have continued on several translations simultaneously.

47. On the date of the Orosius, see Bately, *Old English Orosius*, pp. lxxxvi–xciii.

48. For Alfred's experience with his own generation of officials, see Asser, chapter 106. Asser alludes to the school in chapters 75 and 76, and refers to the financial support it received from the king in chapter 102.

49. A passage in Alfred's translation of St Augustine's *Soliloquies* (above, p. 141) suggests that the king might on occasion convey instructions to his officials by means of a letter accompanied by a seal. For the possibility that officials with judicial responsibilities were expected to be able to refer to the written laws, see below, p. 275 notes 256 and 259. For an

important discussion of Alfred's interest in spreading literacy, see Wormald, 'Uses of Literacy', pp. 102–7.

50. The use made of written documents in later Anglo-Saxon government is discussed by Keynes, *Diplomas of King Æthelred*, pp. 134–53; but for a different view, see Clanchy, *From Memory to Written Record*, especially pp. 12–17. It should be emphasized in this connection that extensive use was made of written documents for administrative purposes in late-eighth- and early-ninth-century Francia: see Ganshof, 'Use of the Written Word in Charlemagne's Administration'.

51. See Asser, chapters 3, 49, 81, 93 and 102. Several passages in Alfred's law-code presuppose the existence of a number of religious houses during his reign: see, for example, § 2 (above, p. 165).

52. Alfred's preface to his translation of Gregory's *Pastoral Care*, above, p. 126.

53. Some of the tangible products of this 'renaissance' are discussed by Hinton, *Alfred's Kingdom*, pp. 47–57; the most famous, of course, is the Alfred Jewel, described above, Appendix II. For an account of a gilt metal reliquary, which may be another product of Alfred's reign, see Hinton et al., 'The Winchester Reliquary'.

54. See Dolley and Blunt, 'Coins of Ælfred the Great', pp. 78–82; North, *English Hammered Coinage*, pp. 72–3 and 92–3; and Lyon, 'Some Problems in Interpreting Anglo-Saxon Coinage', pp. 180–81.

55. For Æthelred and Æthelflæd, see Asser, chapter 75, and below, p. 256 note 145.

56. There may be a reference to such an oath in Alfred's law-code, § 1 (above, p. 164).

57. Alfred's regnal styles are discussed below, p. 227 note 1.

58. See Wormald, '*Lex Scripta* and *Verbum Regis*', especially p. 132.

59. The date of the compilation of the *Anglo-Saxon Chronicle* is discussed in more detail below, pp. 277–9.

60. See Wallace-Hadrill, 'The Franks and the English in the Ninth Century', especially pp. 209–12; Bullough, 'Educational Tradition in England', p. 461; and Parkes, 'The Parker Manuscript of the *Chronicle*', pp. 163–6.

61. Bately, *Old English Orosius*, pp. xc–xci; the Orosius translation may have been completed before the 'publication' of the *Chronicle*, but if both works proceeded from the circle of learned men around the king it is possible that the translator of the one had some prior knowledge of the other. It has been shown, however, that the two works were not produced by the same man: ibid., pp. lxxxiii–lxxxvi.

62. Wallace-Hadrill, 'The Franks and the English in the Ninth Century', especially pp. 210–11 and 213–14, shows effectively how an interest in the past was often cultivated by dynasties under threat, and he argues

that the *Chronicle* was a product of such circumstances and reflects the urgent political need of the West Saxon dynasty. Sawyer, *Age of the Vikings*, p. 20, and Davis, 'Alfred the Great: Propaganda and Truth', pp. 180–82, extend the argument and portray the *Chronicle* as a dynastic history designed to persuade the West Saxons to support their king. The objection to the latter view is essentially that it does not accord with the wider conception of history presented in the *Chronicle* and with Alfred's sense of responsibility towards his non-West Saxon subjects; see also Whitelock, 'Battle of Edington', pp. 6–9, and *EHD*, pp. 123–4. Davis returns to the matter in 'Alfred and Guthrum's Frontier', p. 805.

63. See further below, p. 230 note 12.

64. *S* 223 (*EHD* no. 99).

65. *S* 1628; for an important discussion of this document, see Dyson, 'Two Saxon Land Grants for Queenhithe'.

66. See Lees, *Alfred the Great*, p. 459, and Stanley, 'The Glorification of Alfred', pp. 103–4.

67. Above, p. 191. Æthelweard's generous reference to Alfred is especially interesting, since he was descended from Alfred's brother Æthelred, king of Wessex 865–71, and might therefore have had cause to resent the eclipse of his branch of the West Saxon royal family by Alfred and his descendants.

68. *EHD* no. 239(a).

69. This is inferred from the dates of the surviving manuscripts of the various translations; for details, see Ker, *Catalogue*.

70. *EHD* no. 239(i).

71. Chibnall, *Ecclesiastical History of Orderic Vitalis* II, p. 241.

72. The accounts of King Alfred given by these and other post-Conquest historians are assembled in Conybeare, *Alfred in the Chroniclers*; for further discussion, see Miles, *King Alfred in Literature*, pp. 17–38.

73. For a detailed account of the origins and development of this story, see Parker, *Early History of Oxford*, especially pp. 39–52.

74. Harmer, *Anglo-Saxon Writs*, no. 107.

75. See Arngart, *The Proverbs of Alfred*; Stone, *The Owl and the Nightingale*, pp. 189, 191 and 193; and Stanley, *The Owl and the Nightingale*, p. 34. In the middle of the twelfth century the poetess Marie de France produced a translation of a series of English fables which she attributed to King Alfred.

76. For Alfred's part in the myth of the 'Norman yoke', see C. Hill, *Puritanism and Revolution*, pp. 50–122, especially 95–9.

77. For further details, see Miles, *King Alfred in Literature*, pp. 48–115; Stanley, 'The Scholarly Recovery of the Significance of Anglo-Saxon Records', p. 227 note 13; and idem, 'The Glorification of Alfred'. The exploitation of Alfredian themes by artists in the eighteenth and nine-

teenth centuries is described and illustrated by Strong, *And When Did You Last See Your Father?*, pp. 114–18.

78. The statue, by Count Gleichen, was unveiled in 1877. It bears the inscription: 'Alfred found learning dead, and he restored it. Education neglected, and he revived it. The laws powerless, and he gave them force. The Church debased, and he raised it. The land ravaged by a fearful enemy, from which he delivered it. Alfred's name will live as long as mankind shall respect the past.' The millenary of Alfred's birth also spawned the remarkable 'Jubilee Edition' of *The Whole Works of King Alfred the Great*, edited in two volumes by J. A. Giles, but now to be used with caution.

79. The true date, 26 October 899, was established by Stevenson, 'The Date of King Alfred's Death', in 1898; but it took a while for his views to gain general acceptance.

80. The statue was the work of Hamo Thornycroft. The celebrations of 1901 are recounted in great detail by Bowker, *The King Alfred Millenary*; they included the launch of the most powerful armoured cruiser of her day, H.M.S. *King Alfred*.

81. Stevenson (*Asser*, p. lxx) gives examples of the name in Welsh records. Note, however, that *Asser filius Marchiud* is to be dated considerably later than Stevenson supposed: he flourished in the mid tenth century (see Davies, *The Llandaff Charters*, p. 121), and cannot therefore be identical with our Asser.

82. de Lagarde et al., *S. Hieronymi Presbyteri Opera*, pp. 61 (*Aser: beatitudo vel beatus*), 130, 139 and 159.

83. Lapidge, 'The Study of Latin Texts', pp. 111–13 and 135 note 72.

84. See below, p. 298 note 2.

85. See R. Page, 'Anglo-Saxon Episcopal Lists, pt III', pp. 9, 14, 20 and 24.

86. See O'Donovan, 'Episcopal Dates, pt II', p. 104. Asser is also the beneficiary of *S* 380 (below, p. 317 note 20).

87. See below, p. 294 note 1.

88. See below, p. 264 note 193; cf. O'Donovan, 'Episcopal Dates, pt I', p. 35, and idem, 'Episcopal Dates, pt II', p. 104. See also below, p. 240 note 55.

89. Morris, *Nennius*, pp. 49 and 90, from the *Annales Cambriae*. For the likelihood that the *Annales Cambriae* were being kept at St David's, see Hughes, 'The Welsh Latin Chronicles', and idem, 'The A-Text of the *Annales Cambriae*'.

90. *ASC* MSS 'A', 'B' s.a. 909; MSS 'C', 'D' s.a. 910. 'Florence' of Worcester states, clearly in error, that Asser, bishop of Sherborne, died in 883 and was succeeded by 'Suithelmus', who took the alms of King Alfred to St Thomas in India (B. Thorpe, *Chronicon* I, pp. 98–9). In fact it was Sigehelm who took Alfred's alms to India (below, p. 266 note 198); it seems that in the twelfth century some believed that this Sigehelm was

the same man as the Sigehelm who was bishop of Sherborne *c.* 925 (O'Donovan, 'Episcopal Dates, pt II', pp. 104–5), and 'Florence' evidently thought that he had succeeded Asser by the time he set out for India.

91. The arguments are summarized and discussed by Stevenson, *Asser*, pp. xcv–cxxv, and Whitelock, 'Recent Work', pp. cxl–clii.

92. Galbraith, 'Who Wrote Asser's Life of Alfred?', especially pp. 91–103.

93. Whitelock, *The Genuine Asser*.

94. For a study of Leofric's career, see Barlow et al., *Leofric of Exeter*, pp. 1–16.

95. The bone of contention is that 'Florence' of Worcester refers to Leofric as *Brytonicus* (B. Thorpe, *Chronicon* I, p. 199); however, as Barlow points out, this may mean no more than that Leofric was born in a Welsh-speaking area and need not imply that he was a Welsh-speaker (*Leofric of Exeter*, pp. 2–3). The name Leofric is unquestionably English.

96. The books present in Leofric's library are listed in a document which records the bishop's bequests to the church at Exeter: see Chambers et al., *Exeter Book*, pp. 10–32; Robertson, *Charters*, pp. 226–31; and Barlow et al., *Leofric of Exeter*, pp. 32–42. Sedulius's *Carmen Paschale* and Gregory's *Regula Pastoralis* are, in fact, the only two books cited by Asser of which copies are actually known to have been present in Leofric's library; cf. Galbraith, 'Who Wrote Asser's Life of Alfred?', pp. 100–101. Several manuscripts containing one or other of these works are known to have been written or owned in Anglo-Saxon England: see Gneuss, 'A Preliminary List', passim.

97. One of the books in Leofric's library is described as *liber Oserii* ('the book of Oserius'), and it has been suggested that this might be an error for *liber Aserii*, that is, Asser's *Life of King Alfred*. It is far more likely, however, that *liber Oserii* is a garbled reference to a work by Isidore of Seville: see Chambers et al., *Exeter Book*, p. 29 note 111.

98. See Lloyd, *History of Wales* I, p. 226 note 159.

99. L. Thorpe, *Gerald of Wales: The Journey through Wales*, p. 162.

100. The charter is printed by Evans and Rhys, *Book of Llan Dâv*, pp. 236–7; see also Davies, *The Llandaff Charters*, pp. 63 and 123–4. Hywel was king of Glywysing, and the bishop in question was Cyfeilliog, who is said elsewhere to have been consecrated by Æthelred, archbishop of Canterbury (870–88), and who was active in south-east Wales in the late ninth and early tenth centuries. It may seem unlikely that Asser of St David's would have attested such a charter, but one should bear in mind that he was apparently in Caerwent in 885 (above, note 24).

101. In addition to his stays at Dean (chapter 79) and *Leonaford* (chapter 81), Asser had been to the battle-site at Ashdown (chapter 39), Countisbury (chapter 54) and Athelney (chapter 94); his general knowledge of English

topography is revealed on many occasions (see chapters 1, 4, 5, 30, 35, 39, 42, 49, 52, 57, 66 and 92); he knew that there was a monastery on Sheppey (chapter 3), and that Chippenham, Reading and Wedmore were royal estates (chapters 9, 35, 52, 56). He alludes to those who had given him information (chapters 12, 15, 37, 97), and he says he had often seen the king's mother-in-law (chapter 29). In addition to his personal experience of King Alfred's love of learning (chapters 24–5, 88–9), Asser discussed recent history with the king (chapter 13), frequently saw him hunting (chapter 22) and read his correspondence (chapter 91).

102. For further details, see Lindsay, *Early Welsh Script*.

103. See below, p. 258 note 159.

104. For example, the words *consertoque . . . proelio* in chapter 67 are clearly indebted to *Aeneid* II, 397–8 (*multaque per caecam congressi proelia noctem/conserimus*); see also below, p. 272 note 234. It is worth mentioning that King Alfred's translation of Boethius – in which Asser reportedly collaborated – shows familiarity with Virgil's *Aeneid* and *Georgics* (see Wittig, 'King Alfred's *Boethius* and its Latin Sources').

105. See Lapidge and Herren, *Aldhelm: The Prose Works*, pp. 1–3, and below, p. 258 note 161 and p. 269 notes 210, 213 and 214.

106. See below, p. 229 note 6 and p. 232 note 20.

107. See below, p. 231 note 16.

108. See below, p. 254 note 139.

109. See below, p. 265 note 195.

110. For examples of sprawling sentences, see chapters 76 (lines 1–12 and 50–70 in Stevenson, *Asser*, pp. 59–62) and 93; for examples of confusing exposition, see chapters 74 (and below, p. 255 note 143) and 97. Several examples of obscure syntax are discussed in the notes to Asser's *Life*. See also Stevenson, *Asser*, pp. lxxxix–xci. Some of the infelicities in Asser's Latin can doubtless be attributed to the incomplete state of the work or to faulty transmission of the text, but the overall impression remains of an author struggling with his medium.

111. Stevenson (*Asser*, pp. xci–xciii) described this aspect of Asser's style as 'Hisperic'. Since Stevenson's time, however, much work has been done on the style of Insular Latin authors, and it is no longer appropriate to describe Asser's style as 'Hisperic' or to imply any connection between him and the *Hisperica Famina*; see Lapidge, 'The Hermeneutic Style'.

112. Stevenson, *Asser*, pp. xciii–xciv. Stevenson included the word *curtus*, '(royal) court', in his list, but it should be noticed that in Frankish sources the word is invariably feminine (*curtis*), whereas Asser appears to be unique in taking the word as a masculine noun (chapters 22, 75, 81, 100). Stevenson's list could be extended to include *singularis* for 'boar' (cf. modern French *sanglier*), used in lieu of Classical Latin *aper* (chapter

68), and *Signe* for the river Seine, in lieu of Classical Latin *Sequana* (chapter 82).

113. See above, note 25. At the time he was writing his *Life of King Alfred* in 893, Asser's mastery of English was far from complete: note the list of his errors in understanding the *Anglo-Saxon Chronicle* given by Stevenson, *Asser*, pp. lxxvii–lxxviii.

114. Attention is drawn to Asser's knowledge of Frankish affairs in the notes to chapters 68, 70, 82, 84 and 85. See also chapter 65 (cf. *ASC* 883).

115. For discussion of Asser's indebtedness to Einhard, see Schütt, 'Literary Form'. The possibility has also been raised that Asser was influenced by Thegan's *Vita Hludowici Imperatoris* and by the Astronomer's *Vita Hludowici Imperatoris* (both biographies of Louis the Pious): see Stevenson, *Asser*, pp. lxxx–lxxxii; Wallace-Hadrill, 'The Franks and the English in the Ninth Century', p. 212; and Bullough, 'Educational Tradition in England', pp. 455 note 2 and 458 note 11. It has not, however, been shown conclusively that Asser knew either of these works.

116. It could be argued, of course, that Asser's version of the *Chronicle* did not extend beyond 887; but see below, pp. 278–9.

117. For one possible line of speculation, see below, p. 287 note 9.

118. See Stevenson, *Asser*, p. cxxxi, and Schütt, 'Literary Form', p. 210; see also above, note 110, and below, p. 242 note 72. Stevenson commented on the curious mixture of present and imperfect tenses in references to Alfred, and attributed the confusion to alterations made inconsistently by the scribe of the Cotton manuscript (*Asser*, pp. xlix–l); cf. Galbraith, 'Who Wrote Asser's Life of Alfred?', pp. 110–17. Confusion of tenses is not, however, a serious mistake, and it only adds to the evidence that the received text is not in a finished state. Kirby has argued that the *Life* as we have it is an 'imperfect conflation of several separate shorter treatises on the king, all written originally at different times' ('Asser and his Life of King Alfred', p. 13); he proceeds to identify three such treatises, arguing that the received text of the *Life* is a conflation of these three treatises with some further material, including a translation of the *Chronicle* up to 887. The argument is certainly ingenious, but it does not seem that such a complicated theory is really necessary. The somewhat muddled nature of the *Life* is again most easily explained on the assumption that what we have is a draft as opposed to a polished work.

119. For other examples of Asser's use of Welsh names, see below, p. 250 note 115.

120. See Lapidge, 'Byrhtferth of Ramsey and the Early Sections of the *Historia Regum*', p. 121, and Stevenson, *Asser*, pp. lviii–lix.

121. See Campbell, *Encomium Emmae*, pp. xxxv–xxxvii.

122. Stevenson, *Asser*, pp. lv–lvii.

123. See above, p. 199.

124. Stevenson, *Asser*, pp. lvii–lviii; see also below, p. 243–53, notes 77, 90–91 and 135. Hart, 'The East Anglian Chronicle', pp. 261–4, argues that the chronicler did use the Cotton manuscript.

125. Translated from Brewer, *Giraldus Cambrensis Opera* III, p. 422.

ASSER'S LIFE OF KING ALFRED (pp. 67–110)

The only manuscript of Asser's *Life of King Alfred* which survived into modern times was that designated Otho A.xii in the library of Sir Robert Cotton (1571–1631); but all that is now known of it has to be reconstructed from accounts given by those who saw the manuscript before its destruction by fire on 23 October 1731.

The manuscript was written at an unidentified centre, about the year 1000 (see further below). Its history during the medieval period cannot be traced, but there is some evidence that it was used by a Ramsey chronicler in the early eleventh century and by a Worcester chronicler in the early twelfth century (see above, pp. 56–8). The manuscript was in the possession of the antiquary John Leland in the 1540s, and it is likely that he had acquired it from the library of a religious house at the time of the Dissolution of the Monasteries. Some time after Leland's death in 1552 it passed into the hands of Matthew Parker, Master of Corpus Christi College, Cambridge (1544–53), and Archbishop of Canterbury (1559–75), and while in his possession the manuscript was annotated extensively and served as the basis of the first printed edition published in 1574. Parker bequeathed the greater part of his library to Corpus Christi College, but the Asser manuscript was for some reason not included in the gift, and by 1600 it was to be found in the library of Lord Lumley. One scholar who saw the manuscript there described it as 'written by two diverse scribes at the least', and though the second was considered later than the first, both were apparently pre-Conquest (Stevenson, *Asser*, p. xxxviii note 1); another scholar who saw it at the same time stated that it was filled out with appended pieces of paper in modern handwriting, presumably a reference to some of Parker's interpolations (ibid., p. xxxix note 1). It is apparent that at this stage the manuscript was made up of fifty-six folios: the text of Asser's *Life* occupied fols. 1–55r, two charms in Latin and Old English were entered on fol. 55v, and these items were bound up with some material relating to Edward I (Scragg, *Battle of Maldon*, p. 2). By 1621 the

manuscript had passed into the hands of Sir Robert Cotton, and
while in his possession it was seen and used by Archbishop Ussher
(Stevenson, *Asser*, p. xli): he was evidently of the opinion that it was
written in the Anglo-Saxon period, and he too referred to the inserted
pieces of paper, stating that they contained material derived from
annals wrongly attributed to Asser (the *Annals of St Neots*). Cotton
was in the habit of binding together manuscripts, or parts of manuscripts, that originally had no connection with each other, and it was
presumably he who bound up a number of items (mainly hagiogra-
phical, but including the fragment of the Old English poem on the
Battle of Maldon) with the copy of Asser; a catalogue of the Cotton
library published in 1696 describes the manuscript in its augmented
form, and other evidence shows that it was then made up of 155
folios (Scragg, *Battle of Maldon*, pp. 1–4).

The most detailed and valuable information on the Cotton manuscript of Asser derives from a letter written by the palaeographer
Humphrey Wanley in 1721, and from the edition of the *Life* published
by Francis Wise in 1722. Wanley indicates, in response to queries
from Wise, that the manuscript 'is not written by one hand, but by
several, and much about the same time, according to the custom of
writing books of old'; he states that the first hand was 'the best and
stanchest', and likens it to that of an original charter of King Æthelred
the Unready, dated 1001. (Wanley's letter is printed by Sisam, *Studies
in the History of Old English Literature*, p. 148 note 3.) Wise cites
Wanley's opinions in his edition of the *Life*, and provides some further
information on the manuscript, supplied to him by the antiquary
James Hill: Hill collated the manuscript against a copy of Camden's
printed text of 1602 and reported its readings to Wise, and it is
evidently on Hill's authority that Wise states that a portion of the text
from near the beginning of chapter 88 to the end of chapter 98 was
written by a 'more recent hand', though it remains uncertain whether
the scribe (or scribes) who completed the text was (or included) the
first, whose work was described and dated by Wanley. Hill also
supplied a facsimile of the opening page of the manuscript, published
in Wise's edition (opposite p. 137) and reproduced above, p. 66.
This reveals that Asser's dedication was written in Rustic capitals,
that the text itself began with a large initial followed by a line of
slightly smaller inscriptional capitals, that the second line of the text
was again in Rustic capitals, and that the hand thereafter was Caroline

minuscule (used in England for Latin texts from the middle of the tenth century onwards). It is significant that a very similar lay-out, employing the same range of scripts, is often found in manuscripts written in the late tenth and first half of the eleventh centuries (see Wormald, 'Anglo-Saxon Initials', p. 64, and Temple, *Anglo-Saxon Manuscripts*, plates 71–5 and 290); the quality of the facsimile is not adequate for the purposes of dating the script, but the layout represented is thus seen to be entirely compatible with Wanley's dating of the manuscript about the year 1000.

In 1712 the Cotton library was removed from Cotton House (near Old Palace Yard, Westminster) to Essex House in the Strand, and in 1730 it was moved again to Ashburnham House (Little Dean's Yard, Westminster). A fire broke out there on the morning of Saturday, 23 October 1731, and of the 958 volumes in the library 114 were reported destroyed and ninety-eight damaged. The Cotton manuscript of Asser's *Life of King Alfred* was among those described as 'lost, burnt, or intirely spoiled'. The surviving books were moved to their present location in the British Museum upon its foundation in 1753, and now form part of the British Library.

The text of Asser's *Life* is known to this day in part from the extensive extracts incorporated in certain medieval chronicles, and in part from the transcripts and editions based on the Cotton manuscript before its destruction by fire. The most important of the transcripts occurs in Cambridge, Corpus Christi College MS 100, made for Parker's use in the third quarter of the sixteenth century; it is of particular value because it reproduces the text of Asser as it stood in the Cotton manuscript before Parker's annotations were added and before the passages from other sources had been inserted. Another useful transcript, B.L. Cotton Otho A.xii*, represents the state of the Cotton manuscript at a slightly later stage, since it incorporates some of the Parkerian interpolations as if they formed part of the text itself. Two further transcripts, Cambridge, University Library Add. 3825, and Cambridge, Trinity College MS O. 7. 25, are more closely related to Parker's edition of 1574: the former seems to be a fair copy of the text derived either directly from this edition or from something immediately ancestral to it (a set of proofs, or a transcript used by the printer); the latter is no more than a rough copy of Parker's edition, made towards the end of the seventeenth century. For all these transcripts, see Stevenson, *Asser*, pp. li–lv.

The first published edition of Asser's *Life* was Matthew Parker's, bearing the title *Ælfredi Regis Res Gestæ* and printed by John Day at London in 1574. The text incorporates several passages derived by Parker from other sources, notably from the *Annals of St Neots* (which he believed to be the work of Asser himself); the most famous of these interpolations is undoubtedly the story of Alfred and the Cakes (see Appendix I). Parker's text was reprinted by William Camden, *Anglica, Normannica, Hibernica, Cambrica, a veteribus Scripta* (Frankfurt, 1602; 2nd edn, 1603), pp. 1–22, with the notorious addition of a passage describing King Alfred's alleged foundation of Oxford University. The first attempt at a scholarly edition was Francis Wise, *Annales Rerum Gestarum Ælfredi Magni, auctore Asserio Menevensi* (Oxford, 1722). Wise did his best to distinguish between the genuine text and the later additions admitted by Parker and Camden, and he also made use of the extracts from Asser incorporated in the chronicle attributed to Florence of Worcester; but he was dependent for his knowledge of readings in the Cotton manuscript and the Corpus transcript on information supplied to him by friends, and it is apparent that the information he received was often incorrect and incomplete. The next edition was that of Henry Petrie, *Monumenta Historica Britannica* (London, 1848), pp. 467–98, based on Wise but collated more carefully with both the Corpus and the Otho transcripts, and also with 'Florence' of Worcester and the *Annals of St Neots*; Petrie marked the passages that were not present in the Cotton manuscript by enclosing them in square brackets, and thus gave a reasonably clear impression of Asser's genuine text. Petrie's edition was, however, superseded by W. H. Stevenson, *Asser's Life of King Alfred* (Oxford, 1904). Stevenson effectively reconstructed the text from all the available witnesses, distinguishing those parts which were used by 'Florence' of Worcester (printed in Roman type) from the rest (printed in italics), printing the interpolations in small italics and providing a detailed apparatus of variant readings. His edition represents a remarkable editorial achievement, and laid firm foundations for the modern study of Asser's text.

Several translations of Asser's *Life of King Alfred* have been published. Four are based on Petrie's edition: J. A. Giles, *Six Old English Chronicles* (London, 1848); J. Stevenson, *Church Historians of England* II, part 2 (London, 1854); Edward Conybeare, *Alfred in the Chroniclers* (London, 1900); and L. C. Jane, *Asser's Life of King Alfred*

(London, 1908). Stevenson's edition formed the basis of the complete translation by Albert S. Cook, *Asser's Life of King Alfred* (Boston, 1906), and of the extracts included by Dorothy Whitelock in *English Historical Documents* c. *500–1042* (London, 1955); our own translation is also based on Stevenson's edition.

1. Asser here uses a regnal style (*Angul-Saxonum rex*) that appears to have become current during the 880s, probably in connection with the submission to Alfred in 886 of 'all the English people that were not under subjection to the Danes' (*ASC* s.a. 886; cf. Asser, chapter 83, and see also *ASC* s.a. 900, above, p. 120); the style presumably corresponds to the description of Alfred in the dedication as 'ruler of all the Christians of the island of Britain, king of the Angles and Saxons', and it is used by Asser throughout the *Life* (chapters 1, 13, 21, 64, 67, 71, 73, 83, 87). Before Alfred's reign the West Saxon kings were generally styled (if anything) *rex Saxonum, rex Westsaxonum* or *rex Occidentalium Saxonum* in their charters (see also note 5 below), though the political developments of the ninth century find due reflection in styles which also cover the men of Kent and occasionally other 'southern peoples' as well; Egbert (802–39) and Æthelwulf (839–58) are styled *rex Saxon(iorum)* on some of their coins, and one type of Æthelwulf has the fuller style *rex Occidentalium Saxoniorum*; in the *Anglo-Saxon Chronicle*, before the tenth century, the standard terminology is 'king(dom) of the West Saxons'. Whenever Asser refers to Alfred's predecessors he uses the styles *Occidentalium Saxonum rex* (for Ine, chapter 1; for Beorhtric, chapter 14; for Æthelwulf, chapters 7, 9, 68; for Æthelred, chapter 30) or *Saxonum rex* (for Æthelwulf, chapter 5), and in so doing he thus follows correct usage. There is clear evidence that these styles were still in use during Alfred's reign: in *S* 321, a charter dated 880, the king (named as Æthelwulf, in apparent error for Alfred) is styled *rex Saxonum*, and the same style is found in *S* 345 dated 882, in *S* 348 dated 892 (subscription only), and in *S* 350 dated 898 (superscription and subscription); the king is often styled *rex Sax(onum)* on his coins, at whatever period they were issued; he is 'king of the West Saxons' in his will, in his law-code and, on one occasion, in his translation of Boethius, though elsewhere in his literary works he is no more than 'king'. But a group of three charters shows that regnal styles of the type used by Asser in 893, implying an aspiration to wider political authority, were used in the late 880s and early 890s: in *S* 346 (from Worcester, dated 889) Alfred is styled *rex Anglorum et Saxonum*; in *S* 347 (from Glastonbury, dated 891) he is styled *Anglorum Saxonum rex*; and in *S* 348 (from Wilton, dated 892: translated above, p. 179) he is styled *Angol Saxonum rex*. In three other charters, unfortunately undated, Alfred is styled variously *Angulsaxonum rex* (*S* 354, from the Old Minster Winchester), *Anglorum Saxonum rex* (*S*

355, from Abingdon), and *Angol Saxonum rex* (*S* 356, from Malmesbury); it seems reasonable to suppose that *S* 354–6 belong to roughly the same period as *S* 346–8. The fact that the six charters in which the new styles occur were preserved in the archives of six different religious foundations guarantees that the usage is genuinely Alfredian, whatever the status of the texts overall in their received form; for a discussion of *S* 347–8 and 356 in particular, see Whitelock, 'Some Charters in the Name of King Alfred'. An aspiration to authority over 'Angles' (as opposed to 'Saxons' and other 'southern peoples') may be expressed in the unique example of the 'Two Emperors' coin type, on which Alfred is accorded the style *rex Anglo*[.], probably for *rex Anglorum* (but just conceivably for *rex Anglorum Saxonum*, or the like): while there can be no certainty about the date of a coin type known only from a solitary specimen, numismatists appear to favour the period *c.* 880–85; its significance must be linked to the fact that a coin of a similar type is known for Ceolwulf II of Mercia (styled simply *rex*), but just what this does signify is uncertain. It has to be admitted that there need be nothing special about the style *rex Anglorum* beyond its denotation of an English king: it was a common form of address used for Anglo-Saxon kings by their continental correspondents, and so it is that Alfred himself is addressed as *rex Anglorum* in a letter from Fulco, archbishop of Rheims, written in about 886 (translated above, p. 182). But it is its occurrence on a coin that is truly remarkable at this time, and one might suggest that the type signifies Alfred's claim to be regarded as successor to Ceolwulf (874–9) as ruler of English Mercia: a charter from the Worcester archives (*S* 218) reveals that Ealdorman Æthelred regarded Alfred as his overlord already by 883.

2. The statement that Alfred was born at Wantage rests on Asser's authority. The upper Thames valley (an area long disputed between Wessex and Mercia) was seemingly under Mercian control in the early 840s (see *EHD* no. 87), but it presumably fell under West Saxon control in the same decade, if Wantage was a royal estate when Alfred was born; Alfred bequeathed land at Wantage to his wife Ealhswith (above, p. 177). The statement that Alfred was born in 849 also rests on Asser's authority; in the earliest extant versions of the West Saxon Regnal Table (see Whitelock et al., *Anglo-Saxon Chronicle*, p. 4) Alfred is said to have been twenty-three years old on his accession (soon after Easter 871), implying that he was born in 847 (if he was born sometime after Easter) or in 848 (if he was born before Easter).

3. Asser's etymology seems to be correct: see Gelling, *Place-Names of Berkshire* I, pp. 1–2, and III, p. 840.

4. This genealogy is to be understood largely as a product of royal ideology: it traces Alfred's ancestry through the heroes of the West Saxon past to the pagan god Woden and beyond, and is given Christian respectability

by the claim of ultimate descent from Adam himself. It is based on the genealogy of Æthelwulf in *ASC* s.a. 855, but Asser seems either to have used a version that was significantly different from the versions in the manuscripts of the *Chronicle* that have survived, or to have made his own modifications to the version in front of him in the light of other information. Thus, for example, he 'omits' Esla between Elesa and Gewis, and Wig, Freawine and Frithugar between Gewis and Brand, in these respects differing from the *Chronicle* (though M S 'D' omits Esla); but it is interesting to find that the same names do not occur in other versions of the West Saxon royal genealogy preserved outside the context of the *Chronicle*. (For more detailed discussion of this complex matter, see Sisam, 'Anglo-Saxon Royal Genealogies', especially pp. 301–2, and for the other versions of the West Saxon genealogy, see Dumville, 'Anglian Collection', pp. 34 and 37.) Towards the end of the genealogy, Asser's 'Seth', son of Noah, corresponds to the Sem of Luke iii, 36–8 (cf. Genesis v, 32) and to the Sceaf of *ASC* MSS 'B', 'C' and 'D'; see further Magoun, 'King Æthelwulf's Biblical Ancestors'.

5. Bede, writing in 731, said of the West Saxons that 'in early days they were called the Gewisse' (*HE* iii, 7), and indeed he uses the term several times in the *Ecclesiastical History*; the kings of Wessex are occasionally styled *rex Gewisorum* in charters of the eighth century and later (for example *S* 256, 262), probably as a form of antiquarian affectation, but it is interesting to find the usage suppressed in the Old English translation of Bede's *Ecclesiastical History*, which was prepared during Alfred's reign. On the other hand, Asser's statement that the Welsh (*Britones*) call the West Saxons the Gewisse is well supported by references in Welsh writings: see Williams, *Armes Prydein*, pp. xv–xvi.

6. The Geta mentioned in this poem was a character in Roman comedy, a Greek slave who appears in Terence's *Adelphoe* and *Phormio*. Needless to say, perhaps, the character in Roman comedy has nothing whatsoever to do with the Geat of the genealogy. The source for Asser's statement that Geat was worshipped by the pagans as a god appears to have been the ninth-century *Historia Brittonum*, chapter 31 (Morris, *Nennius*, p. 67).

7. The office of butler (*pincerna*) was a distinguished one, and its holders were likely to have been important figures in the royal court and household: for occurrences of the term in Anglo-Saxon charters and glossaries, see Keynes, *Diplomas of King Æthelred*, pp. 158–61 and p. 150 note 234. Nothing more is known of Oslac, though he may be the Oslac who attests a charter of King Æthelberht in 858 (*S* 328).

8. By describing Oslac as a Goth Asser succumbs to the mistaken notion that the Goths were ethnically the same as the Jutes; the confusion was perhaps suggested by the designation of Jutland as 'Gotland', as in the account of Ohthere's voyage incorporated in the Old English translation of Orosius's

Historiae adversus Paganos (see Bately, *Old English Orosius*, pp. 16 and 195). Asser is probably trying to convey the information that Oslac was of ultimately Danish extraction.

9. *Wihtgarabyrig* (the form in *ASC* s.a. 530; the text of Asser has *Guuihtgaraburhg*) has been identified in the past as Carisbrooke, but strong objections to this were raised by Stevenson, *Asser*, pp. 172–5; the place must remain unidentified.

10. The information in the latter part of this chapter is a rather garbled version of *ASC* s.a. 530 ('In this year Cerdic and Cynric captured the Isle of Wight and killed a few men in *Wihtgarabyrig*') and 534 ('In this year Cerdic died; and his son Cynric ruled for twenty-seven years. And they gave the Isle of Wight to their two kinsmen, Stuf and Wihtgar'). In describing Cynric as Cerdic's son Asser thus follows the *Chronicle*, but contradicts the genealogy provided in chapter 1 which makes Cynric son of Creoda and grandson of Cerdic: it seems likely from other considerations that Creoda was inserted in the West Saxon royal genealogy at a relatively late stage, as part of a politically convenient dynastic fiction, and that the annals themselves remained untouched in the process.

From this point until the end of chapter 86 Asser follows the annals in the *Anglo-Saxon Chronicle* for the years 851–87, though he inserts into this framework a fair amount of information on his own authority, especially in chapters 12–17, 22–5, 29, 37–9 and 73–81; from chapter 87 to the end the information is all original, and if Asser once intended to return to the *Chronicle* for the events of 888–92 he apparently changed his mind, or left his work in this respect incomplete (see above, p. 56).

11. Asser's indications of Alfred's age in a given year follow from the declaration in chapter 1 that the king was born in 849, making that the first, and 851 the third, year of his life. However, errors in the calculation of the king's age soon appear: in chapter 7, for 853, Alfred is said to be in his eleventh year, which is quite eccentric; in chapter 32, for 870, 'twenty-first' is repeated from chapter 31, for 869, introducing an error of one year; in chapter 49, for 876, 'twenty-sixth' is repeated, turning the cumulative error into one of two years; owing to omission of the annal for 877 (below, note 94), the error becomes one of three years in chapter 52, for 878; in chapter 66 the author intended to describe events which occurred in 884, in the king's 'thirty-third' (for 'thirty-sixth') year, but either he or his copyist accidentally followed the chronological information with the events of 885 (so that in this case 'thirty-third' has to be emended to 'thirty-seventh'); this last error is not of the cumulative type, so that the remaining statements of Alfred's age, in chapters 82 and 84, are only three years out. Such errors are purely mechanical, and they are silently corrected in this translation.

12. The word here translated 'Vikings' is *pagani*, literally 'pagans'. In the

Anglo-Saxon Chronicle the invaders are described as 'the heathens' in the annals 851–66, as 'the raiding army' (*here*) or 'the Danes' in the annals 867–96, and as 'the Vikings' in the annals 879 and 885; some of these distinctions are necessarily lost in our translation. Asser may have had good reason for preferring the first usage of the chronicler(s): he regularly refers to the English forces as 'Christians' (a usage found in the *Chronicle* only in the annals for 893 and 896), and his juxtaposition of 'pagans' and 'Christians' creates an impression of religious warfare which was probably intentional (see above, p. 42); see also Page, 'The Audience of *Beowulf* and the Vikings', pp. 118–19. We have chosen, nevertheless, to translate *pagani* as 'Vikings' throughout, in the belief that it identifies them more clearly.

13. Possibly Wigborough, near South Petherton, Somerset, as Stevenson (*Asser*, pp. 175–6) suggests; but as Whitelock et al., *Anglo-Saxon Chronicle*, p. 42 note 14, point out, 'the name Wicga is so common in Devon names that a "Wicga's hill" may well once have existed there'.

14. In *ASC* MSS 'B', 'C', 'D' and 'E', Thanet, not Sheppey, is named as the wintering place; in *ASC* s.a. 855 it is stated that the Vikings stayed 'for the first time' on Sheppey, so it looks as though Asser is here mistaken (cf. Asser, chapter 10). *ASC* MS 'A' does not name the wintering place in 851, and it may be that the manuscript used by Asser was similarly defective at this point.

15. The reference is to Minster in Sheppey, a nunnery founded by St Seaxburh, daughter of Anna, king of East Anglia (*c.* 636–54), and wife of Eorcenberht, king of Kent (640–64); she later became abbess of Ely. Asser seems to imply that the nunnery was still active at the time of writing (893), though the island is known to have been visited by Vikings in 835 and 855–6; they were there again in 1016, and the island was ravaged by the forces of Godwine and Harold in 1052. The nunnery was allegedly re-occupied in the late eleventh century.

16. The words 'and London' were omitted in the manuscript of Asser, but the omission was evidently accidental, since the passage that follows is clearly descriptive of London. The statement that London belongs to Essex is probably derived from Bede (*HE* ii, 3, which refers to the early seventh century). London subsequently became a Mercian town; see also chapter 83.

17. This has been identified as Ockley in Surrey, being the only suitable name in that county; but early spellings of Ockley suggest the meaning 'Occa's clearing', and are incompatible with *Aclea* (which, as Asser states, means 'oak wood' or 'glade where oaks grow', and which should emerge as Oakley: there are many examples throughout England, though none survives in Surrey).

18. Æthelstan was the son of King Æthelwulf, and is styled 'king' in the

Chronicle: he had been made king of Kent, Essex, Surrey and Sussex in 839, and he attests his father's charters as king in the 840s (for example *S* 293 and 296); he is not heard of again after 851.

19. It is difficult to believe the chronicler's claim, here repeated by Asser, that Alfred was anointed king so early, and a letter written by Pope Leo IV (847–55) to King Æthelwulf describes more precisely what happened on this occasion: 'We have now graciously received your son Alfred, whom you were anxious to send at this time to the threshold of the Holy Apostles, and we have decorated him, as a spiritual son, with the dignity of the belt [*or* sword] and the vestments of the consulate, as is customary with Roman consuls, because he gave himself into our hands' (*EHD* no. 219; but for the suggestion that this letter is an eleventh-century forgery, contrived by Pope Gregory VII in his attempt to establish a feudal relationship with William the Conqueror, see Nelson, 'Problem of King Alfred's Royal Anointing'). In the belief that only someone outside the king's circle would have misunderstood the nature of the ceremony, or conversely, that only someone within the king's circle would have misrepresented it, this claim that Alfred was anointed king in 853 is regularly cited in the discussion about the authorship of the *Anglo-Saxon Chronicle*; but whether the error is deliberate or not, the chronicler probably intended merely to convey that Alfred had been marked out for kingship when still a young boy, in much the same way as heavenly signs attended the birth of those who were to become saints (and therefore the claim signifies no more than that this annal in its received form was written while Alfred was king).

20. Asser's source for the Welsh name of Thanet was probably the ninth-century *Historia Brittonum*, chapter 31 (see Morris, *Nennius*, p. 67).

21. This statement, that the marriage took place at Chippenham (in Wiltshire), rests on Asser's authority. Chippenham was indeed a royal estate during Alfred's reign: see Alfred's will (above, p. 177), and below, p. 321 note 65. The daughter in question was called Æthelswith: see *ASC* s.a. 888 (above, p. 113), and below, p. 281 note 3. King Burgred is known to have corresponded with Pope John VIII: see *EHD* no. 220.

22. See above, note 14, and Asser, chapter 3.

23. Asser here seems to imply something rather different from the *Anglo-Saxon Chronicle*. The chronicler states that the king 'booked' (conveyed by charter) the tenth part of his land throughout all his kingdom, in praise of God and for his own eternal salvation, which suggests that the king granted this proportion of his own land either directly to religious foundations, or to laymen who could thereby enjoy the land free from the customary obligations (for example, the provision of sustenance for the king and his officials, and the payment of various taxes, but with the exception of the duties associated with national defence) and who would

at the same time be enabled to convey the land themselves to the Church. Asser, on the other hand, in stating that the king freed a tenth part of the whole kingdom from these obligations, implies that he intended an overall reduction in the assessment of land for public dues, whereby every landowner would benefit from, as it were, a ten per cent cut in taxes. It is presumably the chronicler whose word should be accorded greater authority. Various charters have survived which purport to have been issued in connection with Æthelwulf's 'decimation' or 'tithing', and they should throw further light on its operation. The so-called 'First Decimation' charters (*S* 294, 314, 322) refer to an occasion at Winchester on 5 November 844 when the king announced a general reduction – by a tenth – in the assessment of land, in return for a specified programme of weekly prayer to be conducted by the clergy on behalf of the king and his ealdormen; the so-called 'Second Decimation' charters (*S* 302–5, 307–8) refer to an occasion at Wilton on Easter Day 854 when the king conveyed a tenth part of his lands throughout the kingdom to religious foundations, allowing the laymen actually living on the lands in question to hold them free from the public dues, again in return for prayers. The charters in each of these groups are cast in essentially the same terms, but they are replete with various textual difficulties, and many of the constituent formulae belong to the tenth and early eleventh centuries; moreover *S* 308, the only one of them extant in its 'original' form, is written in an obviously imitative hand apparently of the eleventh century. It seems most likely that these Decimation charters derive ultimately from one forged in the eleventh century in an attempt to recover privileges that had been conceded by Æthelwulf but that had been lost in the turmoil of succeeding generations; why the forged documents were dated 844 and 854 when the *Chronicle* (and Asser) place the Decimation in 855 is uncertain, but the fact that they were so dated does not exactly encourage one's belief in their authenticity. There is, however, one charter associated with Æthelwulf's Decimation which does satisfy the available tests of authenticity: *S* 315 (*EHD* no. 89), dated 855, is a grant by the king to his thegn Dunn, made 'on account of the tithing of lands which, by the gift of God, I have decided to do for some of my thegns'; the same document records that Dunn gave the land to his wife, with reversion after her death to the church of Rochester. The charter supports the *Chronicle* in implying that the Decimation involved a distribution of a tenth of the king's lands to his thegns, who could then transfer the land to a religious foundation if they so desired. It is interesting, and it may be significant, that in describing the Decimation Asser uses the terminology of charters: for example, his statement that it was 'made over . . . to the Triune God' may be compared with the invocation in *S* 315 ('In the name of the Triune Deity'), and his statement that this was done 'on the cross of Christ' is probably a reference to the form of the king's subscription, again as in *S* 315 ('I, King Æthelwulf, have strengthened and subscribed this my donation and privilege with the sign of the Holy Cross of Christ'); note also that Asser's phrase *in sempiterno graphio* ('as an everlasting inheritance') and the dispositive verb *immolare* ('to make over') are common in Celtic Latin charters (see Davies, 'The Latin Charter-Tradition', pp. 268–74).

24. The statement that Alfred accompanied Æthelwulf to Rome in 855–6, making this Alfred's second journey, rests on Asser's authority; cf. Nelson, 'Problem of King Alfred's Royal Anointing', pp. 161–2, for the view that Alfred went only once, in 855–6. Æthelwulf's passage through the lands of Charles the Bald (840–77) is mentioned in the *Annals of St Bertin* for 855: 'Charles also received with honour Æthelwulf, king of the Angles and Saxons [*rex Anglorum Saxonum*], as he was hastening to Rome, and presented him with everything belonging to royal estate, and had him escorted to the frontiers of his kingdom with the attendance fitting for a king' (*EHD* no. 23). His arrival in Rome, accompanied by his followers, is recorded in the Life of Pope Benedict III (855–8) entered in the *Liber Pontificalis*, and the same source lists the splendid gifts that the king gave to the pope on this occasion (quoted by Stevenson, *Asser*, p. 194 note 2).

25. Æthelwulf's marriage to Judith is recorded in the *Annals of St Bertin* for 856: 'Æthelwulf, king of the western English [*rex occidentalium Anglorum*], on his way back from Rome, was married on 1 October in the palace of Verberie to Judith, daughter of King Charles, to whom he had been betrothed in the month of July; and, when the diadem had been placed on her head (Hincmar, bishop of Rheims, giving the blessing) he honoured her with the name of queen, which hitherto had not been customary with him and his people; and when the marriage had been solemnized with royal magnificence on both sides and with gifts, he returned by ship with her to Britain, to the control of his kingdom' (*EHD* no. 23). The order of service composed by Hincmar for the blessing of Judith is printed in Boretius and Krause, *Capitularia*, pp. 425–7.

26. This account of a plot against Æthelwulf during his absence abroad rests on Asser's authority; it is not mentioned in the *Anglo-Saxon Chronicle*, possibly because the chronicler was embarrassed by the event for personal reasons (see Stenton, 'South-Western Element', pp. 113–14), or because he wished to brush over this expression of recent discord within the royal family. The plot was probably connected in some way with Æthelwulf's marriage to Judith: Æthelbald may have considered the marriage a threat to his own interests, and others may have resented her consecration as queen in defiance of current West Saxon practice; for other interpretations, see John, *Orbis Britanniae*, p. 43, and Enright, 'Charles the Bald

and Æthelwulf of Wessex'. According to the *Liber Pontificalis* (see above, note 24) Æthelwulf came to Rome having lost his own kingdom, which may be a garbled reference to measures taken before his departure (see next note), or to developments during his absence and on his return.

27. Æthelwulf apparently divided his kingdom between his two eldest surviving sons before his departure for Rome, to judge from Asser's reference here to 'King' Æthelbald and to judge from the subscription of 'King' Æthelberht to *S* 315 (855); the *Chronicle* accords Æthelbald a reign of five years, and since he died in 860 this takes his accession back to 855. It would appear that on Æthelwulf's return, Æthelberht gave up his kingship and the kingdom was divided between Æthelwulf (assigned Kent, Surrey, Sussex and Essex) and Æthelbald (assigned Wessex, presumably having held it since 855).

28. See the passage from the *Annals of St Bertin*, quoted in note 25 above. As Asser goes on to explain, this custom originated with Eadburh's disgrace after the death of her husband King Beorhtric in 802, and he writes as if it was still observed in the 890s, though it had obviously been set aside for Judith and was always a controversial issue. The evidence of the charters, so far as it goes, supports the view that the West Saxon queen, or rather 'king's wife', was kept firmly in the background in the ninth century. Eighth-century charters reveal that the situation obtaining before Eadburh's disgrace was fairly normal: we occasionally meet in the witness lists to charters of Ine and Æthelheard women who are described as 'queen' (*regina*), and one might add that the *Chronicle* contains a reference to Ine's queen (*cuen*) in the annal for 722, and a reference to Æthelheard's queen (*cuen*) in the annal for 737; Eadburh herself occurs as *regina* during Beorhtric's reign. But we do not find any references to the wife of Egbert or to Æthelwulf's first wife; Judith does seem to occur, albeit in dubious charters, during the reign of Æthelbald (whom she married after Æthelwulf's death), but this only confirms that her position as a consecrated queen was exceptional; there is no reference to a wife of Æthelberht, and none to a wife of Æthelred, though a mysterious 'Wulfthryth regina' makes a solitary appearance in *S* 340 (King Æthelred, dated 868); and there is no reference to Alfred's wife in his charters, discounting *S* 349, which is a magnificently blatant forgery. The evidence is inevitably negative, but the scarcity of references to West Saxon queens in ninth-century charters does seem to support Asser, particularly when contrasted with the references in eighth-century contexts and also with the numerous references to queens in Mercian charters of the eighth and ninth centuries. During the tenth century the status accorded to the queen seems to have improved: the service used for the inauguration of the kings during this period incorporates a service for the consecration of a queen, and certain royal women begin to make

regular appearances in the charters. See further Stafford, 'King's Wife in Wessex'.

29. Offa was king of Mercia from 757 to 796. He was quite as formidable and powerful a king as Asser would suggest (see Stenton, *Anglo-Saxon England*, pp. 201–38). The great dyke, known in Welsh tradition as *Clawdd Offa* (Offa's dyke), stands to this day as one of the most remarkable monuments of the Anglo-Saxon period (see Fox, *Offa's Dyke*).

30. This marriage, which took place in 789, had an important political dimension. At the time, both Offa and Beorhtric may have felt threatened by the Egbert who subsequently succeeded Beorhtric as king of the West Saxons: Egbert was potentially a thorn in Offa's side, since his father Ealhmund had recently managed to gain recognition as a king in Kent, towards the end of a period when Kent enjoyed a measure of freedom from Mercian overlordship (776–85); but as a descendant of Ingild, brother of Ine (see Asser, chapter 1), Egbert was also a dynastic rival for Beorhtric, who had become king of the West Saxons in 786. To judge from *ASC* s.a. 839, the marriage in 789 was part of a pact between the kings of Wessex and Mercia, whereby Beorhtric received Offa's daughter in marriage (to strengthen his own position), and in return helped Offa to drive Egbert into exile (to their mutual advantage); there are, one should add, no grounds for supposing that the marriage meant the subjection of Wessex to Mercia (cf. Stevenson, *Asser*, p. 205, and Stenton, *Anglo-Saxon England*, pp. 209–10).

31. Beorhtric died in 802. Charlemagne (that is, Charles the Great, but here called simply Charles; cf. below, note 135) became king of the Franks in 768 and was crowned emperor in 800; he died in 814. The son of Charlemagne mentioned in the story that follows was probably Charles the Younger, who had been made a king in western Francia in 789 or 790, and who died in 811. On a previous occasion Charlemagne had tried to arrange a marriage between Charles and a daughter of Offa (see *EHD* no. 20), but it is unlikely that Eadburh was the daughter in question (see Stenton, *Anglo-Saxon England*, p. 220 note 4).

32. The name of the nunnery entrusted to Eadburh is not known; she was evidently ejected from it before 814, but she must have lived for a good many years thereafter if Asser himself knew people who had seen her. Pavia was on the pilgrims' road to Rome, so there would have been many opportunities for stories of Eadburh's last days to get back to England; Alfred's sister Æthelswith, who died in 888, was buried in Pavia (*ASC*, above, p. 113).

33. The document described by Asser was evidently a version of the king's will, and the details given may be compared with the references made to the same or a similar document in the will of Alfred (see above, pp. 15–16). It is interesting that although Æthelwulf was at this stage technically

king of Kent, Surrey, Sussex and Essex (see Asser, chapter 12, and note 27 above), he had nevertheless retained the authority to make arrangements for both the eastern and the western parts of the kingdom. Note also that a clear distinction is made between the kingdom itself (to be divided between his two eldest surviving sons, presumably Æthelbald and Æthelberht) and Æthelwulf's own property (to be shared among various members of his family); the information in Alfred's will concerns only the latter aspect of Æthelwulf's will (below, p. 314 note 3). In making his provisions, Æthelwulf may have been taking his cue from the various arrangements made in the first half of the ninth century for the division of the Carolingian empire.

34. Asser is referring here to bequests made by the king for the good of his soul, as explained in more detail in what follows.

35. These words echo the preface of Einhard's *Vita Caroli*: see below, note 139.

36. A hide (here *manens*) was a unit of assessment of land for various administrative purposes, but its actual area on the ground varied in different places and at different times, according to local custom, the quality of the land, and the degree to which it was exploited; moreover, a king might choose to reduce the assessment of an estate as a sign of favour to its holder. When we first meet the term, in the seventh century, it was the area of land considered adequate for the support of one household or family; in the later Anglo-Saxon period a hide was sometimes equivalent to 120 acres, sometimes more, sometimes less.

37. A mancus was both a unit of gold weight and an accounting unit of thirty silver pence. Gold coins of that name seem to have been minted for special purposes (at weights close to three contemporary silver pence), though very few survive: the earliest is from Offa's reign and the first to bear royal authority is from Edward the Elder's (see Lyon, 'Denominations and Weights', pp. 207–9). Offa himself had promised to send the pope 'every year as many mancuses as the year had days, that is, 365 . . . for the support of the poor and provision of lights' (*EHD* no. 205). But neither Offa's nor Æthelwulf's grant seems to have been the origin of the tax which came to be known as Peter's Pence; see further note 206 below.

38. Æthelwulf died in 858 (on 13 January, according to 'Florence' of Worcester). He was buried at Steyning in Sussex, though his body was afterwards moved to Winchester (see Whitelock, *Genuine Asser*, p. 9). A gold finger-ring, found in Wiltshire and inscribed 'King Æthelwulf', is now in the British Museum (see Wilson, *Ornamental Metalwork*, no. 31, and Okasha, *Hand-List*, no. 70). After his death, Æthelberht became king of Kent, Surrey, Sussex and Essex in succession to his father (see above, note 27), and Æthelbald retained Wessex itself.

39. Æthelbald's marriage to Judith is recorded also in the *Annals of St Bertin* s.a. 858 (*EHD* no. 23). For the Christian case against marriage to one's stepmother, see Pope Gregory's reply to St Augustine's fifth question reported by Bede, *HE* i, 27; Asser seems mistaken, however, in implying that the practice was not permitted among the heathen – in the seventh century the pagan king Eadbald of Kent had married Bertha, the Frankish widow of his father Æthelberht, but he gave her up on becoming a Christian (*HE* ii, 5, 6).

40. For the length of Æthelbald's reign, see note 27 above. After his death, Judith returned to Francia, staying initially at Senlis under her father's protection 'with all the honour due to a queen'; but in 862 she eloped with Baldwin, count of Flanders, and soon married him (*Annals of St Bertin* s.a. 862, 863).

41. Asser is here mistaken. Æthelberht was already king of Kent, Surrey, Sussex (and Essex), and it was the late Æthelbald's Wessex that he annexed, thereby reuniting the whole kingdom (see notes 27 and 38 above).

42. This victory over the Vikings is recorded also in the *Annals of St Bertin* s.a. 860 (*EHD* no. 23).

43. The *Anglo-Saxon Chronicle* places these events in 865. It should be remembered that the chroniclers who compiled the annals for the second half of the ninth century seem to have calculated the new year from a point in the (previous) autumn (see below, p. 281), so *ASC* 865 refers to events which occurred in a year beginning in the autumn of 864.

44. The 'great Viking fleet' (literally 'great fleet of pagans', representing the phrase 'great heathen army' used in the *Chronicle*) arrived towards the end of 865 and spent the winter of 865–6 in East Anglia (quite distinct, of course, from the kingdom of the East Saxons, but Asser may only have meant the kingdom of the eastern Saxons, i.e. the East Angles). The statement that the fleet came from the Danube rests on Asser's authority and makes no sense; it is possible that he was simply recording his belief or assumption that it came from Denmark, and made a mistaken connection between Danes and the Danube. According to the chronicler Æthelweard, the Viking force was led by 'the tyrant Igwar', i.e. Ivar, and 'came from the north' (*CÆ*, p. 35); to judge from later Scandinavian tradition, this Ivar was Ivar the Boneless, one of the sons of Ragnar Lothbrok. Ivar is usually identified with the Imar active in Dublin in the 850s and early 860s, and it has been suggested that he came over from Ireland to Northumbria in about 864 and there awaited the main Viking army, which came to England by prior arrangement and which then moved north in 866 to join forces for the attack on York (see Smyth, *Scandinavian Kings*, pp. 169–77); the identification is certainly attractive, though it has been questioned (see Ó Corráin, 'High-Kings', pp. 314–

20). Ivar was associated in the leadership of the Viking army with his brother Halfdan and also it seems with a certain Ubbe (possibly another brother); but there were apparently other important men in the army besides these, including at least one other king and several earls (see Asser, chapters 37–9). One might assume that the Viking armies active in England during Alfred's reign came direct from Scandinavia; many of the men who made up the armies may have done so, but others probably came from Ireland and the Continent.

45. The nautical metaphor for literary composition, used here and in chapter 73, was current in classical and medieval Latin literature: see Curtius, *European Literature and the Latin Middle Ages*, pp. 128–30, and Stevenson, *Asser*, pp. 218–19. In particular the metaphor was favoured by Insular Latin writers, such as Aldhelm (*Carmen de Virginitate*, lines 2801–11: ed. Ehwald, *Aldhelmi Opera*, pp. 466–7), Alcuin (*Versus de Sanctis Euboricensis Ecclesiae*, lines 1649–58), and Æthelweard (*CÆ*, p. 38). For another nautical image, see chapter 91.

46. Asser's curious statement, that Alfred remained 'ignorant of letters until his twelfth year [860], or even longer', may conceal an important stage in the process of Alfred's education. As a young boy, Alfred was evidently dependent on the services of teachers, who read out English poems to him, and he was adept at committing the poems to memory (chapters 22–3). It is possible, however, that it was in about 860 that he learnt how to read English, for this would explain how he was able to read aloud from books in English and to give instruction in literacy to the children of the royal household, apparently in the period preceding the recruitment of helpers from Mercia and elsewhere (chapter 76). At about this stage he still needed to have certain works read out to him (chapters 76–7, 81, 88), and these were presumably in Latin; in 887, under guidance from Asser and others, he finally mastered the reading and translation of Latin, and at the same time resolved to use these skills for the instruction of others (chapters 87–9).

47. This sentence, cast partly in the present tense, seems somewhat out of place here and may have been inserted by Asser at a later stage in the composition of the *Life*; it breaks the otherwise obvious connection between the previous sentence and the following chapter.

48. *magistrum adiit et legit*, where either *et* is an error for *qui* (in which case the master 'read' the book to Alfred) or *legit* means 'absorbed its contents' or 'learnt' (as here translated). The event probably took place some time before 856, since Alfred's mother was presumably dead by then (when his father remarried); it follows that Alfred could not yet read (above, note 46), so he must have needed his teacher's help in memorizing the book.

49. For a more detailed account of this book, see chapters 88–9.

50. Alfred's complaints about the lack of teachers, mentioned here and in chapter 25 (and cf. chapter 76), may be compared with his remarks in the preface to his translation of Gregory's *Pastoral Care* (above, p. 125); see also *EHD* no. 229. Similarly, his reported comments in chapter 25 on the cares of kingship may be compared with his remarks in the preface to his translation of Boethius's *Consolation of Philosophy* (above, p. 131).

51. Asser provides a full account of Alfred's illnesses in chapter 74.

52. Stevenson wanted to omit the passage in brackets, but this seems unnecessary: Asser is saying, admittedly in a somewhat muddled way, that Alfred did not desist from the desire from infancy up to the present day, that he still does not desist from it, and that he will not desist from it (in Asser's opinion) right up to the end of his life.

53. In the manuscript of Asser's *Life*, the scribe wrote *Karoli* (that is '. . . King Charles's life'), but this careless slip (whether Asser's or the scribe's) was afterwards corrected to *Alfredi*.

54. Various later sources with access to northern material give more precise dates for the events described in chapters 26–7: the Vikings occupied York on 1 November (866, or 867 in a year calculated from the previous autumn: cf. note 43 above), according to Simeon of Durham's *Historiae Dunelmensis Ecclesiae* (Arnold, *Symeonis Monachi Opera Omnia* I, p. 55) and according to Roger of Wendover's *Flores Historiarum* (*EHD* no. 4); the battle for York took place on 21 March (867), according to Simeon (loc. cit.) and the *Historia Regum* (Arnold, *Symeonis Monachi Opera Omnia* II, p. 106), or on Palm Sunday (23 March) according to Roger (loc. cit.) and the anonymous *Historia de Sancto Cuthberto* (Arnold, *Symeonis Monachi Opera Omnia* I, p. 202).

55. Asser himself added the word 'honourably' to the record of Ealhstan's death (otherwise derived from *ASC* s.a. 867), and it may be that he was defending one of his predecessors from the charges of complicity in the plot against King Æthelwulf mentioned in chapter 12; it is not certain, however, that Asser was bishop of Sherborne at the time of writing.

56. The term here translated 'heir apparent' is *secundarius* (also used in chapters 38 and 42); it is equivalent to Old Welsh *eil*, meaning 'second', as applied to the heir to the throne. Since no such formal status or office appears to have existed in Anglo-Saxon England, Asser may simply have been applying to Alfred a term with which he had become familiar in Wales, on the assumption that during Æthelred's reign Alfred was in fact the designated heir. See Dumville, 'The Ætheling', pp. 1–2 and 24, and below, p. 315 note 7.

57. The *Gaini* cannot be identified, but they were presumably one of the old tribal groups of the Mercians. Subscriptions of an ealdorman called Mucel occur in charters issued by the Mercian kings between 814 and 866, with two attesting in the 830s and 840s. It seems likely that one

Mucel attests from 814 to the 840s, and he may be the Mucel son of Esne mentioned in *S* 190 (*EHD* no. 85), dated 836; his father was presumably the Ealdorman Esne who attests Mercian charters in the late eighth and early ninth centuries. The second Mucel, therefore, would attest from the 830s until 866, and it is conceivable that he was the son of the first Mucel; it is presumably this second Mucel who became Alfred's father-in-law, and who attested two charters issued in 868 (the year of the wedding) in company with West Saxon dignitaries (*S* 340 and 1201).

58. This Eadburh is quite distinct, of course, from the daughter of Offa mentioned in chapters 14–15. The name of her daughter (Alfred's wife), curiously not given by Asser, was Ealhswith. Ealhswith had a brother called Æthelwulf, who was an ealdorman (see *ASC* s.a. 901), and whose relationship to the Mercian royal family is suggested by *S* 1442, thus confirming Asser's statement that Eadburh was of Mercian royal stock.

59. 'Nottingham' (*Snotengaham*) signifies literally the *ham* (settlement) of the people of a person called Snot; but Nottingham was renowned for its ancient cave dwellings, and *Tig Guocobauc* does mean precisely 'cavy house' in Old Welsh (see Gover et al., *Place-Names of Nottinghamshire*, pp. 13–14). There is no obvious reason, however, why the Welsh should have had a special name for Nottingham, and it may perhaps have been Asser's invention, based on his own knowledge of the place.

60. The transmitted text seems corrupt here: for *non segnius promissione* read *non segnius promissionem adimplentes*, or the like.

61. King Edmund was killed on 20 November 869 (870 in a year reckoned from the autumn). According to later tradition, the Viking leader on this occasion was Hinguar, that is, Ivar, though some sources mention Ubbe as well (see note 44 above, and Whitelock, 'Fact and Fiction in the Legend of St Edmund'). The chronicler Æthelweard states that Ivar died in the same year as Edmund (*CÆ*, p. 36), but for the suggestion that he returned to Northumbria in 870 and to Dublin in 871 (where he died in 873), see Smyth, *Scandinavian Kings*, pp. 233–6.

62. Ceolnoth's burial at Canterbury is not mentioned in the *Chronicle*, but Asser's statement is supported by Æthelweard (*CÆ*, pp. 36–7) and confirmed by Gervase of Canterbury (see Stevenson, *Asser*, p. 233). For the dates of his archiepiscopate (833–70), see O'Donovan, 'Episcopal Dates, pt I', pp. 30–31.

63. Land at Reading was bequeathed by Æthelflæd, second wife of King Edmund (939–46), to the king (Edward the Martyr or Æthelred the Unready) in the later 970s or 980s (*S* 1494); it was a royal estate during the reign of Edward the Confessor (*DB* fol. 58r).

64. Asser here uses a Latin equivalent of the Welsh idiom, *i parth dehou*, 'on the right hand', which would be the normal way for a Welshman to refer to something lying to the south; see also chapters 79 and 80. Similarly, in

chapters 52 and 79 he uses a Latin equivalent of the Welsh idiom, *i parth cled*, 'on the left hand', referring to something lying to the north.

65. *ASC* MSS 'B', 'C', 'D' and 'E' name the earl as Sidroc, doubtless in error; two earls called Sidroc were in fact killed in the battle of Ashdown later on in the same year (see chapter 39).

66. The chronicler Æthelweard (*CÆ*, p. 37) states that Æthelwulf's body was carried away secretly into Mercia and buried in Derby; Æthelwulf had been an ealdorman under the Mercian kings, before the transfer of Berkshire to Wessex (cf. above, note 2).

67. Despite Stevenson's arguments to the contrary (*Asser*, pp. 234–8), Asser's etymology may be correct: see Gelling, *Place-Names of Berkshire* I, pp. 2–4, where it is also shown that 'Ashdown' was applied to the whole line of the Berkshire Downs. The site of the battle cannot therefore be identified precisely, though see idem, *Place-Names of Berkshire* II, p. 495 (and p. 499).

68. 'Core of the army' translates *mediam partem exercitus*; *mediam* may be an error for *unam* or *primam* (as Stevenson suggests), avoiding the implication that there was a central section (and therefore two wings), but Asser may merely have intended by the use of *mediam* to convey the idea that the part of the army assigned to the kings was the more important. In the *Chronicle*, the two kings are named as Bagsecg and Halfdan; the former is otherwise unknown, but the latter was the brother of Ivar (see note 44 above, and chapter 54).

69. We follow Stevenson's emendation of the nonsensical *belli sortem sumere debere sciret* to *belli sortem subiret*; see his *Asser*, pp. 238–9, for an explanation of how the corrupt reading may have arisen.

70. As Williams, *Armes Prydein*, p. xxix note 2, points out, Asser's choice of the phrase 'like a wild boar' to express Alfred's bravery may have been suggested by his knowledge of early Welsh poetic vocabulary, in which *twrch* ('boar') is used for a brave warrior.

71. Stevenson adds a sentence here, derived from 'Florence' of Worcester: 'Eventually, when he had finished the prayers in which he had been engaged, King Æthelred arrived and, once he had invoked the head of the universe, soon joined in the battle.' One cannot be sure, however, that 'Florence' derived this sentence from the text of Asser; he could have added it himself in order to make explicit what Asser may have left implicit.

72. In the manuscript, this chapter began with the words *Quibus cum talia praesentis vitae dispendia alienigenis perperam quaerentibus non sufficerent*, which make no sense on their own: 'To whom (?), since such losses of the present life were not enough for the misguided foreigners . . .'. It is as if Asser originally intended to begin the chapter with a remark to the effect that the Vikings nevertheless came back for more punishment, but then

decided on consulting the *Chronicle* that such a remark would be inappropriate at this point. He forgot, however, to delete his original opening words, and these were then copied in good faith by the scribe of the Cotton manuscript.

73. Asser implies that this new army arrived after the battle of Basing; but a comparison of his account with the *Chronicle* reveals that he has omitted (accidentally or otherwise: see below, note 78) an intervening battle. After its mention of the battle of Basing, *ASC* s.a. 871 continues: 'And two months afterwards, King Æthelred and his brother Alfred fought against the army at *Meretun* [unidentified, but cf. *ASC* s.a. 757], and they were in two divisions; and they put both to flight and had the victory for a long time during the day; and there was a great slaughter on both sides, and the Danes had possession of the battlefield; and Bishop Heahmund [of Sherborne] was killed there and many important men.' (The chronicler Æthelweard adds that Heahmund was buried at Keynsham, in Somerset: *CÆ*, p. 38.) According to *ASC*, it was after this battle that the new army arrived, at Reading; it presumably came towards the end of March or in early April, and joined forces with the army already based there. The chronicler calls it *micel sumorlida*, that is, a 'great summer army' (cf. *CÆ*, p. 39), implying that it was only active during the 'summer' and so that it returned whence it came for the winter; but *sumorlida* may be used here as a general term for a force of Vikings (cf. Old Norse *sumarliði*, and Asser's *paganorum exercitus*), without any necessary implication that it did not come to stay. Indeed, it seems likely that the army did remain in England, and that its leaders were the kings Guthrum, Oscetel and Anwend named in *ASC* s.a. 875 (Asser, chapter 47): see Smyth, *Scandinavian Kings*, pp. 240–54.

74. Alfred's position during Æthelred's reign may have approximated to that of the Welsh 'heir apparent' (see above, note 56), but it is difficult to believe that he was accorded the same position earlier on.

75. Compare Alfred's own remarks, in his translation of Boethius's *Consolation of Philosophy*, that he had no particular desire for earthly rule: see above, p. 132. These remarks were, however, in part suggested by the original text: see Watts, *Boethius: The Consolation of Philosophy*, p. 72.

76. Asser provides the Old Welsh form (*Guilou*) of the river Wylye; see Ekwall, *English River-Names*, pp. 457–60, and Gover et al., *Place-Names of Wiltshire*, p. 11.

77. We follow Stevenson in preferring the reading of the *Annals of St Neots* (*paucitatem persequentium despicientes*) to the reading of the Cotton manuscript (*peraudacitatem persequentium decipientes*, that is, 'outwitting the great daring of the pursuers').

78. *ASC* has nine, so Asser's figure makes it appear that his omission of *Meretun* was deliberate; but in fact only six battles are recorded (Engle-

field, Reading, Ashdown, Basing, *Meretun* and Wilton). The chronicler Æthelweard describes the first five of these battles, and then refers to a battle which took place while Alfred was attending his brother's funeral; he states that nine battles were fought, not including those that he mentions, and adds that eleven earls and one king were killed (*CÆ*, pp. 37–40).

79. The expression 'made peace with the Vikings' can probably be taken to imply that Alfred paid them a sum of money in return for their guarantee of departure. Peace had been purchased by the men of Kent in 865 (*ASC*; Asser, chapter 20).

80. A document dated 872 refers to 'the very pressing affliction and immense tribute of the barbarians, in the same year when the Vikings stayed in London' (*EHD* no. 94), so there can be no doubt that the Mercians had to purchase their peace; the chronicler Æthelweard states that the Mercians 'fixed cash payments' (*CÆ*, p. 40).

81. The Vikings probably went north to quell a Northumbrian revolt against Egbert, the king whom they had installed there in 867 (see *EHD* no. 4); the Vikings wintered at Torksey in Lindsey (*ASC* s.a. 873).

82. The *Schola Saxonum* (*Angelcynnes scolu* in Old English) was not, as its name might imply, an educational establishment: the term originated as applied to the contingent of Saxons, or Englishmen, who served in the militia of Rome, beside similar 'schools' of other Germanic nations. Its foundation was traditionally associated with either Ine of Wessex or Offa of Mercia in the early or late eighth century; in time it developed into a form of hostelry or reception centre for Englishmen with any business in Rome. It was situated on the Vatican Hill, and was served by the church of St Mary-in-Saxia (where the church and hospital of Santo Spirito in Sassia was later established). The *Schola Saxonum* burnt down in 817 (*ASC*), and again early in the pontificate of Leo IV (847–55); Pope Marinus (882–4) freed it from taxation at Alfred's request (see Asser, chapter 71); it came to an end in 1204 (see Stevenson, *Asser*, pp. 243–7).

83. Although the chronicler (and Asser) call Ceolwulf a 'foolish king's thegn', he was clearly more than a puppet king: he issued charters in his own name (for example *EHD* no. 95), and he issued coins, sharing types and moneyers with Alfred, which suggests some degree of mutual recognition. A Mercian regnal list assigns him a reign of five years (presumably 874–9); he is not known to have had any successor as king, and by 883 we find Mercia under the control of Ealdorman Æthelred (*S* 218).

84. The army that went to Northumbria, under the leadership of Halfdan, was presumably made up of the remnants of the army that had arrived in 865; the army that came to East Anglia, under the leadership of Guthrum,

Oscetel and Anwend, was presumably the army that had arrived in 871. See Smyth, *Scandinavian Kings*, pp. 243–4.

85. Seven, according to *ASC* and the version of Asser's *Life* used by the *Annals of St Neots*.

86. The chronicler Æthelweard seems to imply that the army from Cambridge joined forces at Wareham with a 'western army'; see *CÆ*, p. 41, and Stenton, 'The Thriving of the Anglo-Saxon Ceorl', p. 387. A division of the Viking army into a land force and a naval force is further suggested by *ASC* 877 (below, note 94).

87. Wareham is one of the sites listed in the *Burghal Hidage* (above, p. 193); it may not have been fortified in 876, but Asser's description of it as a *castellum* suggests that it had been fortified by the time he was writing, in 893. The site is rectangular, defined on the west, north and east sides by massive earthworks, and on the south side by the river Frome: see Royal Commission on Historical Monuments, *Dorset* II, pt 2, pp. 322–4. Very little is known of the nunnery at Wareham: it was allegedly founded in the late seventh century, and the death of an abbess Wulfwyn of Wareham is recorded in *ASC* MS 'C', s.a. 982. *Durngueir* is the Old Welsh name for Dorchester, derived from the Romano-British form *Durnovaria*; 'Dorset' (OE *Dornsæte*, 'the *Dorn* people') shares the same first element; see Mills, *Place-Names of Dorset* I, pp. 347–8. Asser's name for the river Frome – *Frauu* – is also Old Welsh; see Ekwall, *English River-Names*, pp. 166–8.

88. The chronicler Æthelweard (*CÆ*, p. 41) states that King Alfred gave money to the Vikings as part of the deal.

89. In *ASC* MSS 'B', 'C', 'D', 'E' the reference is to hostages (*gislas*) 'who were the most important men next to their king in the army'; the chronicler Æthelweard similarly refers to hostages 'who then seemed choice men in the army in the regard of their kings' (*CÆ*, p. 41). *ASC* MS 'A' omits the mention of hostages on this occasion. Asser's reference to 'as many picked hostages as he alone chose' seems however to anticipate the reference to hostages (*foregislas*: see below, p. 285 note 2) in *ASC* 877, 'as many as he wished to have': the annal for 877 appears to have been omitted accidentally in the copy of the *Chronicle* used by Asser (see below, note 94), and it is possible that the copyist had in the process inadvertently transferred the description of the hostages in his exemplar's annal for 877 to his own version of the annal for 876.

90. The received text of Asser may be corrupt at this point. The comment 'on which they had never before been willing to take an oath to any race' can hardly have been intended to apply to Alfred's Christian relics, and indeed reference to the equivalent passage in the *Chronicle* shows that it should apply to the 'holy ring' (a sacred ring, sometimes associated specifically with the worship of Thor, on which the Vikings swore their oaths:

see Pálsson and Edwards, *Eyrbyggja Saga*, p. 40, and Davidson, *Gods and Myths*, pp. 76–8). Either Asser mistook a pagan ring for Christian relics and then failed to appreciate the implications of what followed, or we have to suppose that he added the reference to relics on his own initiative and that an intervening reference to the ring has somehow dropped out. Both relics and ring are mentioned in the corresponding passage in the *Annals of St Neots*, and it is possible that this is closer to Asser's original text.

91. Reading *obsides* for *equites*, since it is obviously inconceivable that the Vikings killed all their horse-soldiers; for the probability that the Vikings had received hostages from Alfred, see below, note 108. The text may, however, be corrupt in a different way: the *Annals of St Neots* read *occidentem* for *occidit*, and although what follows cannot be construed as it stands, the original sense was perhaps that the Viking cavalry then turned westwards (*occidentem versus*) and went to Devon.

92. Again, Asser provides Old Welsh forms for Exeter and the river Exe; see Ekwall, *English River-Names*, pp. 153–6.

93. Halfdan did not stay in England for long: he died in 877 attempting to regain control of Dublin (see Smyth, *Scandinavian Kings*, pp. 259–66). The Viking settlements in Northumbria were concentrated between the rivers Humber and Tees (Yorkshire). Much of the land between the Tees and Tyne (County Durham) was soon acquired from the Danish conquerors by the community of St Cuthbert, as related in the *Historia de Sancto Cuthberto* (above, p. 211 note 11): see *EHD* no. 6, and Craster, 'The Patrimony of St Cuthbert', pp. 188–92. The area north of the Tyne (Northumberland) remained, at least for a while, under the control of native rulers based at Bamborough.

94. In Stevenson's edition of Asser's *Life of King Alfred*, chapter 51 reads as follows: 'That year, in the month of August, the army went to Mercia and gave the province of the Mercians in part to Ceolwulf, a certain foolish king's thegn, and in part they divided it up among themselves.' This represents just the last sentence of the annal for 877 in the *Anglo-Saxon Chronicle*, which reads in full: 'In this year the Viking army from Wareham came to Exeter, and the naval force sailed west along the coast and encountered a great storm at sea; 120 ships were lost there at Swanage. King Alfred rode after the mounted Viking army with the English army as far as Exeter, but he was not able to overtake them from behind before they were in the fortress where they could not be reached; and they gave him hostages there – as many as he wished to have – and they swore great oaths and then kept a firm peace. Then in the harvest season the Viking army went into Mercia and shared out some of it, and gave some to Ceolwulf.' (The chronicler Æthelweard adds that they set up *ategias* – huts, or tents – in the town of Gloucester: *CÆ*, p. 42.)

There is reason to believe that Stevenson's chapter 51 was not present in the Cotton manuscript of Asser's *Life*, that it may not have formed part of Asser's original text, and indeed that the whole of the annal for 877 was missing in his copy of the *Chronicle*. The Corpus transcript (of the Cotton manuscript of Asser) passes directly from chapter 50 to chapter 52, and the scribe indicates that the annal for 877 is wanting. It seems that the deficiency in the Cotton manuscript was then made good by the insertion of material derived from two different sources: Stevenson's chapters 50b and 50d are from the *Annals of St Neots*, and chapter 50c is from a thirteenth-century St Albans chronicle. Of these, chapter 50c was inserted into the Corpus transcript on a separate slip, but all three occur in the Otho transcript as if they formed part of the main text; Wise (writing in 1722) states that the three sections were not in the 'old' Cotton manuscript, but had been inserted by a 'more recent', or modern, hand. The textual status of Stevenson's chapter 51 should be judged against this background. The non-occurrence of the chapter in the Corpus transcript suffices to show that it was not present in the ('old') Cotton manuscript, even though it is printed by Wise without any indication that it too is an interpolation. It is, however, found in the *Annals of St Neots*, and the simplest explanation for its presence in Wise's edition is that it was inserted from the *Annals* into the Cotton manuscript, along with chapters 50b and 50d, in order to provide coverage of the events of 877; one has to assume, therefore, that James Hill (who collated the Cotton manuscript on Wise's behalf) failed to notice or record the fact (not in itself unlikely: see Stevenson, *Asser*, p. xxix–xxx). If chapter 51 is thus regarded as another interpolation (presumably effected under Parker's auspices, since it does occur in the Otho transcript and in the edition of 1574), a serious contradiction which would otherwise arise in Asser's text can be avoided: chapter 49 leaves the Vikings at Exeter, but chapter '51' brings them to Mercia, while chapter 52 has them still at Exeter before coming to Chippenham. If, furthermore, we assume that the annal for 877 was carelessly omitted in Asser's copy of the *Chronicle*, it becomes easier to understand why he (mistakenly) brought the Vikings direct from Exeter to Chippenham in chapter 52: he was merely trying to lend continuity to his narrative. The account of the events of 876–8 given by 'Florence' of Worcester confirms the impression that *ASC* 877 was not represented in Asser's *Life*: 'Florence' normally quotes verbatim from the *Life*, but in this case he was obliged to provide his own translation of *ASC* 877; he accommodated Asser's statement that the Vikings came to Chippenham from Exeter by stating himself that only part of the army went from Exeter into Mercia, leaving part at Exeter.

95. For Chippenham, see below, p. 321 note 65. According to the *Chronicle*,

the Viking army came to Chippenham 'in midwinter after twelfth night
[7 January]'.

96. For this Welsh idiom, see above, note 64.

97. Another Old Welsh form; see Ekwall, *English River-Names*, pp. 21–3.

98. It was at this point in the narrative that Archbishop Parker interpolated
the famous story of Alfred and the Cakes: for further details, see
Appendix I.

99. The brother in question is not named in *ASC*, but later tradition
identified him as Ubbe (see above, note 44). According to *ASC*, he was
killed 'and 800 men with him and forty [MSS 'A', 'D', 'E'; 'B', 'C' read
'sixty'] men of his army', which may imply some distinction between
the mass of his followers and his personal retinue; MSS 'B', 'C', 'D',
'E' add that the 'Raven' banner was captured on this occasion. The
chronicler Æthelweard (who names the Viking leader – incorrectly – as
'Halfdan, the brother of the tyrant Ivar') identifies the besieged English
leader as Odda, ealdorman of Devon, and, curiously enough, assigns
victory to the Danes (*CÆ*, p. 43). It seems likely that this invasion was
timed to coincide with the descent of the other Viking army on Chippenham: see Smyth, *Scandinavian Kings*, pp. 248–9.

100. Another Old Welsh form; see Gover et al., *Place-Names of Devon* I, pp.
62–3.

101. For an account of the Welsh hill-forts which may have suggested this
comparison to Asser, see Laing, *Archaeology of Late Celtic Britain and
Ireland*, pp. 106–10.

102. Asser describes the natural advantages of the site at Athelney in more
detail in chapter 92. According to the chronicler Æthelweard, Alfred
was assisted at this time by Æthelnoth, ealdorman of Somerset, with a
small force, and otherwise only by 'servants who had royal maintenance',
i.e. members of the king's household (*CÆ*, p. 42). It was near Athelney
that the Alfred Jewel (reproduced on the cover of this book) was discovered: for further details, see Appendix II.

103. *Coit Maur* is Old Welsh for 'great wood'. The exact location of Egbert's
Stone has never been securely established, though not for lack of trying.
It evidently lay somewhere on a route between Athelney in Somerset
and (the vicinity of) Warminster in Wiltshire (below, note 105), presumably at a point where the men of Somerset, Wiltshire and Hampshire
would be likely to have congregated; one cannot improve on Stevenson's
suggestion (*Asser*, p. 269) that it may have been near Penselwood, where
the boundaries of Somerset and Wiltshire meet. 'Alfred's Tower', near
Stourton, Wiltshire (Grid ref. ST 745351), built *c.* 1722 to mark the
presumed site of Egbert's Stone, is certainly in the right area.

104. The words 'and all the inhabitants of Hampshire – those who had not
sailed overseas for fear of the Vikings' represent the words 'and (all the

people) of Hampshire – that part of it which was on this side of the sea' in *ASC*, where the sea in question may be Southampton Water (as opposed to the English Channel) and so where the reference may be to the inhabitants of west Hampshire.

105. Iley Oak (a place-name now lost) was formerly the meeting-place of the Hundreds of Warminster and Heytesbury, and is to be identified with the present Eastleigh Wood in Sutton Veny, Wiltshire: see Gover et al., *Place-Names of Wiltshire*, pp. 154–5.

106. Edington in Wiltshire, mentioned in King Alfred's will (above, p. 177).

107. The stronghold in question was probably Chippenham (see chapter 52).

108. It was clearly an unprecedented feature of this treaty that Alfred gave no hostages to the Vikings; this suggests, therefore, that the earlier treaties of 876 and 877 had involved the *exchange* of hostages. On the *choice* of hostages, see above, note 89, and below, p. 285 note 2. Alfred's treaties with the Vikings should be compared with those concluded between Carolingian rulers and the Vikings in the second half of the ninth century: see, for example, the *Annals of St Bertin* s.a. 862 and 873.

109. 'As is his wont' translates Asser's *suatim utens*, a curious expression which recurs in chapters 74 and 106.

110. The procedure whereby one ruler stood sponsor to another at baptism or confirmation was widely practised in Anglo-Saxon England, from the seventh century onwards. It established a formal yet personal relationship between the rulers concerned, and often expressed the political superiority of the sponsor. For other examples, see Asser, chapter 80, and *ASC* s.a. 893 (above, p. 116); see also below, p. 288 note 25, the *Annals of St Bertin*, s.a. 873, and *ASC* s.a. 943 and 994.

111. Asser is translating an OE idiom by which Guthrum is described as 'one of thirty men', which would literally imply that he came with twenty-nine men; but the idiom was used loosely in the ninth century, so that Asser's translation and the chronicler's intention probably come to the same thing.

112. The reference is to the custom whereby the white robes and fillet put on at baptism were ceremonially removed on the eighth day following; according to the chronicler Æthelweard, Ealdorman Æthelnoth (of Somerset) took part in the proceedings (*CÆ*, p. 43). Guthrum took the baptismal name Æthelstan (*ASC* s.a. 890: above, p. 113).

113. Wedmore in Somerset, mentioned in King Alfred's will (above p. 175).

114. The word here translated 'treasures' is *aedificia*, used elsewhere by Asser in chapters 76, 91 and 101. It is not obvious what Asser meant by the word, if indeed he always meant the same thing; its sense normally, of course, is 'buildings'. In the present context, it corresponds to *ASC*'s *feoh*, '(movable) property', 'goods', 'riches', 'money'; Asser qualifies the *aedificia* as *optima*, so 'treasures', or something similar, would seem

most appropriate. In chapter 76 the king is said to have made (according to his own design) *aedificia . . . nova* which were said to be *venerabiliora et pretiosiora* than any tradition of his predecessors: again the qualifying adjectives, and the context, suggest finely made objects of value rather than 'buildings'. In chapter 91 the king is said to have made 'gold and silver' *aedificia*, and while in this case the context certainly suggests 'buildings', the adjectives again suggest precious objects of some sort (unless buildings decorated internally with gold and silver are meant). In chapter 101 Asser refers to the king's craftsmen (*operatores*), assembled from many races, who were skilled in every earthly *aedificium*, and here the intended meaning would seem to be 'craft'. Plummer, *Life and Times of Alfred*, pp. 46–7, suggests that by *aedificia* Asser may have meant articles of goldsmith's work, and perhaps in particular shrines and reliquaries (which were often constructed in the form of buildings in miniature); for an example of a reliquary apparently of this period, see Hinton et al., 'The Winchester Reliquary'.

115. The Old Welsh name for Cirencester occurs also in the tenth-century Welsh poem *Armes Prydein* in the form *Kaer Geri*: see Williams, *Armes Prydein*, pp. xxviii, 6 and 42, and see also Smith, *Place-Names of Gloucestershire* I, pp. 60–62. Asser has now provided Welsh forms for eleven English names (see chapters 9, 30, 42, 49, 52, 54, 55, 57, and notes), a sure sign that he was writing with a Welsh audience in mind (above, p. 56); see also Stevenson, *Asser*, pp. lxxvi–lxxvii and 249, and Jackson, *Language and History*, pp. 239–40.

116. The ancient kingdom of the Hwicce covered an area which roughly corresponds to Gloucestershire, Worcestershire and part of Warwickshire; its boundaries appear to have been perpetuated in the medieval diocese of Worcester. The kingdom was absorbed into Mercia in the late eighth century, so the area was not under Alfred's jurisdiction.

117. Asser seems actually to imply that the newly arrived army joined up with Guthrum's army, but this is incompatible with his statement that it wintered at Fulham and thereafter left the country (chapter 61).

118. There was a partial solar eclipse on 26 March 879, but it would not have been visible in Wessex and could not be described as lasting for one hour (*ASC*), nor as occurring between nones and vespers (Asser). It is altogether more likely that *ASC* and Asser are referring to the total eclipse of 29 October 878, and that the chronicler placed it in 879 because he calculated each year from the previous autumn (see below, p. 281).

119. The Viking army which had arrived in 878, and which had spent the winter of 878–9 at Fulham (chapter 58), was active on the Continent from 879 until 892, when it returned to England (*ASC* s.a. 892, above p. 114). The course of its campaign abroad can be reconstructed in

some detail from various continental chronicles (notably the *Annals of St Vaast*): see D'Haenens, *Les Invasions normandes en Belgique au IXe siècle*, pp. 45–61. Some general information on its movements was brought to England and was incorporated in the *Chronicle* (in part duly translated by Asser, chapters 61–3, 65–6, 69, 82 and 84); comparison with the continental chronicles shows that this information was in the main correct, though simplified.

The Vikings sailed for the Continent in the summer of 879. After sacking Thérouanne and the monastery of St Bertin (in Saint-Omer) in July, they reached Ghent in November and spent the winter of 879–80 there. At the beginning of 880 they set off on a raiding expedition up the river Scheldt, and struck further south across the river Oise to Rheims, before returning to their base at Ghent.

120. The Vikings left Ghent in November 880 and spent the winter of 880–81 at Courtrai on the river Lys. They ravaged extensively in and around Flanders, and in the summer they crossed the river Somme and penetrated as far as Beauvais; but on 3 August 881 they were defeated by Louis III at Saucourt, and they returned briefly to Ghent to repair their ships. Louis's victory is celebrated in the poem *Ludwigslied*, translated by Bostock, *Handbook*, pp. 239–41.

121. In the autumn of 881 the Vikings left the Scheldt and moved eastwards from Flanders into Lotharingia, taking up winter quarters for 881–2 at Elsloo on the river Meuse (as correctly stated by Æthelweard, *CÆ*, p. 44); in the first half of 882 they ravaged extensively in the area between the rivers Meuse, Rhine and Moselle, though on one occasion they reached as far south as the diocese of Rheims. In the summer of 882 they were besieged at Elsloo by Charles the Fat (see note 133 below), and once they had come to terms with him they returned westwards to the Scheldt.

122. The Vikings took up winter quarters at Condé on the river Scheldt in October 882, and from there raided to the south and south-west; they left Condé in the spring of 883 and set about ravaging along the coast of Flanders for the next five months or so.

123. Emended from 884: Asser, or his copyist, wrote '884', but then proceeded to give the events of 885. The annal for 884 in the *Chronicle* ('In this year the Viking army went up the Somme to Amiens, and stayed there a year') is thus accidentally omitted. The Vikings moved from the coast of Flanders to the river Somme in the late autumn of 883, taking up winter quarters at Amiens; Carloman (see note 130 below) sued for peace and paid tribute to them, but the Vikings ravaged in the vicinity none the less.

124. The Vikings moved from Amiens to Boulogne towards the end of 884 and then decided to split up. One part went eastwards and set up winter

quarters at Louvain on the river Dyle (as correctly stated by Æthelweard, *CÆ*, p. 44), while the other party crossed the channel and attacked Kent, returning to the Continent in the summer of 885.

125. The chronicler Æthelweard (*CÆ*, pp. 44–5) preserves here a passage that was accidentally omitted in the version of the *Chronicle* that underlies Asser (and the surviving manuscripts). It reveals that only part of the Viking army returned to the Continent at this point. Another part stayed behind and came to terms with the English, though it raided none the less in the vicinity of the Thames estuary; the Vikings who had previously settled in East Anglia then gave support and together the two forces established a base at Benfleet in Essex. But there a quarrel broke out, with the result that some of the Vikings (presumably those who had come from Boulogne in the first place) set sail for the Continent.

126. Alfred's attack on the Vikings of East Anglia was presumably intended to punish them for helping the other Vikings who had come from the Continent (see note 125).

127. Sixteen, according to *ASC*: Asser, or his copyist, has evidently misread 'xvi' as 'xiii'.

128. The Cotton manuscript at this point read *dormiret*, which yields the somewhat peculiar sense, '. . . as the victorious royal fleet was about to go to sleep . . .'. This sense is adopted by the compiler of the later *Historia Regum* (see Whitelock, *Genuine Asser*, p. 19 note 5). However, *dormiret* is evidently a scribal error for *domum iret* ('was about to go home'), as suggested by the corresponding clause in Asser's source: 'when they turned homeward' (*ASC* s.a. 885).

129. Asser's word for 'boar' is *singularis* (the root of modern French *sanglier*), a word which did not exist with this meaning in Classical Latin, where the word for 'boar' is *aper*. Perhaps this is another example of Asser's familiarity with Frankish Latin terminology (see above, p. 54).

130. For Judith, see Asser, chapters 11, 13 and 17. Her father, Charles the Bald, son of Louis the Pious (son of Charlemagne), was allotted the western kingdom (France) at the Treaty of Verdun in 843; he was crowned emperor at Rome on 25 December 875 in succession to his nephew Louis II, and he died on 6 October 877. He was himself succeeded in France by his son Louis the Stammerer, who died on 10 April 879 (for the eclipse, see above, note 118). Louis was succeeded by his sons Louis III (who died on 5 August 882) and Carloman (who died on 12 December 884); see further below, note 133. Asser displays a good knowledge of Frankish affairs by naming Carloman correctly (where *ASC* has Charles) and by naming his brother Louis (unnamed in *ASC*).

131. The territory of the Old Saxons was in fact part of 'Germany'; Plummer, *Life and Times of Alfred*, pp. 40–41, cites evidence which suggests that by *Germania* Asser may have meant Norway.

132. These battles involved an army (or armies) of Vikings different from the one mentioned previously. According to Frankish sources, a Viking army had wintered at Duisburg on the river Rhine in 883–4 and then went eastwards into the land of the Old Saxons; this army was defeated by Henry of Saxony and Arno, bishop of Würzburg, early in 884, and Henry won other battles against the Vikings during the same year. The Frisians fought the Vikings at Norden towards the end of the year, and in 885 a Viking army was defeated when caught between a Saxon and a Frisian force. The Anglo-Saxon chronicler, and Asser, seem therefore to be referring to a combination of events which took place in 884 and 885.

133. Charles the Fat had become king of Alemania (the future Swabia), Alsace and Rhaetia following the death of his father Louis the German (brother of Charles the Bald) in 876. He was crowned emperor at Rome in February 881, and he succeeded to the German territories of his brother Louis the Younger in 882. When Carloman of France died in 884 (see above, note 130), there was no suitable member of Carloman's own branch of the Carolingian dynasty to take his place (since Charles the Simple was considered too young), and so, by general agreement, in June 885 Charles the Fat assumed control of the western kingdom as well. The far-flung empire established by Charlemagne, inherited by Louis the Pious, and then divided up among Louis's sons, was thus largely reconstituted in the hands of Charles the Fat. Asser again displays a good knowledge of Frankish affairs in specifying that Charles was king of the Alemanni and that he succeeded to the re-united empire by general consent (worthy of comment since so much of recent Carolingian history had been beset with inter-dynastic rivalries).

134. The 'marine gulf' (*marinum sinum*) referred to here is the North Sea; Asser's source (*ASC*) speaks merely of Charles's territories 'beyond this sea', apparently a reference to the English Channel. Asser's modification of his source thus implies some knowledge of continental topography, just as he seems to have been well-informed on Frankish history (above, notes 130 and 133). It is conceivable that his knowledge was direct and personal, but it is perhaps more likely that he derived it from a Frankish informant such as Grimbald; see above, p. 55. On the term 'Gauls' (*Galli*) for the inhabitants of Francia, see below, note 156.

135. According to Wise, the Cotton manuscript at this point read *Hlothwic vero ille filius Pipini sive Caroli*, which makes historical nonsense; the Corpus transcript of the Cotton manuscript reads *Lodovic vero ille filius Pipini*. The *Annals of St Neots*, whose compiler may have had access to a different manuscript of Asser's *Life of King Alfred* (above, p. 57), read: *Hlodwicus vero ille filius Karoli magni, et antiqui atque sapientissimi, qui etiam fuit filius Pipini*. This was probably the reading

of·Asser's original text (see Whitelock, *Genuine Asser*, p. 18 note 2), and accordingly we adopt it in our translation. Hart, on the other hand, believes that the compiler of the *Annals of St Neots* used the Cotton manuscript itself and in this case corrected the text by referring directly to the *Anglo-Saxon Chronicle* ('The East Anglian Chronicle', p. 263). The difficulty with this view, however, is that the reading in the *Annals of St Neots* has the support of the *Historia Regum* (attributed, wrongly, to Simeon of Durham); this in turn may imply that the compiler of the *Historia Regum* had access to a copy of Asser's *Life*, but further work is needed to verify this point.

136. On Pope Marinus (882–4) and the *Schola Saxonum*, see above, note 82.

137. For other gifts of pieces of the Cross, see Harbert, 'King Alfred's *Æstel*', pp. 108–10. Alfred may have entrusted his piece to his foundation at Shaftesbury: see Whitelock, *Wills*, pp. 169–70. A reference to Marinus's gift was inserted in certain manuscripts of *ASC* (though not in that used by Asser) s.a. 883; but the record of Alfred's gift of alms to Rome, apparently inserted in the same annal at the same time, seems to refer to 886 (see below, note 198).

138. For this nautical metaphor, see above, note 45.

139. The last half of this chapter (from 'about the life, behaviour . . .' to the end) is clearly based on Einhard's preface to his *Vita Caroli* (see Halphen, *Éginhard. Vie de Charlemagne*, p. 2, and L. Thorpe, *Two Lives of Charlemagne*, p. 51); there are other reflections of Einhard's wording in chapters 16 and 81. Asser's use of Einhard is particularly remarkable, for there is no other evidence of knowledge of the *Vita Caroli* in Anglo-Saxon England; perhaps Asser owed his knowledge of the work to one of Alfred's continental helpers, such as Grimbald. See further Bullough, 'Educational Tradition in England', p. 458 note 11.

140. The Cotton manuscript here read *fauore*, which gives the opposite sense to what is required by the context. It is not easy to conjecture what the (presumed) scribal error might conceal; perhaps *furore*, 'inspired frenzy', and hence by extension 'incantation' or 'spell'.

141. Nothing whatever is known of this St *Gueriir* or his church in Cornwall besides what Asser here states; it has been suggested, however, that the text's *Gueriir* may be a scribal error for *Guenyr*, that is, Gwinear, an originally Irish saint whose cult was celebrated in the far west of Cornwall (see Doble, *St Neot*, pp. 39–40).

142. Stevenson (*Asser*, pp. 55 and 297) regarded this reference to St Neot as a later interpolation into Asser's text; but it is not impossible that Asser himself was responsible for the remark. According to the eleventh-century *Vita S. Neoti* (on which see further Appendix I), Neot studied first at Glastonbury and then became a hermit in Cornwall at a place called *Neotestoc*, said by the hagiographer to be 'about 10 mile-stones

[*lapidibus*] from the monastery of St Petroc'; *Neotestoc* is probably identical with modern St Neot, Cornwall, which is some eight miles from Bodmin, where St Petroc was venerated (though the identifications are not certain). Neot's fame spread to the extent that he was sought out by King Alfred, whom he duly chastised for his evil behaviour. Neot died thereafter and was buried in his own church at *Neotestoc*, though he appeared posthumously to King Alfred in dreams and even guided the victory at Edington. It is difficult to estimate how much (if any) of this account has a factual basis; but at least it shows that an eleventh-century hagiographer could draw on a tradition which made St Neot a contemporary of Alfred's early years and the patron of a church in Cornwall. If we assume that this tradition originated in the ninth century, it is possible that it was Asser who made the allusion to the saint's Cornish resting-place. If, on the other hand, the allusion *is* an interpolation, it would seemingly have to have been one made in a copy of the text that antedated the Cotton manuscript, for St Neot's remains may no longer have been at *Neotestoc* when this manuscript was written, *c.* 1000: they were translated to Eynesbury (soon renamed St Neots) in Huntingdonshire, sometime after the foundation of the priory there *c.* 980 (see Hart, *Early Charters of Eastern England*, pp. 28–9), but before the compilation in the early eleventh century of a list of saints' resting-places which gives St Neot's as Eynesbury (see Rollason, 'Resting-Places', pp. 64–5 and 90). The words *sublevatus est* ('he has been taken up') were apparently added in the Cotton manuscript near the reference to St Neot, presumably by someone in the eleventh century or thereafter who felt it necessary to draw attention to the fact that the saint's remains were no longer in Cornwall; see Plummer, *Life and Times of Alfred*, pp. 29–30.

143. Earlier commentators have regarded this account of Alfred's illnesses as incredible and confused, and hence as evidence for a later forger's work, for the unfinished state of the text, or for conflation of separate traditions (see, for example, Galbraith, 'Who Wrote Asser's Life of Alfred?', pp. 113–16; Kirby, 'Asser and his Life of King Alfred', pp. 14–15; Plummer, *Life and Times of Alfred*, pp. 27–8 and 214). In fact Asser's account is adequately coherent (as recognized by Schütt, 'Literary Form', pp. 214–15), so long as one does not expect it to be entirely explicable in medical terms and so long as one admits some degree of rhetorical embellishment. He recounts the stages of Alfred's medical history in reverse order: (1) as a youth, Alfred was unable to suppress carnal desire, and so prayed to God for an illness to strengthen his resolve, and contracted piles (*ficus*); (2) subsequently, on a visit to Cornwall, he asked God to replace the piles with a less severe illness but one not outwardly visible, whereupon he was cured of piles; (3) at his

wedding (aged nineteen, in 868) he was struck suddenly by the new, unidentified, illness which lasted from his twentieth to his forty-fifth year. Here, and in chapters 25 and 91, Asser presents a picture of the king as one so obsessed with his poor health that one begins to suspect that the illness was in part psychological. The picture is supported to a considerable extent by Alfred's own writings: he alludes to his illness in the preface to his translation of Boethius (above, p. 131), and in chapter 35 of the same work he remarks, as if from his own experience, that 'bodily sloth and vices often trouble the mind with forgetfulness and lead it astray with a mist of error so that it cannot shine as brightly as it would' (Sedgefield, *King Alfred's Old English Version of Boethius*, p. 95). Elias, patriarch of Jerusalem, is known to have sent medical advice to Alfred, perhaps in response to the king's request; certainly the advice seems appropriate to his case (see further below, note 220).

144. The text is evidently corrupt here. Possibly a numeral (specifying the number of Alfred's children who died in infancy) has fallen out after *est*, as Stevenson conjectured. Wheeler ('Textual Emendations', p. 87) points to other examples of numerals having fallen out (in chapters 35 and 56), and suggests reading *quis* for MS *cuius*; our translation follows this suggestion.

145. Æthelred (wrongly called 'Eadred' in the transmitted text) seems to have succeeded Ceolwulf (above, note 83) as ruler of Mercia. He appears for the first time in a charter dated 883 (*S* 218), and had clearly by then acknowledged Alfred's overlordship (cf. Asser's remark at the end of chapter 80). His efforts to extend his authority into Wales are mentioned in chapter 80. In 886 Alfred made him responsible for London (chapter 83); *Ætheredes hyd*, the old name for Queenhithe, may preserve his name, and Aldermanbury may be where he had his residence (see Ekwall, *Street-Names of the City of London*, pp. 35–6 and 195). He was known as 'lord of the Mercians', and died in 911 (*ASC*). His wife Æthelflæd was clearly a remarkable woman: for an account of her crucial contribution to the 'reconquest' of the eastern Danelaw, during the reign of Edward the Elder, see Wainwright, 'Æthelflæd, Lady of the Mercians'. She died in 918 and, like her husband, was buried at Gloucester (*ASC*).

146. In fact, Alfred made her abbess of his own foundation at Shaftesbury (chapter 98); according to Shaftesbury tradition (represented by *S* 357), she took the veil on account of bad health.

147. Æthelweard received generous provision in Alfred's will (above, p. 175); he attests several charters during the reign of his brother Edward; according to 'Florence' of Worcester, he died on 16 October '922' (?920) and was buried at Winchester; according to William of Malmesbury, he had two sons, Ælfwine and Æthelwine, who were killed at the battle of *Brunanburh* in 937 and who were buried at Malmesbury.

148. Not a school in the strict sense of the word (see Stevenson, *Asser*, p. 300); compare the custom on the Continent whereby young noblemen were brought up and educated together with the monarch's children at the royal court (Riché, *Les Écoles et l'enseignement dans l'Occident chrétien*, pp. 287–313); see also Bullough, 'Educational Tradition in England', pp. 455–60. On Alfred's educational schemes, see his remarks in the preface to his translation of Gregory's *Pastoral Care* (above, p. 126), as well as Asser's further remarks in chapters 76 and 102.

149. Edward the Elder. He is the main beneficiary in Alfred's will (above, p. 175); he attests a few charters in the latter part of Alfred's reign (for example *S* 348, above, p. 181), and in one (*S* 350, dated 898) is styled *rex*, which (if not merely a copyist's anachronism) may suggest that Alfred had by then entrusted him with a share in royal government; he played some part in the warfare against the Vikings in the 890s (see above, p. 189). He succeeded Alfred as king of Wessex in 899; during his reign he skilfully extended the burh-building activities of his father, and, in collaboration with his sister Æthelflæd, continued the process whereby the kings of Wessex extended their authority into the Danelaw; he died in 924 (see *ASC*).

150. According to the chronicler Æthelweard (*CÆ*, p. 2), Alfred sent Ælfthryth to marry Baldwin II, count of Flanders; this must have taken place after 893, since she was evidently still in England when Asser was writing. See further Stenton, *Anglo-Saxon England*, p. 344.

151. An excellent illustration of Alfred's direction of government amid the 'interruptions of this present life' is found in an Old English letter addressed to Edward the Elder, concerning the history of Fonthill in Wiltshire. The author of the letter describes how a case of litigation concerning the estate was formerly brought to King Alfred: 'and the king stood in the chamber at Wardour – he was washing his hands' (*EHD* no. 102). The king characteristically dealt with the matter on the spot.

152. For other instances of Alfred's creative intelligence, see Asser, chapter 104 (horn lantern), *ASC* s.a. 895 (double fortification blocking a river) and *ASC* s.a. 896 (new long-ships).

153. *aedificia*: see above, note 114.

154. For a more detailed account of what celebration of the Divine Office entailed, see Tolhurst, *Monastic Breviary* VI, especially pp. 7–14. Alfred's daily (*cotidie*) participation in the 'day-time and night-time offices' reveals exceptional devotion in a layman (see also chapter 24); but Asser's account is supported by the suggestion that Alfred was responsible for translating part of the Psalter (see above, p. 31).

155. Alfred's generosity to foreigners is mentioned again by Asser in chapter 101. His curiosity is well illustrated by a passage in the Old English

Orosius (on which see above, p. 33), which incorporates a report made orally to King Alfred concerning a voyage to the White Sea by a man called Ohthere; this is followed by a report of a voyage around the Baltic by a man called Wulfstan, though it is not certain that this report was made to the king. Both are translated by Swanton, *Anglo-Saxon Prose*, pp. 32–7; see also Bately, *Old English Orosius*, pp. lxxi–lxxii.

156. It is not clear why Asser should here wish to distinguish Franks (*Franci*) from Gauls (*Galli*); see also chapter 70, and Stevenson, *Asser*, p. 292. Since he appears to make no geographical distinction elsewhere, Asser may here be adverting simply to a distinction between Germanic and Romance speakers.

157. There is good evidence for the presence at Alfred's court of all these foreign peoples, excepting only Bretons (and taking Franks and Gauls together); *Britones*, here translated 'Welshmen', could include the inhabitants of Cornwall. The Franks would include Grimbald (see the letter of Fulco to Alfred, above, p. 185, and Asser, chapter 78); it is possible that many Frisians came to England in the 880s to escape the consequences of Viking attack, and some are found fighting in Alfred's ships in 896 (*ASC*, above, p. 119); the 'Vikings' (*pagani*) would include the Norseman Ottar (Ohthere), who addressed his report to 'his lord, King Alfred' (above, note 155); Asser himself, of course, was a Welshman; and for three Irish visitors to Alfred's court, see *ASC* s.a. 891 (above, p. 113). There were certainly close connections between England and Brittany in the first half of the tenth century: see, for example, *EHD* nos. 24–5.

158. These 'officials' (*ministeriales*) would be men with duties in the royal household: see further chapter 100.

159. It is interesting that the wording of Asser's quotation differs from that of the Vulgate (that is, Jerome's translation of the Bible), but agrees with the so-called Old Latin translation, an earlier version of the Bible which seems to have originated in Africa in the second century, which was widely known in the British Isles in the early Middle Ages (it is quoted by St Patrick and Gildas, for example), but which was eventually superseded by the Vulgate (see Cross, *Oxford Dictionary of the Christian Church*, pp. 996–7 and 1451–2). That Asser should quote from the Old Latin version indicates that its text was still current at St David's in the second half of the ninth century; see also below, note 241, and Stevenson, *Asser*, pp. xciv–xcv.

160. Stevenson (following Wise) emends *quo adiutores* (the reading of the two transcripts of the Cotton manuscript) to *coadiutores*, beginning a new sentence; but *quo* is required to govern the following subjunctive *acquireret*, so that the sentence in progress continues.

161. The *locus classicus* for the image of the clever bee in the early Middle

Ages was Aldhelm's prose *De Virginitate*, chapters V–VI (ed. Ehwald, *Aldhelmi Opera*, pp. 233–4; trans. Lapidge and Herren, *Aldhelm: The Prose Works*, pp. 62–3), which passage Asser was imitating verbally. (Compare the image in Symons, *Regularis Concordia*, p. 3.) For other verbal debts to Aldhelm's *De Virginitate*, see below, notes 210, 213 and 214.

162. Alfred's feelings on the lack of scholars in his own kingdom were stated earlier in chapters 24–5 (and see above, note 50).

163. Werferth was bishop of Worcester from *c.* 872 to *c.* 915: see O'Donovan, 'Episcopal Dates, pt II', pp. 112–13. He is named as a beneficiary in Alfred's will (above, p. 177), which may signify some special relationship with the king.

164. On Werferth's translation of Gregory's *Dialogues*, see above, p. 32; Alfred himself contributed a preface, translated above, p. 123. Asser's phrase 'sometimes rendering sense for sense' (*aliquando sensum ex sensu ponens*) derives from a well-known Latin tag, which occurs notably in Gregory the Great's *Registrum Epistularum* I, xxix (*rogo: non verbum ex verbo sed sensum ex sensu transferte*); cf. Gregory's *Dialogi, prefatio*, and Jerome's *Epistola* lvii. A similar phrase is used on two occasions by Alfred himself, in the prefaces to his translations of Gregory's *Pastoral Care* (above, p. 126) and of Boethius's *Consolation of Philosophy* (above, p. 131); see Whitelock, 'Prose of Alfred's Reign', p. 79. Since Asser and Alfred are known to have collaborated closely, this should occasion no surprise.

165. Plegmund became archbishop of Canterbury in 890; but Asser makes it plain that he (like the others) came to Alfred before the king began to read, that is, before 887 (chapter 87). He was one of those who assisted in the translation of Gregory's *Pastoral Care* (above, p. 126). He died on 2 August 923.

166. Æthelstan attests *S* 352 (?879, but probably not reliable) and *S* 350 (898), as well as a few charters issued in the early years of Edward the Elder's reign; it may have been he who was appointed bishop of Ramsbury *c.* 909 (see *EHD* no. 229). Werwulf attests *S* 348 (892; translated above, p. 179) and *S* 356 (undated); in 899 Bishop Werferth of Worcester leased an estate to the priest Werwulf 'on account of our ancient association and his faithful friendship and obedience' (*S* 1279); he continues to attest charters in the early years of Edward the Elder's reign.

167. It is not surprising that Alfred should have turned to Mercia for learned men trained in Latin, since it is an area for which there is some (albeit meagre) record of intellectual achievement during an otherwise barren century. Various writings in Old English have been attributed to ninth-century Mercia, including the poetry of Cynewulf (see Sisam, *Studies*

in the History of Old English Literature, pp. 1–28), a *Life of St Chad* (see Vleeskruyer, *The Life of St Chad*), and the Old English prose *Martyrology* (see Kotzor, *Das altenglische Martyrologium*, pp. 443–54). The Old English translation of Bede's *Ecclesiastical History* was made by a Mercian contemporary of Alfred's (see Whitelock, 'The Old English Bede', and above, p. 33).

168. The 'summoning' of Grimbald was not quite as simple a matter as Asser implies: see above, pp. 26–7, and the letter of Fulco, archbishop of Rheims, to King Alfred, translated above, pp. 182–6. Grimbald had been a monk at the monastery of St Bertin's (in the town of Saint-Omer, Flanders) where Fulco had previously been abbot (878–83), and the archbishop was reluctant to part with Grimbald's services. Nevertheless, and no doubt after some negotiation, Grimbald came over to England, probably in 886. Little is known of his activities in England: he helped Alfred to understand and translate the *Pastoral Care* (above, p. 126); he allegedly declined the offer of the archbishopric of Canterbury in 888; he may have been involved in the planning if not the actual foundation of the New Minster, Winchester. For the possibility that Grimbald brought certain identifiable manuscripts to England, see above, p. 214 note 26, and for the possibility that he was involved in the compilation of the *Anglo-Saxon Chronicle*, see above, p. 40. Grimbald died in England on 8 July 901. See further, Stevenson, *Asser*, pp. 307–11; Grierson, 'Grimbald of St Bertin's'; and Bately, 'Grimbald of St Bertin's'.

169. This John is probably the same as the 'John, a priest and monk of Old [that is, continental] Saxon origin', whom Alfred appointed abbot of Athelney (chapters 94–7); but see the remarks of Bately, 'Grimbald of St Bertin's', p. 2. He was one of those who assisted Alfred in the translation of Gregory's *Pastoral Care* (above, p. 126). He attests *S* 348 (892; translated above, p. 179), and that he survived as a priest into Edward the Elder's reign is shown by *S* 364 (dated 901). An acrostic poem, addressed by 'John' to 'Æthelstan' (son of Edward the Elder), can be attributed to him with some plausibility, and two other acrostics addressed to Alfred (translated above, p. 192) may also be his work: see Lapidge, 'Some Latin Poems', pp. 72–83.

170. For this Welsh idiom, see above, note 64.

171. For the date of Asser's first visit to Alfred, see above, p. 27.

172. For Dean as a royal estate, see below, p. 319 note 41.

173. The act of becoming a king's *familiaris* (a member of the royal household) probably involved a formal undertaking by both parties; see, in general, Magnou-Nortier, *Foi et fidélité*.

174. Asser says simply *sine consilio meorum*; the translation 'people' is supplied for the sake of clarity. It is possible that Asser required their advice

because at St David's he was a member of a religious community controlled by a family group, and needed his kinsmen's permission to spend so much time in England; for accounts of monastic life in Wales in the early Middle Ages, see Lloyd, *History of Wales* I, pp. 205–16; Davies, *An Early Welsh Microcosm*, pp. 128–30; and Victory, *The Celtic Church in Wales*. If Asser were actually bishop of St David's (above, p. 52), the difficulty of his position would be the more easy to understand.

175. The text reads *in Wintonia civitate*. In Celtic-Latin texts, *civitas* is often used to designate a monastery rather than a town or city. The most obvious translation for *Wintonia* would be Winchester, but it is difficult to believe that Alfred would not have known about Asser's illness (and would have needed to communicate with him by letter) had he been all the while in Winchester, or even had he merely contracted the illness there and had then been taken back to Wales (it being unclear whether Asser struggled for a year and a week in *Wintonia*, or in the fever). However, it is quite possible that *Wintonia* is an English scribe's spelling of *Guentonia*, which is the Latin name for Caerwent in Cambro-Latin texts such as the *Liber Landavensis* (see Evans and Rhys, *Book of Llan Dâv*, pp. 220, 222) and the *Life* of St Tatheus, the patron saint of Caerwent (see Wade-Evans, *Vitae Sanctorum Britanniae et Genealogiae*, pp. 272, 274, 282, 284).

176. There were good political reasons why Asser's service with Alfred could be of benefit to St David's; in particular, the support of Alfred would provide security for the community against the depredations of Hyfaidd ap Bleddri, king of Dyfed, as Asser goes on to explain. See Kirby, 'Asser and his Life of King Alfred', pp. 18–20.

177. Stevenson considered the word *rudimenta* to be corrupt. However, *rudimentum* in the sense of 'teaching' or 'learning' is attested elsewhere in Cambro-Latin texts. In a curious note preserved in an early ninth-century Welsh manuscript, the following statement occurs: *Nemnivus istas reperit literas, vituperante quidem scolastico saxonici generis quia Brittones non haberent rudimentum* ('Nemnivus devised these letters when a scholar of the English race was alleging that the Welsh did not have learning': see Dumville, ' "Nennius" and the *Historia Brittonum*', p. 90). If Asser knew of this note, there would be nice irony in his statement that England would be helped *per rudimenta Sancti Degui* – a fitting riposte to the unknown English scholar who thought the Welsh lacked *rudimentum*!

178. Asser speaks of the 'learning of St David', whereas we would more naturally say 'of St David's' in modern English. By Celtic writers in particular, the patron saint of a monastery was regarded as its living head (see Davies, *An Early Welsh Microcosm*, pp. 140–41).

179. It is at least worth asking if Asser intended the terms *tribulationes et*

iniurias in a technical and legal sense. The word *tribulatio* is not so used in texts of the Welsh laws, but *iniuria* (for Welsh *sarhad*) is the normal word for the legal offence of insult and for the compensation payable to the offended (see Jenkins and Owen, *The Welsh Law of Women*, p. 216, and Emanuel, *The Latin Texts of the Welsh Laws*, index, under Insult and Insult-fine).

180. Hyfaidd was king of Dyfed, which included St David's; he died in 892 or 893, according to the *Annales Cambriae* (Morris, *Nennius*, pp. 49 and 90), which at that time were being kept at St David's (see above, p. 219 note 89).

181. As used by Celtic-Latin authors of this period, the term *parochia* (here translated 'jurisdiction') means the jurisdiction of a church over its dependent lands as well as its rights in general. For a discussion of the term and its historical context, see Hughes, *The Church in Early Irish Society*, pp. 57–90, and Davies, *An Early Welsh Microcosm*, pp. 146–9; see also below, note 193. Attacks on the church in Wales by kings and by the aristocracy were by no means uncommon at this time: see Davies, *An Early Welsh Microcosm*, pp. 111–12 and 133, and idem, 'Land and Power in Early Medieval Wales'.

182. As we learn from two entries in the *Annales Cambriae*, Nobis was bishop of St David's from 840 until his death in 873 or 874. Nothing further is known of him. Although its etymology is uncertain, the name is recorded elsewhere in Welsh sources, for example in the *Liber Landavensis* (Evans and Rhys, *Book of Llan Dâv*, p. 216) and in a ninth-century entry in the so-called Book of Chad or Lichfield Gospels (see Stevenson, *Asser*, p. 316 note 4). The title 'archbishop' given by Asser to Nobis is to be understood as honorific (Whitelock, *Genuine Asser*, p. 15); it does not imply metropolitan status, and there is no evidence that the bishops of St David's had any sort of authority over other Welsh sees (see Lloyd, *History of Wales* I, p. 204 note 43, and II, p. 486, and Davies, *An Early Welsh Microcosm*, p. 149).

183. The political events recorded in this chapter are rather complex, but, as far as can be judged, they constitute an accurate survey of Welsh history in the 880s and early 890s. Rhodri Mawr ('the Great') had succeeded his father Merfyn in 844 as king of Gwynedd, and had extended his kingdom to include Powys (?in the 850s) and Ceredigion (in the 870s). He died in 878 (killed by the English, according to the *Annales Cambriae*) and his overlordship was shared between his surviving sons. Anarawd is presumed to be the senior from the fact that he succeeded to the paternal inheritance of Gwynedd. He and his brothers then applied pressure on the southern Welsh kingdoms, forcing the rulers of Dyfed and Brycheiniog to turn to Alfred for protection; the rulers of Glywysing and Gwent were compelled more particularly by

pressure from Ealdorman Æthelred of Mercia to do the same. This process must have been complete by the mid-880s, and it was probably at about this time that Anarawd formed an alliance with Guthfrith, the Viking king of York. The alliance of these two northern powers was potentially very threatening to Alfred. However, because (according to Asser) Anarawd derived no advantage, only misfortune, from the alliance, he broke it and himself submitted to King Alfred; this probably took place in, or shortly before, 893. The political stability which resulted was thus of benefit to Alfred in his struggles against the Vikings, and also to the community of St David's. See further Lloyd, *History of Wales* I, pp. 324–30; Kirby, 'Asser and his Life of King Alfred', pp. 16–20; idem, 'Northumbria in the Reign of Alfred the Great', pp. 341–5; and Loyn, 'Wales and England in the Tenth Century', pp. 285–6.

184. The text specifies six (*sex*) sons of Rhodri, but there is at least a suspicion that this numeral derives in some way from a misreading of an original *filiorum Rotri vi compulsus*, where *vi* ('by the might') gave rise to the impression that there were six (*vi*) sons and ultimately to the received text *sex filiorum Rotri vi compulsus* (as in the Otho transcript of the Cotton manuscript); the reading of the Corpus transcript (*sex filiorum Rotricum pulsus*) supports the possibility that there was some confusion in the manuscript at this point. Asser would otherwise be the only contemporary authority for Rhodri's 'six' sons: four (of whom one was already dead when Asser was writing) are mentioned in the *Annales Cambriae*, though these and six others are known from later medieval Welsh genealogical tracts. See further Dumville, 'The "Six" Sons of Rhodri Mawr'.

185. Again Æthelred is wrongly called 'Eadred' in the transmitted text; cf. above, note 145.

186. The word *suapte*, a curious archaism, is simply the possessive adjective *sua* and the enclitic *-pte*. However, it is not clear why Asser chose the feminine form *sua*: perhaps he understood a feminine noun such as *voluntate*, or perhaps he took *suapte* to be an adverb (cf. *suatim*, above, note 109); the same word is used as an adverb in chapter 103.

187. By 'Northumbrians' Asser is here referring to the Viking kingdom of York; see above, note 183. Anarawd's 'brothers', mentioned previously, might have included his kinsmen, since in Celtic Latin *fratres* often had this more general meaning: see Charles-Edwards, 'Some Celtic Kinship Terms', p. 117 note 3.

188. For this procedure, see above, note 110.

189. It is possible that Asser, in spelling out the terms of the alliance (*amicitia*) with Alfred (presumably for the benefit of his Welsh audience at St David's), was consciously drawing on the technical vocabulary with

which such alliances were agreed: the king had formally undertaken to provide *amor*, *tutela* and *defensio*. One could compare this terminology with that of the obligations created by the contract of vassalage in later times: see Ganshof, *Feudalism*, pp. 83–4, and Hollyman, *Le Développement du vocabulaire féodal*, pp. 52–3.

190. This place cannot be identified; Stevenson, *Asser*, pp. 318–20, makes a case for Landford in Wiltshire.

191. Translating *duas epistolas, in quibus erat multiplex supputatio omnium rerum, quae erant in duobus monasteriis*. These documents presumably comprised inventories of the movable property (relics, church furnishings, treasures, manuscripts, livestock, etc.) belonging to the monasteries; for comparable documents see Robertson, *Charters*, pp. 248–57.

192. Little is known of these monasteries at Congresbury and Banwell (formerly in Somerset, now in Avon, some ten miles south-west of Bristol), though Congresbury is mentioned in an eleventh-century source as the place where St Congar was buried (Rollason, 'Resting-Places', p. 92), and in the twelfth century it was claimed to have been the original site of the see of Somerset. Both places were apparently given to Asser as his personal property, but when he died in 909 they were probably assigned with the Somerset estates of his see of Sherborne to the new bishopric of Wells. Some information on their later history is provided in an account of the endowment of the bishopric of Wells written by Bishop Giso (1061–88), incorporated in the twelfth-century *Historiola de Primordiis Episcopatus Somersetensis* (see Hunter, *Ecclesiastical Documents*, pp. 9–28, especially 15–20). They seem to have come back into royal possession during the tenth or early eleventh century (cf. *S* 373 and 806 for Banwell), for we learn from this account that they were given by the king (?Cnut) to Duduc, sometime before Duduc became bishop of Wells (in 1033); during the reign of Edward the Confessor (1042–66), Duduc gave them to the bishopric, but after his death in 1060 they were seized by Earl Harold. *Domesday Book* shows that both places did indeed belong to Harold before 1066, and Bishop Giso endeavoured to recover them (cf. *S* 1042). In 1086 Congresbury belonged to King William, but Banwell to the bishop of Wells (*DB* fols. 87r, 89v); the former was recovered by the bishopric during the reign of King John. See further Whitelock, *Genuine Asser*, pp. 13–14.

193. Alfred granted to Asser the monastery of Exeter together with all the *parochia* which belonged to it in Wessex and Cornwall, that is, complete with its jurisdiction over its dependent lands and with all its rights; the word *parochia* (above, note 181) would not have been used by Asser in the sense of 'episcopal diocese'. There is accordingly no necessary implication that the gift of Exeter *ipso facto* laid on Asser the episcopal charge of Cornwall and Devon (cf. Finberg, *Lucerna*, pp. 109–10).

However, Asser was certainly a bishop before he succeeded Wulfsige at
Sherborne (see above, p. 49), and it is possible that he was at first made
a suffragan bishop within the Sherborne diocese; Alfred may have
based him at Exeter because he would be particularly well qualified to
look after the interests of the native element in the population of the
south-west, because there was already a monastery there (on which see
Rose-Troup, 'The Ancient Monastery of St Mary and St Peter at
Exeter, 680–1050'), and because he wanted a representative at a place
much exposed to Viking attack. Subsequently, as bishop of Sherborne,
Asser himself presided over the enormous south-western diocese,
though on his death in 909 it was divided up into the three bishoprics of
Sherborne, Wells and Crediton, serving Dorset, Somerset, and Devon
and Cornwall respectively (see *EHD* no. 229). Galbraith's interpretation
of this passage ('Who Wrote Asser's Life of Alfred?', pp. 93–9), that it
would promote the interests of someone who wanted to have the episcopal see of the Devonshire diocese moved from Crediton to Exeter,
depends on the assumption that *parochia* means 'diocese'; see above, pp.
50–51.

194. These words echo the preface of Einhard's *Vita Caroli*: see above,
note 139.

195. Asser's account (in chapters 79 and 81) of the circumstances in which
he entered King Alfred's service is curiously similar to the account,
given in the anonymous *Vita Alcuini* (Arndt, 'Vita Alcuini', especially p.
190), written in the 820s, of how Alcuin entered the service of Charlemagne; we are indebted to Dr Pierre Chaplais for drawing our attention
to this point. The similarities include the presentation of the discussion
between king and scholar, the scholar's declaration of his need to get
permission from his own people to leave them, and the king's grant of
two monasteries to the scholar to strengthen his resolve to stay. If all
this is anything more than an interesting coincidence, it may be that
Asser saw his position at Alfred's court as analogous to that of Alcuin at
Charlemagne's (and perhaps Alfred felt the same way); the analogy
would have been flattering to them both. Acquaintance on Asser's part
with the *Vita Alcuini* would add further to the already extensive evidence
for his knowledge of Frankish history and literature.

196. The territory which the Vikings left is not specified in the transmitted
text, but that of the eastern Franks must be intended: Asser is now
continuing the account of the Viking army last mentioned in chapter 66.

197. The Vikings who had wintered at Louvain on the river Dyle in 884–5
(above, note 124) attacked Rouen in the summer of 885 and then moved
further up the river Seine: after attacking Pontoise in November, they
reached Paris and proceeded to besiege the city. The siege of Paris
lasted from November 885 until November 886, and the story of its

heroic defence (under the leadership of Count Odo in particular) is told in detail in a long poem by Abbo of St Germain: see Wacquet, *Abbon: Le Siège de Paris par les Normands*. Asser clearly had access to information on the siege not given in *ASC*.

198. In chapter 72 Asser had said that the Viking army in East Anglia broke the peace with King Alfred (from *ASC* s.a. 885); here he seems to be saying that it was this violation of the peace that caused Alfred to restore London and turn it into a major bulwark against the Vikings. A misplaced addition in the annal for 883 in certain manuscripts of *ASC* (though not, apparently, in that used by Asser; see also above, note 137) refers to an occasion when Sigehelm and Æthelstan took to Rome the alms promised by King Alfred (and also alms destined for the shrines of St Thomas and St Bartholomew in 'India' or 'Judea') 'when they [the English] were encamped against the Viking army at London; and there – by God's grace! – their prayers were well fulfilled after that promise'. It seems likely that this addition properly belongs to 886 (see Stenton, *Anglo-Saxon England*, p. 258 note 3, and below, note 206), and it shows that Alfred had to use force to recover London.

199. *aut cum paganis sine captivitate erant*: Stevenson (following Wise and the Otho transcript of the Cotton manuscript) emends *sine* to *sub*, thereby implying that the English who *were* in captivity submitted to Alfred, which is nonsensical and which contradicts *ASC*. Wise himself states that the Cotton manuscript read *sine*, and this is confirmed by the Corpus transcript; we follow the original and intended reading.

200. This submission to Alfred may have been marked by the taking of a general oath of loyalty to the king (see further below, p. 306 note 6). It was clearly a major political event, and it probably finds due reflection in the regnal styles employed in Alfred's charters (see above, note 1), and in the issue of a series of pennies bearing the king's portrait on the obverse and a monogram representing 'London' on the reverse, struck at a new, higher weight-standard (see Lyon, 'Some Problems in Interpreting Anglo-Saxon Coinage', pp. 181 and 183). It was perhaps in connection with the 'restoration' of London that the burh at Southwark was built (above, p. 193), and it must have been soon afterwards that Alfred concluded his treaty with the Danish king Guthrum (above, p. 171). For Ealdorman Æthelred, see above, note 145.

201. Chézy(-sur-Marne) is not described as a royal estate in *ASC*, so this is yet another example of Asser's superior knowledge of Frankish affairs. The place in question is sometimes identified as Chessy, near Lagny.

202. This chapter appears to refer to the events of 886–9 (cf. *ASC* s.a. 887, which mentions only two winters, 886–7 and 887–8; but Æthelweard (*CÆ*, p. 46) mentions three). The Vikings left Paris in November 886, with a promise of tribute and with Charles the Fat's permission to

ravage Burgundy during the winter. They went further up the river
Seine, and then up the river Yonne, laying siege to Sens. In the opening
months of 887 they ravaged Burgundy between the rivers Loire and
Saône, and then they returned to Paris to collect their tribute. From
Paris they came back up the Seine, along the river Marne, and established a camp at Chézy, ravaging places as far as the river Meuse, as
well as part of Burgundy. In 888 they besieged Meaux, some distance
down-river from Chézy, and at the end of the year they transferred
their camp to the banks of the river Loing, a tributary of the Seine not
far from the Yonne; they would thus appear to have spent 888–9 in the
vicinity of the Yonne.

203. The dismemberment of the empire of Charles the Fat (above, note 133)
was in fact a rather more complex process, apparently set in motion in
the autumn of 887 when Arnulf, the bastard son of Carloman (brother
of Charles the Fat), was proclaimed king, effectively of the eastern
kingdom (Germany); Charles the Fat was not formally deposed until 11
November 887, and he died several weeks later on 13 January 888. Other
men were then proclaimed kings in other parts of Charles's empire, in
the opening months of 888: Rudolf, formerly count of upper Burgundy,
became ruler over much of Burgundy; Odo, count of Paris, became ruler
of the western kingdom (France); Guy, duke of Spoleto, was at first a
rival candidate for the throne of France, though he presently turned his
attention towards Italy; and Berengar, count of the march of Friuli, was
raised to the kingship of Italy. Guy and Berengar then fought against
each other for control of Italy: the latter defeated the former at Brescia
in the autumn of 888, but the former defeated the latter at Trebbia in
the spring of 889; for some while thereafter Guy was dominant in Italy,
though Berengar remained in the north-east. For these events, see Halphen, *Charlemagne and the Carolingian Empire*, pp. 329–35.

204. Asser's remarks about the priority of Arnulf (derived, but also developed, from *ASC*) represent a point of view that would not have been
shared by everyone on the Continent; Odo, Rudolf and Berengar came
to terms with Arnulf in different ways during 888, and Guy may have
done the same, but they are unlikely to have seen Arnulf's position in
quite such clear terms as Asser implies. Both the chronicler and Asser
had evidently been given a version of events that was decidedly favourable to Arnulf.

205. These last remarks may have been intended to apply to Berengar and
Guy in particular (above, note 203), and not to all five rulers collectively.
The events recorded in chapter 85 thus cover a period from late 887 to
early 889; Asser simply follows *ASC* in placing them all in the annal for
887, though neither he nor the chronicler necessarily implies by so
doing that all the events took place in 887 itself.

206. A record of a similar payment of alms to Rome was entered in certain manuscripts of *ASC*, s.a. 883, probably referring to events of 886 (above, note 198); the present statement presumably refers to 887, and further related statements occur in *ASC* s.a. 888, 889 and 890 (above, p. 113). These payments of alms may represent the origin of the tax later known as Peter's Pence: see Stenton, *Anglo-Saxon England*, p. 217 note 1 (and cf. above, note 37). The payments may have been made with coins specially struck for the purpose: see Dolley and Blunt, 'Coins of Ælfred the Great', pp. 77–8. For some reason Asser does not use *ASC* after this point, even though his copy probably extended to 892: see below, p. 278.

207. For an interpretation of this statement, see above, p. 28, and note 46.

208. Asser referred to Alfred's 'little book' in chapter 24, and he gives further details of it in chapter 89 (where it is called his *enchiridion*, or 'hand-book'); it seems likely that this 'little book' is identical with the *Handboc* of King Alfred mentioned by William of Malmesbury in his *Gesta Pontificum* (written *c.* 1125) and with a volume known as the *Dicta* of King Alfred which was apparently preserved at Worcester (for details, see Whitelock, 'Prose of Alfred's Reign', pp. 71–3, and idem, 'William of Malmesbury on the Works of King Alfred', pp. 90–91). The book seems thus to have existed in the twelfth century, but unfortunately it has not survived to the present day; it would obviously have transformed our knowledge of the spiritual and intellectual interests of the king. One gains the impression from Asser that it was principally filled with Alfred's favourite prayers and psalms, but the references to it in chapters 88–9 show that it also contained many other miscellaneous extracts from various sources. Indeed, it emerges from William's account that it contained information on the lineage of Aldhelm (perhaps in the form of a West Saxon royal genealogy) and on Aldhelm's public performance of vernacular poetry; and the references to the *Dicta* suggest that it contained a West Saxon regnal list as well as some information on St Jerome. (The possibility that the references to Alfred's *Handboc* and *Dicta* are simply to a manuscript of Alfred's translation of St Augustine's *Soliloquies*, with additional material appended, and not to the 'little book' described by Asser, is discussed by Whitelock, ibid.)

209. According to Wise (above, p. 224), there was a change of hand at this point in the manuscript. The second hand, which Wise describes as a *manus recentior*, continued to the end of chapter 98. Unfortunately, Wise does not state whether the scribe who then continued from chapter 99 onwards was the same scribe who had written the first part of the manuscript (up to this point in chapter 88). If it was, it may be assumed that this scribe and that of the *manus recentior* were collaborating and

hence were contemporaries; if not, it is possible that the Cotton manuscript was written over a lengthy period of time. See further Stevenson, *Asser*, pp. xliii–xlvi.

210. Once again Asser borrows a sequence of phrases from Aldhelm's prose *De Virginitate*, chapter I (ed. Ehwald, *Aldhelmi Opera*, p. 229; trans. Lapidge and Herren, *Aldhelm: The Prose Works*, p. 59).

211. A quire or gathering at this period would normally have consisted of four sheets of parchment folded in the middle to make a booklet of eight leaves.

212. The source of this quotation is unknown.

213. The image of the fecund bee is Aldhelmian in inspiration: see above, note 161. The allusion to the 'flowers' of Holy Scripture is also Aldhelmian: compare his description of his method of compiling the prose *De Virginitate* – *purpureos pudicitiae flores ex sacrorum voluminum prato decerpens*, 'plucking crimson flowers of purity from the meadow of holy books' (ed. Ehwald, *Aldhelmi Opera*, p. 249; trans. Lapidge and Herren, *Aldhelm: The Prose Works*, p. 76). Alfred himself used the same image when he described his translation of St Augustine's *Soliloquies* as 'blooms' (*blostman*).

214. *subnixis precibus*: another Aldhelmian tag (see Ehwald, *Aldhelmi Opera*, pp. 201, 281 and 300, from the prose *De Virginitate*; pp. 406, 433 and 436, from the *Carmen de Virginitate*; and pp. 485, 491 and 497, from Aldhelm's letters).

215. The reading *aut* is nonsensical and is best to be understood as a misspelling of (*h*)*aut* or *haud*, whence *Hic haud aliter* = 'Not otherwise did the king . . .'.

216. The transmitted text (*quos*) is nonsensical and is duly marked as corrupt by Stevenson; since the infinitives *discere* and *redigere* apparently depend on *praesumpsit incipere*, we suggest reading *illosque* or *et illos* for *quos*, thus taking everything from *Hic* (?)*haud aliter* to *ad magnitudinem unius psalterii perveniret* as one sentence.

217. The source of this hexameter is unknown. It does not (apparently) occur in any classical author, and may be a medieval remodelling of Statius, *Thebaid* III, 3–4 (. . . *invigilant animo* scelerisque parati / supplicium exercent *curae*); cf. Theodulf of Orleans, *Carmina* ii (*Ad Episcopos*), 221 (*Cura regendarum quibus est concessa animarum*). Stevenson, *Asser*, p. 327, makes the unwarranted statement that the hexameter may be of Frankish origin because the word *pius* was 'an exceedingly favourite one with the Frankish writers of Latin verse'.

218. It is this remark that provides the basis for the date of Asser's *Life of King Alfred*: by Asser's standard calculation, Alfred's forty-fifth year would be 893. He presumably knew that he was writing in 893, and expressed the date as normal in terms of Alfred's age; it would be

perverse to imagine that Alfred's age is the primary dating criterion, giving 893–4 (calculating from Asser's 849 as the year of his birth), or 891–2 or 892–3 (calculating from 847 or 848: see above, note 2).

219. The transmitted text (*de cotidiana nationum*) is evidently corrupt, as Stevenson recognized. Wheeler ('Textual Emendations', p. 86) reasonably conjectures that a word such as *sollicitudine* has fallen out after *cotidiana*, and our translation incorporates his suggestion.

220. There is evidence that Elias, patriarch of Jerusalem (*c.* 879–907), sent a circular letter to western rulers asking for money to help restore churches in his province; one such letter was received in 881 by Charles the Fat, and another may have reached Alfred and have been seen by Asser (see Stevenson, *Asser*, pp. 328–9). A specific link between Alfred and Elias is afforded by the '*Leechbook* of Bald', a collection of medical texts in Old English possibly compiled during Alfred's reign (above, pp. 33–4 and 215 note 40). In book II, chapter 64, of this collection we find a group of medical remedies which 'Dominus Elias, patriarch at Jerusalem, ordered to be told to King Alfred'; unfortunately, owing to the loss of leaves in the manuscript, the opening part of the chapter has not survived, but its original contents can be reconstructed from the list of chapter headings (see Cockayne, *Leechdoms* II, pp. 174–5, 288–91). Elias sent Alfred remedies for constipation, pain in the spleen, diarrhoea, and 'internal tenderness', among other disorders, and also a 'White Stone for all unknown illnesses'; see Meaney, 'Alfred, the Patriarch and the White Stone', and above, note 143. For Alfred's contacts with Ireland, see Asser, chapter 76, and *ASC* s.a. 891 (above, p. 113). It is interesting that the three Irishmen mentioned in *ASC* as visiting Alfred presently set out for Rome and were intent on proceeding thence to Jerusalem (below, p. 282 note 13), so it may be that contacts between the extremities of the western world were more frequent than we might expect.

221. *aedificia*: see above, note 114.

222. Asser presumably means that existing stone buildings were demolished, and the materials incorporated in new and better-situated buildings. We need not imagine that the buildings were 'moved' long distances: such reconstructions took place within the confines of an established royal estate (see, for instance, below, p. 317 note 25).

223. Stevenson's text reads *Qui*, though he recognized that this was nonsensical; both the Corpus and Otho transcripts of the Cotton manuscript read *quid* (see Stevenson, *Asser*, p. 77). Wheeler ('Textual Emendations', p. 87) proposes the reading *quid de*, thus making another rhetorical question in the series *Quid loquar de* . . .; our translation incorporates this suggestion.

224. This sentence, and the passage that follows, afford a clear indication of

the problems that confronted Alfred in persuading his subjects to accept the heavy burdens he had to place on them for the defence of the kingdom; for the suggestion that the *Anglo-Saxon Chronicle* was a work of propaganda compiled under the king's auspices to assist his cause, see Davis, 'Alfred the Great: Propaganda and Truth'. In a letter written in 877 or 878 (*EHD* no. 222), Pope John VIII gave encouragement to Æthelred, archbishop of Canterbury, apparently in connection with the archbishop's resistance to (unspecified) demands made by the king.

225. Assuming that Asser's copy of *ASC* extended to 892 (see below, p. 278), this remark may have been suggested by the reference to a 'half-made' fortification surprised by the Vikings in 892 (above, p. 114). For Alfred's network of fortifications, see the *Burghal Hidage*, above, p. 193.

226. Stevenson's text reads *per hanc rem . . .*, though again he recognized that this was nonsensical; the Corpus transcript of the Cotton manuscript reads *per hac reecheu*, so it is apparent that the manuscript was corrupt at this point. A noun is needed to determine the genitive *eulogii* ('fine utterance', or 'excellent authority') which follows, and which apparently refers to the Scriptural authority quoted above. We conjecture *per exemplum . . . eulogii* and translate accordingly.

227. Asser's language suggests that the reference here may be to a former reluctance on the part of the king's subjects to perform, specifically, the three common burdens (military service, bridge building and fortress building) incumbent upon them; see further below, p. 328 note 7.

228. It is not known for certain when Athelney was founded, but it was presumably sometime after Alfred's sojourn there in 878 (Asser, chapter 55); a charter of Alfred's in favour of the monastery (*S* 343, dated '852') cannot be authentic in its received form. For Alfred's church at Athelney, see Clapham, *English Romanesque Architecture*, pp. 147–8. That there was still a religious community at Athelney during the 930s is suggested by *S* 432 and *S* 1207, and it was certainly flourishing in the late tenth and first half of the eleventh centuries (for instance, *S* 921, 929). See further Page, VCH *Somerset* II, pp. 99–103.

229. This is a reference to the fortification at Lyng, mentioned in the *Burghal Hidage* (above, p. 193); see Hill, 'The Burghal Hidage – Lyng'. The other fortification was that built by Alfred at Athelney itself, in 878 (Asser, chapter 55). The causeway (*pons*) between them may have been a construction similar in form to the wooden bridge at Ravning Enge in Jutland, built *c.* 979 during the reign of Harold Bluetooth, king of Denmark (on which see Roesdahl, *Viking Age Denmark*, pp. 47–8).

230. Asser's remarks on the decline of monasteries may have been prompted by Alfred, who seems to have made similar remarks in a letter to Fulco,

archbishop of Rheims (as reported in Fulco's reply, translated above, p. 182).

231. For John, see above, note 169.

232. These people probably included refugees forced to flee France by the Viking armies active on the Continent in the 880s; according to the *Annals of St Vaast*, s.a. 882, one effect of the depredations was that people were sold 'across the sea'.

233. Stevenson (*Asser*, pp. 334–5) makes the attractive but unprovable conjecture that this young man of Danish extraction was none other than Oda, who subsequently became bishop of Ramsbury (928–41) and archbishop of Canterbury (941–58). On Oda, see further Robinson, *St Oswald and the Church of Worcester*, p. 41, where attention is drawn to some chronological difficulties implicit in Stevenson's conjecture.

234. Asser here interestingly conflates biblical weeds – cockle in the midst of the wheat (Matthew xiii, 25: *zizania in medio tritici*) – with Virgil's crops, which are overcome by the wretched tare (*Georgics* I, 152–4: *intereunt segetes . . . infelix lolium et steriles dominantur avenae*).

235. The reading of the text here, *auditoribus*, means 'listeners' rather than 'accomplices', but 'listeners' in modern English lacks the point of Asser's Latin phrase. In spite of our translation, we do not mean to imply that *adiutoribus* should be read for *auditoribus* in the text.

236. It is not precisely clear what Asser means by *dispoliatis gladiis. Dispoliare* properly means 'to rob' or 'to strip (of clothing)'; perhaps by extension the swords are stripped of their sheaths, or laid bare.

237. As in the case of Athelney, it is not known for certain when Shaftesbury was founded; Asser's remark that the abbey was built 'near the east gate of Shaftesbury' suggests that the burh there was already in existence, and if the burh was built in 880 (see below, p. 340 note 6) it would follow that the abbey was founded between 880 and 893 (when Asser was writing). Alfred's foundation charter (*S* 357) would appear to belong to a date in the 870s, but it is plainly spurious. Two charters of King Æthelstan in favour of Shaftesbury (*S* 419, 429) show that the community was still flourishing in the 930s, and it continued to prosper thereafter, so that by the close of the Anglo-Saxon period it was easily the richest nunnery in the country. This was doubtless due in part to the close connection it always enjoyed with the royal family: Ælfgifu, wife of King Edmund (939–46), was buried there in 944 and soon came to be venerated as a saint (see *CÆ*, p. 54), and the abbey also became the centre of the cult of King Edward the Martyr (975–8), whose remains were translated there in 979 (*ASC*). See further Page, VCH *Dorset* II, pp. 73–9.

238. A feminine singular relative pronoun, *quae*, modifying *meditationem* and serving as the subject of the past participles *incepta . . . inventa . . .*

servata, has apparently fallen out after *meditationem* and before *non inaniter*.

239. The passage is probably corrupt through dittography. We delete the second occurrence of the words *decimam sibi multipliciter redditurum fuisse* from our translation. An alternative solution would be to take the second *redditurum* as a scribal error (by dittography) for *redditum*, and to translate: 'For he had once heard a passage in scripture to the effect that the Lord had promised to repay His tithe many times over, and had faithfully kept His promise, and had indeed repaid the tithe many times over.' But the solution is not clear since the 'passage in scripture' cannot be identified.

240. The king's revenues in the late ninth century would have been derived, directly and indirectly, from a variety of sources: for example, the annual food-rents due from all folkland, which though originally paid in kind might by this time have been commuted for cash; the profits which accrued from the king's estates, for instance from the sale of excess produce; the proceeds of justice over folkland; the proceeds of justice derived from fines for particularly heinous crimes, which the king reserved to himself; the sale of bookland or of privileges over bookland; tolls on trade; the profits of coinage; tribute from Welsh rulers who had accepted the king's overlordship; and miscellaneous bequests from the king's subjects. (For the terms 'folkland' and 'bookland', see below, p. 308 note 23). A proportion of this income would naturally have been diverted in the king's service at a local level, but the rest would have come to his treasury: see further below, note 246.

241. Again Asser quotes from the Old Latin translation of the Bible, rather than from the Vulgate; see above, note 159.

242. For some further information on King Alfred's household officials, see below, p. 289 note 34, p. 290 note 39 and p. 330 note 15.

243. King Alfred's organization of his household in these three rotating shifts may be compared with his division of the army, described in *ASC* s.a. 893: see above, p. 115, and below, p. 285 note 4.

244. There seems to be a reference to this annual distribution in Alfred's will (above, p. 177): 'And to the men who serve me, *to whom I have just now given money at Eastertide*, 200 pounds are to be given and divided between them, to each as much as will belong to him *according to the manner in which I have just now made distribution to them.*' From this we may perhaps infer that the annual distribution took place regularly at Easter; that the amount of payment varied according to the individual fits precisely with what Asser himself says.

245. *in omni terreno aedificio*: see above, note 114.

246. 'Treasury' translates *fiscus*. At this period it is unlikely that the royal treasury was very much more than a chest (or chests) which followed

the king on his travels round the kingdom, kept in the custody of one of his household officials; for Ælfric, King Alfred's 'treasurer', see below, p. 330 note 15. In the tenth century the revenues of the West Saxon kings increased, once they became kings of all England, and there is evidence that King Eadred (946–55) deposited a large part of his wealth in monasteries throughout his kingdom; it is only in the eleventh century that evidence emerges for Winchester as the main and permanent repository of the king's treasures (see, for example, *ASC* s.a. 1035 and 1043, and Hollister, 'The Origins of the English Treasury', p. 263).

247. The quotation is paraphrased from Gregory's *Regula Pastoralis* III, 20: *unde et necesse est, ut sollicite perpendant, ne commissa indigne distribuant; ne quaedam quibus nulla, ne nulla quibus quaedam, ne multa quibus pauca, ne pauca praebeant quibus impendere multa debuerunt* (*PL* 77, col. 84). The passage is translated in Alfred's Old English version of the *Pastoral Care* (on which Asser collaborated: above, p. 126): see Sweet, *Pastoral Care* II, p. 320.

248. On this school, see above, note 148.

249. The passage in question is not found in Holy Scripture (if that is what Asser means by *divina scriptura*), but in Augustine's *Enchiridion*, §20: *Qui enim vult ordinate dare eleemosynam, a seipso debet incipere* (*PL* 40, col. 268). Cf. Galbraith, 'Who Wrote Asser's Life of Alfred?', p. 101.

250. The transmitted *divinis* is meaningless here; we conjecture *divitiis* and translate accordingly.

251. Possibly these would have included the chaplains Æthelstan and Werwulf, named in chapter 77.

252. Stevenson supplies a lengthy note (*Asser*, pp. 338–41) on the construction of these lanterns; after sifting evidence for horn-lamps in antiquity and the early Anglo-Saxon period, he concludes that Alfred 'may really be the inventor of the horn lantern as we know it'. See also Langenfelt, *The Historic Origin of the Eight Hours Day*, especially pp. 17–21, and idem, 'King Alfred and the First Time-Measurer'.

253. See the letter to Edward the Elder (*EHD* no. 102; cited above, note 151), which gives a contemporary account of Alfred's scrupulous care 'in establishing the truth in judicial hearings'. The extent of the king's personal involvement in such affairs is suggested by a remark made in the letter: 'and if one wishes to change every judgement which King Alfred gave, when shall we have finished disputing?' Some clauses in Alfred's law-code may have originated as judgements given by the king in particular cases: see Wormald, '*Lex Scripta* and *Verbum Regis*', p. 113.

254. The transmitted text is corrupt; we follow Wheeler ('Textual Emendations', p. 87) in supplying the words *utilitati studebat* at the end of the sentence.

255. The transmitted *studebat* is meaningless, and the reading probably arose in connection with the corruption at the end of the previous sentence. We follow Wheeler ('Textual Emendations', p. 87) in reading *sedebat*.

256. Stevenson (*Asser*, pp. 342–3) was of the opinion that, since ealdormen and reeves 'had no judicial powers apart from the courts of which they formed part', Asser had been mistaken in implying that such persons themselves acted as judges. But there is, in fact, substantial evidence showing that ealdormen and reeves had judicial authority in their own right (as pointed out by Whitelock, 'Recent Work', pp. cxlv–cxlvii). The opening statement in Edward the Elder's first law-code reads: 'King Edward commands all the reeves that you give such just judgements as you know most right and as it stands in the law-book' (Attenborough, *Laws*, pp. 114–15); for the 'law-book', see below, p. 311 note 34. A passage in a late-tenth-century Anglo-Latin poem gives a detailed account of an ordeal presided over by a reeve (see Whitelock, 'Wulfstan *Cantor* and Anglo-Saxon Law', pp. 87–9).

257. The transmitted text here (*quamvis per vim lege et stipulatione venire coactus esset*) is difficult, and Stevenson rightly marked *lege* as corrupt. We suggest reading *legis* (which has, in fact, the support of the Otho transcript) and *stipulationem*, and translate accordingly.

258. Alfred may have been influenced by the strong continental tradition of royal concern with judicial malpractice: see, for example, King, *Law and Society in the Visigothic Kingdom*, especially pp. 117–18, and Ganshof, 'Charlemagne's Programme of Imperial Government', pp. 63–4. In the late thirteenth century the story was told of how King Alfred had forty-four judges hanged in one year for their false judgements (see Whittaker, *The Mirror of Justices*, pp. 166–71); needless to say, the story is completely fictitious, but it does afford some idea of Alfred's reputation as an arbiter of justice.

259. On Alfred's interest in spreading literacy, see above, pp. 35–6. It seems clear from the context that one purpose of the exercise was to ensure that those of the king's officials with judicial authority would be able to absorb the wisdom and justice contained in the written laws; in the reign of Edward the Elder, reeves were certainly expected to be able to consult the 'law-book' (see above, note 256).

260. The abruptness of the ending suggests that the *Life* may have been left unfinished; see above, p. 56.

THE ANGLO-SAXON CHRONICLE, 888–900
(*pp. 113–20*)

The *Anglo-Saxon Chronicle* provides the foundation for our knowledge of Anglo-Saxon secular history from its traditional beginnings in the middle of the fifth century to its conclusion in 1066; indeed, the *Chronicle* was still kept up at certain places after the Norman Conquest, and one version extends as far as 1154. Before using it as a source, however, it is important to have some understanding of the manner of its composition and of the stages of its growth. Its title is potentially misleading, in two ways. First, it seems to suggest that the work as we see it printed is in some sense a single continuous text, composed by a presumably long series of chroniclers writing year by year and each responsible for a certain part of the whole. Secondly, it can be taken to imply that the work in some sense embodies an 'official' view of Anglo-Saxon history, an inference seemingly strengthened by the terseness and apparent objectivity of the language often employed by the chroniclers, who are themselves personally unobtrusive and anonymous. At first sight, therefore, the *Chronicle* creates the impression that it has a consistent character and uniform authority throughout, but one does not have to penetrate its surface very far to realize that the reality is rather different.

The '*Anglo-Saxon Chronicle*' is in fact a term applied by modern scholars, for the sake of convenience, to a group of chronicle texts, now represented not only directly by the several manuscripts which preserve the annals in their original Old English form, but also indirectly by material embedded in various Latin chronicles and histories, which can be shown to derive from manuscripts of the *Chronicle* that have not survived. There are seven manuscripts of the *Chronicle* itself, conventionally designated as follows: MS 'A' (Cambridge, Corpus Christi College MS 173), also known as the 'Parker Chronicle', first written in the late ninth or early tenth century and continued thereafter by a succession of scribes, at Winchester and (in the late eleventh century) at Christ Church, Canterbury; MS 'B' (B.L. Cotton Tiberius A. vi), written by one scribe in 977 or 978, probably at Abingdon (though the manuscript seems later to have been at Ramsey, and then at Canterbury); MS 'C' (B.L. Cotton Tiberius B. i), written by two scribes in the 1040s, apparently at Abingdon, and continued intermittently thereafter up to 1066; MS 'D' (B.L. Cotton Tiberius B. iv), written by several scribes around the middle of the eleventh century, possibly at Worcester; MS 'E' (Oxford, Bodleian Library, Laud Misc. 636), written at Peterborough in the 1120s, with a continuation extending to 1154; MS 'F' (B.L. Cotton Domitian viii), a bilingual (Latin and Old English) version written by one scribe at Christ Church, Canterbury, towards the end of the eleventh century; and M S 'G' (B.L. Cotton Otho B. xi, almost entirely destroyed in the fire of 1731), a direct copy of M S 'A' made at Winchester in the early eleventh century. Among the Latin works which incorporate material derived from lost copies of the *Chronicle* are: Asser's *Life of King Alfred*; the chronicle written by Æthelweard, ealdorman of the western shires, in the 980s; the chronicle compiled at Worcester in the first half of the twelfth century, commonly known as that of Florence of Worcester but now regarded as the work of John of Worcester; the histories written by William of Malmesbury and Henry of Huntingdon at about the same time; and the so-called *Annals of St Neots*, apparently compiled at Bury St Edmunds in the second quarter of the twelfth century. The proper assessment of the information in the *Chronicle* depends on the study of the relationship between all these versions, each of which represents a slightly different stage in the development of the text; it is a complex task, made the more uncertain by the knowledge that there were several other copies of the *Chronicle* of which no trace has survived beyond (say) a mention in a medieval library catalogue, any one of which could have affected the reconstruction of the *Chronicle*'s textual history in some important way. The general object of the exercise is to identify and characterize the discrete elements of chronicling activity which together make up the *Chronicle* as a whole, in the expectation that the elements represent the work of different chroniclers and are the products of different circumstances. Some chroniclers might have been better informed than others; some might have been writing year by year, while others might have written blocks of annals at one time; overall, their interests and horizons would naturally have differed. The authority of the various elements would vary accordingly.

For our present purposes, it is only necessary to pursue this study in so far as it concerns the annals for the reign of King Alfred the Great. The fact that Asser, writing in 893, made use of a copy of the *Chronicle* that extended at least as far as 887 provides us with the essential point of departure: the *Chronicle* must have existed in some form already during Alfred's reign. Indeed, recent studies of the vocabulary used in the *Chronicle* (see Bately, 'The Compilation of the Anglo-Saxon Chronicle', especially pp. 109–16) suggest that the initial work of compilation was done by a team of collaborating annalists, who assembled and edited a range of earlier materials and then added some annals of their own: it is particularly interesting that the annals centring on the 870s and those centring on the 880s seem to have been written by two different men, though one cannot tell whether the 880s annalist was acting on his own, continuing an earlier compilation, or whether he too was collaborating with the others. At all events, the various manuscripts of the *Chronicle* share essentially the same material up to 890 or 892, so it was probably about this time that the *Chronicle* was first 'published', in the sense that a completed text was made available for copying.

The precise extent of this common stock (that is, the original compilation in the form in which it was first 'published') is a matter for argument. It is odd that Asser himself does not use the *Chronicle* after 887, but this need not imply that his copy extended no further. Asser leaves the *Chronicle* in 887 because in that year Alfred learnt how to read (chapter 87), and this occasions a long and rambling account of the king's various domestic activities and achievements, which occupies Asser from chapter 88 to the end of the work; see also above, p. 56. It may be that by this stage (chapter 106) Asser had said what he most wanted to say about the king, and could not bring himself to return once again to the more mundane task of translating the remaining entries in his copy of the *Chronicle*, particularly when the material available would only be anti-climactic; so instead he left the work in its rather unfinished state. Some scholars see a significant textual break after annal 890, because annal 891 is not present in MS 'E', suggesting the existence of a version that once extended to 890 but no further. Others would place the break in annal 891, because the first scribe in MS 'A' gives way to the second towards the end of the annal, as if all that follows is continuation; it is indeed puzzling that he should have done so, but the explanation probably lies in the complex history of this particular manuscript (which, it should be said, is already some stages removed from the original) and does not reflect on the textual history of the *Chronicle* itself. A strong case can, however, be made for 892 as being the last annal in the original compilation. The evidence is essentially textual. In the first place, while the version of the *Chronicle* behind MS 'E' seems not to have contained annal 891 (perhaps omitted accidentally), it did contain annal 892, but not the remaining annals for Alfred's reign. (MS 'D', which also descends from the version behind 'E', does have all the annals for the 890s, but it probably received those for 893 onwards at a later stage, by conflation with another version of the *Chronicle*.) Secondly, the copy of the *Chronicle* used by Æthelweard in the late tenth century had the annals up to and including 892, but not the annals for 893–6 that follow in MSS 'A', 'B', 'C' (and 'D'); since it is known that Æthelweard's copy was in some ways closer to the original than any of the surviving manuscripts, this evidence is particularly important. So, MS 'E' and Æthelweard both suggest that there was a significant textual break after annal 892. The case for 892 as the last annal in the original compilation derives some support from a simple historiographical consideration: the chronicler provides information on the movements during the 880s of the Viking army that had left England in 879, and it could be argued that his concern to record this information is a sure sign of his awareness that it was this army that returned to England in 892 (see Sawyer, *Age of the Vikings*, p. 19); but the chronicler's sustained interest in its movements could be attributed to fear that it might return (as part of it did, briefly, in 885). Whatever the case, the textual evidence suffices to show that the *Chronicle* originally extended to 892: the work of compilation may have begun in the late 880s, but it was only after the Vikings arrived in Kent in the autumn of 892 that a text was made available for copying. (For further discussion, see above, pp. 39–41 and 41–2, and below, p.283 note 18.)

The annals for 893 onwards should thus be regarded as a continuation of the original common stock. As such, they have to be distinguished clearly from the annals up to and including 892, since it is likely that the annals on each side of 892/3 are the work of different chroniclers; considerations which apply to the common stock will not therefore necessarily apply to the material from 893 on, and vice versa. A further distinction in the annals for 893 onwards has to be recognized, between those for 893–6 and those for 897 and 900. There can be little doubt that the annals for 893–6 were the work of one chronicler, writing in 896. They are unusually long and detailed, and display a literary technique that represents a marked change in narrative style when compared with what has gone before (providing, incidentally, another reason for placing the break after annal 892): the syntax becomes more complex, with free use of subordination, a wider range of connectives, and some rhetorical patterning (for example in the use of antithesis); for an excellent description, see Clark, 'The Narrative Mode of *The Anglo-Saxon Chronicle*', pp. 221–4. It is,

moreover, a sure sign of the separate authorship of this section that
the annals begin with the full phrases 'In this year . . .', 'And then
immediately after that, in this year . . .', 'In the same year . . .', and
'Then afterwards, in the summer of this year . . .', whereas the annals
before 893 and after 896 begin with the conventional adverb *Her*
(literally, 'In this place (in the annals)', but translated 'In this year').
So far as its content is concerned, the 893–6 continuation provides a
justly celebrated account of Alfred's campaign against the Vikings
who arrived in 892 (see above, pp. 42–3). The chronicler is not, however, content simply to report events, for he frequently enlarges on
the king's *motives* for doing something, and is willing also to express
his own opinions and to offer his own interpretations; this adds
enormously to the interest of his account, though there is no reason to
believe that the personal intrusion of the chronicler represents anything more than the private view of an independent, unofficial observer. It is apparent, finally, that the 893–6 chronicler was writing at
one time, presumably in or soon after 896: the annals are bound
together by various recurrent phrases which militate against the sup-
position that they were composed year by year, and the chronicler
himself clearly saw them as forming a composite whole, as in annal
896 when he reflects on the events of 'those three years' (893, 894,
895).

The annals for 897 and 900 belong to what might be called the
second continuation, that is to say the next identifiable section of the
Chronicle which appears to have had a distinctive history. This continuation extended from 897 to 914 and was essentially concerned
with the opening stages of Edward the Elder's campaign to conquer
the Danelaw. There is no guarantee that it is all the work of one man;
it probably accumulated piecemeal in the early years of the tenth
century, in continuation of the 893–6 section, but it clearly reaches its
climax with the events of 912–14.

Our division of the annals for 888–900 into three sections, in the
translation above, is thus intended to reflect the stages in the growth
of the *Chronicle*, and thereby to emphasize the point that the annals
were not all composed under similar circumstances. Annals 888–92
represent the closing part of the original common stock, translated
here because they were not incorporated by Asser in his *Life of King
Alfred*; annals 893–6 represent the first continuation, written by a
new chronicler, and have to be seen as a distinct unit; annals 897–900

represent the opening part of the second continuation, and are again likely to be the work of someone new.

It should be noted that the chroniclers for Alfred's reign did not begin the year, as we do, on 1 January: rather, they began it some time in the previous autumn, possibly in September (see further below, p. 329 note 9), so that an annal dated '874' would refer to the period from early autumn 873 to late summer 874.

Our translation is based on MS 'A', though significant variant readings from the other manuscripts are recorded in the commentary. The text is printed by Plummer, *Two Chronicles* I, pp. 80–92, and by Smith, *Parker Chronicle*, pp. 38–52. There is a complete translation of the *Chronicle* by Garmonsway, *Anglo-Saxon Chronicle*; this follows the pagination and layout of Plummer's edition, and has the advantage of being readily available. It is better, however, to use the translation by Whitelock et al., *Anglo-Saxon Chronicle* (also in *EHD* no. 1), in which the similarities and differences between the various manuscripts are clearly displayed, and in which the chronology is corrected; this translation is also accompanied by an authoritative discussion of the work as a whole.

ANNALS 888–92 (*pp. 113–14*)

1. Nothing more is known of Beocca. An Ealdorman 'Bucca' attests a charter of King Alfred's reign which may have a genuine base (*S* 345, dated 882); an Ealdorman Beocca attests a Winchester document in Edward the Elder's reign (*S* 1286, dated 904); and an Ealdorman 'Byocca' occurs in a spurious text which appears to combine elements from charters of Alfred and Æthelstan (*S* 351).

2. For these payments of alms to Rome, see above, p. 268 note 206.

3. Æthelswith had married Burgred, king of Mercia, in 853 (*ASC*; Asser, chapter 9); she had perhaps accompanied her husband to Rome in 874 (*ASC*; Asser, chapter 46). A gold finger-ring, found in Yorkshire and inscribed 'Queen Æthelswith', is now in the British Museum (see Wilson, *Ornamental Metalwork*, no. 1, and Okasha, *Hand-List*, no. 107).

4. He succeeded Ceolnoth as archbishop of Canterbury in 870 (see Asser, chapter 34); he died on 30 June 888.

5. The chronicler Æthelweard gives this name (in error) as Æthelbald, and describes him as ealdorman of Kent (*CÆ*, p. 47). Subscriptions of an Ealdorman Æthelwold occur in *S* 321 (dated 880) and in *S* 345 (dated 882), the former in a Kentish context; see also *SEHD*, p. 90.

6. There are several subscriptions of an Abbot Beornhelm in Kentish contexts

in the 870s and 880s; he was apparently abbot of St Augustine's, Canterbury (A. H. Davis, *Thorne's Chronicle*, p. 34).

7. Guthrum was regarded as the first *of the Danes* to settle in East Anglia: see Asser, chapters 56 and 60, and the Treaty between Alfred and Guthrum (above, p. 171). Guthrum issued coins in East Anglia using his baptismal name Æthelstan: see North, *English Hammered Coinage*, no. 479. According to the *Annals of St Neots*, he was buried at the royal estate at Hadleigh (Suffolk).

8. The Viking army on the Continent had spent the winter of 888–9 on the banks of the Loing (see above, p. 266 note 202). In 889 they ravaged extensively in Burgundy, Neustria and part of Aquitaine. Around autumn they returned to Paris, but were intercepted by King Odo and came to terms: they left the Seine and went westwards to Brittany, laying siege to Saint-Lô (in what is now Normandy) in the winter 889–90. Saint-Lô fell to the Vikings early in 890, but they were then defeated by the Bretons and were forced to return to the Seine. The river in which some of the Vikings were drowned was probably the Vire.

9. Towards All Saints' Day (1 November) 890, the Viking army left the Seine, went eastwards up the river Oise, and established a camp at Noyon, ravaging extensively during the winter months. In the spring of 891 they left Noyon and spent some time on the Flanders coast; in June they appeared at Liège, and in the same month they surprised and defeated a Frankish army nearby. The Vikings then went to establish a camp for the winter at Louvain, on the river Dyle. Arnulf, king of eastern Francia (see above, p. 267 note 203), came to meet them, and defeated them in battle on (?)31 August 891; but he then returned to Bavaria, and the Vikings duly took up their winter quarters for 891–2 at Louvain.

10. The chronicler calls them 'Scots', which was the normal term for Irishmen in the late ninth century; cf. Bede, *HE* i, 1, and ii, 4.

11. Holy men from Ireland often chose pilgrimage as the ultimate expression of their religious zeal: see Hughes, 'Irish Pilgrimage', and Charles-Edwards, 'The Social Background to Irish *Peregrinatio*'. Bede tells the story of St Fursa, who came from Ireland to East Anglia in the second quarter of the seventh century, 'anxious to live the life of a pilgrim for the Lord's sake, wherever opportunity offered' (*HE* iii, 19).

12. The boat was evidently a currach, made from animal hides stretched over a wooden frame. Compare the description of St Brendan's boat in the late-eighth-century *Navigatio Sancti Brendani*: Webb and Farmer, *The Age of Bede*, p. 214.

13. Their visit to Alfred's court was clearly a celebrated event, and it improved in the re-telling: according to the chronicler Æthelweard, the three pilgrims were welcomed by the king and then set out for Rome, proposing to go on from there to Jerusalem (*CÆ*, p. 48). Other evidence

for the presence of Irishmen in England in the late ninth and tenth centuries is assembled by Hughes, 'Contacts between the Churches of the Irish and English', pp. 59 and 65–6. Some Irish pilgrims are known to have reached Jerusalem in the ninth century: see Tierney, *Dicuili Liber de Mensura Orbis Terrae*, p. 62.

14. The death of 'Suibne, son of Maelumai, anchorite and excellent scribe of Clonmacnois', is recorded in the *Annals of Ulster*, s.a. 890 (for 891). There was a memorial slab to Suibne at Clonmacnois (Macalister, *Corpus Inscriptionum Insularum Celticarum*, no. 776), but it was lost in the nineteenth century; for a drawing of it, see Macalister, *Memorial Slabs*, p. 97. One imagines that news of Suibne's death was brought to England by the three Irish pilgrims; if so, this might be taken to imply that the chronicler responsible for the entry in *ASC* was associated with Alfred's court.

15. In 891 the Rogation Days (Monday, Tuesday and Wednesday before Ascension Day) fell on 10–12 May.

16. This comet was also seen on the Continent in 891; more remarkably, Chinese sources report the appearance of a comet on 12 May, and Japanese sources on 11 May, 891 (see Ho Peng Yoke, 'Ancient and Mediaeval Observations of Comets', p. 177).

17. As a rule, a comet has a single tail pointing away from the sun; but under certain circumstances a comet can develop multiple tails. The 'some men' cited by the chronicler could have observed one of these more unusual comets, or they could have been acquainted with Pliny's description of the various types of comet in his *Natural History*. The Latin word *cometa* itself derives from a Greek word meaning 'long-haired'.

18. Note this unusual personal intrusion of the chronicler. It is possible that he makes the connection explicit at this point in order to highlight the reason for having included all the information on the movements of the Viking army on the Continent: it was this army that now returned to England (cf. Asser, chapter 61). But it could be argued that the remark suggests that some interval had elapsed since the writing of the material up to 891. In either case, the annal for 892 is shown to belong with the preceding annals, and not to be part of the 893–6 continuation.

19. The Viking army which spent the winter of 891–2 at Louvain was based there for much of 892; meanwhile another Viking force (apparently a part of the main army which had been made responsible for looking after the ships) went ravaging down the Rhine, and then returned to the coast. The main army itself (some part of which may also have been involved in this expedition) was then compelled by a famine to leave the vicinity of Louvain, and it too returned to the coast. The Vikings assembled at Boulogne, where they were 'provided with ships' (which may imply that their own were no longer adequate, and that they had to obtain others locally); and so in the autumn of 892 (according to the *Annals of St*

Vaast) they left Francia and crossed the Channel to England. The names of the army's leaders on its return to England are unknown; while on the Continent it had been led by two kings, Guthfrith and Sigefrith, but the former had died in 885 and the latter in 887. The army had a king at the battle of Farnham in 893 (*ASC*), and a certain Hun(c)deus went back to the Continent with part of the army in 896 (see below, p. 288 note 25).

20. Limen (Lympne) is the old name for the Rother, though the river's course near the coast has changed. It rises near Rotherfield in Sussex, and it seems that it originally flowed north of the isle of Oxney, past Appledore (described in annal 893 as 'on the Limen estuary'), along the edge of Romney Marsh and into the sea near Lympne and Hythe; see further below, note 22.

21. '250' is the reading of MSS 'A', 'E' and 'F', against MSS 'B', 'C' and 'D', which read '200'; the *Annals of St Neots* specify '350'; the chronicler Æthelweard does not mention the number of ships in the fleet. For textual reasons it seems likely that '250' represents the original reading.

22. It is difficult to identify this fortification, not least because one cannot be sure that the chronicler meant *exactly* what he said. A good case, however, has been made for an earthwork at Castle Toll, Newenden, Kent: see Davison, 'The Burghal Hidage Fort of Eorpeburnan' (and Brooks, 'Unidentified Forts', pp. 81–6). The identification assumes that the mouth of the Limen estuary was reckoned to be at Appledore; Castle Toll lies on the end of a mile-long peninsula jutting out from the forest into Romney Marsh, about six miles further upstream. Davison also suggests that this earthwork may be the *Eorpeburnan* mentioned in the *Burghal Hidage* (above, p. 193): according to this document, *Eorpeburnan* was assessed for defence at 324 hides, indicating a defensive line of about 1,336 feet, a figure which corresponds well with the distance across the Castle Toll peninsula on the only side adjoining firm land.

23. Literally, 'churlish men', that is, men of the *ceorl* class (on which see below, p. 307 note 16).

24. This is the reading of MSS 'A', 'E' and 'F'. The reading of MSS 'B', 'C' and 'D' ('. . . and there they attacked a fortification. Inside in that fortress there were a few commoners, and it was only half-made') is unlikely to be original, not least because it incurs a redundant preposition *on*. The reference to the 'half-made' fortification may be compared with Asser's remark (chapter 91) about fortifications which had not been finished in time for them to be of any use against the enemy.

25. Milton Regis, near Sittingbourne, Kent. The arrival of this force in the north of Kent brought to England a second Viking army, different in its origins from the 'great army'. Hastein (or Hadding: it is not quite certain which Old Norse name is represented by the forms *Hæsten* in *ASC* and *Hastingus* – or A(l)stingus – in continental sources) had been active on

the Continent for many years prior to his arrival in England. His earliest reported exploits belong more to legend than to history: after raiding in Francia for a while, he became one of the leaders of the Viking expedition (of 859–62) which entered the Mediterranean and sacked Luna (modern Luni) in north Italy, thinking it to be Rome; he was then allegedly active on the rivers Loire and Sarthe in 866, and would seem to have remained in the vicinity for some years thereafter. He is introduced more certainly to history in the 880s. He made a treaty with Louis III in 882 and left the Loire for 'coastal parts', though perhaps not for long; he may have been involved to some extent in the activities of the 'great army' during the 880s. He was at Argoeuves, on the Somme, in 890–91, and at Amiens in 891–2; when he crossed to England in 892 he was clearly acting in collusion with the 'great army'. For the most recent account of his career, in history and legend, see Amory, 'The Viking Hasting'.

26. In other words, the 'great army', which had previously attacked the half-made fortification in the Limen estuary, came back towards the mouth of the estuary and made a fortification for itself at Appledore.

ANNALS 893–6 (*pp. 114–19*)

1. This is a reference to the winter camp established by the Vikings at Louvain in 891–2 (see above, p. 282 note 9), which was not actually mentioned by the previous chronicler.

2. The word here translated 'hostage' is *foregisel*, literally 'preliminary hostage', that is, one given as security for the subsequent performance of an oath. The same word is used in *ASC* for the hostages given by the Vikings to King Alfred in 877 (see above, p. 245 note 89) and 878; Asser, chapter 56, translated the word in the 878 annal as 'chosen hostage', which may imply that he understood *fore-gisel* to mean a prominent or distinguished hostage. Note incidentally that the syntax of the opening sentence of this annal is unclear in the original, and that our translation omits the transmitted *ond* after *foregisla vi*.

3. The 'burhs' (OE *burh* or *burg*, whence modern English 'borough') were the fortified sites established by King Alfred throughout southern England, and organized for the defence of the kingdom as described in the *Burghal Hidage*: see above, pp. 24–5 and 193–4.

4. Note that this statement is provided by way of explanation: Alfred could have reorganized his army at any time during the previous decade or so. The statement is too general to afford a clear idea of how the Alfredian system operated, and at least two interpretations are possible (taking into account the information provided later in this annal). In the first place, it may be that at any time one part of the total number of men liable for military service was 'at home', defending and otherwise looking after the

land, while another part was out on service against the Vikings, leaving a third part to defend (but also to operate offensively from) the burhs; and that the two parts of the army proper served in rotation, so that the part 'at home' replaced the part in the field when the latter had completed its appointed term of service. Such a system would be analogous to the organization of the king's household, as described by Asser, chapter 100. Alternatively, it may be that of the total number of men available, apart from those reserved for the burhs, half were reckoned to be always 'at home', where they were responsible for equipping and in other ways supporting the other half, who were always out on service and who might themselves have been organized in relays. This would mean that the standing army was a professional body of men, and therefore, perhaps, as effective as it could be. Such a system would then be analogous to that employed in Charlemagne's Francia, where each man who served in the army was supported by a certain number of men responsible for equipping him; see Ganshof, *Frankish Institutions*, p. 61. The Alfredian system can be compared with that of the Amazon queens Marpesia and Lampeto, described in the OE translation of Orosius's *History*, made in Alfred's reign: 'They divided their army in two parts, the one to be at home to defend their land, the other to go out to fight'; but one need not imagine that Alfred modelled his system on theirs (see Bately, *Old English Orosius*, pp. 30 and 220).

5. The chronicler's presentation of this and the following events is made obscure by the rather confusing way in which he describes the activities of the various Viking armies involved. As we learn later in this annal, Alfred had attempted to defuse the dangerous situation posed by the two armies at Appledore and Milton by coming to terms with Hastein while he was at Milton: the king had given him money and had received one of his sons as a godson (and Ealdorman Æthelred the other), and Hastein for his part had given hostages and oaths. Hastein then crossed the Thames and established camp at Benfleet in Essex, and at once set about ravaging from his new base. It seems that the other Viking army sent its ships to join Hastein's army in Essex, and set off ravaging inland on its own account. So in this case it is the Appledore army that seizes the booty and then wishes to cross the Thames to meet its ships (which were apparently at Mersea, an island off the coast of Essex, before they joined the others at Benfleet). For further discussion of this annal, see Shippey, 'A Missing Army'.

6. The chronicler Æthelweard gives a more detailed, but very confusing, account of the battle of Farnham (in Surrey), and names the English leader as Edward (the Elder): see above, p. 189.

7. Æthelweard identifies this island as Thorney, and gives a rather different account of the events which follow: see above, p. 190.

8. Note this allusion to Alfred's reorganization of the army: see above, note 4.

9. For these raids, see Smyth, *Scandinavian York and Dublin* I, pp. 32–7. The fortification (*geweorc*) in Devon was perhaps the burh at Pilton, named in the *Burghal Hidage*; Exeter is another of the burhs named there (see above, p. 193). Asser, chapter 81, says that Alfred had given him the monastery at Exeter: one wonders, therefore, whether there is any connection between this siege of Exeter in 893 and the fact that Asser apparently broke off writing his *Life of King Alfred* in the same year.

10. 'Townsmen' translates *burgware*, which means literally 'inhabitants of a burh': the reference here is presumably to a detachment from the military garrison of the burh at London.

11. Benfleet, in Essex. This place had been used once before as a Viking base, in 885; see above, p. 252 note 125. It is conceivable that Hastein had been present at Benfleet on this earlier occasion (see above, p. 284 note 25); but it seems that the events described by the chronicler in the present annal do belong exclusively to 893, and should not be taken to imply that Hastein's sons had been baptized in 885 (cf. above, note 5).

12. Æthelred, ealdorman of Mercia, and King Alfred's son-in-law: see Asser, chapter 75. For the practice of standing sponsor at baptism or confirmation, see above, p. 249 note 110.

13. For Ealdorman Æthelred, see previous note; for Ealdorman Æthelhelm, see below, p. 328 note 4. Æthelnoth was ealdorman of Somerset: see above, pp. 190, 248 note 102, and 249 note 112.

14. This apparent allusion to burhs north of the Thames and west of the Severn serves to remind us that the *Burghal Hidage* affords only a partial (essentially West Saxon) view of the burghal network: there must have been several others under Mercian jurisdiction that are not mentioned in this document.

15. For relations with Wales during Alfred's reign, see Asser, chapters 80–81 and notes. The fact that 'some part' only of the Welsh people are said to have been fighting on the English side may indicate that Anarawd had not yet submitted to Alfred. If so, it was probably the defeat of the Danes and their East Anglian and Northumbrian allies at Buttington that made him submit (Asser, chapter 80).

16. This is sometimes identified as Buttington Tump, in Tidenham, near Chepstow, Gloucestershire, where the river Wye flows into the Severn estuary; but this is hardly compatible with the statement that the Vikings arrived at the Severn from the Thames, and then went *up along the Severn*. The alternative, Buttington near Welshpool in Montgomery, therefore seems preferable.

17. Nothing more is known of this man.

18. The words 'and there was a mighty slaughter of the Danes there' were omitted accidentally in *ASC* MS 'A'; they are supplied here from MSS 'B', 'C' and 'D'.

19. Chester was an ancient Roman city; its name is given as *Legaceaster*, 'city of the legions'. A battle was fought there in 616, between Æthelfrith, king of Northumbria, and the Britons (Bede, *HE* ii, 2), and the city may have been deserted for some time thereafter; it is difficult to believe, however, that it was still unoccupied in the late ninth century, though it was not until 907 that its defences were 'restored' (*ASC* MSS 'B', 'C', 'D').

20. See above, note 10; Chichester is one of the burhs named in the *Burghal Hidage*.

21. This fortification must have been in or near Hertford. The phrase 'in the same year' used by the chronicler would most naturally refer to 894; it is uncertain, however, whether this was his intention, or whether he has simply, and absentmindedly, written 'in the same year' when he meant 'in this year'.

22. See above, note 10; presumably men from the burh at London are meant.

23. This tactic had been used against the Vikings by the Carolingians (see Hassall and Hill, 'Pont de l'Arche: Frankish Influence on the West Saxon Burh?'), but we may suppose that Alfred was intelligent enough to think of it for himself; see also Brooks, 'Development of Military Obligations', p. 72. The same tactic was used by Edward the Elder in the first quarter of the tenth century.

24. 'Without property' translates *feohleas*. *Feoh*, 'property', had been used by the chronicler in his annal for 893 in a context which clearly implies that movable goods are meant: the Vikings 'made safe their women and their ships and their property in East Anglia', before setting out for Chester. The property in question was presumably the proceeds of their ravaging, that is, money and valuable goods, and perhaps livestock as well. Those who had 'property' would have been able to use it to acquire land on which to settle; those who had none were obliged to return to the Continent, where they might still hope to make their fortunes. See further Sawyer, *Age of the Vikings*, pp. 100–101.

25. The return of part of the Viking army to the Continent is recorded in the *Annals of St Vaast* for 896. They came with their leader Hun(c)deus in five large ships (*barchis*) to the river Seine, and proceeded to do much damage; by Christmas they had established a camp at Choisy on the Oise. In the following year they ravaged as far as the Meuse, before returning to the Seine; but then at Easter (27 March) Hun(c)deus was baptized, with King Charles (the Simple) standing as his sponsor. See further Lyon and Stewart, 'Northumbrian Viking Coins in the Cuerdale Hoard', pp. 116–18, for the possibility that he subsequently returned to Northumbria.

26. An entry, unfortunately of dubious authority, in one of the versions of the *Annales Cambriae* (Morris, *Nennius*, pp. 49 and 90), records, s.a. 896: 'Bread failed in Ireland. Vermin like moles with two teeth fell from the air and ate everything up; they were driven out by fasting and prayer.'

27. Swithwulf's earliest subscription as bishop is in a charter dated 880. He is one of the bishops who is known to have received a copy of King Alfred's translation of Gregory's *Pastoral Care*: see below, p. 294 note 1.

28. Nothing more is known of this Ceolmund, though there are several subscriptions of a thegn called Ceolmund in Kentish charters dating from the earlier part of Alfred's reign.

29. By the terms of the treaty between Alfred and Guthrum (above, p. 171), Essex would have been under Danish control – so this reference to an ealdorman of Essex is rather interesting. It may imply that Alfred managed to regain control of at least part of Essex at some time during the period 893–5. For possible occurrences of Beorhtwulf in charters, see Whitelock, 'Some Charters in the Name of King Alfred', pp. 85–6.

30. Nothing more is known of this Wulfred, though see below, p. 329 note 11.

31. Ealhheard's earliest subscription as bishop is in a charter dated 888. The bishopric which became that of Dorchester had been moved from Leicester, apparently in the 870s to escape the Viking invasions; the description of Ealhheard as 'bishop *at* Dorchester' may indicate that at the time of writing Dorchester had still not been confirmed as the new episcopal see.

32. Eadwulf is otherwise unknown.

33. Beornwulf is otherwise unknown, though a thegn of this name attests *S* 321 (dated 880). As town-reeve (*wicgerefa*) of Winchester he would probably have been the king's representative in the city, with general responsibility for supervising judicial, financial and administrative affairs; see Biddle, *Winchester in the Early Middle Ages*, pp. 422–6.

34. Ecgwulf is probably the person who attests *S* 345 (dated 882) and *S* 356 (undated); he may be the Ecgwulf mentioned in King Alfred's will (above, p. 175). As the king's horse-thegn he would probably have been responsible for the care of the king's horses, and perhaps also for the king's transport arrangements; he was certainly far more than a groom, and could be regarded as the precursor of the royal marshal.

35. Another example of the king's creative intelligence (cf. *ASC* s.a. 895, and Asser, chapters 76 and 103–4). One can only speculate about the details of Alfred's design for the new ships. The capture of the Viking ships on the Lea in 895 would have given him an opportunity to study their construction closely, and might have precipitated his decision to build a new fleet; the captured ships perhaps included some of those acquired by the Vikings at Boulogne in 892, so not all would necessarily have been of 'Danish' design. The chronicler's distinction between 'Danish', 'Frisian' and the Alfredian ships is more tantalizing than helpful. By 'Danish' he presumably meant a round-hulled, slender boat with fully developed keel and steeply curving stem and stern, represented

generally by the Gokstad ship from Norway and the Ladby and Skuldelev ships from Denmark. By 'Frisian' he probably meant a flat-bottomed, full-bodied boat with a less pronounced keel and relatively straight, but steeply inclined, stem and stern, represented in its developed form by the medieval cog; alternatively, he meant a banana-shaped, keel-less boat without stem-posts or stern-posts, represented by an example from Utrecht and, in its developed form, by the medieval hulk. Alfred's ships possibly derived certain of their features from each of these types. They clearly differed in being unusually long, and this might have given them their extra speed; their greater stability implies width and a relatively flat bottom; their greater height might have made them more seaworthy, and would have given the crews a distinct advantage over other ships in battles fought at sea. However, it clearly took a while to learn how to handle the new ships, as shown by the account of their first recorded engagement. The chronicler's reference to Alfred's building of long-ships is often taken to represent nothing less than the foundation of the navy: although West Saxon kings had deployed naval forces before (see, for instance, *ASC* s.a. 851), Alfred may well have been the first to have ships built specifically for fighting the Vikings at sea; Charlemagne seems to have done the same in the early ninth century (see Ganshof, *Frankish Institutions*, pp. 64 and 157). One would like to know whether King Alfred's designs had any influence on later English ships. It is perhaps worth mentioning in this connection that the Graveney boat, found in Kent and dating from around 930, stands apart in various respects from ships of the presumed 'Danish' and 'Frisian' types (though it seems itself to have been essentially a trading vessel): for details, see Fenwick, *The Graveney Boat*. Moreover, there is evidence that ships of around sixty oars were the norm in the first half of the eleventh century: see Keynes, *Diplomas of King Æthelred*, p. 225. Finally, the English ships depicted in the Bayeux Tapestry seem to differ from the Norman ships in having a break in the row of oar-holes, and apparently a raised deck, amidships. For a general account of the various types of ship in this period, see Crumlin-Pedersen, 'The Vikings and the Hanseatic Merchants', and idem, 'Viking Shipbuilding and Seamanship'.

36. It is not possible to identify the estuary in question. Suggestions include Poole Harbour in Dorset, and various estuaries flowing into the Solent and Southampton Water.

37. Lucuman is otherwise unknown. As 'king's reeve' he may have been in charge of one of the king's estates.

38. These Frisians are otherwise unknown; cf. Asser, chapter 76, for Frisians in King Alfred's service.

39. Æthelferth is otherwise unknown. A king's *geneat* would be one of his associates or companions, probably a member of the royal household;

such a man, though not necessarily of noble birth, might nevertheless have had a wergild of 1,200 shillings (see the laws of Ine, *EHD* no. 32, § 19).

40. If 120 Danes, from three ships, were killed, and there were still enough survivors to row the ships away, each ship must originally have had a crew of at least forty-five men.

41. This statement presents some difficulties. The Danish ships would presumably have been beached soon after high water; the English ships evidently ran aground when the tide was falling, though some time before low water. The English ships, therefore, must have been nearer the low-tide level than the Danish ships (as well as nearer the mouth of the estuary), and yet we are told that the incoming tide reached the Danish ships first. The simplest explanation (provided by Binns, 'The Navigation of Viking Ships', pp. 109–10) is that the Danish ships, having been deliberately beached, were on rollers, so that the survivors were able to push them down to the water; the English ships, which may anyway have drawn more water, had gone aground accidentally, so that their crews would have had to wait until there was sufficient water to float them.

42. Wulfric is otherwise unknown, though the name occurs several times among the witnesses to Alfred's charters. For horse-thegn, see above, note 34. The term 'Welsh-reeve' does not occur elsewhere, and various interpretations are possible: he may have been responsible in some way for the Welsh, or Cornish, border; or for the Welshmen at court or in the kingdom (cf. Ine's law-code, §§ 23–4 and 32, and Asser, chapter 76); or in his capacity as a horse-thegn he may have been in charge of the king's Welsh horsemen, who carried the king's messages (cf. Ine's code, § 33, assuming such men still existed in Alfred's day). See Faull, 'Old English *Wealh*', pp. 28–9.

ANNALS 897–900 (*p. 120*)

1. For Æthelhelm, see below, p. 328 note 4.

2. It is uncertain when Heahstan became bishop of London. He is one of the bishops who is known to have received a copy of King Alfred's translation of Gregory's *Pastoral Care*: see below, p. 294 note 1.

3. King Alfred died on 26 October 899, reckoned as 900 by a chronicler who calculated the new year from the previous autumn (below, p. 329 note 9). He was buried in the Old Minster, Winchester, but his body was translated by Edward the Elder to the New Minster, Winchester, soon after its foundation, together with that of Alfred's wife Ealhswith (who died on 5 December 902).

4. The chronicler's obituary notice of Alfred seems curiously restrained.

The late-tenth-century chronicler Æthelweard was more lavish in his praise of the king: see above, p. 191.

5. Edward the Elder (899–924): see Asser, chapter 75. He was crowned on 8 June 900 (*CÆ*, p. 51).

6. Æthelwold was the son of King Æthelred, King Alfred's elder brother. His rebellion against his cousin Edward most probably arose from a feeling that he had been denied his rights or expectations under the terms of King Alfred's will (see above, p. 173).

7. Wimborne Minster, Dorset, where King Æthelred was buried (*ASC*; Asser, chapter 41). The monastery there had been founded by Cuthburh, sister of King Ine, in the early eighth century (*ASC* s.a. 718; see also *EHD* no. 159). It was a royal estate in the reign of Edward the Confessor (*DB* fol. 75r).

8. Twynham, now Christchurch, Hampshire. This was one of the burhs named in the *Burghal Hidage*. It was a royal estate in the reign of Edward the Confessor (*DB* fol. 38v).

9. For this sentence in MS 'A', MSS 'B', 'C', 'D' read: 'And then the atheling Æthelwold, his father's brother's son, seized the residences at Wimborne and Twynham, against the will of the king and his councillors.'

10. Badbury Rings, an Iron Age hill-fort in the parish of Shapwick, Dorset.

11. For this sentence in MS 'A', MSS 'B', 'C', 'D' read: 'Then meanwhile the atheling rode away during the night, and came to the Viking army in Northumbria, and they received him as their king and submitted to him.' This probably represents the original form of the annal: in MS 'A' the acceptance of Æthelwold as *king* in Northumbria was suppressed, perhaps to obscure this evidence of dissension within the West Saxon royal dynasty. The chronicler Æthelweard records that in 899 there was a great dissension among the English in Northumbria (above, p. 191), and this may well be related to Æthelwold's acceptance as king; but it is interesting that Æthelweard says nothing about Æthelwold's rebellion, perhaps because it embarrassed him (he was, after all, himself descended from Æthelwold's father, King Æthelred). The rebellion was short-lived: Æthelwold came south to Essex in 901, and after ravaging in Mercia and Wessex was killed at the battle of the Holme (unidentified, but somewhere in East Anglia) in 902.

12. Taking a nun from a nunnery, without the permission of the king or the bishop, was expressly forbidden in Alfred's law-code (§ 8), and it incurred a fine of 120 shillings.

13. Ealdorman Æthelred is otherwise unknown; cf. below, p. 329 note 12.

THE PREFACE TO WERFERTH'S TRANSLATION OF GREGORY'S DIALOGUES (*p. 123*)

Werferth's translation of the *Dialogues* is preserved in two complete copies (Cambridge, Corpus Christi College MS 322 and B.L.

Cotton Otho C. i, vol. 2) and one fragment (Canterbury, Cathedral Library, Add. 25), none of which is earlier than *c.* 1000. Another manuscript preserves a redaction of the text rather than a copy of it (Oxford, Bodleian Library, Hatton 76). The standard edition is Hecht, *Dialoge*, in which the text and the redaction are printed in parallel columns; our translation is based on Hecht's edition of the Cambridge manuscript.

1. Asser (chapter 77) states that Werferth alone translated the *Dialogues*; but 'friends' here implies more than one translator. Given the Anglian dialectal forms in the translation, one thinks inevitably of the other Mercians in Alfred's circle who are named by Asser: Plegmund, Æthelstan and Werwulf (chapter 77; and cf. above, p. 34). Of these three, it is interesting to note that Werwulf in particular enjoyed a close relationship with Werferth, for in 899 Werferth leased an estate to Werwulf 'on account of our ancient association and his faithful friendship and obedience' (*S* 1279). In view of their friendship, it is tempting to think that Werwulf was Werferth's collaborator in producing the translation of the *Dialogues* (cf. Whitelock, 'Prose of Alfred's Reign', pp. 67–8).

2. There is an obvious parallel between the Lombard invasions in sixth-century Italy which shattered Gregory's longing for tranquillity, and the Viking attacks in late-ninth-century England which similarly destroyed Alfred's tranquillity. In fact Alfred's words here (*betwih þas eorðlican gedrefednesse hwilum gehicge þa heofonlican*) reflect a dominant concern of Gregory's *Dialogues*: like Alfred, the pope was 'disturbed by the tribulations of this world' (Werferth's translation reads *onstyred mid þam gedrefednyssum þissere worulde*: Hecht, *Dialoge*, p. 5), and therefore wished to contemplate the lives of holy men who had abandoned this present world (ibid., p. 6). The 'virtues and miracles of holy men' in effect occupy Books I–III of the *Dialogues*, with Book II being devoted entirely to St Benedict of Nursia.

FROM THE TRANSLATION OF GREGORY'S PASTORAL CARE (*pp. 124–30*)

Alfred's translation of the *Pastoral Care* survives in some six manuscripts. Two of these were probably written during Alfred's lifetime: B.L. Cotton Tiberius B.xi (now badly damaged by fire but known from an early antiquary's transcript) and Oxford, Bodleian Library, Hatton 20 (which survives intact). For a facsimile edition of the two manuscripts, see Ker, *The Pastoral Care*. The edition we have used is Sweet, *Pastoral Care*: this is based on the two oldest manuscripts, and includes a complete translation of Alfred's text. For a translation of the prose and verse prefaces, see *EHD* no. 226.

1. It is probable that in Alfred's original, no name was given at this point, but that the name of the bishop to whom a particular copy was to be sent would be added as the copy was being made. Interestingly, Cotton Tiberius B.xi has no name at this point, and there is some possibility that it was the exemplar from which copies were made at Alfred's central writing office. A note formerly to be found in Tiberius B.xi stated that 'Archbishop Plegmund [of Canterbury] has been given his book, and Bishop Swithwulf [of Rochester] and Bishop Werferth'. Of the surviving manuscripts, Hatton 20 is evidently the copy which was sent to Werferth at Worcester. Two other surviving manuscripts are later copies of books sent to Heahstan of London (B.L. Cotton Otho B.ii, of *c.* 1000) and Wulfsige of Sherborne (Cambridge, University Library, Ii.2.4, of the second half of the eleventh century). No name is preserved in the remaining two manuscripts (Cambridge, Corpus Christi College MS 12, and Cambridge, Trinity College R.5.22). If each bishop in the kingdom were to receive a copy, at least ten would have been needed; and we may assume that other important monastic centres (such as Athelney and Shaftesbury, both of which were founded by Alfred: Asser, chapters 92 and 98) would have been sent copies as well. Nevertheless, the number of surviving manuscripts is surprisingly high, and indicates that Alfred's procedure for circulating the work proved successful. On manuscript evidence for the publication and circulation of Alfred's *Pastoral Care*, see Sisam, *Studies in the History of Old English Literature*, pp. 140–47.

2. These remarks on the 'happy times' of the past probably refer to the latter part of the seventh century, and seem to have been suggested in particular by Bede's account of the age of Theodore, archbishop of Canterbury 668–90 (*HE* iv, 2).

3. Alfred is here alluding to his own activities in the 880s, when it was necessary to seek learned men from outside the kingdom of Wessex (Asser, chapter 76) – from Mercia (chapter 77), Francia (chapter 78) and Wales (chapter 79).

4. Alfred seems to be thinking in terms of a general decline of learning throughout the eighth and ninth centuries, leading up to the desperate situation which obtained at the time of his accession in 871. He implies, however, that the effect of the decline was more pronounced in Wessex (south of the Thames) than in Mercia (north of the Thames but south of the Humber) and Northumbria. The implication is interestingly corroborated by the evidence of the archiepiscopal writing office at Canterbury during the period after the sack of Canterbury by the Vikings in 851, and in particular by the career of one scribe who appears in Canterbury charters between 855 and 873. The latest of his productions, a charter of 873 (*S* 344), is miserably written and gives twice the witness-list of an earlier transaction while omitting that for 873, suggesting that this scribe,

by then the principal scribe of the Canterbury writing office, could barely see what he had written: a striking confirmation of Alfred's words that there was not a single man of learning south of the Thames when he succeeded to the kingdom in 871 (see Brooks, 'England in the Ninth Century', pp. 15–16).

5. Alfred reverts to the slightly better situation at the time of writing (*c*.890).

6. This is presumably a reference to the Viking invasions of the central decades of the ninth century; in common with many Christian authors before and after him, Alfred regarded the invasion of hostile peoples as a form of divine punishment for decadence and decay.

7. These words are a version of a sentence of St Augustine which was frequently quoted during the Middle Ages: *non se autem glorietur Christianum, qui nomen habet et facta non habet* (see Cross, 'The Name and Not the Deeds').

8. Alfred is now referring, it seems, to the earlier part of the ninth century, before the worst of the Viking attacks.

9. This quotation is normally punctuated so as to include the sentence which follows; but see Shippey, 'Wealth and Wisdom', especially pp. 347–9. Alfred is saying, in effect, that the learned men of the late seventh century had loved wisdom and had accordingly accumulated an abundance of treasures and books which they had passed on to their successors; these successors in the earlier part of the ninth century had the treasures and books as evidence of their ancestors' activities, but they did not have the ability themselves to make any use of them.

10. Alfred goes a stage further: the negligence of the men in the earlier part of the ninth century has been punished by the Viking invasions, and consequently in Alfred's own day the English lack not only the wisdom but also the wealth (the treasures and the books). Note that Alfred's image of following the track refers to hunting; as Asser tells us (chapter 22), Alfred was an enthusiastic huntsman whose skill and success in that activity were unsurpassed.

11. It is true there are no English prose translations *in extenso* of Latin texts before Alfred's time, but it is worth recalling that Bede was engaged in translating the gospel of John into English at the time of his death (see Colgrave and Mynors, *Bede's Ecclesiastical History*, pp. 582–3); Bede's translation, however, was intended to encompass only the first six chapters of that text, and it has not survived.

12. There is no certainty about what translations Alfred is here referring to. The Bible was translated into Gothic by Ulfilas in the fourth century, but Alfred is unlikely to have known of this work. It is more likely that he knew of one of the translations made in Germany during the ninth century: a prose translation of the gospel story (based on Tatian's *Diatessaron*) in East Franconian made at Fulda *c*. 830; a metrical version of the

same gospel story (similarly based on the *Diatessaron*) in Old Saxon made during the decade 830–40, perhaps at Werden, known as the *Heliand*; and a metrical version of the gospels in Rhenish Franconian made by the monk Otfrid of Weissenburg sometime between 863 and 871. See Bostock, *Handbook*, pp. 157–83 and 190–212. Alfred may have known of one or all of these translations through his continental helpers, Grimbald and John the Old Saxon. See also Wormald, 'Uses of Literacy', p. 106.

13. On Alfred's choice of books most necessary for all men to know, see above, p. 28–35. It is not clear whether Alfred means simply that he himself has been moved to undertake this task, or whether he is instructing his bishops to begin the work of translation themselves.

14. These words have a verbal parallel in Asser (chapter 75): *ut antequam humanis artibus uires haberent.* For discussion of this passage, see Bullough, 'Educational Tradition in England', p. 458 note 10.

15. Again, these words have a verbal parallel in Asser (chapter 77): *aliquando sensum ex sensu ponens*; see above, p. 259 note 164.

16. For these men see Asser, chapters 77–9, and accompanying notes above, pp. 259–61.

17. On *æstel* (roughly a 'book-marker') see Appendix II, p. 205.

18. The verse preface is printed as prose by Sweet, *Pastoral Care*, p. 8; it is edited by Dobbie, *Anglo-Saxon Minor Poems*, p. 110. On the relation of the verse to the prose preface, see Sisam, *Studies in the History of Old English Literature*, pp. 144–5.

19. The convention of the book speaking in the first person is common in Old English poetry; cf. the metrical preface composed by Wulfsige to accompany Werferth's translation of the *Dialogues*, above, p. 187, and below, p. 333 note 1.

20. In the two preceding chapters Gregory has stressed that no one ought to undertake teaching unless he is first properly instructed, and especially that someone in holy orders ought not to lead others by bad example.

21. I Kings xv, 1–35.

22. II Kings xi, 1–27.

23. I Kings xxiv, 1–23.

24. IV Kings xx, 1–21.

25. Daniel iv, 1–34.

FROM THE TRANSLATION OF BOETHIUS'S CONSOLATION OF PHILOSOPHY (*pp. 131–7*)

Alfred's Boethius translation is preserved in two manuscripts: Oxford, Bodleian Library, Bodley 180 (of the first half of the twelfth century) and B.L. Cotton Otho A.vi (of the mid tenth century; now badly fire-damaged, but known from a transcript made by the seventeenth-century antiquary Junius). These manuscripts apparently record two different stages in the preparation of the translation. In what is apparently the earlier stage (represented, paradoxically, by the later manuscript, Bodley 180), Boethius's metres are translated into simple English prose. In the other manuscript, the metres have been rendered into Old English verse (the verse being based directly on the Old English prose version, without further recourse to the Latin). There seems no reason to doubt that these Old English verse translations were made by Alfred himself, for he refers to them in the prose preface (see below, note 3); but they have not been translated here. William of Malmesbury notes that Asser expounded the text of Boethius to King Alfred 'in simple prose' (see below, note 2). Because the translation at many points provides information not found in the original (such information is usually explanatory, as, for example, of Boethius's mythological references), much scholarly enterprise has been devoted to identifying the sources consulted by the king and his helper(s). Until recently it has been assumed that the translation was based on a manuscript of Boethius which was fully glossed, the marginal and interlinear glosses providing all the additional explanatory material found in the translation; and attention has been drawn to one particular manuscript (now in the Vatican Library, MS lat. 3363) which was written in the Loire region sometime during the ninth century but had travelled to England at latest by the mid tenth century (see Parkes, 'A Note on MS Vat. lat. 3363'). The manuscript contains many annotations in Welsh minuscule of late-ninth-century date, and scholars have (not unnaturally) thought of Asser in this connection. However, the annotations do not always correspond to information given in Alfred's translation, and it is more reasonable to think, as Wittig has argued ('King Alfred's *Boethius* and its Latin Sources'), that Alfred and his helper(s) were drawing on a range of standard reference works such as Isidore and Servius rather than on a single glossed manuscript. The general characteristics of Alfred's Boethius translation have been well studied by Otten, *König Alfreds Boethius*, and Payne, *King Alfred and Boethius*. Our translation is based on the text of Sedgefield, *King Alfred's Old English Version of Boethius* (the chapter numbers are from this edition); the entire work has also been translated into modern English by Sedgefield, *King Alfred's Version of the Consolations of Boethius*.

1. For this phrase see Asser, chapter 77 (and above, p. 259 note 164), and Alfred's preface to the *Pastoral Care*, above, p. 126.

2. William of Malmesbury reports (on the basis of unknown evidence) that Asser expounded the text of Boethius to the king 'in simple prose' (*planioribus verbis elucidavit*: Hamilton, *Willelmi Malmesbiriensis Monachi De Gestis Pontificum*, p. 177), which Alfred presumably 'mastered' and then rendered into English.

3. Interestingly, the sole manuscript which preserves this prose preface (Bodley 180) does not preserve Alfred's metrical versions of Boethius's metres. It seems clear that Alfred first turned the Latin metres into simple English prose (as they are found in Bodley 180), then subsequently turned his English prose into English verse without further resort to the Latin. We must assume that Bodley 180 is a copy of the translation made at the stage when the preface had been drafted but before the metrical versions of the metres had been interpolated. See Sisam, *Studies in the History of Old English Literature*, pp. 293–7.

4. This passage replaces an autobiographical passage in Boethius (II, pr. iii).

5. The song in question is II, m. vi (*Novimus quantas dederit ruinas*). This present chapter of Alfred's Boethius is also translated in *EHD* no. 237 (b).

6. The division of society into three orders was a widespread notion during the Middle Ages, particularly in continental writers of the eleventh century and later. However, it appears to be attested for the first time here in Alfred's translation. A century later than Alfred, Ælfric speaks on several occasions of the threefold division of *oratores, bellatores* and *laboratores*; see discussion by Dubuisson, 'L'Irlande et la théorie médiévale des "trois ordres" ', pp. 37–41. The notion has recently been treated at length by Duby, *The Three Orders*; see especially pp. 99–109 for discussion of Alfred and the Anglo-Saxon evidence.

7. These words have often been taken as an explicit statement of Alfred's personal credo; but in fact the words must be read in the context of Boethius's discussion, for Wisdom goes on to explain that desire for worldly renown is a trivial concern if man will only reflect on the size of the universe, whence follows the famous comparison of the earth's mighty expanse to a pin-point in relation to the expanse of the heavens.

8. The Junius transcript of Cotton Otho A.vi has the variant reading *hi* for *hine* at this point which, if accepted, would mean 'they cannot from all their wealth grant virtue to those who love them'.

9. Alfred drastically alters Boethius's meaning at this point. Boethius (III, pr. x) is explaining that by achieving divinity men may by participation be gods, though by nature there is only one God; Alfred takes Boethius's statement on 'gods' (Latin *deos*, Old English *goda*) as a point of departure for a disquisition on 'goods' (also *goda* in Old English).

FROM THE TRANSLATION OF AUGUSTINE'S SOLILOQUIES (*pp. 138-52*)

Alfred's translation of Augustine's *Soliloquies* survives in a single manuscript, now B.L. Cotton Vitellius A.xv, ff. 4-59, of mid-twelfth-century date and unknown origin. Because so much time lies between the date of Alfred's translation and the date of the manuscript, it is not surprising that the text as preserved contains numerous errors and lacunas and at least one substantial dislocation, as well as being incomplete at beginning and end. By the same token, the language has been modernized in certain respects. Nevertheless, these difficulties hardly hinder the reader from appreciating the work essentially as Alfred wrote it, even if the meaning of particular words and phrases must sometimes remain in doubt (such passages are treated in the accompanying notes). Our translation is based on the edition of Carnicelli, *King Alfred's Version of St Augustine's* Soliloquies; the entire work has been translated by Hargrove, *King Alfred's Old English Version of St Augustine's* Soliloquies, and there are extracts in *EHD* no. 237 (a).

1. The work begins acephalously; the word 'then' (*þonne*) seems to imply a sequence of previous statements which have been lost. It is difficult to say how much has been lost, but the coherent argument of the preface as it stands suggests a fairly small loss.

2. Metaphors drawn from everyday life are frequent in Alfred's writings (cf. below, note 9). With this metaphor of tools compare two passages in Alfred's translation of Boethius (Sedgefield, *King Alfred's Old English Version of Boethius*, pp. 30, lines 9-10, and 40, lines 9-25; the latter passage is translated above, pp. 132-3) and Asser's statement that Alfred was able to construct *aedificia* to his own specifications (chapter 76).

3. The sentiments expressed here recur frequently in Alfred's writings; see the prefaces to the *Pastoral Care* (above, p. 126) and the *Boethius* (above, p. 131).

4. Alfred here gives clear indication of the sources on which he drew in compiling the present work. In addition to Augustine's *Soliloquia* he used that author's *Epistola* 147 (*De Videndo Deo*), Gregory's *Dialogi*, *Regula Pastoralis* and *Homilia in Evangelia*, and Boethius, *De Consolatione Philosophiae*. Carnicelli (*King Alfred's Version of St Augustine's* Soliloquies, pp. 29 and 105) suggests that Alfred also used Jerome's *Expositio quattuor evangeliorum* for certain points pertaining to Dives and Lazarus; the work in question is not by Jerome (though it may have travelled under Jerome's name during the Middle Ages) but possibly by an Irish author of the seventh century.

5. On the nature of 'bookland', see below, pp. 308-9, notes 23-4.

6. Alfred's translation here is entirely opposed to the sense of Augustine's original, where the stress is on 'pure solitude' (*solitudo mera*) as the condition necessary for composition.

7. The prayer here placed in the mouth of St Augustine is in fact an addition based on Boethius (see Carnicelli, *King Alfred's Version of St Augustine's* Soliloquies, p. 100). The wording closely resembles certain passages in Alfred's *Boethius*, and it is likely that the Boethius translation was earlier than the *Soliloquies* (ibid., pp. 29–37).

8. Alfred again departs from Augustine's text to insert a homiletic passage on man's need to love God.

9. Alfred seems to have had an especial fondness for nautical imagery. In addition to the present passage see above, p. 142 (Faith, Hope and Charity as the three anchors which hold fast the ship, etc.), together with close parallels in the Boethius translation (Sedgefield, *King Alfred's Old English Version of Boethius*, p. 144, lines 28–32) and the *Pastoral Care* (Sweet, *Pastoral Care*, p. 445, lines 9–14).

10. The passage clearly implies some form of written document accompanied by a seal (not necessarily attached to the document) to guarantee its authenticity. We know that Alfred conducted much of his business by letter: Asser reports having received letters (*indiculos*) from the king (chapter 79), and the *Anglo-Saxon Chronicle* for 889 mentions letters sent by Alfred to Rome (above, p. 113). See further Keynes, *Diplomas of King Æthelred*, pp. 136–7.

11. A similar statement is found in Alfred's *Boethius*, chapter XLII (Sedgefield, *King Alfred's Old English Version of Boethius*, p. 147, lines 12–17; translated above, p. 136).

12. The meaning of this phrase is obscure; see Carnicelli, *King Alfred's Version of St Augustine's* Soliloquies, p. 77 note 15. Our translation involves construing *buton* with the accusative and punctuating as follows: . . . *buton þæt an – þæt he lufað*, 'except for the one (fact), that he loves (them all)'; but this solution is not entirely satisfactory.

13. A similar statement concerning God's two eternal creatures is found in the Boethius translation (above, p. 136). As in the case of the Boethius passage, the statement is an addition to the text.

14. From this point onwards, Alfred ceases to follow Augustine's *Soliloquia* altogether.

15. The transmitted text is obviously corrupt here, the second question in the sequence having been omitted by scribal error. We follow Carnicelli's suggestion (*King Alfred's Version of St Augustine's* Soliloquies, p. 86, note to lines 1–4) in supplying the words *hweðer ðu a lifde*.

16. There is a gap in the manuscript at this point. The words 'so that they could rejoice in the future life when the body and soul' (*þæt hi fægnian mosten ðæs toweardan lifes, siððan se lichama and seo sawl*) were supplied

by Endter and adopted by Carnicelli (*King Alfred's Version of St Augustine's* Soliloquies, p. 87, note to lines 10–11).

17. The manuscript reading *hu* is incomprehensible; we follow Carnicelli in reading *huru*, 'indeed'.

18. See above, p. 145.

19. This text is in fact Augustine's *Epistola* 147 (printed *PL* 33, cols. 596–622).

20. At this point in the manuscript there is a serious dislocation of text, resulting apparently from the misbinding of leaves in an exemplar. We follow Carnicelli's rearrangement of the text (see *King Alfred's Version of St Augustine's* Soliloquies, p. 92, note to lines 21 ff.); several gaps remain, however (see below, note 23).

21. We follow Carnicelli in understanding *aletan byd* as 'delivered' or 'released'; the syntax of the sentence is far from clear, however.

22. The 'weaker testimony' is evidently the testimony of other men.

23. It is necessary to assume a lacuna in the manuscript (or its exemplar) at this point.

24. The story of Dives and Lazarus is also recorded in Gregory's *Dialogues* and *Pastoral Care*, whence Alfred would have been easily familiar with it; see Carnicelli, *King Alfred's Version of St Augustine's* Soliloquies, p. 106.

25. Our translation omits the words *næfre ne* supplied by editorial conjecture in Carnicelli's text.

FROM THE PROSE TRANSLATION OF
THE PSALTER (*pp. 153–60*)

The West Saxon prose version of the first fifty psalms of the Psalter is preserved in a single manuscript, now Paris, Bibliothèque Nationale, lat. 8824, of mid-eleventh-century date and unknown origin. The translation bears no indication of authorship. However, William of Malmesbury tells us (Stubbs, *Willelmi Malmesbiriensis Monachi De Gestis Regum Anglorum* I, p. 132) that Alfred set out to translate the Psalter but was prevented by death from finishing the task. There is therefore some possibility *a priori* that the translation in the Paris Psalter is Alfred's, and it has recently been demonstrated beyond reasonable doubt that the Psalter translation shares so many lexical and stylistic features with Alfred's genuine works that it is to be regarded as certainly his (see Bately, 'Lexical Evidence for the Authorship of the Prose Psalms in the Paris Psalter'). BN lat. 8824 also includes a Latin text of the entire Psalter together with verse translations of Psalms 51–150. These verse translations were apparently composed sometime in the late tenth or early eleventh century and were appended – probably by the scribe of the manuscript – to Alfred's translation of the first fifty in order to provide a complete Psalter in English. In any case, the Latin text of the Psalter preserved in this manuscript cannot have been the text on which Alfred's translation was based (see Ramsay, 'The Latin Text of the Paris Psalter'). In fact Alfred's translation was based on a copy of the so-called Roman version of the Psalter (edited by Weber, *Le Psautier romain*) which had been contaminated at many places by Gallican readings. His translation is for the most part fairly literal, though a few additions and alterations were incorporated (see notes below). Concerning the Introductions which preface each psalm: it has long been recognized (see Bright and Ramsay, 'Notes on the "Introductions" ') that the principal source of these Introductions was a compilation which passes under the name *In Psalmorum Librum Exegesis* and is printed among the works of Bede in *PL* 93, cols. 483-1098. For each psalm this compilation provides: (a) a historical introduction, based largely on Theodore of Mopsuestia's Greek commentary on the psalms which was known to the Latin West through a Latin translation attributed to Julian of Aeclanum (see de Coninck, *Theodori Mopsuesteni Expositionis in Psalmos Iuliano Aeclanensi Interprete in Latinum versae quae supersunt*); (b) explanatory notes derived from the so-called *Tituli Psalmorum* (see Salmon, *Les 'Tituli Psalmorum' des manuscrits latins*); and (c) line-by-line commentary on each psalm based on the earlier commentaries by Arnobius and Jerome. The compilation cannot be by Bede, and it has been suggested that it is a product of seventh-century Ireland (see Fischer, 'Bedae de titulis psalmorum liber', pp. 93–7 and 107). How the compilation became available to Alfred is by no means clear, but it is interesting to recall Alfred's connections with Irish pilgrims (*ASC* s.a. 891: above, p. 113). The entire question has been discussed by O'Neill, 'Old English Introductions to the Prose Psalms of the Paris Psalter'. Finally, note that the numbering of the verses in Alfred's translation does not correspond to numbering in the Vulgate. Our translation is based on the edition by Bright and Ramsay, *Liber Psalmorum: The West-Saxon Psalms*.

1. The sources of this prose Introduction are discussed by Bright and Ramsay, 'Notes on the "Introductions" ', pp. 527–31.
2. The Old English word *ealdormenn* (translating Latin *principes*) is used here in a general rather than a technical sense.

3. The first sentence of this verse (*hwæt forstent heora spræc, cwæð se witega, þeah hi swa cweðen*) has no counterpart in the Latin and was presumably added by Alfred for the sake of clarification. The Psalmist's transitions are frequently very abrupt and in need of some explanation.

4. For the sources of this Introduction, see Bright and Ramsay, 'Notes on the "Introductions" ', p. 531.

5. These words (*ac hit nis na swa hy cweðað*) were added by Alfred, again, presumably, for clarification.

6. These words (*for þam þu eart min God*) are also Alfred's addition.

7. For the sources of this Introduction, see Bright and Ramsay, 'Notes on the "Introductions" ', p. 536.

8. In the Latin text of the Roman Psalter it is the enemies' unholy name (*impius nomen eorum*) which perishes; possibly Alfred was working from a corrupt copy of the Psalter, or else he misunderstood the sentence.

9. This passage bears little resemblance to the Latin (*inimici defecerunt framea in finem*); Alfred possibly misunderstood the word *framea* ('sword').

10. The word 'cities' (OE *ceastra*) is wanting in the manuscript, but was supplied by Thorpe, the first editor, by recourse to *ciuitates* in the Latin text.

11. The Latin reads *in portis filiae Syon* ('in the gates of the daughter of Sion'); Alfred's alteration was probably made for the sake of clarity.

12. For the sources of this Introduction see Bright and Ramsay, 'Notes on the "Introductions"', p. 537; note that Alfred repeats the error in his source by calling Rabsaces 'king of the Assyrians' (see I V Kings xvi–xviii).

13. For the sources of this Introduction, see Bright and Ramsay, 'Notes to the "Introductions"', p. 554.

14. Alfred here expands the rather cryptic words in the Latin text: *sonauerunt et turbatae sunt aquae eius conturbati sunt montes in fortitudine eius.*

EXTRACTS FROM THE LAWS OF KING ALFRED
(*pp. 163–70*)

The composite law-code of Alfred and Ine survives complete in two manuscripts. The earliest is Cambridge, Corpus Christi College MS 173, best known as the 'A' manuscript of the *Anglo-Saxon Chronicle*; the code, written (probably at Winchester) by two mid-tenth-century scribes, originally followed the annal for 920 (misdated 923), but it now follows the final annal (for 1070) of the continued chronicle. The complete code otherwise occurs in the Textus Roffensis, a manuscript compiled in the time of Ernulf, bishop of Rochester (1115–24), and preserved at Rochester Cathedral. Portions of the code are preserved in four other early, but now damaged or incomplete, manuscripts: B.L. Cotton Otho B.xi, of which the relevant part was written at Winchester in the early eleventh century; B.L. Cotton Nero A.i, of which the relevant part was written at an un-identified centre at about the time of the Norman Conquest; B.L. Burney 277, fol. 42, probably written in Kent in the second half of the eleventh century; and Cambridge, Corpus Christi College MS 383, probably written at St Paul's, London, in the late eleventh or early twelfth century. A transcript of Otho B.xi was made by Laurence Nowell in 1562, before the manuscript was badly damaged in the Cotton fire, and is now B.L. Add. 43703: this provides the complete text of the code as it originally stood in Otho B.xi, and is therefore of considerable importance (see further note 8 below). It is unusual for a law-code to be preserved in so many manuscripts, and this fact may suggest that the Alfred–Ine code was quite widely disseminated in the Anglo-Saxon period.

The date of the code is uncertain, but on general historical grounds it is more likely to date from the 880s or 890s than from the 870s. If one accepts that the passage (Int. 49.7) about synods was suggested by Fulco's letter (see note 3 below), it must have been issued after *c*. 886. Asser does not mention the code, but this need not suggest that it was issued after 893; indeed, it would be strange if the king, whose interest in legal affairs is described by Asser in chapters 105–6, had not already set about codifying the law at the time Asser was writing.

The text is edited by Liebermann, *Gesetze* I, pp. 16–123, and in part (with translation) by Attenborough, *Laws*, pp. 36–61 (Ine) and 62–93 (Alfred), and by Whitelock et al., *Councils & Synods* no. 7; for another translation, see *EHD* nos. 32 (Ine) and 33 (Alfred).

1. It is important to appreciate that Ine's laws are clearly regarded, on the evidence of the chapter headings, as an integral part of Alfred's legislation. The division into 120 chapters is often effected with apparent disregard for content, and it may well be that the number had some symbolic meaning; Wormald, '*Lex Scripta* and *Verbum Regis*', p. 132, offers an attractive interpretation based on 120 as the age at which Moses died.

2. The quotations are sometimes translated fairly freely from the source, to bring the Mosaic law more into line with Anglo-Saxon practice, or to make it more readily comprehensible to an Anglo-Saxon audience; see Liebermann, 'King Alfred and Mosaic Law'. There may be some connection between Alfred's extracts and the eighth-century Irish *Liber ex lege Moysi*, a work which includes a very similar collection of extracts from Exodus and which was apparently known in England at about this time; see Fournier, 'Le *Liber ex lege Moysi*', especially p. 230.

3. This passage about synods may have been suggested by the letter of Fulco, archbishop of Rheims, to King Alfred: see above, p. 184. Among the manuscripts possibly brought to England in the late ninth century (above, p. 214 note 26) is one that includes a substantial collection of conciliar decrees (Oxford, Bodleian Library, Hatton 42).

4. Statements to the same effect were made in some other early Germanic law-codes (for instance Visigothic and Lombardic), and derive ultimately from the seventh *Novella* of the sixth-century Byzantine emperor Justinian; see Wormald, '*Lex Scripta* and *Verbum Regis*', p. 113.

5. Alfred's concern to incorporate the best of the laws of Ine (king of Wessex, 688–726), Offa (king of Mercia, 757–96) and Æthelberht (king of Kent, 560–616) perhaps reflects a sense of responsibility on his part not only for the West Saxons but also for the others (such as Mercians and the men of Kent) not under Danish rule. The laws of Æthelberht survive independently (*EHD* no. 29), and were used principally for the section on compensation for bodily injury (see below, note 33). The laws of Ine are appended (see below, note 34). One would expect the reference to the laws of Offa in this context to imply their existence as a separate document, but they have not survived in this form and it is accordingly difficult to assess Alfred's indebtedness to them. There are, however, several similarities between Alfred's code and the capitulary incorporated in the report of the legates to Pope Hadrian (describing their activity in England in 786: *EHD* no. 191); see, for example, notes 12 and 15 below. Though apparently drafted by the legates and first promulgated in Northumbria, the capitulary was later read out, both in Latin and in the vernacular, in a Mercian council convened by Offa. It could thus be said that the capitulary was written in the days of Offa, and since he and the Mercians are known to have undertaken to observe its statutes it is conceivable that Alfred's reference may simply be to the capitulary itself (as suggested by Wormald, '*Lex Scripta* and *Verbum Regis*', p. 112 note 40). On the other hand, it is also possible that Offa subsequently issued his own law-code, and that he drew for this purpose on the legates' capitulary (see Whitelock et al., *Councils & Synods*, p.18). In a letter written in 797, Alcuin urged a Mercian ealdorman to 'admonish all the race of the Mercians diligently to observe the good, moderate and chaste customs (*mores*) which Offa of blessed memory established (*instituit*) for them' (*EHD* no. 202), and the reference here would seem to be to such a code. There are, moreover, a few traces of Mercian vocabulary in Alfred's code (see below, notes 15 and 20) which, if they do not merely reflect some Mercian help with the drafting, may have arisen from the use of a vernacular code issued by Offa; the evidence is admittedly slight, but one should add that some of the traces occur in parts of Alfred's code which would not have been

derived from a vernacular version of the legates' capitulary. For further possible evidence of the use of a Mercian source, see below, note 24.

6. This law would presumably cover all oaths and pledges made in the normal course of affairs, on which order in Anglo-Saxon society depended; but Alfred may have had uppermost in his mind an oath of loyalty sworn to him by his subjects. In *S* 362 (*EHD* no. 100) we hear of an Ealdorman Wulfhere who 'deserted without permission both his lord King Alfred and his country in spite of the oath which he had sworn to the king and all his leading men', and who suffered forfeiture of his property in consequence. A law-code of Edward the Elder (Attenborough, *Laws*, p. 120) states that everyone who breaks the oath and pledge 'which the whole people has given' must pay compensation in accordance with the 'law-book', and since the 'law-book' in question was undoubtedly the code of Alfred it follows that the 'oath and pledge' therein was regarded as one sworn by all. It may have been Alfred, consciously following Carolingian example (on which see Ganshof, 'Charlemagne's Use of the Oath'), who first introduced a general oath of loyalty to the king; later Anglo-Saxon kings themselves followed suit (see Campbell, 'Observations on English Government', pp. 46–7).

7. Alfred is here reiterating a principle formerly enunciated by Bede (and before him, by Origen), that it is better to leave an oath unfulfilled if performance of it will entail a worse crime than the act of oath-breaking itself: see Bonner, 'Bede and Medieval Civilization', p. 75.

8. These opening words of this clause were accidentally omitted in the earliest manuscript (Cambridge, Corpus Christi College MS 173), and are supplied from the Textus Roffensis. It is interesting that the words do occur in B.L. Add. 43703, showing that they were present in B.L. Cotton Otho B.xi: one might have supposed that the Otho text was copied directly from Corpus 173 (since its text of the *Anglo-Saxon Chronicle* was certainly derived, by the same scribe, directly from this manuscript), but this reading shows that the Otho scribe, or a later corrector, had access to another text of the code, now lost.

9. In his translation of St Augustine's *Soliloquies*, Alfred alludes to men in prison on the king's estate: see above, p. 144 (and p. 151).

10. The reference is presumably to those monasteries to which Alfred assigned a portion of his annual revenues: see Asser, chapter 102.

11. This seems to mean those of the king's men who are plotting against his life.

12. In other words, he is to forfeit his life and his possessions; similar provisions were enacted subsequently by Æthelstan (*EHD* no. 35, § 4) and Æthelred (*EHD* no. 44, § 30; Robertson, *Laws*, p. 102, § 37). The strength of Alfred's feelings on this matter may be gauged also from Int. 49.7 and from § 42.5–6; he may have been influenced, directly or

indirectly, by the capitulary in the report of the legates to Pope Hadrian (*EHD* no. 191), chapter 12.

13. Wergild (literally 'man-price') was the sum due to a dead man's kindred as compensation for his death. It varied according to the rank of the dead man (see note 16 below), and could be paid in cash or kind; the slayer, his own kinsmen and his associates (if any) were collectively responsible for its payment, and it was shared between the dead man's maternal and paternal kindred; see further Whitelock, *Beginnings of English Society*, pp. 39–47, and Loyn, 'Kinship', pp. 203–5. The precise figure for the king's wergild in late-ninth-century Wessex is not known, but would probably have been at least 30,000 pence (or 6,000 shillings), which was the sum paid for a West Saxon atheling in 694 (*ASC*); the wergild of a Mercian king was of the same order, though that of a Northumbrian king was rather higher (see *EHD* no. 51). An oath equivalent to the king's wergild would thus have been one sworn by the number of men whose wergilds collectively amounted to 6,000 shillings (or more).

14. The phrase 'both *ceorl* and noble' renders the traditional rhyming formula *ge ceorle ge eorle*; for an account of the social hierarchy thus covered, see note 16 below.

15. Alfred's legislation on this subject may have been derived from Offa's code: the capitulary in the report of the legates to Pope Hadrian (*EHD* no. 191) includes a clause prohibiting marriage with nuns (chapter 15) and one declaring children of such unions to be illegitimate (chapter 16), and if similar provisions were incorporated in a code of Offa's this might account for the appearance in Alfred's code of a word (*lefnys*, 'permission' – also used in § 20) that otherwise occurs only in the (Mercian) translation of Bede's *Ecclesiastical History*; cf. *ASC* s.a. 900 (above, p. 120).

16. This clause encapsulates the basic social distinctions recognized among the West Saxons in the ninth century. The 'twelve-hundred man' was a man with a wergild of 1,200 shillings, and would be a substantial land-owner (though the actual amount of land such men owned would doubt-less have varied considerably). He would originally have been termed an *eorl* ('noble', as in the archaic formula mentioned in note 14 above), but in Ine's laws he appears as a *gesith* (literally 'companion'), and by Alfred's time was coming to be known as a 'thegn' (a word embodying the concept of *service* to the king which was a characteristic of the class: see Asser, chapter 100). The 'six-hundred man' was a man with a wergild of 600 shillings. In Ine's laws this was the wergild assigned to a Welsh-man with five hides of land (*EHD* no. 32, § 24.2), but it may also have applied to Englishmen of 'noble' stock who had less than five hides of land, or no land at all. The same was perhaps true in Alfred's day, but the class disappears altogether in the tenth century, presumably because these distinctions were then no longer recognized. The *ceorl* or

'commoner' was an ordinary freeman. He had a wergild of 200 shillings and would probably have held in his own right between one and five hides of land; in the tenth century, and perhaps also in Alfred's day, a *ceorl* who acquired five hides of land and an office in the king's hall became entitled to the rights of a thegn, and this rank became hereditary after three generations (see *EHD* no. 51 (a) and (b)).

17. For these meetings presided over by a reeve, see Asser, chapter 106, and above, p. 275 note 256.

18. The text of the code in the Textus Roffensis adds 'and he [the reeve] is to succeed to the fine'.

19. The purpose of this clause was presumably to ensure that all traffic within and across the frontiers of the kingdom was carefully regulated: there was always a danger that men up to no good might masquerade as traders (see the Treaty between Alfred and Guthrum, § 5).

20. The word for 'district' is *boldgetale* (literally 'a number of dwellings'), which otherwise occurs only in Bishop Werferth of Worcester's Old English version of Pope Gregory's *Dialogues* (e.g. Hecht, *Dialoge*, p. 45), where it translates *provincia*. The use of the word in Alfred's code would thus seem to be another sign of Mercian influence, either in the drafting or from the use of a Mercian written source.

21. This clause may be compared with an analogous clause in Ine's code (*EHD* no. 32, § 39), which states that a man who moves without permission from one shire to another is to return whence he came and pay sixty shillings to his lord. Alfred thus seeks to discourage such illicit moves by imposing a heavy fine on the would-be new lord, to be used for the king's purposes in each of the shires involved; he does not, however, insist that the man should return whence he came. The notion of 'service' in a shire probably represents the man's assessment there for the various public obligations (not that he was some kind of local official).

22. Note the distinction made here between the *burg* or *burh* ('residence', with the implication that it was protected or fortified in some substantial way) of the king, etc., and the *edor* ('hedge' or 'fence' enclosing a dwelling) of the *ceorl*.

23. 'Bookland' was land held according to the privileges stated or implied in a 'book', or charter (see the example translated above, p. 179); typically, the privileges were that the land was immune from the customary burdens (for example, payment of food-rent to the king), with the exception of bridge-work, fortress-work and military service, and that the owner had full power to bequeath it to anyone of his choosing. In these respects bookland was distinguished from 'folkland', or land subject to all the customary burdens and not alienable outside the owner's kindred (see also p. 325 note 103 below). Bookland, as a form of tenure, originated in the seventh century as a means to serve the interests of the Church, by

enabling laymen to grant their land to religious foundations (for the good of their souls), and by entitling these foundations to hold the land free from all but the most essential public burdens.

24. Although bookland could normally be bequeathed to anyone of the owner's choosing, the original grantor (the king) or the owner might on occasion stipulate that it could not in fact be alienated outside the kindred. For during the eighth century bookland was increasingly created not so much to enable a layman to endow a church, as to entitle him to hold his land free from the public burdens (with the exception of bridge-work, etc.); and in such cases it might be advisable to protect the long-term interests of the kindred by explicitly restricting the owner's powers of alienation. Thus a charter of Offa, king of Mercia, restricts the scope of alienation to the original beneficiary's kindred (*S* 114, dated 779), and one of Burgred, king of Mercia, restricts it further to a male representative of the paternal line (*S* 214, dated 869); for examples of similar stipulations made by the owners themselves, see the will of King Alfred (above, p. 178) and the will of Ealdorman Alfred (*EHD* no. 97). This practice may well have originated in eighth-century Mercia, suggesting the possibility that it was an analogous clause in Offa's code that gave rise to the present clause in Alfred's.

25. The meaning of this statement is not entirely clear. It may be (as is normally supposed) that a person (presumably a disappointed kinsman) who challenges the owner's power to dispose of the bookland outside the kindred is required to adduce the evidence supporting his case, in the stated circumstances. On the other hand, it may be that it is the owner of the bookland who is required to announce in public the existence of the special restrictions on his powers of alienation, so as to prevent him from disregarding them at the expense of his kindred. Since the clause is phrased as if directed towards the owner himself, the second explanation is perhaps to be preferred.

26. In the list of chapter-headings prefixed to the code the title of this clause is 'Concerning the feud', so the enemy in question would be someone against whom the man has a legitimate blood-feud. Alfred was evidently concerned that the practice of feuding might get out of hand and thus jeopardize domestic order; his regulations were intended to ensure that all feuds would be settled peaceably, by payment of wergild, and not by endless bloodshed.

27. This refers back to § 5: if a man involved in a blood-feud reaches a church which a bishop has consecrated, he is to be safe there for seven days (as long as he can survive without food, and provided he does not himself violate the church's sanctuary); if the religious community need their church, he is to be transferred to another building (which must not have more doors than the church); if he is willing to give up his weapons,

his opponents are to keep him for thirty days, and send notice about him to his kinsmen.

28. In other words, he is to pay the appropriate wergild if the man is killed, or he is to pay compensation for any wounds inflicted on the man (presumably following the tariff set out at the end of the code).

29. In other words, if the person pursuing the 'enemy' attacks him once he has surrendered, he (the pursuer) is to pay compensation and is no longer entitled to avenge his kinsman (in respect of whom the blood-feud had arisen). An alternative (but rather less natural) interpretation is suggested by Attenborough, *Laws*, pp. 85 and 198: if he is willing to surrender and to give up his weapons, and after that anyone (that is, as it transpires from the end of the sentence, a kinsman of the 'enemy') fights against him (the pursuer, to whom the 'enemy' has surrendered), he (who does so) is to pay wergild or wound in accordance with what he has done, and a fine, and is to have ruined his kinsman (that is, the outcome of his action is that his kinsman – the 'enemy' who surrendered – is no longer guaranteed the protection otherwise afforded to him by the law).

30. This placing of loyalty to one's lord above loyalty to one's kinsman is graphically illustrated, though in different circumstances, by a story told in the *Anglo-Saxon Chronicle*: a West Saxon atheling called Cyneheard attacked and killed Cynewulf, king of Wessex; the king's thegns came to confront the atheling, who offered them terms and told them that he had kinsmen of theirs on his side; the thegns replied that 'no kinsman was dearer to them than their lord and that they would never serve his slayer'; so they attacked the atheling and killed him along with his men (*ASC* s.a. 757, recounting events which took place in 786).

31. The reference here to slaves and 'unfree labourers' (*esnewyrhtan*) suggests that there was some technical distinction between the two classes, but there can have been little difference in reality. *Esne* is used on its own to signify 'slave' or to translate *servus*, 'slave', but it also occurs with the meaning 'man' or 'young man'; *wyrhta* means 'labourer'; *esnewyrhta* occurs elsewhere as a translation of *mercenarius*, 'hireling'. The *esnewyrhta* of Alfred's code was perhaps a poor man who eked out a living by working for a master, and who was neither free nor able to move elsewhere.

32. The 'four Ember weeks' were those in which the Ember days fell: the Wednesday, Friday and Saturday following (a) the first Sunday in Lent, (b) Whit Sunday, (c) Holy Cross Day (14 September), and (d) St Lucy's Day (13 December). The days were observed by the Church as days of fasting and abstinence.

33. A similarly detailed tariff of compensations for bodily injuries occurs in the law-code of Æthelberht, king of Kent (560–616), and clearly served as the model for the tariff in Alfred's code; for full translations of both,

see Attenborough, *Laws*, pp. 9–15 and 87–93. The Alfredian tariff covers almost every part of the human anatomy, from the head to the little toe; the compensations range from 100 shillings (for a serious wound to the neck) to one shilling (for knocking off the nail of the little finger). It is possible that the compensation was sometimes paid in kind: see Okasha, *Hand-List*, no. 36.

34. For a translation of Ine's code, see *EHD* no. 32. By re-issuing Ine's code as an integral part of his own, Alfred clearly intended to supplement existing West Saxon legislation, and not to supersede it. There are many important provisions in Ine's code for which there are no corresponding provisions in Alfred's, and in these cases one imagines that the earlier legislation remained in force; but there are also several discrepancies between Alfred's code and Ine's, and here one imagines that Alfred's legislation took precedence. The fact that such discrepancies were allowed to stand suggests that the received text of Ine's code was respected, and was not edited by Alfred to suit his own purposes. The several appeals to the 'law-book' in codes issued by Edward the Elder (899–924), Æthelstan (924–39) and Edgar (959–75) seem to refer to the composite Alfred–Ine code, and suggest that it remained valid as a whole well into the tenth century.

THE TREATY BETWEEN ALFRED AND GUTHRUM
(pp. 171–2)

This document is preserved in a collection of Anglo-Saxon legal texts (Cambridge, Corpus Christi College MS 383), probably written at St Paul's, London, in the late eleventh or early twelfth century. It occurs in this manuscript in two forms, one (p. 6) slightly shorter than the other (pp. 83–4); our translation follows the longer version. The text is edited by Liebermann, *Gesetze* I, pp. 126–9, and (with translation) by Attenborough, *Laws*, pp. 98–101; it is translated in *EHD* no. 34.

1. This is the boundary which separates Wessex and English Mercia from the Danelaw, and it presumably represents a modification of the boundary established when the Vikings divided Mercia with Ceolwulf in 877 (see above, p. 246 note 94): Alfred took control of London in 886, and in the new settlement the city is left on the English side. The treaty must therefore have been drawn up in or soon after 886; Guthrum died in 890 (*ASC*, above, p. 113). Watling Street was an important Roman road, now known as the A 5. The boundary may not have remained on the line described for very long: see Davis, 'Alfred and Guthrum's Frontier', pp. 803–6, and above, p. 289 note 29.

2. In other words, the wergild (see above, p. 307 note 13) of the slain man,

whether Englishman or Dane, was eight half-marks of gold. A mark was a Scandinavian unit of weight and account containing eight 'ores', and an ore apparently came to be regarded in England as synonymous with an ounce. Eight half-marks would thus be equivalent to thirty-two ounces, and this amount of gold, since the ratio of gold to silver was about 10:1, would represent about 320 ounces of silver, or (at four shillings to the ounce), 1,280 shillings (see Lyon, 'Denominations and Weights', pp. 210–11 and 216). It would appear, therefore, that the treaty envisages the Englishmen and Danes in question as men of high standing, since in Alfred's Wessex 1,200 shillings was the wergild of the highest social class (see above, p. 307 note 16).

3. 'The *ceorl* who occupies rented land' would seem to mean one of the class of ordinary freemen who did not have land of his own, and this would imply that the *ceorl* with his own land was included in the previous class with the higher wergild; by contrast, the wergild for a *ceorl* in Wessex was 200 shillings. One effect of the clause as a whole would thus have been to place an unusually high price on the lives of all free and independent Englishmen who came into contact with the Danes, presumably for their better protection; another would have been to place the same high price on all Danish freemen, so they too would be well protected; the English *ceorl* on rented land was assigned the normal *ceorl*'s wergild, as was the Danish freedman. The clause would thus have been advantageous to Englishmen and Danes alike, and one imagines that its intention was to discourage clashes between men of the two races within Guthrum's kingdom itself, and between Guthrum's Danes and Alfred's Englishmen in general; a similar provision was included in King Æthelred the Unready's treaty with the Vikings in 994 (*EHD* no. 42, § 5). See further, Maitland, *Domesday Book and Beyond*, p. 44 note 1, and for a different interpretation see Davis, 'East Anglia and the Danelaw', pp. 33–4.

4. In other words, the accused man must be able to produce twelve king's thegns prepared to support his oath of denial.

5. This seems to mean that a man accused of some other misdemeanour (theft, for example) involving a sum of more than four mancuses should adopt the same procedure for clearing himself as in cases of manslaughter; but if he cannot clear himself in this way, he is to pay compensation at three times the value (of the stolen property).

6. In other words, anyone involved in the purchase of men (slaves), horses and oxen was to ensure that he had a warrantor to the transaction.

7. 'Army' is here used in the sense of 'Danish settlers', and it does not imply that Alfred's subjects might be allowed to join the Viking army. The purpose of the agreement was simply to ensure that Alfred's subjects did not visit or settle in the Danelaw, and that Guthrum's subjects did not visit or settle in Alfred's territories, without due permission, thereby

reducing the risk of clashes between the two peoples. The sentence that follows shows that both parties would countenance such traffic for the purposes of trade, so long as it was carefully controlled; the danger (from Alfred's point of view) was presumably that Viking raiders might try to pass themselves off as traders.

8. Literally, 'that one has a clean back'.

THE WILL OF KING ALFRED (*pp. 173–8*)

The will of King Alfred (*S* 1507) was preserved in the archives of the New Minster, Winchester. It occurs in the New Minster *Liber Vitae* (B.L. Stowe 944, fols. 29v–33v), written during the reign of Cnut (1016–35), probably in 1031. This manuscript begins with an account of the early history of the monastery, from its foundation by Edward the Elder, and there follow various lists of persons deemed worthy of remembrance by members of the community in their prayers. Alfred's will was entered by the original scribe immediately after these lists, as the first of a series of miscellaneous texts. The reason for its inclusion is not immediately apparent. A copy of the will may have been entrusted to the New Minster by Edward the Elder, or one may have been secured deliberately by the community when they subsequently acquired an interest in certain of the estates mentioned (see below, notes 29 and 36); the availability of so singular a document would then have been sufficient justification for its inclusion, while its close associations with Edward the Elder would have made it especially attractive. In later tradition Alfred himself came to be regarded as the prime mover in the foundation of the New Minster, and indeed a copy of the will (apparently derived from the *Liber Vitae*) was entered in the fourteenth-century *Liber Monasterii de Hyda* as if it were in some way the foundation charter.

The will was drawn up after 872, if that is the year of Werferth's accession to the bishopric of Worcester (see above, p. 259 note 163), and before 30 June 888, when Archbishop Æthelred died (*ASC*). It must have been drawn up several years after the king's marriage in 868, since he already had five children; the fact that special bequests are made to Werferth and to Æthelred, ealdorman of the Mercians, suggests a date in the 880s, by which time these men had come to be closely associated with the king.

The text is edited (with translation) in *SEHD* no. 11; it is translated in *EHD* no. 96.

1. The phrase 'by the grace of God' normally qualifies the tenure of some God-given office, but the word 'and' which follows this phrase precludes what would otherwise be the more natural translation ('I Alfred, king by the grace of God . . .'); the same consideration arises later in the will, when Alfred names himself again, so it is unlikely that the 'and' is simply an error. It seems that the phrase (which should have been part of the king's title) was taken by the person who wrote out the original document to apply in some way to the process of making the will; cf. *SEHD*, p. 92.

2. Æthelred became archbishop of Canterbury in 870, and he died on 30 June 888: see O'Donovan, 'Episcopal Dates, pt I', p. 31.

3. This statement represents just one aspect of the provisions made by King Æthelwulf in his will. We know from Asser, chapter 16, that Æthelwulf arranged a division of the kingdom between his two eldest (surviving) sons: Æthelbald was assigned the western kingdom (Wessex itself, having held it since 855), and Æthelberht was assigned the eastern kingdom (Kent, Surrey, Sussex and Essex, having acted as king of this area in 855–6). At the same time, Æthelwulf made arrangements for the disposal of his own inheritance 'between his sons, daughter and kinsmen', and the references in Alfred's will are to a part of these arrangements. The fact that Æthelberht is not mentioned in this connection probably signifies that Æthelwulf had made separate provision for him, by giving him the greater part (if not all) of his property in the eastern kingdom with the intention that Æthelberht should establish a permanently separate and distinct dynasty there. The inheritance bequeathed jointly to Æthelbald, Æthelred and Alfred probably comprised King Æthelwulf's personal, or private, holdings of 'bookland' (above, p. 308 note 23), of which he would have been free to dispose as he pleased; as such, it would have been quite distinct from the rest of the king's property, comprising his folkland (the descent of which was governed by customary laws) and also any land earmarked for the support of the king (which would have passed automatically to the next holder of the office). Cf. below, note 103. Æthelwulf clearly intended that this 'personal' property should be kept intact, and since it seems to have been considered desirable that the reigning king should hold it himself (in addition to the other royal estates), it is likely that Æthelwulf had also intended that the kingship too should pass from Æthelbald to each of his brothers in turn (in so far as they survived each other). For further discussion of these matters, see John, *Orbis Britanniae*, pp. 40–44; Dumville, 'The Ætheling', pp. 21–4; and A. Williams, 'Royal Succession', pp. 145–9.

4. Æthelwulf's plan for the division of the kingdom was, it seems, necessarily set aside after the early death of Æthelbald in 860 (*ASC*; Asser, chapter 18), perhaps because Æthelred and Alfred were still too young for either to assume the office of kingship; so Æthelberht, already holding the eastern kingdom, succeeded to Wessex as well. But Æthelberht made an

arrangemeht with his brothers whereby he would enjoy the estates in
Wessex during his lifetime (since he would now want them for his own
purposes), undertaking to restore them (and anything obtained from the
use of them) to Æthelred and Alfred after his death, along with 'that
which he had himself acquired'. This seems to imply that just as Æthelberht was to hold the property in both kingdoms, so too would Æthelred and
Alfred eventually succeed to Æthelberht's property in the east, as well as
recover their own in the west; perhaps it was already known, therefore, that
Æthelberht had no prospect of male heirs to continue his line.

5. Æthelberht died, apparently without issue, in 865 (*ASC* s.a. 860; Asser,
   chapter 19). His successor Æthelred became king in the latter part of the
   same year (*ASC* s.a. 866, that is, covering a year from 24 September 865;
   Asser, chapter 21).

6. The distinction made in the will between the *inherited* property and the
   acquired property is rather interesting: the same distinction, albeit in a
   different context, was made in Eadred's reign (see Keynes, *Diplomas of
   King Æthelred*, p. 148 note 224), and it seems to anticipate the practices
   governing succession to property in Anglo-Norman England (on which
   see Holt, 'Politics and Property', especially p. 12).

7. Alfred appears to have wanted his share of the joint inheritance during his
   brother's lifetime, perhaps because he was aware that Æthelred had
   children of his own who might stake a claim to the whole on their father's
   death. But such a division of the joint inheritance would have been contrary
   to the terms of Æthelwulf's will, and perhaps for that reason it could not be
   effected (or that at least may have been the excuse). So Alfred had to be
   satisfied with an assurance that the joint property (and anything acquired in
   addition by Æthelred) would pass to him after Æthelred's death. This
   arrangement would have meant, in effect, that Alfred was now regarded as
   heir apparent: see Asser, chapter 29, and above, p. 240 note 56.

8. The reference is to the 'great heathen army' which had arrived in England
   in 865 (*ASC* s.a. 866; Asser, chapter 21) and which invaded Wessex in
   870–71 (*ASC* s.a. 871; Asser, chapter 35).

9. Unidentified (see *EHD*, p. 534 note 1). The meeting presumably took
   place after the beginning of the Viking invasion of Wessex in the autumn
   of 870 and before the death of Æthelred soon after Easter 871.

10. In a time of uncertainty, provision was made for the children of Æthelred
    and Alfred. Under the existing arrangement, the joint property and
    whatever else was acquired from the use of it would pass from Æthelred
    to Alfred (and so, presumably, to Alfred's heirs), leaving only Æthelred's
    own estates for his own children; or (if Alfred predeceased Æthelred)
    the property would pass from Æthelred to his children, leaving only
    Alfred's own estates for his own children. Under the new agreement, the
    joint property would be retained as before by the surviving brother

(presumably passing eventually to his own heirs), but any additional property acquired from the use of it, together with the estates given by Æthelwulf to the surviving brother individually, would be given by the surviving brother to the children of the deceased brother. In other words, the children of the deceased brother, instead of receiving only the property given to their father individually by Æthelwulf, and whatever else their father bequeathed to them, would now receive in addition everything acquired from the use of the joint property as well as the property given to the surviving brother individually by Æthelwulf. By way of compensation for the latter, the surviving brother would receive all the personal property of the deceased brother (for instance, what he had acquired by bequests from other members of the family), except that part of it which the deceased brother had bequeathed to his own children. It is possible that these negotiations were affected by the expectation that Alfred would predecease Æthelred, since he had been afflicted by a mysterious illness in 868 (Asser, chapter 74): the new agreement ensured more generous provision for the children of the brother who died first, so Alfred would have done his best for any children that he already had or might have in the future; but the children of the surviving brother would ultimately have the advantage of possession of the joint property, so Æthelred's concessions would not have seriously damaged the interests of his own heirs.

11. Æthelred died soon after Easter (15 April) in 871 (*ASC*; Asser, chapter 41).

12. This remark implies either that Alfred had himself failed to fulfil his obligations to Æthelred's children arising from the *Swinbeorg* agreement, or that Æthelred's children themselves chose to question the terms of that agreement by claiming a share of the joint property which would now be held by Alfred. Since Alfred's response was to refer to the will of King Æthelwulf, it would appear that it was Alfred's title to the joint property that was disputed.

13. Unidentified (see *EHD*, p. 535 note 1); a place called *Langandene* is mentioned in the boundary clause of *S* 601, which concerns land at Ippleden in Devon.

14. The reference is to Æthelhelm and Æthelwold, sons of Alfred's brother Æthelred, who receive bequests later in the will.

15. Literally 'hear', in accordance with the earlier statement that Æthelwulf's will was read out to the councillors.

16. 'Sign manual' translates *handseten*: the word normally applies to the act of witnessing a written document, probably by touching the cross beside the witness's name (both actually written by the scribe of the document itself), but it is not clear in this case that subscriptions to a document were involved; perhaps some simple gesture associated with making the pledge is meant.

17. Edward the Elder, king of Wessex (899–924): see Asser, chapter 75.

18. Stratton, Cornwall, where one hide (though with land for thirty ploughs) was held by Osbern (later bishop of Exeter) and Alfred the Marshal before 1066 (*DB* fol. 121v); 'Triggshire' represents the Domesday Hundred of Stratton, later divided into three smaller Hundreds called Stratton, Lesnewth and Trigg. The information given here and in the notes which follow is intended to show what is known about the later history of all the estates named in the will, up to the end of the Anglo-Saxon period; see further below, note 100. The phrase 'before 1066' translates the formula *T.R.E.* ('in the time of King Edward') used in *Domesday Book*, and refers to the period immediately preceding the Norman Conquest.

19. Hartland, Devon, where nine hides (land for 110 ploughs) were held by Earl Harold's mother before 1066 (*DB* fol. 100v).

20. From their position in the will, one might judge the estates in question to have been in Devon or Somerset. There are no charters of Edward disposing of land in Devon, and only one disposing of land in Somerset (*S* 380: Wellington, West Buckland and Bishop's Lydeard given to Asser in exchange for the minster at Plympton in Devon); but see also *S* 1705 and 1707–8. Nothing is known of the Leofheah to whom Alfred had apparently leased the estates.

21. Carhampton, Somerset, which was evidently a major royal estate before 1066 (*DB* fol. 86v); see also *S* 806.

22. Kilton, Somerset, where $10\frac{1}{2}$ hides were held by a certain Ælfweard and Leofric before 1066 (*DB* fol. 96r).

23. Burnham, Somerset, where four hides were held by a certain Brixi before 1066 (*DB* fol. 95r).

24. Wedmore, Somerset. Wedmore is named as a royal estate by Asser, chapter 56. Land there was given by Edward the Confessor to Giso, bishop of Wells (see *S* 1115, and cf. *S* 1042); Giso held ten hides at Wedmore before 1066 (*DB* fol. 89v), as part of the royal manor of Cheddar (*DB* fol. 86r).

25. Cheddar, Somerset, was a royal estate in the tenth century, and meetings of the king's councillors were held there in ?941, 956 and ?968 (*S* 511, 611, 806); it was held by Edward the Confessor before 1066 (*DB* fol. 86r). Its status in the latter part of the ninth century is not so clear. It may have been a royal estate: the 'community' there to which the will refers could be the permanent household which looked after the estate on the king's behalf, and Alfred was perhaps concerned merely to ensure that the residents accepted Edward as his successor on terms previously agreed; the land itself may have passed automatically to the new king along with other property tied to the royal office. Alternatively, the reference may be to a religious community established at Cheddar which

had agreed to accept Edward's patronage, perhaps with the implication that in the process Cheddar itself would become a royal estate; according to S 806, Edward gave certain estates in Somerset to the 'community' at Cheddar, and since this reference must be to a religious community the second interpretation makes better sense. The excavations conducted at Cheddar in the early 1960s revealed a not unimpressive 'Long Hall' in the Alfredian and Edwardian period, which could (but need not) be 'royal'. More significantly, however, they showed that the site underwent a major re-arrangement during the 930s or thereabouts: a stone chapel was built where the 'Long Hall' had stood, and a more imposing hall was constructed slightly to the south-west of the old one. See Rahtz, *Saxon and Medieval Palaces at Cheddar*, especially pp. 13–18, 49–57 and 373–6 (and Hinton, *Alfred's Kingdom*, pp. 43–5). This re-arrangement suggests that it was not until Æthelstan's reign that Cheddar was developed as an important royal estate, arguably supporting the view that it had not then been a royal estate for long.

26. Chewton Mendip, Somerset, where fourteen hides (land for forty ploughs) were held by Queen Edith before 1066 (*DB* fol. 87r).

27. Cannington, Somerset, which was evidently a major royal estate before 1066 (*DB* fol. 86v).

28. Bedwyn, Wiltshire (an estate which may have included the hill-fort at Chisbury, one of the sites listed in the *Burghal Hidage*); a manuscript containing two acrostic poems on King Alfred was at Bedwyn in the middle of the tenth century (below, p. 338). In the later tenth century Bedwyn was one of the estates earmarked for the support of kings' sons; King Edgar gave it to Abingdon abbey, but it was recovered for the crown after his death (see *S* 756, 937). Bedwyn was evidently a major royal estate before 1066 (*DB* fol. 64v).

29. Pewsey, Wiltshire. King Edmund gave thirty hides at Pewsey to the New Minster, Winchester, in 940 (*S* 470), and the church held the estate before 1066 (*DB* fol. 67v).

30. Hurstbourne Tarrant, Hampshire. In the later tenth century Hurstbourne was one of the estates earmarked for the support of kings' sons; King Edgar gave it to Abingdon abbey, but it was recovered for the crown after his death (see *S* 689, 937). Hurstbourne was still a royal estate before 1066 (*DB* fol. 39r).

31. Probably Bishop's Sutton, Hampshire, where Earl Harold held twenty-five hides before 1066 (*DB* fol. 44v); other possibilities are Sutton-by-Cheam, Surrey (*DB* fol. 32v) and Sutton-by-Guildford, Surrey (*DB* fol. 36v).

32. Leatherhead, Surrey. The estate is not entered separately in *Domesday Book*, though the church at Leatherhead was attached to Ewell, apparently a royal estate before 1066 (*DB* fol. 30v).

33. Probably Carshalton, Surrey, where twenty-seven hides were held by five free men from King Edward before 1066 (*DB* fol. 36r); other possibilities are Alton Priors, Wiltshire (*DB* fol. 65v; see also *S* 1513), and Alton, Hampshire (*DB* fol. 43r). It is also possible that the *Aweltune* of the will signifies 'the *tun* (estate) at Ewell'; if so, the association between Leatherhead and Ewell (above, note 32) may date back to the ninth century.

34. These cannot be identified; King Eadred similarly bequeathed all his booklands in Kent (and Surrey and Sussex) to his mother, Queen Eadgifu (*S* 1515).

35. Hurstbourne Priors, Hampshire, where the bishop of Winchester held thirty-eight hides before 1066 (*DB* fol. 41r).

36. Chisledon, Wiltshire. According to certain charters of dubious authority, land at Chisledon was given by the Old Minster, Winchester, to Edward the Elder, who gave it to the New Minster, Winchester: see *S* 359, 366, 370 and 1417. Forty hides at Chisledon were held by the New Minster before 1066 (*DB* fol. 67v).

37. The Old Minster claimed that Æthelwulf had promised the estates to the church with effect from Alfred's death; the bishop then gave up his rights in Alfred's favour, in return for help in paying tribute to the Vikings, but Alfred himself granted the reversion of the estates to the church in exchange for land in Berkshire (*S* 354); see also *S* 358–9.

38. 'Private property' translates *sundorfeoh*: *feoh* normally means movable property of some kind, in which case the reference might be to the livestock on the estate, but it is also possible that the reference is to a separate estate at Stoke by Hurstbourne (see *S* 359).

39. Æthelweard: see Asser, chapter 75.

40. Arreton, Isle of Wight, a minor royal estate before 1066 (*DB* fol. 39v).

41. Presumably the same place as the 'royal estate which is called Dean', in Sussex, where Asser first met King Alfred (Asser, chapter 79), and probably to be identified as East or West Dean in west Sussex. Neither is entered separately in *Domesday Book*, but both were perhaps assessed with Singleton (which lies between them), where 97½ hides were held by Earl Godwine before 1066 (*DB* fol. 23r). In the early eleventh century the whole estate was known as *Æðelingadene*, or 'Dean of the athelings', so it had apparently become an estate associated in particular with kings' sons; see Keynes, *Diplomas of King Æthelred*, p. 187 note 117. King Æthelred gave sixty hides there to Wherwell abbey in 1002 (*S* 904), but the land was presumably taken from the abbey at a later date by Earl Godwine. A less likely identification for the Dean of the will is East or West Dean, near Eastbourne, east Sussex, where Countess Goda (Edward the Confessor's sister) and others held relatively small estates before 1066 (*DB* fols. 19rv, 21r); cf. Stevenson, *Asser*, pp. lxxii, 312.

42. East or West Meon, Hampshire. In the tenth century Kings Æthelstan, Eadwig and Edgar disposed of various estates in East and West Meon to individuals (*S* 417, 619, 754, 811), but by the end of the Anglo-Saxon period the land had for the most part been acquired by the Old Minster, Winchester (*DB* fols. 38r, 40v).

43. Amesbury, Wiltshire. Land at Amesbury was bequeathed by King Eadred to his mother Queen Eadgifu (*S* 1515), and meetings of the king's councillors were held there on various occasions in the tenth century; it was evidently still a major royal estate before 1066 (*DB* fol. 64v).

44. Probably West Dean in Wiltshire, a small estate held by a certain Godric before 1066 (*DB* fol. 72r); perhaps also East Dean, just across the border in Hampshire, where various people held small estates from King Edward before 1066 (*DB* fols. 38v, 42r, 48rv).

45. Sturminster Marshall, Dorset, where Archbishop Stigand held thirty hides before 1066 (*DB* fol. 80r).

46. Yeovil, Somerset, where various people held estates of two and six hides before 1066 (*DB* fols. 93r, 96v).

47. Crewkerne, Somerset, where Edith, wife of Edward the Confessor, held a substantial estate (land for forty ploughs) before 1066 (*DB* fol. 86v).

48. Probably Whitchurch Canonicorum, Dorset, if only to judge from its position in the will – and on the ground – between Crewkerne and Axmouth; the church was held by the abbey of St Wandrille, Normandy, at the time of the Domesday survey (*DB* fol. 78v). Other possibilities are Whitchurch, Devon (*DB* fol. 115r), and Whitchurch, Somerset (perhaps assessed with Queen Edith's large estate at Keynsham: *DB* fol. 87r).

49. Axmouth, Devon, which was apparently a minor royal estate (land for twelve ploughs) before 1066 (*DB* fol. 100v).

50. Branscombe, Devon, where five hides were held by the bishop of Exeter before 1066 (*DB* fol. 102r).

51. Cullompton, Devon, where one hide was held by a certain Turbert before 1066 (*DB* fol. 104r).

52. Tiverton, Devon, where $3\frac{1}{2}$ hides (land for thirty-six ploughs) were held by Earl Harold's mother before 1066 (*DB* fol. 100v).

53. Probably Silverton, Devon (in preference to Milborne Port, Somerset, which, though a large royal estate before 1066 (*DB* fol. 86v), would be out of place at this point). There was a small holding in Silverton known as Burn (*DB* fol. 117r), and Silverton itself was a large royal estate (land for forty-one ploughs, and three mills) before 1066 (*DB* fol. 100r).

54. Exminster, Devon, apparently a royal estate assessed at one hide (land for twenty ploughs) before 1066 (*DB* fol. 100r).

55. Probably the *Sutreworde* (Southbrook) of *Domesday Book*, which has been identified as Lustleigh, Devon; a certain Asgar held one virgate (land for twelve ploughs) at Southbrook before 1066 (*DB* fol. 111v).

56. Lifton, Devon, was held by Queen Edith before 1066, assessed at 3½ virgates though with land for twenty-five ploughs (*DB* fol. 100v); two estates, at *Lanliner* (Landinner) and *Trebichen* (Trebeigh), are said to have belonged to it, and these are probably (among?) the Cornish lands to which the will refers (for 'Triggshire', see note 18 above). There was a meeting of the king's councillors at Lifton in 931 (*S* 416).

57. Æthelflæd: see Asser, chapter 75.

58. Perhaps East Wellow, Hampshire, where a certain Agemund held five hides from the king before 1066 (*DB* fol. 50r); other possibilities are Wellow, Somerset, and West Wellow, Hampshire. There was a meeting of the king's councillors at 'Wellow' in 931 (*S* 1604).

59. Æthelgifu: see Asser, chapters 75 and 98.

60. Kingsclere, Hampshire, still a royal estate before 1066 (*DB* fol. 39r; see also fols. 43r, 45r, 48v, 50v); land at Kingsclere was bequeathed by King Eadred to the New Minster, Winchester (*S* 1515); see also *S* 1504.

61. Probably Preston Candover, Hampshire, where there were several small estates held from King Edward, Queen Edith and Earl Harold before 1066 (*DB* fols. 44v, 45v, 47rv, 49v); land in Brown and Chilton Candover was held by the Old and New Minsters, Winchester, before 1066 (*DB* fols. 40v, 42r).

62. Ælfthryth: see Asser, chapter 75.

63. Wellow, Isle of Wight, where two hides were held by a certain Coolf from the king before 1066 (*DB* fol. 52r).

64. Probably Ashton Keynes, Wiltshire, where the church of Cranborne held twenty hides before 1066 (*DB* fol. 67v); it seems unlikely that the reference is to Steeple Ashton, Wiltshire, since King Edgar had to book this estate to himself in 964 (*S* 727), suggesting that it would have been folkland, not bookland, in Alfred's reign.

65. Chippenham, Wiltshire. It is named as a royal estate by Asser, chapters 9 and 52; there were meetings of the king's councillors at Chippenham on various occasions in the tenth century (*S* 405, 422–3, 473, 1445); it was evidently a major royal estate before 1066 (*DB* fol. 64v).

66. Son of Æthelred, but probably not the Æthelhelm who was ealdorman of Wiltshire (see below, p. 328 note 4); nothing more is known of him.

67. Aldingbourne, Sussex, where the bishop of Selsey held thirty-six hides before 1066 (*DB* fol. 16v); see also *S* 1291.

68. This could be one of several Comptons in Sussex, Surrey and Hampshire. If only to judge from positions on the ground and in the will, Compton, near Harting in west Sussex, is perhaps the most likely; there was an estate of ten hides there (held from Earl Godwine) before 1066 (*DB* fol. 24r; see also fol. 34r). Other possibilities are Compton in West Firle, east Sussex, Compton in Surrey and Compton in Hampshire, where various

people held estates from the king before 1066 (*DB* fols. 21r, 36r, 48v respectively).

69. Crondall, Hampshire. King Edgar is alleged to have given forty-five hides at Crondall to the Old Minster, Winchester (*S* 820); see also *S* 1485 and 1491. The Old Minster held fifty hides there before 1066 (*DB* fol. 41r).

70. Upper Beeding, Sussex, a substantial royal estate before 1066 (*DB* fol. 28r).

71. Beddingham, Sussex, a substantial royal estate before 1066 (*DB* fol. 20v).

72. Probably Eastbourne, Sussex, a substantial royal estate before 1066 (*DB* fol. 20v); for the identification, see Mawer et al., *Place-Names of Sussex* II, p. 426.

73. Thunderfield, Surrey: not in *Domesday Book* (nor is Horley, under which it was probably assessed). There was a meeting of the king's councillors at Thunderfield during the reign of Æthelstan.

74. Eashing, Surrey (one of the sites listed in the *Burghal Hidage*): not entered separately in *Domesday Book*, but probably assessed under Godalming (see note 76 below).

75. Son of Æthelred; for his rebellion against Edward the Elder following Alfred's death, see *ASC* s.a. 900 (above, p. 120).

76. Godalming, Surrey, a substantial royal estate before 1066 (*DB* fol. 30v).

77. Guildford, Surrey, which had a mint at least from the reign of Edward the Martyr and which was a borough by the end of the Anglo-Saxon period (see *DB* fol. 30r).

78. Steyning, Sussex, where the king held eighteen hides, three virgates before 1066 (*DB* fol. 28r); Edward the Confessor had allegedly given a much larger estate there to the abbey of Fécamp, though Earl Harold held it in 1066 (see *S* 1054 and *DB* fol. 17r). It was at Steyning that King Æthelwulf was originally buried: see above, p. 237 note 38.

79. Osferth's relationship to Alfred is uncertain. He may have belonged to his mother Osburh's family, or he may have been a son of the Oswald *filius regis* who occurs in *S* 340, 1201 and 1203 and who was perhaps a son of Alfred's brother Æthelred. It is presumably this Osferth who attests charters in 898 (*S* 350) and in the opening years of Edward's reign (for example, *S* 364 and 367, in a position which suggests some relationship to the royal family); who is styled 'king's brother' (mistakenly) in *S* 1286 and 'king's kinsman' in *S* 378; and who occurs as an ealdorman between 909 and 934.

80. Beckley, Sussex: not entered separately in *Domesday Book*, but probably covered by the entry for Glossams, where three unnamed men held 1½ hides before 1066 (*DB* fol. 20r).

81. Rotherfield, Sussex, where Earl Godwine held three hides (land for twenty-six ploughs) before 1066 (*DB* fol. 16r).

82. Ditchling, Sussex, a substantial royal estate before 1066 (*DB* fol. 26r).

83. Sutton, Sussex, where five unnamed men held 8½ hides before 1066 (*DB* fol. 23v).

84. Lyminster, Sussex. A meeting of the king's councillors was held there in 930 (*S* 403), and it was a substantial royal estate before 1066 (*DB* fol. 24v).

85. Angmering, Sussex, where two estates of five hides each were held by Earl Godwine and by three unnamed men before 1066 (*DB* fol. 24v).

86. Felpham, Sussex. King Eadred gave thirty hides at Felpham to his mother, Queen Eadgifu, in 953 (*S* 562); the abbey of Shaftesbury held twenty-one hides there before 1066 (*DB* fol. 17v).

87. King Alfred's wife: see Asser, chapter 29. She died on 5 December 902 (see *ASC* s.a. 903).

88. Lambourn, Berkshire. The estate later belonged to Æthelflæd, wife of King Edmund, so it may once have been earmarked for the support of royal women; it was returned to the crown after her death (*S* 1494), and it was a substantial royal estate before 1066 (*DB* fol. 57v; see also fols. 61v, 63r).

89. Wantage, Berkshire. This was Alfred's birthplace (Asser, chapter 1); in the mid tenth century it was bequeathed by King Eadred to his mother, Queen Eadgifu (*S* 1515); a meeting of the king's councillors was held at Wantage in 997 (*S* 891); it was still a royal estate before 1066 (*DB* fol. 57r).

90. Edington, Wiltshire. This was the scene of Alfred's victory over the Vikings in 878 (Asser, chapter 56); a meeting of the king's councillors was held there in 957 (*S* 646); land at Edington was given by King Edgar to Romsey abbey in 968 (*S* 765), and Romsey held thirty hides there before 1066 (*DB* fol. 68r; see also fol. 74v).

91. Æthelred, ealdorman of the Mercians: see Asser, chapters 75 and 83. The fact that he is mentioned as if distinct from Alfred's own ealdormen is a sign of his special position as effective ruler of Mercia (and possibly, by this time, as the king's son-in-law).

92. For Alfred's annual division of part of his revenues among members of his household, see Asser, chapters 100–101.

93. References to a Bishop Esne occur in documents associated with Taunton, and he may have served as an assistant to the bishop of Sherborne, with responsibility for Somerset; see Finberg, *Early Charters of Wessex*, p. 126.

94. Werferth was bishop of Worcester and one of Alfred's literary helpers: see Asser, chapter 77.

95. The bishop of Sherborne and the archbishop (of Canterbury) are not named, presumably because the bequests were intended for whoever were the incumbents at the time of Alfred's death; the naming of Esne

and Werferth suggests that their bequests were more for personal services to the king.

96. Alfred was buried initially in the Old Minster, Winchester, but his remains were transferred to the New Minster by Edward the Elder.

97. Perhaps it would be helpful to give a general idea of the sums of which Alfred is talking. A 'pound' of money contained 240 silver pence; so Alfred bequeathed (the equivalent of) 120,000 pence to each of his two sons, 24,000 pence to his wife and to each of his three daughters, 48,000 pence to the members of his household, and 48,000 pence to the mass-priests etc. A 'mancus' was equivalent to thirty silver pence (above, p. 237 note 37); so Alfred bequeathed 3,000 pence to each of his ealdormen (of whom, for the sake of the argument, there were perhaps ten), 3,000 pence each to Æthelhelm, Æthelwold and Osferth, a sword worth 3,000 pence to Ealdorman Æthelred, and 3,000 pence each to the archbishop and three bishops. This would make a grand total of 486,000 pence, or about 2,000 pounds. For comparison, the sums bequeathed by King Eadred in his will (S 1515) must have approached a total of about 3,000 pounds; the first, and smallest, payment made by King Æthelred to the Vikings, in 991, was 10,000 pounds.

98. It is not immediately clear what Alfred means here, since one might expect the amount of his property and the number of his kinsmen to increase with the passage of time. He may have made a will sometime before the meeting at *Langandene*, and (though he does not say so) this meeting may have precipitated a revised settlement for his nephews which left him with less property; the side-effects of the Viking wars in the 870s and the programme of military reform in the 880s must have involved a considerable drain on his own financial resources. The lost kinsmen may have included Oswald (above, note 79), Ælfflæd (below, note 106), and Alfred's children who died in infancy (Asser, chapter 75).

99. This is perhaps a reference to the stipulation in Æthelwulf's will that 'for every ten hides throughout all his hereditary land one poor man . . . should be sustained with food, drink and clothing' (Asser, chapter 16).

100. The information, given in the notes above, on the subsequent history of the estates mentioned in the will should afford at least some idea of the extent to which this preference was observed. We should naturally expect many of the estates left to Edward to remain in royal possession, but it is striking that a substantial proportion of the estates left to the other beneficiaries of the will seem to have come back to the crown in the first half of the tenth century. Æthelweard, Edward's brother, died *c*. 920 and was survived by two sons, Ælfwine and Æthelwine, both of whom were killed at the battle of *Brunanburh* in 937; no other descendants are known, and the estates given originally to their father might then have reverted to the reigning king. Æthelflæd died in 918, and her

daughter Ælfwyn was promptly taken to Wessex under circumstances which would suggest that Æthelflæd's property was then acquired by Edward. There is no sign that the property bequeathed to Æthelgifu, abbess of Shaftesbury, was ever held by the abbey, and it is possible anyway that she did not survive her father. The third daughter Ælfthryth may well have given up (or sold) her title to landed property in England when she married Baldwin of Flanders. The estates bequeathed to Æthelwold would presumably have been forfeited to Edward after his death in 902, if indeed he had ever taken possession of them before his rebellion. Æthelhelm may have predeceased his brother and have left his estates to him, in which case they too would have been forfeited to Edward; if he did not, he or his descendants could have bequeathed them (or some of them) to the reigning king. Osferth, or his descendants (if he had any), may similarly have bequeathed estates to the crown. Ealhswith probably left her property to her son Edward. For another way in which the estates bequeathed to Alfred's daughters and wife could have reverted to the crown, see note 102 below.

101. This expression means, of course, 'in the male line and not in the female line'. Alfred's grandfather was Egbert, king of Wessex (802–39).

102. In other words, it appears that Alfred's male kinsmen (perhaps Edward in particular) were to be given an option to purchase the estates bequeathed to his daughters and wife, if they wanted to take possession of them at any time before the women's deaths; if they did not exercise this option, the land would pass to any suitable male heirs, or, if there were none, back to (?)Edward. A similar provision occurs in the exactly contemporary will of Ealdorman Alfred (*EHD* no. 97).

103. The estates bequeathed by King Alfred were those held by him as bookland, as opposed to folkland (for these terms, see above, p. 308 note 23). Alfred would have been quite entitled to leave such land to whomsoever he pleased, though in the long-term interests of his family he chose to restrict its passage to his kinsmen (in accordance with the situation envisaged in Alfred's law-code, § 41; see also *EHD* no. 97); he did, however, express a further preference for the male line, and he is now reminding his heirs that they have no *right* to the estates bequeathed to the women and must therefore expect to pay for them should they want them. This could be taken to imply that the descent of folkland, by contrast, was restricted to the male line; and it was probably governed by other restrictions which meant that it was never bequeathed by will. One should not suppose, therefore, that the estates mentioned in Alfred's will represent the sum total of his landed property as king. He would have had much more, but held as folkland, which accordingly passed by the customary laws (whatever they were) to his descendants; it is likely that there were also other estates earmarked for the support

of the king and therefore not alienable by will. These additional prop-
erties may have included Reading and *Leonaford* (described by Asser,
chapters 35 and 81, as royal estates), Wardour (see *EHD* no. 102), Benson
(see *S* 217), and Wimborne and Twynham (see *ASC* s.a. 900). It seems
that Alfred's desire to protect the long-term interests of the royal family
was taken further by his successors: royal estates appear to have been
under even tighter control in the tenth century, to judge, for example,
from the fact that King Eadred disposed of far less land in his will (*S*
1515) than Alfred had done, even though he must have had more.

104. The exact meaning of this passage is uncertain, owing to the rarity of
the word *cyrelif*, here translated 'dependant'. Its only other occurrence
is in an ecclesiastical context, where the words 'who dwell in a *cyrelif*'
refer to a body of canons dependent on a bishop for their food and
clothing. Alfred is perhaps referring to people who came to him from
various places for support (cf. Asser, chapters 76 and 101) and who
were then organized into communities, probably of religious character.
The councillors determined that Alfred could do as he liked with them,
and the king decided to grant them the freedom to choose any other
lord after his death.

105. Damerham, Hampshire. This was evidently a religious community of
some nature, since it held land in its own right. King Edmund gave a
large estate at Damerham to his wife Æthelflæd, with reversion after
her death to Glastonbury abbey (*S* 513); she duly bequeathed the property to Glastonbury in her will (*S* 1494), and the abbey held land there
before 1066 (*DB* fol. 66v). Another estate at Damerham was bequeathed by King Eadred to the Old Minster, Winchester (*S* 1515). It
is quite possible, therefore, that Damerham was already a royal estate in
Alfred's reign, and hence the special reference to the community there
in the will; cf. the discussion, in note 25 above, of the community at
Cheddar.

106. Nothing is known of this Ælfflæd. Perhaps she was a kinswoman of
Alfred's who had founded the community at Damerham.

107. Alfred was following a common practice whereby testators arranged for
a certain amount of livestock to be distributed to religious communities
and to others in need, for the good of their souls; cf., for instance, *S*
1494 and 1508. It is not clear whether or not this instruction refers
specifically to the community at Damerham.

KING ALFRED'S CHARTER FOR
EALDORMAN ÆTHELHELM (*pp. 179–81*)

The original charter has not survived. At some date before the
Norman Conquest the land to which it refers passed into the posses-

sion of Wilton abbey, and the charter would have been transferred at that time into the archives of the community. In the fourteenth century the charters which together served as the title-deeds for the abbey's estates were copied into a single manuscript, and this cartulary is now B.L. Harley 436; Alfred's charter for Ealdorman Æthelhelm (*S* 348) occurs on fols. 29v–31r. The text is printed, with detailed discussion, by Whitelock, 'Some Charters in the Name of King Alfred', especially pp. 78–83.

The form of the document needs some explanation. The text would originally have been inscribed on one side of a single sheet of parchment; it is written in Latin, except for the boundary clause, which is in Old English. The document would have been folded inwards, and an endorsement (summarizing the contents, in Old English) would have been written on the outside of the folded parchment; it is likely that the rubric in the cartulary reproduces the wording of the endorsement on the original charter. The text itself begins with a verbal invocation ('In the name of the Lord'). This is followed by the superscription, which names the issuing authority ('I Alfred . . . king of the Anglo-Saxons'), and in turn by the dispositive section, which names the beneficiary and the estate concerned, and in which the terms of the grant are set out. The outer perimeter of the estate is then traced, from one landmark to the next, in the boundary clause. The dating clause follows, and introduces the list of witnesses, beginning with the subscription of the king and continuing with the names of prominent ecclesiastics and laymen who were present when the transaction was performed; the subscriptions would have been written by the scribe of the text, not by the individual witnesses themselves. The document concludes with a combined blessing and sanction, promising an eternal reward for those who respect the terms of the charter and threatening damnation on those who do not. Anglo-Saxon charters of the later ninth century onwards in general conform to the same basic pattern, though one usually finds a proem (for instance, a statement adducing religious considerations which have led to the making of the grant) between the invocation and the superscription, and the sanction (plus blessing, if there is one) is normally positioned immediately before the boundary clause. The whole text can attain much greater length and complication than shown in this relatively straightforward example.

1. 'Booked' is a technical expression meaning 'conveyed by charter (or 'book')': the estate would be held as 'bookland', on which see above, p. 308 note 23.

2. The description of the beneficiary Æthelhelm as 'thegn' (as opposed to 'ealdorman') is probably no more than a slip, made either by the original scribe or by the cartulary copyist.

3. For the significance of this regnal style, see above, p. 227 note 1.

4. Æthelhelm was ealdorman of Wiltshire. He took the alms of King Alfred and of the West Saxons to Rome in 887 (*ASC*; Asser, chapter 86); he took part in the siege of Buttington in 893 (*ASC*, above, p. 116), and he died in 897 (*ASC*, above, p. 120).

5. The phrase 'in eternal inheritance' expresses one of the privileges associated with the tenure of bookland: the beneficiary was free to dispose of the land to whomsoever he pleased, and his successors as holders of the land would be free to do the same.

6. North Newnton in Wiltshire. The land passed eventually to Wilton abbey, probably by gift of one of Æthelhelm's heirs; but to 'improve' their title to the estate, the community subsequently forged a charter (*S* 424) claiming that it was given to them by King Æthelstan in 933. The land is entered as Wilton property in *Domesday Book* (*DB* fol. 67v). For an explanation of the word 'hide', see above, p. 237 note 36.

7. This sentence expresses another of the characteristic features of bookland. Its holder would be exempt from many of the burdens customarily incumbent on land in general, such as the payment of an annual food-rent to the king, and the obligation of providing sustenance for the king's officers going about their business; but the king would not grant immunity from the three burdens that pertained to the defence of the kingdom. Owners of bookland would thus remain liable for military service and for the public building operations that were essential for good communications and security. The three burdens are explicitly reserved in Mercian charters from the late eighth century, and in West Saxon charters from the mid ninth century (see Brooks, 'Development of Military Obligations'); so this provision in Alfred's charter represents a continuation of existing practices.

8. The boundary clause appears to describe a line that corresponds to the modern parish boundary of North Newnton. The survey starts towards the south-east corner of the parish, on the bank of the river Avon; 'stint's ford' (a ford where people were accustomed to take rest?) is probably at the south-east corner itself, grid ref. SU 136568; the survey then proceeds westwards along the lower boundary, past 'rush-slade' (a side-valley where rushes grew: ?SU 115569) to 'Tiolta's ford', probably at the south-west corner of the parish, SU 107569; the survey turns north-west along the

boundary with Wilsford (*wifeles ford*: weevil's or beetle's ford) until it
meets the 'road' (now a footpath) at SU 100579; it follows the road
north-north-east to 'sand hill' (presumably the hill at the north-west
corner of the parish: SU 106591), and thence turns east to 'Bottle' (*botan
wælle*, Bota's well or spring, a name preserved in Bottle Farm) in the
vicinity of SU 112592; the survey then goes south-east 'along the wood',
which would seem to have been a line contiguous with the stream (still
partly wooded) marking the upper boundary of the parish; it goes 'across
the wood' from SU 125579 (though this line is now the northern edge of
North Newton Wood) and then bends south to the 'gore' (the triangle
of land between two branches of the Avon, above their confluence at SU
130574 and below North Newton church), and so back to the starting-
point on the Avon itself.

9. The indiction, as used here, was a reckoning of time based on continuous
cycles of fifteen years; the indiction for each year is its position within
the current fifteen-year cycle. The term derives from the taxation system
instituted by the emperor Constantine the Great (306–37); in its original
form, the indictional year ran from 1 September, and the first fifteen-
year cycle began on that date in 312 (see Harrison, *Framework*, pp. 38–9).
So to calculate the indiction, subtract 312 from the year of grace and
divide by 15: the remainder represents the indiction for the year (for
example, 892 − 312 = 580, ÷ 15 = 38, remainder 10); if the remainder
is 0, the indiction is 15. A modified form of indiction, based on the same
fifteen-year cycles but in which each year ran from 24 September, is
attested in Anglo-Saxon England by Bede; because of its subsequent
adoption under the Holy Roman Empire, this came to be known as the
Imperial, or Caesarean, Indiction (see Harrison, *Framework*, pp. 41–4).
In the *Anglo-Saxon Chronicle*, particularly in the annals for the second
half of the ninth century, the year was sometimes calculated from a point
in the autumn, which could be either the Indiction of Constantine or else
the Caesarean Indiction (but which may be no more than the opening of
a new campaigning year: see Harrison, *Framework*, pp. 117–18); in
charters, however, the year of grace was generally reckoned from 25
December or 1 January, and the indictional year seems to have followed
suit.

10. Wulfsige, bishop of Sherborne. He attests for the first time in 889 (*S*
346), and is one of the bishops known to have received a copy of King
Alfred's translation of Gregory's *Pastoral Care* (see above, p. 294 note
1); he was succeeded by Asser (see above, p. 49).

11. Wulfred, ealdorman of Hampshire. He attests *S* 352 (?879) and *S* 345
(dated 882); he died sometime in the period 893–5 (*ASC*, above, p.
118).

12. Probably the Ealdorman Æthelred of Devon who died in 899 (*ASC*, above,

p. 120); but conceivably Ealdorman Æthelred of Mercia (on whom see Asser, chapter 75).

13. Edward the Elder: see Asser, chapter 75.

14. These two priests are mentioned by Asser, chapters 77–8, as among Alfred's helpers.

15. These three subscriptions, of Deormod, Ælfric and Sigewulf, throw light on Asser's allusions (chapters 76 and 100–101) to officials of the royal household. Deormod *cellerarius* must be the man of this name to whom King Alfred granted an estate at Appleford in Berkshire, probably in the 890s (*S* 355); he attests several of Alfred's charters, and continues to appear in charters in the opening years of Edward the Elder's reign. As a *cellerarius*, he would have been one of the officials responsible for ensuring that provisions were always in good supply; the Old English equivalent of *cellerarius* was *hordere*, 'storekeeper', but in the tenth century the official in question was probably known as a *discthegn*, 'seneschal' or 'steward'. Ælfric *thesaurarius* is doubtless the Ælfric *hræglthegn* ('rail-thegn', or keeper of the wardrobe) mentioned in an Alfredian context in *EHD* no. 102, since the king's treasures were kept in his chamber and custody of the one implies some office in respect of the other; for King Alfred's 'treasury', see Asser, chapter 102. Sigewulf *pincerna* occurs several times as a thegn in Alfred's reign, and was made an ealdorman, probably of Kent, by 898 (*S* 350); he was killed at the battle of the Holme in 902 (*ASC* s.a. 903). As a *pincerna* (OE *byrle*), he was one of the king's butlers (cf. Asser, chapter 2). The subscriptions of these three men, in their putative OE guises, would thus give us a *discthegn*, a *hræglthegn* and a *byrle*, in that order; it is interesting that King Eadred (946–55) makes a bequest in his will to 'each appointed *discthegn*, to each appointed *hrægl-thegn* and to each appointed *byrle*' (*EHD* no. 107).

16. Several of these thegns can probably be identified among the witnesses to charters of the late ninth and early tenth centuries, but nothing is known about any one of them individually. Some of them may have held office in the king's household; others would be friends of the king, or thegns who happened to be present when the charter was drawn up.

17. The wording and placement of this formula suggests Mercian influence on the drafting of the charter (see Whitelock, 'Some Charters in the Name of King Alfred', pp. 88–9); Mercian influence might also account for the elaborate form of the superscription (ibid., pp. 89–90), and for the use of a present participle plus future tense (*concedens . . . dabo*) in the operative part of the dispositive section. It is possible that the Mercians at court sometimes assisted in the drafting of royal documents; so it may well be significant that the Mercian priest Werwulf occurs among the witnesses to the present charter.

THE LETTER OF FULCO, ARCHBISHOP OF RHEIMS, TO KING ALFRED (*pp. 182–6*)

This letter survives as an addition in B.L. Add. 34890, a manuscript of the Gospels written in the first quarter of the eleventh century by a scribe who has been located at Christ Church, Canterbury (see Temple, *Anglo-Saxon Manuscripts*, no. 68); the letter occurs on fols. 158r–160v, written rather later in the eleventh century by a scribe who belonged to the New Minster, Winchester. It seems, therefore, that the manuscript was transferred from Canterbury to Winchester, and that the community of the New Minster regarded a gospel-book as a suitable place for preserving the text of a letter which concerned Grimbald of St Bertin's, who was closely involved in the foundation of their house; owing to the inclusion of the letter, the manuscript itself is sometimes known as the Grimbald Gospels. A copy of the letter also occurs in the *Liber Monasterii de Hyda*, a history of the New Minster (and Hyde abbey) compiled in the fourteenth century.

The text is printed by Whitelock et al., *Councils & Synods*, pp. 6–12; it is translated in *EHD* no. 223. There is an important discussion of the letter by Grierson, 'Grimbald of St Bertin's', pp. 547–52, though we differ on certain points of interpretation.

1. Fulco was abbot of St Bertin's (in Saint-Omer, Flanders) from 878 to 883, archbishop of Rheims from 883 and Charles the Simple's archchancellor from 898; he was assassinated on 17 June 900. For a detailed study of his distinguished career, see Schneider, *Erzbischof Fulco von Rheims*.

2. These remarks on the decline of the ecclesiastical order in the ninth century should be compared with the views expressed by Asser (chapter 93) and Alfred (preface to his translation of the *Pastoral Care*, above, p. 125).

3. It is apparent from Bede's account of St Augustine's mission that certain concessions were indeed made to the people of Kent, in order to ease their acceptance of Christianity: for example, marriage was to be permitted within the third and fourth degrees of relationship (see Bede, *HE* i, 27), and pagan temples were not to be destroyed, but were instead to be converted into Christian churches (*HE* i, 30). See also the remarks attributed to the Northumbrian missionary Aidan in *HE* iii, 5.

4. This reference to the summoning of councils may be the source of the analogous remark in Alfred's laws, Int. 49.7 (above, p. 163).

5. This could be taken to imply that Alfred had specifically named Grimbald in his request for help, and that he had indicated his intention to grant him a bishopric in England; on the other hand, Fulco might simply be

advising the king that the choice of his delegates had fallen on Grimbald, and that it was he, therefore, who was destined to fulfil the role of watchdog over the English. See further below, notes 8 and 10.

6. Grimbald entered the community at St Bertin's during the abbacy of Hugh I (834–44); he styles himself 'deacon and monk' in documents which he drew up there in 867 and 868; he was a priest by 873, and styles himself 'priest and monk' in a document which he drew up at St Bertin's on 8 September 885. For details, see Grierson, 'Grimbald of St Bertin's', pp. 542–3.

7. This passage has been taken to imply that Grimbald had joined Fulco's staff at Rheims (see, for instance, Grierson, 'Grimbald of St Bertin's', p. 551), but Fulco's meaning seems rather to be that he *would* have had Grimbald as a companion and assistant (just as he had had him as a faithful son at St Bertin's), had he been able to fulfil his desire to make him a bishop in his own province. It remains likely, therefore, that Grimbald came to England as a monk from St Bertin's, and not as one who had spent any length of time at Rheims.

8. *Cum suis electoribus*: Grierson ('Grimbald of St Bertin's', p. 549 note 2) takes these *electores* to be 'those who were to elect Grimbald as bishop', but the reference could simply be to those members of the delegation who had actually chosen Grimbald as a suitable person to assist Alfred in his endeavours.

9. Two letters written by Fulco in or soon after 890, one to King Alfred and the other to Plegmund, archbishop of Canterbury, reveal that Fulco did maintain his interest in English ecclesiastical affairs: see Whitelock et al., *Councils & Synods*, pp. 12–13, and *EHD* nos. 224–5.

10. Grierson ('Grimbald of St Bertin's', p. 549) interprets this passage as a suggestion by Fulco that he should himself perform Grimbald's consecration as bishop; in *EHD*, p. 886, the words *ad propriam sedem* (which we translate 'to their own home') are translated 'to his own see', implying, therefore, that Fulco assumed that a bishopric was already waiting for Grimbald. But there is no necessary suggestion that Fulco was proposing to consecrate Grimbald as bishop: rather, he seems to be saying that the members of Alfred's delegation would formally undertake to respect his and Grimbald's teaching, and then, having received Grimbald as one who had been properly ordained (as a priest), would take him back with all due honour to their own home, that is, to England. In the course of his letter, Fulco certainly made clear to Alfred his opinion that Grimbald was worthy of a bishopric, and presumably hoped that he would attain this distinction once in England, but there seems no reason to believe either that Alfred had promised Grimbald a bishopric at this stage or indeed that Fulco understood the king to have made such a promise. It does appear, on the other hand, that Alfred did his best to comply with

Fulco's desires as soon as a suitable post became available. According to Winchester tradition (see Tolhurst, *Monastic Breviary* IV, 289r–290r), Alfred installed Grimbald in a small monastery at Winchester until such time as he could make him a bishop; when Æthelred, archbishop of Canterbury, died (in 888), the king offered the archbishopric to Grimbald, but he declined the offer and recommended that Plegmund should be appointed instead. Grimbald thus remained a priest until he died: Alfred refers to him as 'my mass-priest', Asser styles him 'priest and monk', and the obit of 'the priest Grimbald' is entered in the *Chronicle* for 901; of course the obit suggests that he was regarded as a priest of unusual importance.

BISHOP WULFSIGE'S PREFACE TO THE TRANSLATION OF GREGORY'S DIALOGUES (*pp. 187–8*)

This poem is preserved uniquely in B.L. Cotton Otho C. i, vol. 2, a manuscript of mid-eleventh-century date and Worcester provenance. The poem is found on the first folio of the manuscript and serves as preface to a copy of Werferth's translation of Gregory's *Dialogues* (on which see above, p. 32). Sisam (*Studies in the History of Old English Literature*, pp. 201–3 and 225–31) demonstrated convincingly that Otho C. i vol. 2 is a later copy of an exemplar which Alfred had originally sent to Wulfsige, bishop of Sherborne. As in the case of the *Pastoral Care*, Alfred probably accompanied the gift with a request that it be copied; and in implementing the request, Wulfsige supplied the present metrical preface. Our translation is based on the edition of the poem by Yerkes, 'The Full Text of the Metrical Preface'.

1. The convention adopted here, that of the book speaking in the first person by way of preface to what is to follow, is fairly common in Old English poetry and owes its origin to the tradition of riddles. Other examples are the verse preface which Alfred added to the *Pastoral Care* (above, p. 127) and the poems called by editors 'Thureth' and 'Aldhelm' (Dobbie, *Anglo-Saxon Minor Poems*, pp. 97–8).

2. Through careful study of the manuscript Yerkes was able to supply a part of the first line which previous editors had failed to read. However, the line as restored presents some difficulties, and Yerkes's translation ('he who thinks to read me troubles himself with a good intention') makes little sense. We have taken *teonð* (from the verb *tynan*) simply to mean 'to close' (as used of books, doors, etc.) and assume that the poet is referring to the reward the reader will have gained by the time he has read through the book and finally closed it; but this solution is not entirely satisfactory either.

3. We follow Sisam (*Studies in the History of Old English Literature*, p. 225) in rendering *þas boc begeat* as 'had this copy made'.

4. The manuscript reads *ðas bysene*, 'this exemplar'. However, as Sisam pointed out (ibid.), the reference cannot be to the copy prepared by Wulfsige but must be to the exemplar supplied by Alfred, and hence we translate 'the' rather than 'this'.

ÆTHELWEARD'S ACCOUNT OF THE CLOSING YEARS OF ALFRED'S REIGN (pp. 189-91)

The only manuscript of Æthelweard's *Chronicle* known to have survived into modern times was Cotton Otho A. x, of unknown origin but datable by its script to the beginning of the eleventh century. This manuscript was almost entirely destroyed in the fire at Ashburnham House on 23 October 1731, and the few badly charred leaves which survive are now bound with remnants of other burnt manuscripts in B.L. Cotton Otho A.x and B.L. Cotton Otho A.xii. What little can be read of the text from these burnt leaves has been printed by Barker, 'The Cottonian Fragments of Æthelweard's Chronicle'; the fragments happen to include portions of the passage translated above, though they are not sufficiently continuous to be construed as they stand. Æthelweard's *Chronicle* had, however, been printed from the Cotton manuscript before the fire, by Henry Savile in 1596, and his edition remains the basis of our knowledge of the complete text. The modern editor or translator of Æthelweard is thus confronted with a serious problem. One forms the impression that Æthelweard had little command of Latin grammar but immense stylistic pretensions, particularly when it came to using obscure, learned-sounding words (see Winterbottom, 'The Style of Æthelweard', and Lapidge, 'The Hermeneutic Style', pp. 97-8). At difficult points in the text, therefore, it is virtually impossible to decide whether the difficulty is to be attributed to the author's ignorance of (or disregard for) correct Latin usage, or whether it derives from faulty transmission, by the scribe of the Cotton manuscript or by Savile himself. Accordingly, any translation of Æthelweard must often be purely conjectural; we have drawn attention to some of the difficulties in the following notes, though to discuss them all would be beyond the scope of this book.

The most recent edition of the text, based on Savile and the surviving fragments, is Campbell, *Chronicle of Æthelweard* (*CÆ*), which includes a translation; our own translation is based on this edition (*CÆ*, pp. 49–51), though we differ from Campbell in a number of significant details.

1. The transmitted *pascalique* is incomprehensible. We suggest reading *pascaliaque* (dependent on *post*), where the neuter plural adjective *pasc*(*h*)*alia* is employed as substantive, understanding something like *paschalia sollemnia*.

2. The phrase *de Gallias uenerat partes* suggests that Æthelweard thought *de* should govern the accusative rather than the dative; alternatively, *de* has replaced a preposition such as *per* which would govern the accusative ('they had come by way of Gaulish parts'). One might also expect the adjective *Gallicas*, for *Gallias*.

3. One would expect *Eaduuerdo* and *filio* (both agreeing with the dative *clitoni*), instead of the transmitted *Eaduuerdi* and *filii*, but here as elsewhere it is not clear whether the fault is Æthelweard's or his copyists'.

4. In medieval Latin (unlike Classical Latin) the word *exercitare* means 'to wage war'.

5. Reading *Angli* (nominative) for the transmitted *Anglos*.

6. We follow the reading of the Cotton manuscript and Savile (*induuntur*: 'they are dressed [scil. with arms]'), though it is not entirely happy. Campbell conjectured *inducuntur*, 'are brought in', which is possible, though his translation of the whole sentence ('Later, however, they [the Danes] penetrated Wessex') is quite impossible.

7. The transmitted text (*fit in occursu*) is apparently corrupt: either a noun such as *bellum* or *proelium* governing *fit* has fallen out, or else *occursus* (nominative) is itself the subject of *fit*. We read *fit occursus*, 'the engagement takes place'.

8. It is not clear what *minacibus stridens* is dependent upon (an *occursus* shrieking with threats is improbable). Some words may have fallen out here.

9. This sentence is inscrutable. Æthelweard apparently construed *iuuentus*, 'youth' (singular), with plural verbs (as later on in this annal), so *iuuentus* must be the subject of *insiliunt*; but how *contra* and *facta* are related to *iuuentus insiliunt* is not clear. Here as elsewhere, *iuuentus* probably refers to the English, not the Vikings.

10. Reading *irrupti* for *irrepti*, which would mean 'having crept in (with weapons)' (?); in any case, Campbell's translation ('having slipped on their armour') is quite impossible.

11. The word *sultant* is not Latin, and what it might conceal cannot easily be conjectured.

12. A rather free rendering of *post suetam praedam*; but it is difficult to see what else the words mean, if the parallel with Edward's freeing of the English army is to be upheld.

13. Supplying the preposition *ad* before *pascua*.

14. We understand the syntax of the passage to mean *turmas trans fluuium temese pellunt*. The transmitted word *transpellunt* is not attested elsewhere, and in any case a preposition is needed to govern the accusative *fluuium*. In other words, *turmas trans pellunt fluuium* ('they drive the crowds across the river') is a pretentious Æthelweardian example of hyperbaton.

15. The transmitted *insula pali* is possibly corrupt, though it is conceivable that Æthelweard intended a piece of etymological word play on the name *Thorn-ig*, 'island of the thorn'; *palus* is, however, a poor equivalent for OE *þorn* (a more accurate translation would have been *insula spinae*). Whatever the explanation, *insula pali* cannot mean 'island of marshy land', as Campbell supposed; he was apparently thinking of *paludis* (genitive), not *pali*. Æthelweard's reference to 'Thorney', and the statement in *ASC* that the island lay up the river Colne (above, p. 115), show that the place in question was Thorney, in the parish of Iver, south Buckinghamshire: see Stenton, 'The Danes at Thorney Island'. There are several areas of land thereabouts which could be regarded as 'islands', between the river Colne and Colne Brook, and it is not certain to which one in particular the chronicler and Æthelweard refer.

16. Æthelred, ealdorman of Mercia; he was not, of course, a king.

17. That is, the provinces subject to Ealdorman Æthelred: when Æthelred died, in 911, Edward the Elder 'succeeded to London and Oxford and to all the lands which belonged to them' (*ASC*), so one imagines that these are the provinces to which Æthelweard refers.

18. Mersea is not in Kent but in Essex; *locum Cantiam* is either corrupt or should apply to the Limen estuary (in Kent).

19. Reading *uelis secundis* for the transmitted *uelis secundum*.

20. Reading *curriculo* for the transmitted *ergo*; some such noun must govern the genitive *eiusdem anni* and be governed itself by the preposition *in*.

21. Taking *statuta* as a noun (nominative feminine singular) meaning 'treaty' and serving as the subject of *abrumpitur*. No such noun appears to be attested elsewhere, however, and it is possibly a simple corruption of *status* (cf. *pacis ... foederisque statum* a few lines earlier), meaning 'arrangement', hence 'treaty'.

22. Reading *Britannorum* for the transmitted *Brittannum*.

23. Reading *tum* for the transmitted *cum*. It is also possible that *cum* has been misplaced, and should precede *Æðelnoð* in the next line; but the syntax of this sentence is hopelessly confused.

24. Following Savile's *paratu* for the reading *parauit* of the Cotton manuscript. If *parauit* is to be retained, some noun governing *equestri* must be presumed to have fallen out.

25. Translating *iniciunt bella alterna*. It is also possible that *alterna* (emended to *alterno*) is to be construed with *certamine*.

26. Following Campbell's emendation *nisus* of the transmitted *uisus*.

27. Reading *ineptus* for *inaptus*.

28. Reading *Danica* ('Danish') for the transmitted *Danaa*, which presumably would mean 'Greek' (from *Danai*).

29. Reading *expers* (which takes the ablative) for *experto*, though this solution is doubtful. In any case *experto nutu* is not Latin.

30. Reading *annalem* (construed with *thesaurum*) for the transmitted *annilem*, which is not a Latin word.

31. Possibly a word such as *partibus* or *terra* (dependent on *de*) has fallen out before *Northhimbriorum*; or possibly Æthelweard thought that *de* governed the genitive (cf. above, note 2).

32. Sigeferth is probably the Viking king known to have minted coins at York: see Lyon and Stewart, 'Northumbrian Viking Coins in the Cuerdale Hoard', especially pp. 115-16. Stenton ('Æthelweard's Account', pp. 10-11) connects Sigeferth's expedition with the ravaging of Mercia recorded by Æthelweard in his annal for 894; but Smyth (*Scandinavian York and Dublin* I, pp. 33-7) connects it with the reference in *ASC* 893 (above, p. 115) to a Viking force which besieged a fortress on the north coast of Devon, and he argues that Sigeferth went on from there to Dublin before returning to Northumbria.

33. It is interesting that the same idiom is used in *ASC* 893-5 to indicate the passage of time; the similarity is probably coincidental, given the differences in all other respects between Æthelweard's account of these years and the annals in *ASC*.

34. Æthelnoth was ealdorman of Somerset; it is uncertain whether he was on military or diplomatic business.

35. The transmitted *pandunt* is nonsense, and Campbell's translation of it ('possessed', literally 'opened out') is impossible: *pando* is intransitive and cannot govern the accusative *territoria*. We suggest emending to *praedantur*, 'they plunder'.

36. Stenton ('Æthelweard's Account', pp. 11-12) observed that the area described corresponds to Rutland, and he suggested that it may have formed part of the district controlled from Northampton; the fact that it was ravaged by the Vikings of York would imply some hostility between inhabitants of the different parts of the Danelaw. It is possible, on the other hand, that Rutland had remained under English, or Mercian, control after the Viking settlement of 877 (see Phythian-Adams, 'Rutland Reconsidered', pp. 72-3), and that the Vikings of York were therefore ravaging English territory in the Danelaw.

37. Guthfrith had been king of York since the early 880s: see *EHD* no. 6, and Smyth, *Scandinavian York and Dublin* I, pp. 43-7. For his dealings with Anarawd of Gwynedd, see above, p. 262 note 183. Numismatic evidence suggests that he was succeeded by Sigeferth (above, note 32).

According to one source, the Northumbrian Vikings concluded a peace with Alfred, apparently after Guthfrith's death: see Arnold, *Symeonis Monachi Opera Omnia* II, p. 119 (and cf. above, note 34, for the possibility that Alfred made diplomatic contact with the Northumbrians shortly before Guthfrith's death).

38. Reading *qui* for the transmitted *quae*, and deleting *loca*.

39. Reading *foetidas* (agreeing with *turmas*) for the transmitted *foetidus*. Campbell's explanatory note (*CÆ*, p. 51 note 3) is utterly incomprehensible, as is his translation of the sentence.

40. The cause and nature of this 'dissension' (*discordia*) is unknown, but it may be connected in some way with the readiness of the Northumbrian Vikings to accept the atheling Æthelwold as king in late 899 or 900 (see above, p. 292 note 11). See Stenton, 'Æthelweard's Account', p. 12, and Smyth, *Scandinavian York and Dublin* I, pp. 51–2.

41. Reading *lachrymosos* (agreeing with *motus*, accusative plural) for the transmitted *lachrymosus*.

42. This gives 25 October as the day of Alfred's death; *ASC* (above, p. 120) gives 26 October, which is more likely to be correct.

TWO ACROSTIC POEMS ON KING ALFRED (*p. 192*)

These two poems are preserved uniquely in Bern, Burgerbibliothek MS 671, a gospel-book written at an unidentified centre in the Celtic parts of Britain during the first part of the ninth century. It was in England by *c.* 900 when the two acrostic poems were added (there is a facsimile of the poems in Lindsay, *Early Welsh Script*, plate V), and later in the tenth century it was at Bedwyn, Wiltshire (one of Alfred's estates: see above, p. 318 note 28) where some additions in Old English were made (see Meritt, 'Old English Entries in a Manuscript at Bern'). The poems have been edited, translated and discussed by Lapidge ('Some Latin Poems', pp. 81–3), who attributes them tentatively to John the Old Saxon.

1. Reading *utque* for the manuscript's *atque*.

2. Reading *flectas* for the manuscript's *fletas*.

3. The allusion is to Matthew xxv, 16.

4. The 'fields of foreign learning' (*rura peregrine sophie*) may possibly suggest that Alfred's instructor and the author of this poem was a foreigner. Otherwise it is difficult to see what *peregrine* could refer to: it would hardly be flattering to remind King Alfred in a poem addressed to him that learning was a thoroughly foreign experience for him.

THE BURGHAL HIDAGE (*pp. 193–4*)

There are two versions of the document known as the *Burghal Hidage*. One, hereafter designated 'A', occurs among a group of miscellaneous texts added, apparently during the eleventh century, to a manuscript whose contents included the Old English translation of Bede's *Ecclesiastical History*, a text of the *Anglo-Saxon Chronicle*, and Alfred's law-code; this manuscript (B.L. Cotton Otho B.xi) was largely destroyed in the Cotton fire of 1731 (see above, p. 225), but its contents can be reconstructed from a transcript made by the antiquary Laurence Nowell in 1562 (B.L. Add. 43703). The second version, hereafter designated 'B', is found in six manuscripts which range in date from the early thirteenth to the mid fourteenth century, but which derive ultimately from a presumably pre-Conquest archetype. A text of the *Burghal Hidage* was printed by Thomas Gale in 1691 (*Scriptores*, p. 748): he specified two manuscripts of the 'B' version as his source, but it is clear that he also had access to another version (not necessarily 'A') from which he was able to make good some of the deficiencies in 'B'. For further details, see Robertson, *Charters*, pp. 246–9 and 494–6, and D. Hill, 'The Burghal Hidage: the Establishment of a Text'. The translation is based on 'A', though certain readings are admitted from 'B'; these, and other important variations in 'B' and Gale, are duly recorded in the notes which follow.

The *Burghal Hidage* cannot be dated precisely, but it is likely to be a revised and amplified form, compiled during the reign of Edward the Elder, of a document originally drawn up for administrative purposes in the latter part of Alfred's reign. The inclusion of Oxford and Buckingham in a list that is basically West Saxon suggests that the *Burghal Hidage* was compiled after 911 (when Edward took over the control of these areas following the death of Æthelred, ealdorman of Mercia: see *ASC*), and unless Edward's two burhs at Buckingham represented the strengthening of existing fortifications it cannot be earlier than 914 (when these burhs were built); the other burhs built by Edward in the 910s were on or beyond the Danelaw frontier and may have been assessed separately. On the other hand, the absence from 'A' of Worcester and Warwick (see note 15) might suggest that this version was compiled before 919 (when these – and other – Mercian burhs would have come under Edward's control, following the death of his sister Æthelflæd in 918), while their presence in 'B' could be attributed to a subsequent updating of the text. If, therefore, the 'A' version of the *Burghal Hidage* dates from the period 914–19, it could attest to an overhaul of the Alfredian burghal system undertaken in connection with Edward the Elder's major offensive against the Danes in 917. For different views on the date of the *Burghal Hidage*, see Campbell et al., *The Anglo-Saxons*, p. 152, and Davis, 'Alfred and Guthrum's Frontier', pp. 807–9.

1. *Eorpeburnan* cannot be securely identified; but for the possibility that the name refers to an earthwork at Castle Toll, Newenden, Kent, see above, p. 284 note 22.
2. This is the reading of 'B'; 'A' reads '12 hides', which is obviously incorrect.
3. The entry for Burpham does not occur in 'B'; but Gale includes it, and gives the assessment as '726 hides'.
4. The reference is to an Iron Age hill-fort at Chisbury, near Bedwyn in Wiltshire: see Brooks, 'Unidentified Forts', pp. 75–9.
5. This is the reading of 'B'; 'A' reads '500 hides.'
6. The words 'and to Shaftesbury likewise' are taken from 'B'; their non-occurrence in 'A' is probably due to scribal error. An inscription seen at Shaftesbury by William of Malmesbury in the early twelfth century read: 'In the year of the Lord's Incarnation 880 King Alfred made this town, in the eighth year of his reign'; (Alfred's eighth year was 878–9, but William could have misread *viiii* as *viii*). A rubbing of a small fragment of the inscription is all that now survives, and shows that it *could* date from before the Conquest; but the authority of the inscription must remain uncertain. See Royal Commission on Historical Monuments, *Dorset* IV, pp. 56–7.
7. Twynham (or Twinham) is the old name for Christchurch, Hampshire; see *ASC* s.a. 900 (above, p. 120).
8. The name *Brydian* in 'A' probably refers to Bridport, Dorset; but the burh in question is identified by some as an Iron Age hill-fort at Bredy (about seven miles further east).
9. 'B' adds 'that is Barnstaple'; the reference is probably to the Iron Age hill-fort in Pilton known as Roborough Camp, about a mile north of Barnstaple, Devon. See Pearce, *Archaeology of South West Britain*, pp. 196–8, for other possibilities.
10. 'B' reads '2,200 hides'.
11. 'B' reads '1,500 hides'.
12. 'B' reads '1,300 hides'. It is particularly difficult to choose between 'A' and 'B' in their discrepant readings for Cricklade and Oxford; for some discussion of the matter, see D. Hill, 'The Burghal Hidage: the Establishment of a Text', p. 86 note 13, and Hinton, *Alfred's Kingdom*, p. 37.
13. Sashes is an island in the Thames, near Cookham, Berkshire: see Brooks, 'Unidentified Forts', pp. 79–81.

14. 'B' reads '500 hides'.

15. 'B' continues with the following statement (not present in 'A'): 'That is fully 27,000 hides and seventy which belong to it, and thirty to Wessex.' The meaning of this is apparent only if one assumes that '27,000 hides and seventy' is intended as a grand total of the assessments, and that the 'thirty' refers to the number of burhs regarded as being in 'Wessex' for the purposes of the calculation: including Shaftesbury (see note 6) and excluding Buckingham (outside 'Wessex': the boundary in mind was probably the Thames), thirty burhs have indeed been listed up to this point, and the sum total of their assessments is 27,071 hides, counting Lewes as 1,300 (cf. note 2), counting Chisbury and Shaftesbury as 700 apiece (cf. notes 5–6), and taking Malmesbury, Cricklade, Oxford and Eashing at their assessments in 'A' (cf. notes 10–12, 14). This statement in 'B' is itself followed by a reference to two Mercian burhs: 'And to Worcester 1,200 hides; to Warwick 2,404 hides' (though the figure for Warwick can be explained as a scribe's slip for 2,400). 'B' ends at this point; the second paragraph in the translation occurs only in 'A'.

16. This statement reveals the basis of the assessments provided in the first paragraph. Given that each pole ($5\frac{1}{2}$ yards) of wall was to be manned by four men (that is, one man for just over four feet), and that one man would be supplied from one hide, then the maintenance of an acre's breadth (four poles, or twenty-two yards) of wall would require sixteen men and therefore an assessment of sixteen hides; the maintenance of twenty poles (110 yards, or half a furlong) of wall would require eighty men and therefore an assessment of eighty hides; and so on. By working back from the assessments themselves, it is accordingly possible to calculate for each burh the length of the defences which were to be manned by the intended garrison: for example, Wareham's assessment of 1,600 hides implies a garrison of 1,600 men who, at sixteen men per twenty-two yards, could defend 2,200 yards of wall. In many cases the calculated length can be compared with the length of the defences still measurable on the ground, and the correspondence is generally close: thus the defences enclosing three sides of Wareham measure about 2,180 yards, leaving the fourth side protected by the river; for other examples, see the table in Hill, *Atlas of Anglo-Saxon England*, p. 85. This certainly encourages the belief that the person who compiled the *Burghal Hidage* knew what he was talking about, and (at the risk of compounding a *non sequitur*) this suggests in turn that the text derives from an official administrative document.

Note on Further Reading

The indispensable 'textbook' for Anglo-Saxon history is Dorothy Whitelock, ed., *English Historical Documents* c. *500–1042* (London, 1955; 2nd edn, 1979), complemented by David C. Douglas, ed., *English Historical Documents 1042–1189* (London, 1953; 2nd edn, 1981). These massive volumes contain a large selection of primary sources in translation, and are furnished with valuable commentaries.

The most authoritative modern account of Anglo-Saxon history is F. M. Stenton, *Anglo-Saxon England* (Oxford, 1943; 3rd edn, 1971); but R. H. Hodgkin, *A History of the Anglo-Saxons*, 2 vols. (Oxford, 1935; 3rd edn, 1952), retains its value as an excellent and abundantly illustrated narrative, covering the period up to the death of Alfred the Great. Among the many shorter surveys, differing to some extent in their treatment of the subject, are Peter Hunter Blair, *An Introduction to Anglo-Saxon England* (Cambridge, 1956; 2nd edn, 1977), Christopher Brooke, *The Saxon and Norman Kings* (London, 1963), D. J. V. Fisher, *The Anglo-Saxon Age* c. *400–1042* (London, 1973), and P. H. Sawyer, *From Roman Britain to Norman England* (London, 1978), all of which have been published in paperback editions. An important book which combines lavish illustrations with valuable discussion is James Campbell, Eric John and Patrick Wormald, *The Anglo-Saxons* (Oxford, 1982).

The best surveys covering social, cultural, administrative and economic history are H. R. Loyn, *Anglo-Saxon England and the Norman Conquest* (London, 1962), H. R. Loyn, *The Governance of Anglo-Saxon England* (London, 1984), and Dorothy Whitelock, *The Beginnings of English Society* (Harmondsworth, 1952; 2nd edn, 1954). S. A. J. Bradley, *Anglo-Saxon Poetry* (London, 1982), and Michael Swanton, *Anglo-Saxon Prose* (London, 1975), present selections, in translation, from the literature of the period. The material evidence from Anglo-Saxon England is discussed in David Wilson, *The Anglo-Saxons* (London, 1960; 3rd edn, Harmondsworth, 1981), and David

Wilson, ed., *The Archaeology of Anglo-Saxon England* (London, 1976; paperback edn, Cambridge, 1981); see also D. A. Hinton, *Alfred's Kingdom. Wessex and the South 800–1500* (London, 1977), and Lloyd and Jennifer Laing, *Anglo-Saxon England* (London, 1979; paperback edn, Frogmore, 1979). There are two useful books which guide the reader around sites with Anglo-Saxon associations: Lloyd and Jennifer Laing, *A Guide to the Dark Age Remains in Britain* (London, 1979), and Nigel and Mary Kerr, *A Guide to Anglo-Saxon Sites* (Frogmore, 1982). For a clear, concise and well-illustrated account of the Anglo-Saxon coinage, see Michael Dolley, *Anglo-Saxon Pennies* (London, 1964). David Hill, *An Atlas of Anglo-Saxon England* (Oxford, 1981), presents a wide range of information in various diagrammatic forms, and is of great value, while the Ordnance Survey map, *Britain before the Norman Conquest* (Southampton, 1973), is both instructive and decorative.

The study of Anglo-Saxon history can never proceed without an understanding of contemporaneous developments on the Continent, in Scandinavia, and in the Celtic parts of the British Isles. For a recent account of Frankish history, see Rosamond McKitterick, *The Frankish Kingdoms under the Carolingians 751–987* (London, 1983); see also Lewis Thorpe, trans., *Einhard and Notker the Stammerer: Two Lives of Charlemagne* (Harmondsworth, 1969). For a recent account of Viking history, see P. H. Sawyer, *Kings and Vikings: Scandinavia and Europe A.D. 700–1100* (London, 1982). Peter Foote and David M. Wilson, *The Viking Achievement* (London, 1970), and Else Roesdahl, *Viking Age Denmark* (London, 1982), discuss the Vikings in their homelands; the raids and settlements in England are covered by P. H. Sawyer, *The Age of the Vikings* (London, 1962; 2nd edn, 1971) and H. R. Loyn, *The Vikings in Britain* (London, 1977). For Wales, see Wendy Davies, *Wales in the Early Middle Ages* (Leicester, 1982); for Ireland, see Donncha Ó Corráin, *Ireland before the Normans* (Dublin, 1972).

King Alfred himself has been the subject of several biographies. Charles Plummer, *The Life and Times of Alfred the Great* (Oxford, 1902), though old, and H. R. Loyn, *Alfred the Great* (Oxford, 1967), though short, are of high quality; see also Beatrice Adelaide Lees, *Alfred the Great. The Truth Teller. Maker of England 848–99* (New York, 1915), Eleanor Duckett, *Alfred the Great and his England* (London, 1957), and Douglas Woodruff, *The Life and Times of Alfred the Great* (London, 1974). A major study, by Dorothy Whitelock, is due to be published in 1985, and another, by Patrick Wormald, is in course of preparation. The following articles are of particular importance: N. P. Brooks, 'England in the Ninth Century: The Crucible of Defeat', *Transactions of the Royal Historical Society* 5th ser. 29 (1979), 1–20; R. H. C. Davis, 'Alfred the Great: Propaganda and Truth', *History* 56 (1971), 169–82; R. H. M. Dolley and C. E. Blunt, 'The Coinage of Ælfred the Great 871–99', *Anglo-Saxon Coins. Studies Presented to F. M. Stenton*, ed. R. H. M. Dolley (London, 1961), pp. 77–95; D. P. Kirby, 'Asser and his Life of King Alfred', *Studia Celtica* 6 (1971), 12–35; J. M. Wallace-Hadrill, 'The Franks and the English in the Ninth Century: Some Common Historical Interests', *Early Medieval History* (Oxford, 1975), pp. 201–16; and the several studies on aspects of King Alfred's reign reprinted in Dorothy Whitelock, *From Bede to Alfred. Studies in Early Anglo-Saxon Literature and History* (London, 1980). References to other relevant books and articles are given in the notes above, and all the works thus cited occur in the list which follows. Recent publications on all aspects of Anglo-Saxon England are listed in the annual bibliographies in the journal *Anglo-Saxon England*, ed. Peter Clemoes et al., 1– (Cambridge, 1972–   ).

References

Allott, Stephen, *Alcuin of York, c. A.D. 732 to 804 – His Life and Letters* (York, 1974)

Amory, Frederic, 'The Viking Hasting in Franco-Scandinavian Legend', *Saints, Scholars and Heroes. Studies in Medieval Culture in Honour of Charles W. Jones*, ed. Margot H. King and Wesley M. Stevens (Collegeville, Minnesota, 1979) II, pp. 265–86

Arndt, W., ed., 'Vita Alcuini', *Vitae Aliaeque Historiae Minores*, Monumenta Germaniae Historica, Scriptores XV, pt 1 (Hannover, 1887), pp. 182–97

Arngart, O., *The Proverbs of Alfred*, 2 vols., Skrifter utgivna av Kungl. Humanistiska Vetenskapssamfundet i Lund 32 (Lund, 1942–55)

Arnold, Thomas, ed., *Symeonis Monachi Opera Omnia*, 2 vols., Rolls Series (London, 1882–5)

Attenborough, F. L., ed. and trans., *The Laws of the Earliest English Kings* (Cambridge, 1922)

Barker, Eric E., 'The Cottonian Fragments of Æthelweard's Chronicle', *Bulletin of the Institute of Historical Research* 24 (1951), 46–62

Barlow, Frank, ed. and trans., *The Life of King Edward who Rests at Westminster* (London, 1962)

Barlow, Frank, K. M. Dexter, A. M. Erskine and L. J. Lloyd, *Leofric of Exeter* (Exeter, 1972)

Bately, Janet, ed., *The Old English Orosius*, Early English Text Society, Supplementary Series 6 (London, 1980)

  'Grimbald of St Bertin's', *Medium Ævum* 35 (1966), 1–10

  'The Compilation of the Anglo-Saxon Chronicle 60 B.C. to A.D. 890: Vocabulary as Evidence', *Proceedings of the British Academy* 64 (1980 for 1978), 93–129

  The Literary Prose of King Alfred's Reign: Translation or Transformation? (London, 1980)

  'Lexical Evidence for the Authorship of the Prose Psalms in the Paris Psalter', *Anglo-Saxon England* 10 (1982), 69–95

Biddle, Martin, ed., *Winchester in the Early Middle Ages. An Edition and Discussion of the Winton Domesday*, Winchester Studies 1 (Oxford, 1976)

  'Towns', *The Archaeology of Anglo-Saxon England*, ed. David M. Wilson (London, 1976), pp. 99–150

Bieler, Ludwig, ed., *Anicii Manlii Severini Boethii Philosophiae Consolatio*, Corpus Christianorum Series Latina 94 (Turnhout, 1957)

Binns, Alan, 'The Navigation of Viking Ships Round the British Isles in Old English and Old Norse Sources', *The Fifth Viking Congress*, ed. Bjarni Niclasen (Tórshavn, 1968), pp. 103–17

Bonner, Gerald, 'Bede and Medieval Civilization', *Anglo-Saxon England* 2 (1973), 71–90

Boretius, A., and V. Krause, ed., *Capitularia Regum Francorum* II, Monumenta Germaniae Historica, Legum Sectio II (Hannover, 1897)

Bostock, J. Knight, *A Handbook on Old High German Literature*, 2nd edn (Oxford, 1976)

Bowker, Alfred, *The King Alfred Millenary. A Record of the Proceedings of the National Commemoration* (London, 1902)

Brewer, J. S., ed., *Giraldi Cambrensis Opera* III, Rolls Series (London, 1863)

Bright, James W., and Robert L. Ramsay, ed., *Liber Psalmorum: The West-Saxon Psalms, being the Prose Portion, or the 'First Fifty', of the so-called Paris Psalter* (Boston, 1907)

'Notes on the "Introductions" of the West-Saxon Psalms', *Journal of Theological Studies* 13 (1912), 520–58

Brooks, Nicholas, 'The Unidentified Forts of the Burghal Hidage', *Medieval Archaeology* 8 (1964), 74–90

'The Development of Military Obligations in Eighth- and Ninth-Century England', *England before the Conquest. Studies in Primary Sources Presented to Dorothy Whitelock*, ed. Peter Clemoes and Kathleen Hughes (Cambridge, 1971), pp. 69–84

'England in the Ninth Century: The Crucible of Defeat', *Transactions of the Royal Historical Society* 5th ser. 29 (1979), 1–20

Brown, Peter, *Augustine of Hippo: A Biography* (London, 1967)

Bullough, D. A., 'The Educational Tradition in England from Alfred to Aelfric: Teaching *Utriusque Linguae*', *Settimane di studio del Centro italiano di studi sull'alto medioevo* 19 (1972), 453–94

Burleigh, John H. S., *Augustine: Earlier Writings*, Library of Christian Classics 6 (London, 1953)

Campbell, Alistair, ed., *Encomium Emmae Reginae*, Camden 3rd series 72 (London, 1949)

The Chronicle of Æthelweard (London, 1962)

Campbell, James, 'Observations on English Government from the Tenth to the Twelfth Century', *Transactions of the Royal Historical Society* 5th ser. 25 (1975), 39–54

Campbell, James, Eric John and Patrick Wormald, *The Anglo-Saxons* (Oxford, 1982)

Carnicelli, Thomas A., ed., *King Alfred's Version of St Augustine's Soliloquies* (Cambridge, Mass., 1969)

Chadwick, Henry, *Boethius: The Consolations of Music, Logic, Theology and Philosophy* (Oxford, 1981)

Chambers, R. W., Max Förster and Robin Flower, *The Exeter Book of Old English Poetry* (Exeter, 1933)

Charles-Edwards, Thomas, 'Some Celtic Kinship Terms', *Bulletin of the Board of Celtic Studies* 24 (1970–72), 105–22

'The Social Background to Irish *Peregrinatio*', *Celtica* 11 (1976), 43–59

Chibnall, Marjorie, ed. and trans., *The Ecclesiastical History of Orderic Vitalis* II (Oxford, 1969)

Clanchy, M. T., *From Memory to Written Record. England 1066–1307* (London, 1979)

Clapham, A. W., *English Romanesque Architecture I. Before the Conquest* (Oxford, 1930)

Clark, Cecily, 'The Narrative Mode of *The Anglo-Saxon Chronicle* before the Conquest', *England before the Conquest. Studies in Primary Sources Presented to Dorothy Whitelock*, ed. Peter Clemoes and Kathleen Hughes (Cambridge, 1971), pp. 215–35

Cockayne, Thomas Oswald, ed., *Leechdoms, Wortcunning and Starcraft of Early England*, 3 vols., Rolls Series (London, 1864–6)

Colgrave, Bertram, and R. A. B. Mynors, ed., *Bede's Ecclesiastical History of the English People* (Oxford, 1969)

Collins, Rowland L., *Anglo-Saxon Vernacular Manuscripts in America* (New York, 1976)

Coninck, L. de, ed., *Theodori Mopsuesteni Expositionis in Psalmos Iuliano Aeclanensi Interprete in Latinum versae quae supersunt*, Corpus Christianorum Series Latina 88A (Turnhout, 1977)

Conybeare, Edward, *Alfred in the Chroniclers*, 2nd edn (Cambridge, 1914)

Craster, Edmund, 'The Patrimony of St Cuthbert', *English Historical Review* 69 (1954), 177–99

Cross, F. L., ed., *The Oxford Dictionary of the Christian Church*, 2nd edn (Oxford, 1974)

Cross, J. E., 'The Name and Not the Deeds', *Modern Language Review* 54 (1959), 56

'The Apostles in the *Old English Martyrology*', *Mediaevalia* 5 (1979), 15–59

'The Influence of Irish Texts and Traditions on the *Old English Martyrology*', *Proceedings of the Royal Irish Academy* 81C (1981), 173–92

Crumlin-Pedersen, Ole, 'The Vikings and the Hanseatic Merchants: 900–1450', *A History of Seafaring based on Underwater Archaeology*, ed. George F. Bass (London, 1972), pp. 181–204

'Viking Shipbuilding and Seamanship', *Proceedings of the Eighth Viking Congress*, ed. Hans Bekker-Nielsen, Peter Foote and Olaf Olsen, Mediaeval Scandinavia Supplements 2 (Odense, 1981), pp. 271–86

Curtius, Ernst Robert, *European Literature and the Latin Middle Ages* (London, 1953)

Davidson, H. R. Ellis, *Gods and Myths of Northern Europe* (Harmondsworth, 1964)

Davies, Wendy, *An Early Welsh Microcosm. Studies in the Llandaff Charters*, Royal Historical Society Studies in History Series 9 (London, 1978)

'Land and Power in Early Medieval Wales', *Past and Present* 81 (1978), 3–23

The Llandaff Charters (Aberystwyth, 1979)

'The Latin Charter-Tradition in Western Britain, Brittany and Ireland in the Early Mediaeval Period', *Ireland in Early Mediaeval Europe: Studies in Memory of Kathleen Hughes*, ed. Dorothy Whitelock, Rosamond McKitterick and David Dumville (Cambridge, 1982), pp. 258–80

Davis, A. H., trans., *William Thorne's Chronicle of Saint Augustine's Abbey Canterbury* (Oxford, 1934)

Davis, Henry, *St Gregory the Great: Pastoral Care*, Ancient Christian Writers 11 (Westminster, Maryland, and London, 1950)

Davis, R. H. C., 'East Anglia and the Danelaw', *Transactions of the Royal Historical Society* 5th ser. 5 (1955), 23–39

'Alfred the Great: Propaganda and Truth', *History* 56 (1971), 169–82

'Alfred and Guthrum's Frontier', *English Historical Review* 97 (1982), 803–10

Davison, B. K., 'The Burghal Hidage Fort of Eorpeburnan: A Suggested Identification', *Medieval Archaeology* 16 (1972), 123–7

Deferrari, Roy J., *Paulus Orosius: The Seven Books of History Against the Pagans*, Fathers of the Church 50 (New York, 1964)

D'Haenens, Albert, *Les Invasions normandes en Belgique au IXe siècle. Le phénomène et sa répercussion dans l'historiographie médiévale*, Université de Louvain Recueil de Travaux d'Histoire et de Philologie, 4th ser. 38 (Louvain, 1967)

Dobbie, Elliott van Kirk, ed., *The Anglo-Saxon Minor Poems*, Anglo-Saxon Poetic Records 6 (New York, 1942)

Doble, Gilbert H., *St Neot*, Cornish Saints Series 21 (Exeter, 1929)

Dodwell, C. R., *Anglo-Saxon Art: A New Perspective* (Manchester, 1982)

Dolley, R. H. M., *The Hiberno-Norse Coins in the British Museum*, Sylloge of Coins of the British Isles 8 (London, 1966)

Dolley, R. H. M., and C. E. Blunt, 'The Chronology of the Coins of Ælfred the Great 871–99', *Anglo-Saxon Coins: Studies Presented to F. M. Stenton*, ed. R. H. M. Dolley (London, 1961), pp. 77–95

Domesday Book, ed. Abraham Farley, 2 vols. (London, 1783)

Dubuisson, D., 'L'Irlande et la théorie médiévale des "trois ordres"', *Revue de l'histoire des religions* 188 (1975), 35–63

Duby, Georges, *The Three Orders: Feudal Society Imagined* (London, 1980)

Dumville, David N., '"Nennius" and the *Historia Brittonum*', *Studia Celtica* 10–11 (1975–6), 78–95

'The Anglian Collection of Royal Genealogies and Regnal Lists', *Anglo-Saxon England* 5 (1976), 23–50

'The Ætheling: A Study in Anglo-Saxon Constitutional History', *Anglo-Saxon England* 8 (1979), 1–33

'The "Six" Sons of Rhodri Mawr: A Problem in Asser's *Life of King Alfred*', *Cambridge Medieval Celtic Studies* 4 (Winter, 1982), 5–18

Dyson, Tony, 'Two Saxon Land Grants for Queenhithe', *Collectanea Londiniensia: Studies Presented to Ralph Merrifield*, ed. J. Bird, H. Chapman and J. Clark, London and Middlesex Archaeological Society Special Paper 2 (London, 1978), pp. 200–15

Ehwald, Rudolf, ed., *Aldhelmi Opera*, Monumenta Germaniae Historica, Auctores Antiquissimi XV (Berlin, 1919)

Ekwall, Eilert, *English River-Names* (Oxford, 1928)

Street-Names of the City of London (Oxford, 1954)

Emanuel, Hywel David, *The Latin Texts of the Welsh Laws* (Cardiff, 1967)

Enright, Michael J., 'Charles the Bald and Aethelwulf of Wessex: The Alliance of 856 and Strategies of Royal Succession', *Journal of Medieval History* 5 (1979), 291–302

Evans, J. Gwenogvryn, and John Rhys, *The Text of the Book of Llan Dâv Reproduced from the Gwysaney Manuscript* (Oxford, 1893; repr. Aberystwyth, 1979)

Faull, Margaret Lindsay, 'The Semantic Development of Old English *Wealh*', *Leeds Studies in English* 8 (1975), 20–44

Fenwick, Valerie, ed., *The Graveney Boat: A Tenth-Century Find from Kent*, British Archaeological Reports, British Series 53 (Oxford, 1978)

Finberg, H. P. R., *The Early Charters of Wessex* (Leicester, 1964)

Lucerna. Studies of Some Problems in the Early History of England (London, 1964)

Fischer, B., 'Bedae de titulis psalmorum liber', *Festschrift Bernhard Bischoff*, ed. J. Autenrieth and F. Brunhölzl (Stuttgart, 1971), pp. 90–110

Fournier, Paul, 'Le *Liber ex lege Moysi* et les tendances bibliques du droit canonique irlandais', *Revue Celtique* 30 (1909), 221–34

Fox, Sir Cyril, *Offa's Dyke. A Field Survey of the Western Frontier-Works of Mercia in the Seventh and Eighth Centuries A.D.* (London, 1955)

Galbraith, V. H., 'Who Wrote Asser's Life of Alfred?', *An Introduction to the Study of History* (London, 1964), pp. 88–128

Gale, Thomas, ed., *Historiae Britannicae, Saxonicae, Anglo-Danicae, Scriptores XV* (Oxford, 1691)

Ganshof, F. L., *Feudalism*, 3rd edn (London, 1964)

Frankish Institutions under Charlemagne (New York, 1970)

'Charlemagne's Programme of Imperial Government', *The Carolingians and the Frankish Monarchy. Studies in Carolingian History* (London, 1971), pp. 55–85

'Charlemagne's Use of the Oath', *The Carolingians and the Frankish Monarchy. Studies in Carolingian History* (London, 1971), pp. 111–24

'The Use of the Written Word in Charlemagne's Administration', *The Carolingians and the Frankish Monarchy. Studies in Carolingian History* (London, 1971), pp. 125–42

Garmonsway, G. N., ed. and trans., *The Anglo-Saxon Chronicle* (London, 1953)

Gelling, Margaret, *The Place-Names of Berkshire*, 3 vols., English Place-Name Society 49–51 (Cambridge, 1973–6)

Gibson, Margaret, ed., *Boethius: His Life, Thought and Influence* (Oxford, 1981)

Gneuss, Helmut, 'A Preliminary List of Manuscripts Written or Owned in England up to 1100', *Anglo-Saxon England* 9 (1981), 1–60

Gover, J. E. B., Allen Mawer and F. M. Stenton, *The Place-Names of Devon*, 2 vols., English Place-Name Society 8–9 (Cambridge, 1931–2)

The Place-Names of Wiltshire, English Place-Name Society 16 (Cambridge, 1939)

The Place-Names of Nottinghamshire, English Place-Name Society 17 (Cambridge, 1940)

Grierson, Philip, 'Grimbald of St Bertin's', *English Historical Review* 55 (1940), 529–61

Halphen, Louis, ed. and trans., *Éginhard. Vie de Charlemagne*, 4th edn, Les classiques de l'histoire de France au moyen âge (Paris, 1967)

Charlemagne and the Carolingian Empire (Amsterdam, 1977)

Hamilton, N. E. S. A., ed., *Willelmi Malmesbiriensis Monachi De Gestis Pontificum Anglorum Libri Quinque*, Rolls Series (London, 1870)

Harbert, Bruce, 'King Alfred's Æstel', *Anglo-Saxon England* 3 (1974), 103–10

Hargrove, Henry Lee, *King Alfred's Old English Version of St Augustine's Soliloquies Turned into Modern English*, Yale Studies in English 22 (New York, 1904)

Harmer, F. E., ed., *Select English Historical Documents of the Ninth and Tenth Centuries* (Cambridge, 1914)

Anglo-Saxon Writs (Manchester, 1952)

Harrison, Kenneth, *The Framework of Anglo-Saxon History to A.D. 900* (Cambridge, 1976)

Hart, C. R., *The Early Charters of Eastern England* (Leicester, 1966)

'The East Anglian Chronicle', *Journal of Medieval History* 7 (1981), 249–82

Hassall, J. M., and David Hill, 'Pont de l'Arche: Frankish Influence on the West Saxon Burh?', *Archaeological Journal* 127 (1970), 188–95

Hecht, Hans, ed., *Bischof Wærferths von Worcester Übersetzung der Dialoge Gregors des Grossen*, 2 vols. (Leipzig, 1900–1907)

Hill, Christopher, *Puritanism and Revolution. Studies in Interpretation of the English Revolution of the 17th Century* (London, 1958)

Hill, David, *An Atlas of Anglo-Saxon England 700–1066* (Oxford, 1981)

  'The Burghal Hidage – Lyng', *Proceedings of the Somersetshire Archaeological and Natural History Society* 111 (1967), 64–6

  'The Burghal Hidage: the Establishment of a Text', *Medieval Archaeology* 13 (1969), 84–92

Hinton, David A., *A Catalogue of the Anglo-Saxon Ornamental Metalwork 700–1100 in the Department of Antiquities Ashmolean Museum* (Oxford, 1974)

  Alfred's Kingdom. Wessex and the South 800–1500 (London, 1977)

Hinton, David A., Suzanne Keene and Kenneth E. Qualmann, 'The Winchester Reliquary', *Medieval Archaeology* 25 (1981), 45–77

Hodges, Richard, 'Trade and Market Origins in the Ninth Century: An Archaeological Perspective of Anglo-Carolingian Relations', *Charles the Bald: Court and Kingdom*, ed. Margaret Gibson and Janet Nelson, British Archaeological Reports, International Series 101 (Oxford, 1981), pp. 213–33

Hollister, C. Warren, 'The Origins of the English Treasury', *English Historical Review* 93 (1978), 262–75

Hollyman, K. J., *Le Développement du vocabulaire féodal en France pendant le Haut Moyen Âge* (Geneva, 1957)

Holt, J. C., 'Politics and Property in Early Medieval England', *Past and Present* 57 (1972), 3–52

Ho Peng Yoke, 'Ancient and Mediaeval Observations of Comets and Novae in Chinese Sources', *Vistas in Astronomy* 5 (1962), 127–225

Howlett, D. R., 'The Iconography of the Alfred Jewel', *Oxoniensia* 39 (1974), 44–52

  'Alfred's *Æstel*', *English Philological Studies* 14 (1975), 65–74

Hughes, Kathleen, *The Church in Early Irish Society* (London, 1966)

  'The Changing Theory and Practice of Irish Pilgrimage', *Journal of Ecclesiastical History* 11 (1960), 143–51

  'Evidence for Contacts between the Churches of the Irish and English from the Synod of Whitby to the Viking Age', *England before the Conquest. Studies in Primary Sources Presented to Dorothy Whitelock*, ed. Peter Clemoes and Kathleen Hughes (Cambridge, 1971), pp. 49–67

  'The Welsh Latin Chronicles: *Annales Cambriae* and Related Texts', *Celtic Britain in the Early Middle Ages* (Woodbridge, 1980), pp. 67–85

  'The A-Text of the *Annales Cambriae*', *Celtic Britain in the Early Middle Ages* (Woodbridge, 1980), pp. 86–100

Hunter, Joseph, *Ecclesiastical Documents*, Camden Society (London, 1840)

Jackson, Kenneth, *Language and History in Early Britain: A Chronological Survey of the Brittonic Languages 1st to 12th centuries A.D.* (Edinburgh, 1953)

Jenkins, Dafydd, and Morfydd E. Owen, ed., *The Welsh Law of Women* (Cardiff, 1980)

John, Eric, *Orbis Britanniae and Other Studies* (Leicester, 1966)

Ker, N. R., ed., *The Pastoral Care: King Alfred's Translation of St Gregory's Regula Pastoralis*, Early English Manuscripts in Facsimile 6 (Copenhagen, 1956)

Catalogue of Manuscripts Containing Anglo-Saxon (Oxford, 1957)

Keynes, Simon, *The Diplomas of King Æthelred 'the Unready' 978–1016. A Study in their Use as Historical Evidence* (Cambridge, 1980)

King, P. D., *Law and Society in the Visigothic Kingdom* (Cambridge, 1972)

Kirby, D. P., 'Northumbria in the Reign of Alfred the Great', *Transactions of the Architectural and Archaeological Society of Durham and Northumberland* 11 (1965), 335–46

'Asser and his Life of King Alfred', *Studia Celtica* 6 (1971), 12–35

Kotzor, Günter, *Das altenglische Martyrologium*, Abhandlungen der bayerische Akademie der Wissenschaften, phil.-hist. Klasse 88 (Munich, 1981)

Lagarde, P. de, et al., ed., *S. Hieronymi Presbyteri Opera I. 1: Opera Exegetica*, Corpus Christianorum Series Latina 72 (Turnhout, 1959)

Laing, Lloyd, *The Archaeology of Late Celtic Britain and Ireland* c. 400–1200 AD (London, 1975)

Langenfelt, Gösta, *The Historic Origin of the Eight Hours Day. Studies in English Traditionalism*, Kungl. Vitterhets Historie och Antikvitets Akademiens Handlingar 87 (Stockholm, 1954)

'King Alfred and the First Time-Measurer', *Tekniska Museets Årsbok: Dædalus* (1962), 39–49

Lapidge, Michael, 'The Hermeneutic Style in Tenth-Century Anglo-Latin Literature', *Anglo-Saxon England* 4 (1975), 67–111

'Some Latin Poems as Evidence for the Reign of Athelstan', *Anglo-Saxon England* 9 (1981), 61–98

'Byrhtferth of Ramsey and the Early Sections of the *Historia Regum* Attributed to Symeon of Durham', *Anglo-Saxon England* 10 (1982), 97–122

'The Study of Latin Texts in Late Anglo-Saxon England: (1) The Evidence of Latin Glosses', *Latin and the Vernacular Languages in Early Medieval Britain*, ed. N. P. Brooks (Leicester, 1982), pp. 99–140

Lapidge, Michael, and Michael Herren, trans., *Aldhelm: The Prose Works* (Ipswich, 1979)

Lees, Beatrice Adelaide, *Alfred the Great. The Truth Teller. Maker of England 848–899* (New York, 1915)

Liebermann, F., *Die Gesetze der Angelsachsen*, 3 vols. (Halle, 1903–16)

'King Alfred and Mosaic Law', *Transactions of the Jewish Historical Society of England* 6 (1908–10), 21–31

Lindsay, W. M., *Early Welsh Script* (Oxford, 1912)

Lloyd, Sir John Edward, *A History of Wales from the Earliest Times to the Edwardian Conquest*, 2 vols., 3rd edn (London, 1939)

Loyn, H. R., *The Vikings in Britain* (London, 1977)

'Kinship in Anglo-Saxon England', *Anglo-Saxon England* 3 (1974), 197–209

'Wales and England in the Tenth Century: The Context of the Athelstan Charters', *Welsh History Review* 10 (1981), 283–301

Lyon, Stewart, 'Historical Problems of Anglo-Saxon Coinage – (3) Denominations and Weights', *British Numismatic Journal* 38 (1969), 204–22

'Some Problems in Interpreting Anglo-Saxon Coinage', *Anglo-Saxon England* 5 (1976), 173–224

Lyon, C. S. S., and B. H. I. H. Stewart, 'The Northumbrian Viking Coins in the Cuerdale Hoard', *Anglo-Saxon Coins: Studies Presented to F. M. Stenton*, ed. R. H. M. Dolley (London, 1961), pp. 96–121

Macalister, R. A. S., *The Memorial Slabs of Clonmacnois, King's County* (Dublin, 1909)

Corpus Inscriptionum Insularum Celticarum, 2 vols. (Dublin, 1945–9)

Magnou-Nortier, E., *Foi et fidélité. Recherches sur l'évolution des liens personnels chez les Francs du VIIe au IXe siècle* (Toulouse, 1976)

Magoun, F. P., 'King Æthelwulf's Biblical Ancestors', *Modern Language Review* 46 (1951), 249–50

Maitland, Frederic William, *Domesday Book and Beyond* (Cambridge, 1897)

Mawer, A., and F. M. Stenton, *The Place-Names of Sussex*, 2 vols., English Place-Name Society 6–7 (Cambridge, 1929–30)

Meaney, Audrey L., 'Alfred, the Patriarch and the White Stone', *AUMLA. Journal of the Australasian Universities Language and Literature Association* 49 (1978), 65–79

Meritt, Herbert, 'Old English Entries in a Manuscript at Bern', *Journal of English and Germanic Philology* 33 (1934), 343–51

Migne, J. P., ed., *Patrologiae Cursus Completus. Series (Latina) Prima*, 221 vols. (Paris, 1844–64)

Miles, Louis Wardlaw, *King Alfred in Literature* (Baltimore, 1902)

Miller, Thomas, ed., *The Old English Version of Bede's Ecclesiastical History of the English People*, 4 vols., Early English Text Society, Original Series 95–6 and 110–11 (London, 1890–98)

Mills, A. D., *The Place-Names of Dorset* I, English Place-Name Society 52 (Cambridge, 1977)

Moricca, U., ed., *Gregorii Magni Dialogi Libri IV* (Rome, 1924)

Morris, John, ed. and trans., *Nennius. British History and the Welsh Annals* (Chichester, 1980)

Nelson, Janet L., 'The Problem of King Alfred's Royal Anointing', *Journal of Ecclesiastical History* 18 (1967), 145–63

North, J. J., *English Hammered Coinage*, I: *Early Anglo-Saxon – Henry III*, c. *600–1272*, 2nd edn (London, 1980)

Ó Corráin, Donnchadh, 'High-Kings, Vikings and Other Kings', *Irish Historical Studies* 21 (1978–9), 283–323

O'Donovan, Mary Anne, 'An Interim Revision of Episcopal Dates for the Province of Canterbury, 850–950: part I', *Anglo-Saxon England* 1 (1972), 23–44

    'An Interim Revision of Episcopal Dates for the Province of Canterbury, 850–950: part II', *Anglo-Saxon England* 2 (1973), 91–113

Okasha, Elisabeth, *Hand-List of Anglo-Saxon Non-Runic Inscriptions* (Cambridge, 1971)

O'Neill, Patrick, 'Old English Introductions to the Prose Psalms of the Paris Psalter: Sources, Structure and Composition', *Eight Anglo-Saxon Studies*, ed. J. S. Wittig (Chapel Hill, North Carolina, 1981), pp. 20–38

Otten, Kurt, *König Alfreds Boethius*, Studien zur englischen Philologie n.f. 3 (Tübingen, 1964)

Page, R. I., 'Anglo-Saxon Episcopal Lists, part III', *Nottingham Mediaeval Studies* 10 (1966), 2–24

    'The Audience of *Beowulf* and the Vikings', *The Dating of Beowulf*, ed. Colin Chase (Toronto, 1981), pp. 113–22

Page, William, ed., *The Victoria History of the County of Dorset* II, Victoria History of the Counties of England (London, 1908)

    The Victoria History of Somerset II, Victoria History of the Counties of England (London, 1911)

Pálsson, Hermann, and Paul Edwards, trans., *Eyrbyggja Saga* (Edinburgh, 1973)

Parker, James, *The Early History of Oxford, 727–1100* (Oxford, 1885)

Parkes, M. B., 'The Palaeography of the Parker Manuscript of the *Chronicle*, Laws and Sedulius, and Historiography at Winchester in the Late Ninth and Tenth Centuries', *Anglo-Saxon England* 5 (1976), 149–71

    'A Note on MS Vatican, Bibl. Apost., lat. 3363', *Boethius: His Life, Thought and Influence*, ed. Margaret Gibson (Oxford, 1981), pp. 425–7

Pauli, Rheinhold, *The Life of Alfred the Great* (London, 1853)

Payne, F. Anne, *King Alfred and Boethius: An Analysis of the OE Version of the 'Consolation of Philosophy'* (Madison, 1968)

Pearce, Susan M., *The Archaeology of South West Britain* (London, 1981)

Phythian-Adams, Charles, 'Rutland Reconsidered', *Mercian Studies*, ed. Ann Dornier (Leicester, 1977), pp. 63–84

Plummer, Charles, ed., *Two of the Saxon Chronicles Parallel*, 2 vols. (Oxford, 1892–9)

    The Life and Times of Alfred the Great (Oxford, 1902)

Radford, C. A. Ralegh, 'The Pre-Conquest Boroughs of England', *Proceedings of the British Academy* 64 (1980 for 1978), 131–53

Rahtz, Philip, *The Saxon and Medieval Palaces at Cheddar. Excavations 1960– 62*, British Archaeological Reports, British Series 65 (Oxford, 1979)

Ramsay, Robert L., 'The Latin Text of the Paris Psalter: a Collation and Some Conclusions', *American Journal of Philology* 41 (1920), 147–76

Richards, Jeffrey, *Consul of God. The Life and Times of Gregory the Great* (London, 1980)

Riché, P., *Les Écoles et l'enseignement dans l'Occident chrétien de la fin du Ve siècle au milieu du XIe siècle* (Paris, 1979)

    'Le Psautier, livre de lecture élémentaire d'après les vies des saints mérovingiens', *Études Mérovingiennes* (Paris, 1953), pp. 253–6

Robertson, A. J., ed. and trans., *The Laws of the Kings of England from Edmund to Henry I* (Cambridge, 1925)

    Anglo-Saxon Charters, 2nd edn (Cambridge, 1956)

Robinson, J. Armitage, *St Oswald and the Church of Worcester*, British Academy Supplemental Papers 5 (London, 1919)

Roesdahl, Else, *Viking Age Denmark* (London, 1982)

Rollason, D. W., 'Lists of Saints' Resting-Places in Anglo-Saxon England', *Anglo-Saxon England* 7 (1978), 61–93

Rose-Troup, Frances, 'The Ancient Monastery of St Mary and St Peter at Exeter, 680–1050', *Report and Transactions of the Devonshire Association for the Advancement of Science, Literature and Art* 63 (1931), 179–220

Royal Commission on Historical Monuments (England), *An Inventory of Historical Monuments in the County of Dorset* II, pt 2 (London, 1970), and IV (London, 1972)

Salmon, P., *Les 'Tituli Psalmorum' des manuscrits latins* (Vatican, 1959)

Sawyer, P. H., *Anglo-Saxon Charters. An Annotated List and Bibliography* (London, 1968)

    The Age of the Vikings, 2nd edn (London, 1971)

    Kings and Vikings: Scandinavia and Europe AD 700–1100 (London, 1982)

Schneider, Gerhard, *Erzbischof Fulco von Reims (883–900) und das Frankenreich*, Münchener Beiträge zur Mediävistik und Renaissance-Forschung 14 (Munich, 1973)

Schütt, Marie, 'The Literary Form of Asser's "*Vita Alfredi*"', *English Historical Review* 62 (1957), 209–20

Scragg, D. G., ed., *The Battle of Maldon* (Manchester, 1981)

Sedgefield, Walter John, ed., *King Alfred's Old English Version of Boethius De Consolatione Philosophiae* (Oxford, 1899)

King Alfred's Version of the Consolations of Boethius. Done into Modern English, with an Introduction (Oxford, 1900)

Sherley-Price, Leo, trans., *Bede: A History of the English Church and People* (Harmondsworth, 1955)

Shippey, T. A., 'Wealth and Wisdom in King Alfred's *Preface* to the Old English *Pastoral Care*', *English Historical Review* 94 (1979), 346–55

'A Missing Army: Some Doubts about the Alfredian *Chronicle*', *In Geardagum* 4 (1982), 41–55

Sisam, Kenneth, *Studies in the History of Old English Literature* (Oxford, 1953)

'Anglo-Saxon Royal Genealogies', *Proceedings of the British Academy* 39 (1953), 287–348

Smith, A. H., ed., *The Parker Chronicle 832–900*, 3rd edn (London, 1951)

The Place-Names of Gloucestershire, 4 vols., English Place-Name Society 38–41 (Cambridge, 1964–5)

Smyth, Alfred P., *Scandinavian Kings in the British Isles 850–880* (Oxford, 1977)

Scandinavian York and Dublin. The History and Archaeology of Two Related Viking Kingdoms, 2 vols. (Dublin, 1975–9)

Stafford, Pauline, 'The King's Wife in Wessex 800–1066', *Past and Present* 91 (1981), 3–27

Stanley, Eric Gerald, ed., *The Owl and the Nightingale* (London, 1960)

'The Glorification of Alfred King of Wessex (from the Publication of Sir John Spelman's *Life*, 1678 and 1709, to the Publication of Rheinhold Pauli's, 1851)', *Poetica* (Tokyo) 12 (1981), 103–33

'The Scholarly Recovery of the Significance of Anglo-Saxon Records in Prose and Verse: A New Bibliography', *Anglo-Saxon England* 9 (1981), 223–62

Stenton, F. M., *Anglo-Saxon England*, 3rd edn (Oxford, 1971)

'Æthelweard's Account of the Last Years of King Alfred's Reign', *Preparatory to Anglo-Saxon England*, ed. Doris Mary Stenton (Oxford, 1970), pp. 8–13

'The Danes at Thorney Island in 893', *Preparatory to Anglo-Saxon England*, ed. Doris Mary Stenton (Oxford, 1970), pp. 14–15

'The South-Western Element in the Old English Chronicle', *Preparatory to Anglo-Saxon England*, ed. Doris Mary Stenton (Oxford, 1970), pp. 106–15

'The Thriving of the Anglo-Saxon Ceorl', *Preparatory to Anglo-Saxon England*, ed. Doris Mary Stenton (Oxford, 1970), pp. 383–93

Stevenson, William Henry, ed., *Asser's Life of King Alfred* (Oxford, 1904)

'The Date of King Alfred's Death', *English Historical Review* 13 (1898), 71–7

Stone, Brian, trans., *The Owl and the Nightingale. Cleanness. St Erkenwald* (Harmondsworth, 1971)

Strong, Roy, *And When Did You Last See Your Father? The Victorian Painter and British History* (London, 1978)

Stubbs, William, ed., *Willelmi Malmesbiriensis Monachi De Gestis Regum Anglorum Libri Quinque*, 2 vols., Rolls Series (London, 1887–9)

Swanton, Michael, ed. and trans., *Anglo-Saxon Prose* (London, 1975)

Sweet, Henry, ed., *King Alfred's West-Saxon Version of Gregory's Pastoral Care*, 2 vols., Early English Text Society, Original Series 45 and 50 (London, 1871–2)

Symons, Thomas, ed. and trans., *Regularis Concordia* (London, 1953)

Temple, Elżbieta, *Anglo-Saxon Manuscripts 900–1066*, Survey of Manuscripts Illuminated in the British Isles 2 (London, 1976)

Thorpe, Benjamin, ed., *Florentii Wigorniensis Monachi Chronicon ex Chronicis*, 2 vols. (London, 1848–9)

Thorpe, Lewis, trans., *Einhard and Notker the Stammerer: Two Lives of Charlemagne* (Harmondsworth, 1969)
   Gerald of Wales: The Journey through Wales and The Description of Wales (Harmondsworth, 1978)

Tierney, J. J., ed., *Dicuili Liber de Mensura Orbis Terrae*, Scriptores Latini Hiberniae 6 (Dublin, 1967)

Tolhurst, J. B. L., ed., *The Monastic Breviary of Hyde Abbey, Winchester* IV and VI, Henry Bradshaw Society 78 and 80 (London, 1939–42)

Vaughan, Richard, ed., *The Chronicle Attributed to John of Wallingford*, Camden Miscellany 21, Camden 3rd ser. 90 (London, 1958)

Vercauteren, F., 'Comment s'est-on défendu, au ixe siècle dans l'Empire franc contre les invasions normandes?', *Annales du xxxe Congrès de la Fédération archéologique et historique de Belgique* (Brussels, 1935–6), pp. 117–32

Victory, Siân, *The Celtic Church in Wales* (London, 1977)

Vleeskruyer, Rudolf, ed., *The Life of St Chad. An Old English Homily* (Amsterdam, 1953)

Wacquet, Henri, ed. and trans., *Abbon: Le Siège de Paris par les Normands. Poème du IXe siècle*, 2nd imp., Les classiques de l'histoire de France au moyen âge (Paris, 1964)

Wade-Evans, A. W., *Vitae Sanctorum Britanniae et Genealogiae* (Cardiff, 1944)

Wainwright, F. T., 'Æthelflæd, Lady of the Mercians', *Scandinavian England*, ed. H. P. R. Finberg (Chichester, 1975), pp. 305–24

Wallace-Hadrill, J. M., *Early Germanic Kingship in England and on the Continent* (Oxford, 1971)
   'The Franks and the English in the Ninth Century: Some Common Historical Interests', *Early Medieval History* (Oxford, 1975), pp. 201–16

'The Vikings in Francia', *Early Medieval History* (Oxford, 1975), pp. 217–36

Warner, Rubie D.-N., ed., *Early English Homilies from the Twelfth Century MS. Vesp. D. XIV*, Early English Text Society, Original Series 152 (London, 1917)

Watts, V. E., trans., *Boethius: The Consolation of Philosophy* (Harmondsworth, 1969)

Webb, J. F., and D. H. Farmer, *The Age of Bede* (Harmondsworth, 1983)

Weber, R., ed., *Le Psautier romain et les autres anciens psautiers latins* (Vatican, 1953)

Wheeler, G. H., 'Textual Emendations to Asser's Life of Alfred', *English Historical Review* 47 (1932), 86–8

Whitaker, John, *The Life of Saint Neot, the Oldest of all the Brothers to King Alfred* (London, 1809)

Whitelock, Dorothy, ed., *Anglo-Saxon Wills* (Cambridge, 1930)

The Beginnings of English Society, 2nd edn, Pelican History of England 2 (Harmondsworth, 1954)

English Historical Documents c. *500–1042*, 2nd edn, English Historical Documents 1 (London, 1979)

'Recent Work on Asser's Life of Alfred', *Asser's Life of King Alfred*, ed. William Henry Stevenson, new imp. (Oxford, 1959), pp. cxxxii–clii

'The Old English Bede', *Proceedings of the British Academy* 48 (1962), 57–90

'The Prose of Alfred's Reign', *Continuations and Beginnings: Studies in Old English Literature*, ed. E. G. Stanley (London, 1966), pp. 67–103

The Genuine Asser, Stenton Lecture 1967 (Reading, 1968)

'William of Malmesbury on the Works of King Alfred', *Medieval Literature and Civilization: Studies in Memory of G. N. Garmonsway*, ed. D. A. Pearsall and R. A. Waldron (London, 1968), pp. 78–93

'Wulfstan *Cantor* and Anglo-Saxon Law', *Nordica et Anglica: Studies in Honour of Stefán Einarsson*, ed. A. H. Orrick (The Hague, 1968), pp. 83–92

'Fact and Fiction in the Legend of St Edmund', *Proceedings of the Suffolk Institute of Archaeology* 31 (1969), 217–33

'The List of Chapter-Headings in the Old English Bede', *Old English Studies in Honour of John C. Pope*, ed. Robert B. Burlin and Edward B. Irving, Jr (Toronto, 1974), pp. 263–84

'Some Charters in the Name of King Alfred', *Saints, Scholars and Heroes. Studies in Medieval Culture in Honour of Charles W. Jones*, ed. Margot H. King and Wesley M. Stevens (Collegeville, Minnesota, 1979) I, pp. 77–98

'The Importance of the Battle of Edington A.D. 878', *From Bede to*

Alfred. Studies in Early Anglo-Saxon Literature and History (London, 1980), no. 13

Whitelock, D., M. Brett and C. N. L. Brooke, ed., *Councils & Synods with other Documents relating to the English Church I. A.D. 871–1204, pt 1: 871–1066* (Oxford, 1981)

Whitelock, Dorothy, David C. Douglas and Susie I. Tucker, ed., *The Anglo-Saxon Chronicle. A Revised Translation* (London, 1961)

Whittaker, William Joseph, ed., *The Mirror of Justices*, Selden Society 7 (London, 1895)

Williams, Ann, 'Some Notes and Considerations on Problems Connected with English Royal Succession, 860–1066', *Proceedings of the Battle Conference on Anglo-Norman Studies I: 1978*, ed. R. Allen Brown (Ipswich, 1979), pp. 144–67

Williams, Sir Ifor, with Rachel Bromwich, *Armes Prydein. The Prophecy of Britain, from the Book of Taliesin* (Dublin, 1972)

Wilson, David M., *Anglo-Saxon Ornamental Metalwork 700–1100 in the British Museum*, Catalogue of Antiquities of the Later Saxon Period 1 (London, 1964)

Winterbottom, Michael, 'The Style of Æthelweard', *Medium Ævum* 36 (1967), 109–18

Wittig, J. S., 'King Alfred's *Boethius* and its Latin Sources: a Reconsideration', *Anglo-Saxon England* 11 (1983), 157–98

Wormald, Francis, 'Anglo-Saxon Initials in a Paris Boethius Manuscript', *Gazette des Beaux-Arts* (July 1963), pp. 63–70

Wormald, Patrick, '*Lex Scripta* and *Verbum Regis*: Legislation and Germanic Kingship, from Euric to Cnut', *Early Medieval Kingship*, ed. P. H. Sawyer and I. N. Wood (Leeds, 1977), pp. 105–38

'The Uses of Literacy in Anglo-Saxon England and its Neighbours', *Transactions of the Royal Historical Society* 5th ser. 27 (1977), 95–114

Wright, C. E., ed., *Bald's Leechbook. British Museum Royal Manuscript 12 D. xvii*, Early English Manuscripts in Facsimile 5 (Copenhagen, 1955)

Yerkes, David, 'The Full Text of the Metrical Preface to Wærferth's Translation of Gregory', *Speculum* 55 (1980), 505–13

Zangemeister, C. F. W., ed., *Pauli Orosii Historiarum adversum Paganos Libri VII*, Corpus Scriptorum Ecclesiasticorum Latinorum 5 (Vienna, 1882)

Zimmerman, Odo John, *Saint Gregory the Great: Dialogues*, Fathers of the Church 39 (New York, 1959)

Index